The Color Printing Manual

The Color Printing Manual

Bob Nadler

AMPHOTO
American Photographic Book Publishing Co., Inc.
Garden City, New York

Fourth Printing 1979

Copyright © 1978 by Bob Nadler

Published in Garden City by American Photographic Book Publishing
Co., Inc. All rights reserved. No part of this book may be
reproduced in any form without the written consent of the publisher.

Library of Congress Catalog Card No. 77-90000

ISBN 0-8174-2186-6 (Softbound)

Manufactured in the United States of America

Dedication

It was really much easier to write this book than it is now to decide just how to phrase the thanks I want to express to the many people who were kind enough to help me do it.

Since the most obvious place to start is at the beginning, I will simply offer my heartfelt thanks to my wife, Gardy, who worked just as hard as I did on this book, but who never moaned and groaned about it the way I did.

And a low bow and a tug at the forelock to the best photo fan book editor in the business, Jim Hughes, who had the good taste, enlightened self interest, and splendid judgment to decide to run several large sections of this book in one of his excellent magazines, *35mm Photography.* The sale of a book's first rights to the best magazine in the field is the kind of author encouragement that really counts. Thanks, Jim. Then there was Tom Ridinger and friends. Tom is the Art Director of *35mm Photography* and the man with the incredible patience, skill, and magic needed to convert my rotten line drawings into the clear and understandable pieces of artwork upon which the drawings in this book are based. Thanks, Tom (and friends).

And speaking of patience, fortitude, skill, and such—my thanks too, to the staff members of *35mm Photography,* who all somehow managed to package great, unmanageable chunks of this book in magazine format—and not just once, mind you, but four back-bending times.

My thanks, too, to Art Goldsmith, the Editorial Director of *Popular Photography,* and Burt Kepler, the Editorial Director of *Modern Photography,* both of whom bought much of the material on which this book is based, for use in their respective magazines; and to Shinichiro Tora, *Popular Photography's* Art Director, who suffered with some of the peculiar illustrations that accompanied that work.

So much for the folks in the magazine business and on to my many friends in the photographic hardware and software business who gave so much time and expended so much effort answering my endless queries, who were kind enough to supply me with much of the data that appears between these covers, and who made many of their firm's products available to me for trial and evaluation. I doubt if I could find as nice a bunch of people in any other industry.

Finally, my thanks to the cast of thousands at Amphoto who somehow managed to convert twenty pounds of manuscript into the book you are holding. You're all beautiful ... I love ya.

BOB NADLER

Table of Contents

Table of Black-and-White Illustrations in Chapters 1–8

Table of Color Illustrations

The Page-numbering System

Pages in this book are numbered so that each chapter has its own pagination. This is intended to facilitate the insertion of new material incorporated in the pages of the looseleaf supplement service. Each page has a reference both to its chapter number and to the page sequence number.

Chapters are indicated by 2 groups of Arabic numerals. For example, **2-7** means chapter two, page seven; **9-23** means chapter nine, page twenty-three.

Color pages are numbered differently. Each color sheet will have the letter "C" before the chapter number followed by the page number. Thus, **C3-3** means the third color page in chapter three.

Supplement Page Numbering. Insert pages are distributed through the supplement service for incorporation into this book. Each supplement will have a Newsletter, which will include specific instructions for insertion and removal of new and old pages. When existing pages are revised, they will retain their original numbering. Each page will, however, be imprinted with a reference to the issue number of the supplement with which it is distributed. New page Insertions are identified by decimal notation added to preceding page numbers. Thus, if a new page is to be added between 3-8 and 3-9, it will be identified as 3-8.1. The reverse side will be 3-8.2. In addition, new pages will carry a reference to the supplement with which they are distributed.

PRINTS MADE WITH VARIOUS COLOR-PRINTING TECHNIQUES

If you get bored with an image, try rearranging the colors and see what happens. I printed this tight head shot, which was originally made on Kodachrome II, on Ektacolor 74 RC paper. I liked the peculiar image obtained.

PRINTS MADE WITH VARIOUS COLOR-PRINTING TECHNIQUES

▲ I propped this insect on a houseplant leaf and shot it from all angles using one roll each of Tri-X, Kodacolor II, and High Speed Ektachrome B. This is one of the images made on High Speed Ektachrome B and Type 1993 paper.

▼ When printing this simple image, shot on Kodachrome II, I wanted to supress all background details, saturate and slightly mute the reds, and accentuate the overall contrast. Making the print on Cibachrome material was an easy choice.

▲ I made use of the orange filter built into my 16mm rectilinear fisheye lens to enhance this shot of a pair of ancient schooners living out their days on a New England mud flat. I decided to use the filter after I had already shot several rolls of the subject in a number of different ways. I normally wouldn't have used such an obvious ploy, and I still feel a bit ashamed of myself for doing it, and more so for liking the image. This kind of high-contrast, low-information, brightly colored graphic, made on Kodachrome II, was a natural for printing on Cibachrome material.

► Getting some of the details in this image of Manhattan's murky 42nd Street, made on Kodachrome II, and holding overall contrast to a minimum called for the kind of control I find I can get from Kodak's direct-reversal Ektachrome Type 1993 material.

PRINTS MADE WITH VARIOUS COLOR-PRINTING TECHNIQUES

▲ This aerial of lower Manhattan was shot on Kodachrome II through a 16mm rectilinear fisheye, and proved to be extremely easy to print on Ektachrome Type 1993 paper. No burning, dodging, contrast control, or other manipulative processes were required to make the straight print look almost as good as the chrome.

◄ I made this shot, on High Speed Ektachrome, while on a Washington D.C. peace march during the Vietnam war era. In those days there were no high-quality, direct-reversal printing materials available, so I had to make a 2¼″ × 3¼″ internegative on Ektacolor 6008 internegative film, before I could make the print on Unicolor (Mitsubishi) type-B paper.

Shot through a polarizer, with a very low sun angle, this red Nova Scotia fishing shack took on an incredible hue when rendered first on Kodachrome II, then on Ektachrome Type 1993 paper.

BASIC COLOR SCHEME

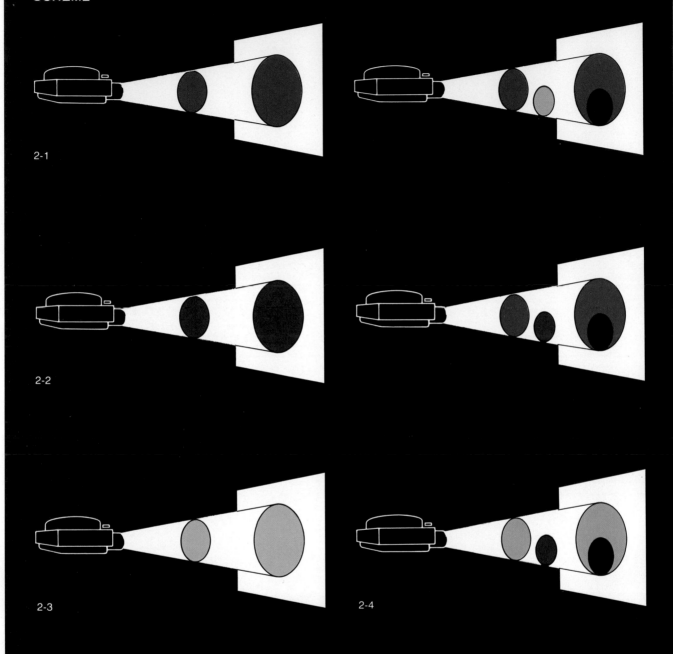

2-1

2-2

2-3

2-4

Fig. 2-1—A red filter lets only the red component of white light through.

Fig. 2-2—A blue filter lets only the blue component of white light through.

Fig. 2-3—A green filter lets only the green component of white light through.

Fig. 2-4—Any two additive primary filters placed over a single source of light will pass no light.

BASIC
COLOR
SCHEME

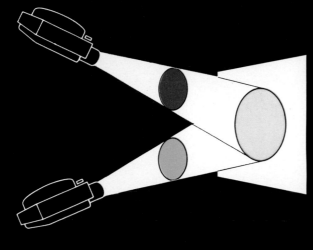

2-5

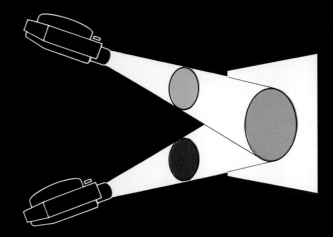

2-6

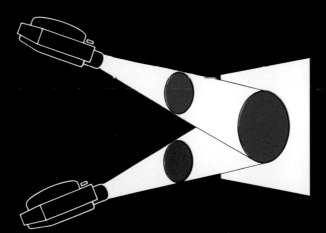

2-7

Fig. 2-5—If you blend equal parts of red and green light, the resulting color seen will be yellow, blue's complementary (exact opposite) color.

Fig 2-6—Similarly, a mixture of green and blue light yields red's complementary, cyan.

Fig. 2-7—Magenta, green's complementary, results from a mixture of blue and red light.

Fig. 2-8—White light is a mixture of equal parts of red, green, and blue light.

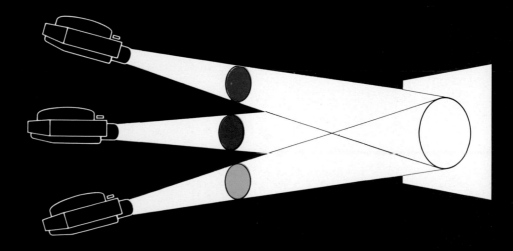

2-8

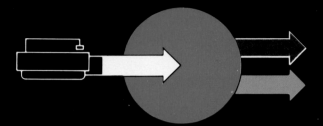

2-9

2-12

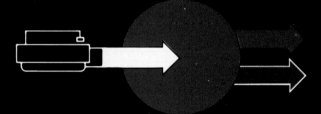

2-10

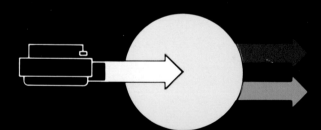

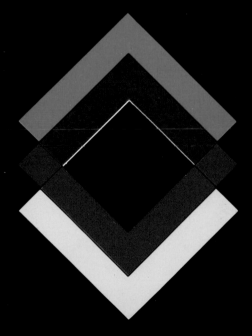

2-11

2-13

Fig. 2-9—Cyan subtracts red, but passes
green and blue.

Fig. 2-10— Magenta subtracts green, but
passes red and blue.

Fig. 2-11- Yellow subtracts blue, but passes
red and green.

Fig. 2-12—Low-density subtractive primary
filters remove only a portion of white light's
three component colors and form low neutral
density (gray)

Fig. 2-13—High-density subtractive filters
remove all of white light's three component
colors for high neutral density (black)

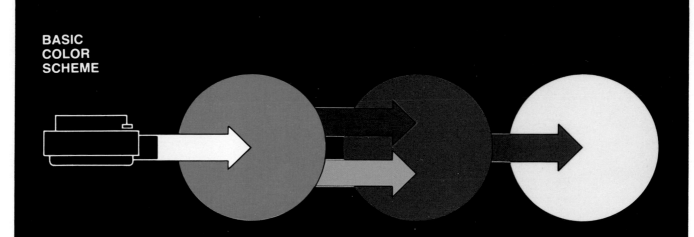

Fig. 2-14—White light passes through a cyan filter and loses its red component. The remaining blue and green light encounters a magenta filter, where the green component is absorbed. This leaves only the blue component of the original beam of white light to pass through to the yellow filter, where it too is absorbed. The result is neutral density.

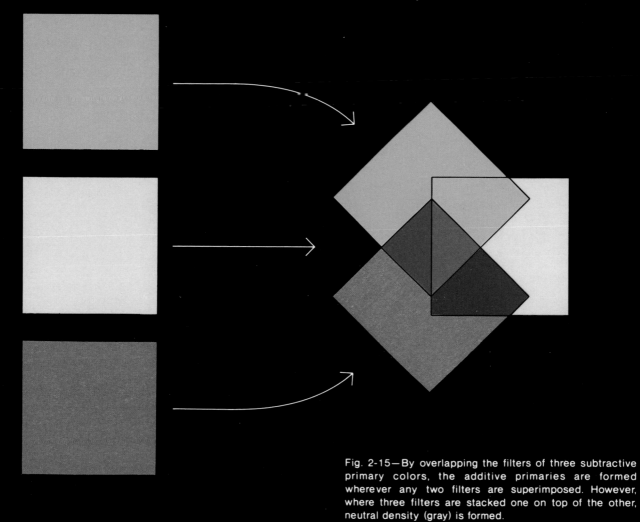

Fig. 2-15—By overlapping the filters of three subtractive primary colors, the additive primaries are formed wherever any two filters are superimposed. However, where three filters are stacked one on top of the other, neutral density (gray) is formed.

EXPOSURE OF TYPICAL COLOR NEGATIVE FILM TO REFLECTED LIGHT

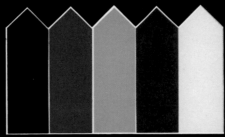

Multicolored board fence

BLK = BLACK
R = RED
G = GREEN
Y = YELLOW
B = BLUE
W = WHITE

LAYER	SENSITIVE TO	BLK	R	G	B	W	DYE COLOR AFTER DEVELOPMENT
		no light					
1	Blue & violet					XXXXXXXXXX XXXXXXXXXX	Yellow
			R	G	some B	R+G+ some B	
2	Not sensitized. Yellow filter.						None. Separates emulsion layers.
			R	G		R + G	
3	Green & blue			XXXXX XXXXX		XXXXX XXXXX	Magenta (plus a yellow coupler for printing filtering).
			R	some G		R + some G	
4	Not sensitized. Clear gelatin.						None. Separates emulsion layers.
			R	some G		R + some G	
5	Red, blue & slightly to green.		XXXXX XXXXX			XXXXX XXXXX	Cyan (plus a reddish coupler for printing filtering).
			some R	some G		some R + some G	
6	Not sensitized. Film base.						None. Acts as support for other layers.
			some R	some G		some R + some G	
7	Not sensitized. Anti-halation layer.						None. Absorbs any light that gets this far.

Fig. 2-16—This diagram represents the exposure of typical color negative film to light reflected from a black, red, green, blue, and white object (xxxx=latent image formed by exposure of silver-halide grains to light of a color to which the grains are sensitive).

**COLOR
NEGATIVE
FILM
AFTER
DEVELOPMENT**

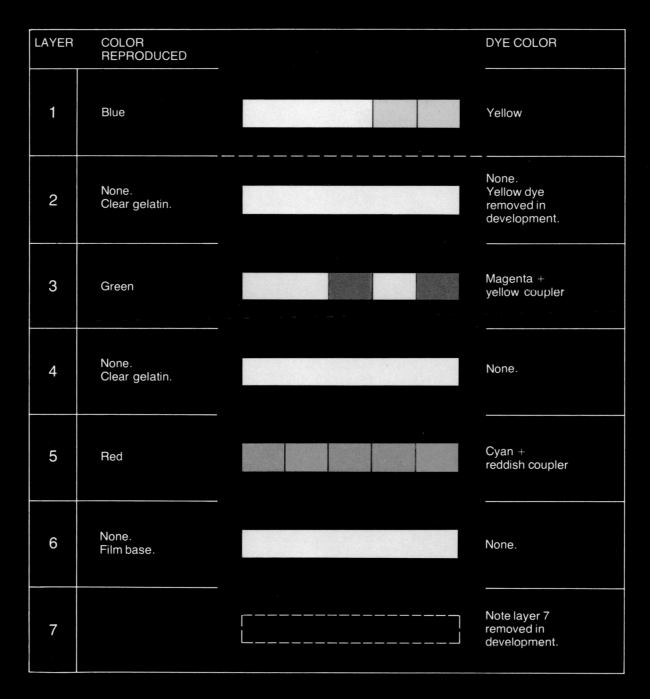

LAYER	COLOR REPRODUCED		DYE COLOR
1	Blue		Yellow
2	None. Clear gelatin.		None. Yellow dye removed in development.
3	Green		Magenta + yellow coupler
4	None. Clear gelatin.		None.
5	Red		Cyan + reddish coupler
6	None. Film base.		None.
7			Note layer 7 removed in development.

Fig. 2-17—In this diagram of the color negative film after processing, note that the second gelatin layer is now clear and that the seventh layer has been removed. The dyes formed are the complementary colors of the light which exposed the film. Yellow couplers remain in unexposed portions of layer three, and orange couplers remain in unexposed portions of layer five.

PRINTING A COLOR NEGATIVE

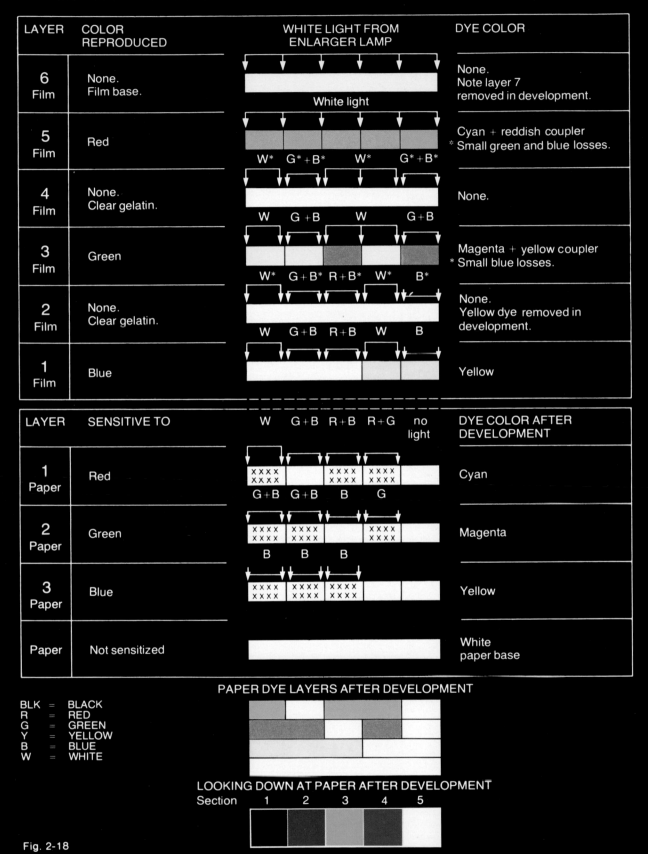

LAYER	COLOR REPRODUCED	WHITE LIGHT FROM ENLARGER LAMP	DYE COLOR
6 Film	None. Film base.	White light	None. Note layer 7 removed in development.
5 Film	Red	W* G*+B* W* G*+B*	Cyan + reddish coupler * Small green and blue losses.
4 Film	None. Clear gelatin.	W G+B W G+B	None.
3 Film	Green	W* G+B* R+B* W* B*	Magenta + yellow coupler * Small blue losses.
2 Film	None. Clear gelatin.	W G+B R+B W B	None. Yellow dye removed in development.
1 Film	Blue		Yellow

LAYER	SENSITIVE TO	W	G+B	R+B	R+G	no light	DYE COLOR AFTER DEVELOPMENT
1 Paper	Red	xxxx xxxx G+B	G+B	xxxx xxxx B	xxxx xxxx G		Cyan
2 Paper	Green	xxxx xxxx B	xxxx xxxx B	B	xxxx xxxx		Magenta
3 Paper	Blue	xxxx xxxx	xxxx xxxx	xxxx xxxx			Yellow
Paper	Not sensitized						White paper base

PAPER DYE LAYERS AFTER DEVELOPMENT

BLK = BLACK
R = RED
G = GREEN
Y = YELLOW
B = BLUE
W = WHITE

LOOKING DOWN AT PAPER AFTER DEVELOPMENT

Section 1 2 3 4 5

Fig. 2-18

C2-8

FORMATION OF A COLOR POSITIVE SLIDE IMAGE

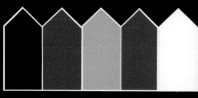

Multicolored board fence

SENSITIVE TO		BLK	R	G	B	W	

BLUE & VIOLET
xxxxxxxxxx
xxxxxxxxxx

Gelatin (w/yellow dye)

GREEN & BLUE
x x x x x   x x x x x
x x x x x   x x x x x

Gelatin

RED & BLUE
x x x x x   x x x x x
x x x x x   x x x x x

Film base

Anti-halation material

Initial exposure of color transparency film, in camera, and subsequent development in black-and-white developer (xxx = metallic silver formed in black-and-white developer).

o o o o o o o o o o o o o o o   x x x x x x x x x x
o o o o o o o o o o o o o o o   x x x x x x x x x x

o o o o o o o o o o o x x x x x o o o o x x x x x
o o o o o o o o o o o x x x x x o o o o x x x x x

o o o o x x x x x o o o o o o o o o x x x x x
o o o o x x x x x o o o o o o o o o x x x x x

Film after reexposure (or chemical fogging) and subsequent development in color developer (ooo = metallic silver formed in color developer).

Film after bleaching and fixing. All metallic silver has been removed and only dye remains.

Looking down at white light shining through the film after processing is complete.

BLK = BLACK
R = RED
G = GREEN
Y = YELLOW
B = BLUE
W = WHITE

Fig. 2-19

FORMATION OF A COLOR POSITIVE PRINT IMAGE

WHITE LIGHT FROM ENLARGER LAMP

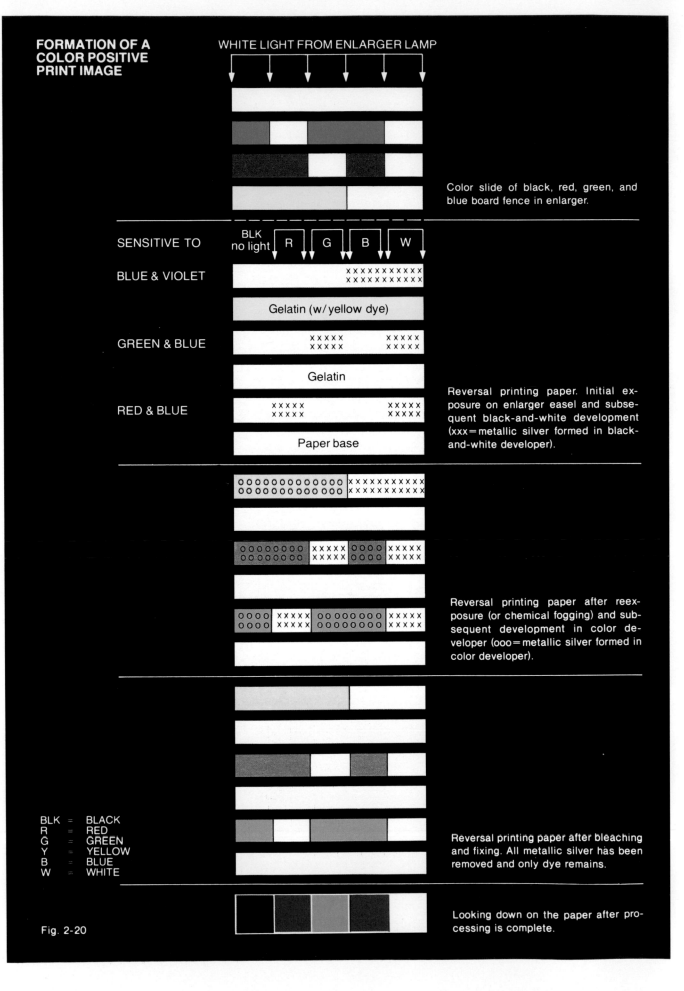

Color slide of black, red, green, and blue board fence in enlarger.

SENSITIVE TO

BLK no light | R | G | B | W

BLUE & VIOLET

Gelatin (w/yellow dye)

GREEN & BLUE

Gelatin

RED & BLUE

Paper base

Reversal printing paper. Initial exposure on enlarger easel and subsequent black-and-white development (xxx = metallic silver formed in black-and-white developer).

Reversal printing paper after reexposure (or chemical fogging) and subsequent development in color developer (ooo = metallic silver formed in color developer).

BLK = BLACK
R = RED
G = GREEN
Y = YELLOW
B = BLUE
W = WHITE

Reversal printing paper after bleaching and fixing. All metallic silver has been removed and only dye remains.

Looking down on the paper after processing is complete.

Fig. 2-20

**FORMATION OF A
COLOR POSITIVE IMAGE
ON CIBACHROME
DYE BLEACH
PRINTING MATERIAL**

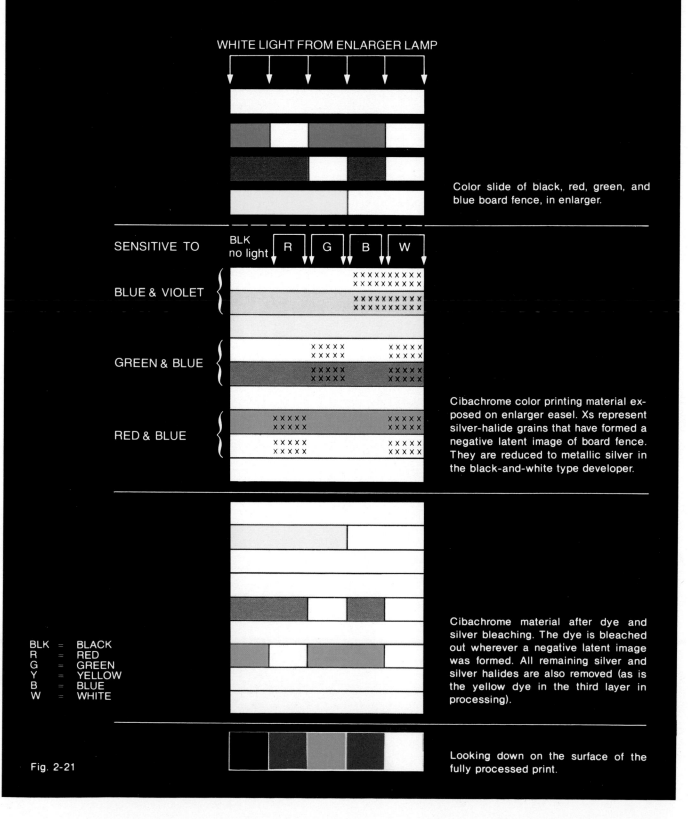

WHITE LIGHT FROM ENLARGER LAMP

Color slide of black, red, green, and blue board fence, in enlarger.

SENSITIVE TO

BLK no light | R | G | B | W

BLUE & VIOLET

GREEN & BLUE

RED & BLUE

Cibachrome color printing material exposed on enlarger easel. Xs represent silver-halide grains that have formed a negative latent image of board fence. They are reduced to metallic silver in the black-and-white type developer.

BLK = BLACK
R = RED
G = GREEN
Y = YELLOW
B = BLUE
W = WHITE

Cibachrome material after dye and silver bleaching. The dye is bleached out wherever a negative latent image was formed. All remaining silver and silver halides are also removed (as is the yellow dye in the third layer in processing).

Fig. 2-21

Looking down on the surface of the fully processed print.

C2-11

TYPICAL CIBACHROME DYE BLEACH PRINTING PAPER CONSTRUCTION

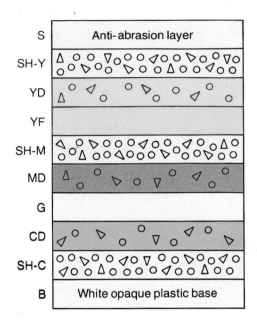

Cibachrome "paper" is comprised of the following labeled layers: (S) the anti-abrasion layer; (SH-Y) contains silver halide that is sensitive to blue light; (YD) contains fully saturated yellow dye and additional blue-sensitive silver halide; (YF) a yellow-dyed gelatin which serves as a blue light-absorbing filter; (SH-M) contains silver halides that are sensitive to green and blue light; (MD) contains fully saturated magenta dye and additional green/blue sensitive silver halide; (G) a simple gelatin layer; (CD) contains fully saturated cyan dye and some red/blue sensitive silver halides; (SH-C) contains silver halides that are sensitive to red and blue light, (B) a white, opaque, triacetate base.

Fig. 2-22

I didn't expect to be in the Kremlin on the night I made this simple shot of the floodlit domes of St. Basil's Church, so I had to work with the equipment I had with me—a handheld camera loaded with daylight-balanced relatively slow Agfa CT18 film. Printed on Cibachrome, for maximum color saturation and high contrast, this simple spur-of-the-moment shot took on added graphic interest.

Chapter 1

Introduction

Before getting to the subject matter of this book, I'd like to introduce myself to you and tell you a bit about why I wrote it.

If I have to describe myself as any one thing, it would be as a writer/photographer for photographic magazines. I have written so many feature articles, test reports, interviews, etc., for publications like *Popular Photography, Modern Photography, Camera 35,* and several others, that I've lost count. As a matter of fact, I spent four years as the technical editor of *Camera 35.*

I don't mention this to impress you with credentials, but only to let you know why this book is written in the first person and has such a peculiar style. I'll just have to blame it on bad habits picked up from long associations with magazines. It's also the style and way of explaining things that comes naturally to me.

With that out of the way, the next thing I want to do is tell you who this book was written for. It is specifically designed for amateur and low-volume professional photographers who want to do their own color printing. This is definitely not meant to be a text for commercial photofinishers, or even for workers who must produce large numbers of prints in well-equipped studios. There is no procedure, process, or material called for between these covers, that can't be successfully dealt with by anyone of normal intelligence, using a kitchen, bathroom, or an under-the-stairs kind of darkroom. Actually, as I will point out later, even a closet will do nicely.

But dear reader, if you do have a big, beautiful darkroom, don't feel slighted. You *will* have an easier time of it than the person who has to make his exposures in a third-floor linen closet, and then run down two flights of stairs to the basement sink to do his print processing. However, there is no reason for you to think that the big, elaborately equipped darkroom will yield better color prints. *Print quality is, to the greatest extent, a function of the skill of the printer, not of the size and equipment of his darkroom.* Put another way, this book is designed to give you the printing skills needed to enable you to produce first-rate prints, if need be, under fifth-rate conditions.

I've presented the information you will need in such a way that you will never have to remember more than six different names of colors and the interrelation of three of these colors to one another. If I have done my work well then you should always be able to arrive logically at any answer to any color printing problem, rather than have to fumble around trying to remember some kind of silly rule (which you don't understand) or have to look up your particular problem in a table of general solutions to general problems (and begin to tear your hair out when you find that you can't find it).

Once you have read this book, you will know why you have a particular problem and what you ought to do about it. The solution will be at hand, because you will know what brought the problem about in the first place, and how to correct such conditions in the second.

From long, hard experience with writing for magazines, I am also well aware that there are many readers who have neither the patience nor the stamina to read the book through prior to heading for the darkroom to try out the few little bits of information that they have picked up before their patience ran out. (If the truth were to be known, I'm probably among them). In order to keep such folks happy, I've provided some sections that will enable them to rush off to start printing color long before they have any considerable understanding of what it is that they are doing in the darkroom. I've even gone to the extent of including color-printing programs that will allow the impatient to function as mindlessly as a computer if so desired. But, hopefully, this sort of printing will become boring and unsatisfying very quickly and the reader will return here for more information.

There was a time in the not-too-distant past when color printing was difficult, time consuming, and uneconomical to do in a small home darkroom. It used to take 48¼ minutes to process a reversal print, and 31 minutes just to process a print made from a negative. Today, both processes can easily be carried out in less than ten minutes. Several years ago you would be thought just slightly mad to try to undertake making color prints without a full, temperature-controlled darkroom sink. Today, a dishpan and a gallon plastic jug will suffice. Frankly, I find that with today's materials, it is easier to make a first-rate color print than it is to make a first-rate black-and-white one.

Throughout this book I shall concentrate on ease of operation. There is no point to doing things the hard way. I hope to be able to help you to avoid some procedures that are unnecessarily complicated and difficult. Wherever possible I will have you working in full white light rather than in darkness, or the near darkness required by some outmoded procedures and equipment.

I'm an opinionated worker. I won't pretend to be objective. If I feel that a product or a process is not all that it should be, you may rest assured that I will let you know. I will also clearly label such pronouncements as what they are, *opinion*. But most, if not all, of my opinions have been come by the hard way. They have been formed when I tried to do certain things, or use some particular process or machine, and found that I was wasting time, effort, or money. I hope that you can agree with my opinions. But, if you do reach an impasse with the material presented here, I have enough faith in what I have written

to believe that in time, you will reconsider and return to this tome. I have so much faith in it that I originally called it *The Color Printer's Bible*.

I firmly believe that the only way any printer will ever get to understand color printing thoroughly, either negative-to-positive, or positive-to-positive, is through an understanding of how the entire process of color photography works. Don't panic! I only intend to explain the color photographic processes in a brief and schematic fashion. I have no intention of boring and confusing a lot of people with a tremendous amount of unnecessary detail and chemical data. If I can get the reader to think of every color image he or she may see in the future as nothing more complicated than three layers of dye, I will have done almost everything that I set out to accomplish.

Because I think such an understanding is the bedrock of color printing success, I intend to open the book with this material. If you are the type of reader I referred to earlier, who can't sit still long enough to read through these basics, but must rush off to the darkroom for some firsthand, if mediocre, experience, then I suggest that you go directly to Chapter 4 entitled "Getting Started," where you will get sufficient instruction to let you get your hands wet. You won't know what you are doing when you are doing it, but have fun, enjoy yourself, then come on back here and sit down and read the "hard" stuff. You will be a better printer for it in the end.

A look at the table of contents will tell you quite quickly and accurately what subjects I have covered, but it won't explain why the book has been loose-leaf bound and why periodic supplements are offered. To understand these arrangements you need only look at the recent developments in amateur color printing. It is a field which, just several years ago, had few sources of supply and a small variety of available equipment. Today, anyone with a few dollars to invest is bringing out some "new," "useful," "revolutionary," or "superior" product about every 30 minutes. All of which means that there is continual ferment going on in the field. To keep abreast of all this continual stirring is virtually a full-time job. I will try to do that job and continue to report my findings on these new and different products and processes to you in future supplements which you can use to keep this text up to date.

Chapter 2

What You Need To Know:
How Color Photography Works

How the Eye Perceives Color

It is refreshing to note that medical science is quite willing to admit that there is really no one proven explanation of how the eye "sees" colors. As a matter of fact, the little that is known does clearly point to the distinct possibility that the eye is not the instrument that perceives color at all. It seems a safer bet that the brain docs this job.

The radiation that the human eye does respond to falls into one tiny portion of the electromagnetic spectrum, right between ultraviolet and infrared radiation. For those of you who are interested, the wavelengths handled by our eyes fall between about 400 and 700 nanometers (a nanometer, formerly called a millimicron, equals a millionth of a millimeter) and there is no known reason why our eyes should respond to this incredibly narrow frequency range the way they do; they just do. When radiation of wavelengths covering all of this 400 to 700 nanometers band stimulate the retina of the eye, the sensation received is that of seeing "white" light. However, the brain really isn't too fussy about the spectral accuracy of what it perceives as white. It seems that the brain doesn't want to trouble its owner unduly, and is willing to perceive a fairly wide variety of portions of the visible spectrum as "white" light. The classic example of this situation is when you shoot color transparency film in the very early morning or late afternoon, not thinking about, or perceiving, the peculiar nature of the light. It is only after the slides get back from the lab that you fully appreciate just how red that "white" light you shot in really was.

As a matter of fact, the eye is almost always too happy to "see" just the color you want it to see. This can be a source of trouble to the color printer, as you will find later in the section pertaining to the use of viewing filters. The eye can't see any one color selectively. That is, it can't, for example, pick the blue portion of white light out of the remainder of the spectral distribution falling upon it as the ear, at least to some extent, can tune in, or concentrate on, one portion of the various audio frequencies that it is receiving. The eye can certainly "see" the color blue when *only* light of the proper frequency (about 430 to 475 nanometers) is present, but it simply doesn't have the ability to "see" that single part of the whole visible spectrum.

Rather than get into a long-winded discussion of what will have to be clearly labeled as supposition and conjecture in the end, I'd like to state simply, that for all practical purposes, and certainly for our own photographic purposes here, the eye and its associated networks of nerves seems to be so arranged that it receives light and transmits it, through nerve networks of incredible complexity, to the brain through three separate color receptor channels. These channels seem designed to separately handle radiation of the color red (approximately 600–700 nanometers), green (approximately 500–600 nanometers), and blue (approximately 400–500 nanometers). But, each of these channels seems to *also* receive and transmit to the brain some of the portion of the spectrum that is handled by the other two channels.

It is all very complicated, but what it boils

2-1

down to, as far as we are concerned here, is that we can make practical use of this apparent three-channel construction of the eye to fool the head into thinking that it is seeing something it isn't. For example, if we stimulate the three receptors of the eye with only one source of red light and one of green light, the eye, or brain if you will, thinks it is seeing yellow light.

Even if the two filters controlling the red and green light falling on the eye are designed to completely remove that small portion of the visible spectrum which is yellow light (575–590 nanometers), the poor eye will still think it is "seeing" yellow light. Similarly, if the eye is supplied with one source of blue light and one of green light, it will see a bluish-green color we will call cyan. And if it is supplied from one source of red light and one of blue light the eye will see a reddish-blue color called magenta. Neither cyan nor magenta are colors in the spectrum.

The Basic Color Scheme Common to All Photographic Systems

The Additive Primaries

The eye's three color channels are tuned to receive and transmit the colors red, green, and blue. Every color film, paper or any other photographic medium anyone presently manufactures is also sensitive to these three colors. These three colors are called the *additive primaries*. The reason for this name is quite simple. The only way that any one of these colors can cause your eye to see anything but its own color is if it is combined in some part with radiation of the frequency of another of the additive primaries. If that is less than clear, try this: In order to see yellow your eyes will have to be stimulated with *both* a source of green *and* a source of red light. (The yellow portion of the spectrum is so narrow that spectral yellow is seldom ever seen in nature, except in rainbows.) To be of any intermediate color-forming use, the additive primaries mut be added, one to the other. The proper addition of the three additive primaries can fool your head into thinking that it is seeing any color at all, even the ones, such as magenta and cyan, that don't occur in nature's spectrum. To do this, however, separate sources of these additive colors are required to stimulate the eye/brain into seeing the synthesized color.

It may be clearer if you consider that a red filter placed in a beam of white light will absorb all radiation except that in the red frequencies from passing (see color section, Fig. 2–1). Similarly, a blue filter blocks everything but blue light and a green filter stops everything but green light from passing through it (see color section, Fig. 2 2 and 2–3). Each filter of an additive primary color manages to block two thirds of the visible spectrum from passing through itself.

If a red filter stops everything but red light from passing through it, then it shouldn't be too hard to comprehend that if you place a flashlight behind a red filter and then place a green filter in front of the red one, no light will manage to get through the pair of filters at all. The flashlight's white light will first encounter the red filter, and that filter will absorb all of the spectral frequencies but those of red. The red light will leave the red filter and encounter the green filter. Since the green filter absorbs all spectral frequencies except green, it will absorb the red light and pass nothing through to the eye.

So, any combination of two filters of the additive primary colors—red/green, red/blue, green/blue—placed over a single source of white light will absorb all of the light and allow you to see nothing (see color section, Fig. 2–4). But, as mentioned earlier, if a red filter is placed over a single flashlight and a green filter is placed over another flashlight, and both flashlights are of equal intensity and are shined at the same spot on a screen, you will see the result of these two colors being added (within the eye/brain combination)—you will see a yellow spot on the screen (see color section, Fig. 2–5). Similarly, adding green light to blue light yields the color cyan (see color section, Fig. 2–6) and adding blue light to red light produces a color called magenta (see color section, Fig. 2–7). When all three of the additive primary colors are added in equal parts the eye/brain perceives the color white (see color section, Fig. 2–8).

I think it will be easy to see that dyes of these additive primary colors are useless for the formation of photographic images, as there is only a single source of white light available for viewing such images; slides are viewed by the light of a single projection lamp, prints are seen by the white light that passes into the print from above and is then reflected from the print.

The way that the additive primaries are used in color photography is actually very similar to the way that nature seems to use them in allowing humans to see colors; *the additive primaries are the colors to which film and paper are sensitive,* just as they are the colors to which the human eye is sensitive; but the dyes within any photographic image are of another set of colors entirely.

The Subtractive Primaries

The *subtractive primaries* are those colors which result from mixing equal amounts of any two additive primary light sources. Separate and equal sources of red and blue light on a screen are perceived as the subtractive primary called magenta. A mixture of equal parts of the additive primaries blue and green yield the subtractive primary called cyan. A blend of equal parts of red and green cause the perception of the subtractive primary called yellow. The wonderful thing about these subtractive primary colors is that they are only half as greedy as the additive primary colors. A filter in any of the additive primary colors will absorb two thirds of the spectral frequencies of white light, allowing only the third containing its particular color to pass. However, a filter of any of the subtractive primary colors will absorb only about one third of the spectral frequencies of white light. The third that they do absorb is perhaps the most wonderful thing about these peculiar colors, which only interior decorators and photographers can appreciate.

Each of the subtractive primaries removes (subtracts) one of the additive primaries. The additive primary it subtracts is called its complementary color. Just as in the case of a black-and-white negative, where the black portions of the negative will print as white highlights on the paper, and the clear (white) portions of the negative will show up as black sections of the print, a cyan portion of a negative will show up in its complementary color, red, on the print. But I'm afraid I'm getting a bit ahead of myself, so back to the concept of complementary colors.

The various sets of complementaries are red/cyan, blue/yellow and green/magenta. A cyan filter will pass green and blue, but hold back red (see color section, Fig. 2-9). A magenta filter will hold back green, but pass red and blue (see color section, Fig. 2-10). A yellow filter will pass green and red, but hold back blue (see color section, Fig. 2-11). And these wonderful subtractive primaries don't require separate sources of light, white or otherwise, to do their thing. They are perfectly happy to subtract their complementaries from a single source of light.

Now we are getting somewhere. These peculiar colored dyes are nicely suited to making photographic images.

If you will recall my earlier statement, we are able to produce any color at all by stimulating the eye's receptor channels with various combinations of the additive primaries. Since the subtractive primaries can be used to accurately control the mixture of additive primaries *in any single source of light,* it follows that by controlling only three layers of dye, one in each of the subtractive primary colors, we can manipulate the additive primaries and cause the eye to perceive any color at all.

A bit more explanation is in order here. A filter has two principal properties: its color and its density. We have been discussing color up to now, but as yet we have said nothing about density. If a filter is made with a little bit of dye of a pure magenta color, it will have a pale magenta appearance and it will absorb only a little of the green component of white light. If the same filter is made with a great deal of magenta dye, it will have a deep magenta appearance and it will remove a great deal of the green component of white light. The same, of course, is true for filters of the other subtractive primaries (see color section, Figs. 2-12, 2-13). Later, when I get into the use of subtractive primary filters for controlling your enlarger's white-light output, I will mention conventional filter densities of 5 to 40 for the standard acetate color printing (CP) filters most often used in color printing. I mention these here just to give you some idea of the amount of subtracting power of such filters. For instance, a 40 magenta filter will subtract about 65 percent of the green content of the white light passing through it. A 5 magenta filter, on the other hand, will only remove about 20 percent of white light's green component. So much for dye density. On to neutral density.

It may not have occurred to you that it is possible to stack several of the subtractive primary filters together to remove more than one additive primary component of white light; however, doing so is entirely possible. You can place a cyan filter over a beam of white light and remove some or all (depending on the cyan filter's density) of the beam's red component. If you then place a magenta filter on top of the cyan one you can also get rid of the beam's green component, and finally, if you place a yellow filter over the other two you will get rid of the beam's blue component (see color section, Fig. 2–14). Now, if you get rid of red, green, and blue, what do you have left? Nothing, so far as our eyes are concerned. And what does nothing equal in any discussion of color? *Neutral density* is the answer.

A much simpler and more readily understood term for neutral density is black. Black is the absence of any light. However, neutral density, as all you users of neutral density camera filters well know, comes in various densities too. Neutral density starts where white leaves off and goes through increasingly darker shades of gray until it hits its maximum density at which point no light, of any color at all, can be transmitted through it. It is always this absence of light that forms the "color" black (see color section, Fig. 2–15).

How Color Films Are Designed and How They Operate

Perhaps the easiest way to think of color film is as three layers of black-and-white film glued together. While that is a gross simplification, it is not too far from being the case. Color film has three separate and distinct silver-halide emulsion layers, one on top of the other, all sitting on one layer of plastic film base. But, unlike black-and-white emulsion, which is panchromatic (it responds to all of the colors of the visible spectrum, more or less equally), each of the emulsion layers on a piece of color film are essentially monochromatic (they respond to one, or mostly to one color alone). The reason for this construction — it's the same, by the way, for almost all color materials (except Cibachrome which I'll get to later) whether they're color printing papers, transparency film, reversal color papers, etc. — is that in photography there are only three different dye colors used to reproduce any and every color. Those dyes colors are the subtractive primaries, cyan, magenta, and yellow.

The basic scheme employed is such that each of the three emulsion layers is specifically designed to respond to exposure by light of one of the additive primary colors. The topmost emulsion layer is sensitive to blue light, the center emulsion layer responds to green light, and the bottom emulsion layer records a latent image when exposed to red light. The effect of light on the emulsion layers is exactly the same as it is in black-and-white photography. Each layer of emulsion that receives exposure is left with a latent image in its silver halide. It is not until after further film processing that any dyes are formed.

In addition to silver halides, each emulsion layer has chemical substances called couplers incorporated in them (except in the case of the Kodachromes, which have both their couplers and dyes added during processing). During one of the chemical processes of development, these couplers react selectively to form dye. For example, where the middle emulsion layer of a color negative film receives exposure from green light and records a latent image in the silver halide, development will reduce that silver halide to metallic silver (just as in black-and-white film), while oxidizing the developer at the same time. The coupler in the center emulsion layer then reacts with components of the oxidized developer to form an amount of magenta dye that is in direct proportion to the amount of green light exposure that the emulsion originally received. Some couplers are also used to form a printing mask (the orange or deep yellow color) in color negatives. This will be explained in more detail later.

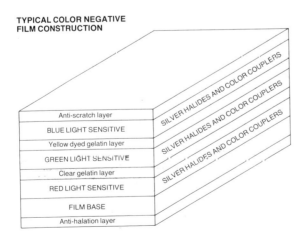

TYPICAL COLOR NEGATIVE
FILM CONSTRUCTION

Anti-scratch layer
BLUE LIGHT SENSITIVE
Yellow dyed gelatin layer
GREEN LIGHT SENSITIVE
Clear gelatin layer
RED LIGHT SENSITIVE
FILM BASE
Anti-halation layer

SILVER HALIDES AND COLOR COUPLERS
SILVER HALIDES AND COLOR COUPLERS
SILVER HALIDES AND COLOR COUPLERS

2-4

All color films incorporate some kind of anti-halation layer. It is provided to insure that any light that manages to reach the film base will not be reflected back up through the emulsion layers. The anti-halation layer can absorb all the radiation of the visual spectrum. The anti-halation layer is the black substance that causes many home processors of 5247 and 5254 Eastman movie film stock a good deal of grief when little bits and pieces of it find their way to the emulsion side of the film during processing.

I should also mention that there are gelatin layers between each emulsion layer. They are there to separate the emulsion layers from one another mechanically and chemically. However, the gelatin layer between the uppermost (blue-sensitive) and middle (green-sensitive) layer also serves as a yellow filter. I'll get to the reason for that quite soon. The yellow dye incorporated in this layer washes out during the film processing, leaving this gelatin layer, too, with only its role as a separator once the film has been processed.

Many films also incorporate a topmost layer of anti-scratch material to protect the tender emulsion layers below it from mechanical damage during the film's transport through the camera.

How Color Printing Papers Are Designed and How They Operate

The major difference between the structure of color film and color paper is that the emulsion layers of the paper material are supported on a layer of opaque, highly reflective and brilliant white paper, instead of on a transparent plastic material as is the case with color films. The reason for this is that color printing is designed to yield an image that will be viewed by reflection, rather than by transmission, as in the case of color transparency films. Another important difference between film and paper is that the emulsion layers are in a different order in color papers meant for use with color negatives. Color negative printing papers have their emulsion layers arranged so that the uppermost layer is sensitive to red, the center layer is sensitive to green, and the bottom layer responds to blue. Reversal papers, which are used to make prints directly from slides, such as Kodak Ektachrome RC Paper, Type 1993, R-14, and Cibachrome's various papers, have their emulsion layers in the same order as the film, with the top layer responding to blue light, the center layer sensitive to green light, and the bottom layer responding to red light.

There are two principal types of color printing papers designed for producing images from color negatives. These are called, simply enough, type-A and type-B. From a practical point of view the difference between the two types is that the type-B paper can be evaluated for print color balance while the print is wet, while type-A prints must be dried before this evaluation can be made. From a structural point of view the difference lies in the way the couplers are incorporated in the paper's emulsion layers. Type-A papers incorporate their couplers incapsulated in tiny oil globules which are dispersed throughout the emulsion layers. Type-B papers keep their couplers from wandering between emulsion layers and from interacting with the silver halides by attaching the coupler molecules to large organic groups.

Another practical material consideration, among the several color-printing paper materials, is the paper's base itself. There are, presently, two different principal types of paper bases available; baryta (barium sulfate) coated and resin (plastic) coated. Most type-B papers are of the former type, while most of the type-A papers are plastic coated. Plastic-coated papers are easier to wash, quick to dry, and lie flat after drying. Baryta-base paper is somewhat less expensive and can provide a surface when air dried, which, at least to this observer, is far better than anything I have seen on resin-coated materials. I prefer the ease of working with plastic-coated papers.

TYPICAL COLOR NEGATIVE PAPER CONSTRUCTION

RED LIGHT SENSITIVE
Clear gelatin layer
GREEN LIGHT SENSITIVE
Clear gelatin layer
BLUE LIGHT SENSITIVE
PAPER BASE

SILVER HALIDES AND COLOR COUPLERS
SILVER HALIDES AND COLOR COUPLERS
SILVER HALIDES AND COLOR COUPLERS

The structure of the entirely plastic-base Cibachrome color printing "paper" is so different from all of the materials discussed here, that it will be taken up separately.

How the Negative-To-Positive System Works

How a Latent Image Is Recorded on Color Negative Film

In order to understand how color relationships are manipulated to achieve a color print, the most logical place to begin is with the generation of a color negative. Figure 2–16 (see color section) represents a cross-sectional view, greatly magnified, of a piece of tri-pack color negative film being used to take a picture of a section of board fence. The first board visible on the left side of the viewfinder is painted matte-black; the board adjacent to it is painted red; the next board is green; the one after is blue; the final board, visible on the right side of the viewfinder, is white.

The light reflected off the fence is focused on the film plane. The first emulsion layer it strikes contains silver salts sensitive to blue and violet. The silver salts are affected where layer No. 1 is struck by the light coming from the blue painted board; the intensity of the blue light is diminished as its energy is consumed in the photochemical reaction, causing the silver salts in this layer to begin to be reduced to metallic silver. Note that there is also a reaction in this emulsion layer where it is struck by light from the white board. White light contains equal parts of red, green, and blue light, and its blue component is diminished as it affects this layer of emulsion. Since this layer is insensitive to the colors red and green, light from the red and green boards will cause no changes. Obviously, there will also be no effect from the black board—black being the absence of light rather than a color.

Layer No. 2 consists of a gelatin containing yellow dye. This layer is nothing more than a yellow filter. Yellow, being the complementary of blue, effectively eliminates any blue light which has passed through the first blue-sensitive layer. Complementary colors, you will recall, yield neutral density (shades of gray through black). Layer No. 3, which is sensitive to both green and blue, must not receive blue light. The yellow layer effectively blocks blue while allowing red and green light to pass through unaffected.

Layer No. 3 now records the image of the green board and the green component of the image of the white board. In doing so, it reduces the intensity of the green light that passes through it and onto layer No. 4. The red light passes through layer No. 3 undiminished.

Layer No. 4 is simply clear gelatin, used to separate emulsion layers No. 3 and No. 5. It has no effect on the light passing through it.

Layer No. 5 is sensitive to red and blue, and only slightly sensitive to green. As all of the blue light has either been absorbed or filtered and most of the green light has been absorbed, only the image of the red board (and the red component of the white board) will be recorded in this layer.

Layer No. 6, the film base, is transparent plastic and serves only as a mechanical support.

Layer No. 7 is an anti-halation backing, which serves to absorb any light energy that has gotten through, thereby preventing this light from being bounced back up through the layers to cause multiple images and/or fog.

How the Latent Image Is Developed to a Color Negative Image

If you have been making references to Figure 2–16 (see color section) while reading the material just before this, you will have noticed a column of information labeled "Dye Color After Development," which I will explain now.

The data simply indicates the color of the dye that will be deposited in each of the emulsion layers during the development process, which is complicated chemical procedure. Briefly, couplers incorporated in each layer of the film's emulsion will selectively combine with the products of oxidation that result when you develop the exposed silver salts. The amount of dye so deposited will be in direct proportion to the amount of exposure received by the emulsion. The couplers used not only insure that the right color dye is deposited in the appropriate emulsion layer, but also form a printing mask which gives most color negatives their characteristic orange color. (I'll explain this masking later.) Once the dye is deposited, all metallic silver and silver salts are removed by bleaching and fixing.

A glance at Figure 2–17 (see color section)

will show that in emulsion layer No. 1, which is used to record the blue image, yellow dye will be formed after development. Yellow, of course, is the complement of blue; remember, this is a negative we are making. Similarly, magenta—green's complement—will be deposited in the green-sensitive layer No. 3, and cyan—red's complement—will be deposited in red-sensitive layer No. 6.

How the Color Negative Image Is Printed

Figure 2–18 (see color section) shows our negative of the multi-colored fence, emulsion side down in an enlarger. A sheet of color printing paper is shown below it in position to be printed. Below the cross-sectional views of the film and paper is an additional cross-sectional view of the paper's dye layers after development, and a plan view (looking down at the emulsion side) of the paper as it will appear after development. You will note that the topmost film layer illustrated is layer No. 6, the film base (the anti-halation layer is dissolved and removed during film processing). White light from the enlarger lamp is shown falling on the film base. Since the film base is clear, the white light passes through unaffected.

Film layer No. 5 is now a dye layer, containing two sections of cyan dye that control the exposure of the red-sensitive emulsion of the printing paper. Where the white light passes through the cyan dye deposits, the red component is filtered out (cyan being red's complementary color), leaving only the green and blue components to pass through to film layer No. 4. (For the moment let's ignore the asterisks shown below this layer in Figure 2–18. We will return to them later.) Film layer No. 4 is clear gelatin and does not affect the light passing through it.

Film layer No. 3 is responsible for controlling the exposure of the green-sensitive emulsion of the printing paper. It contains two magenta sections that remove the green component of the light that passes through them.

Now, let's stop and look at the light that falls on layer No. 2. The first pair of arrows on the left (section 1) is shown as white light, since these have not passed through any dye deposit to this point. The next pair of arrows (section 2) is labeled green + blue, because the white light these arrows started out as has passed through cyan dye in film layer No. 5. The next pair of arrows (section 3) is shown as red + blue, because

their original white light has passed through magenta dye in film layer No. 3. The next pair of arrows (section 4) is indicated as white light because they have not passed through any dye at this point. The final pair of arrows (section 5) on the right are labeled blue, because the white light from which they originated has passed through cyan dye in film layer No. 5 (where the red component was lost) and magenta dye in film layer No. 3 (where the green component was lost). Once again, I have ignored the asterisks, we will return to them later as well.

Layer No. 2 is the gelatin that contained yellow dye before development. It is now quite clear, as all of its yellow dye was removed in the development process. Therefore, the light reaching film layer No. 1 is unchanged from the light that falls on film layer No. 2. Film layer No. 1 is responsible for controlling the exposure of the blue-sensitive emulsion of the printing paper. It contains two contiguous sections of yellow dye that will remove the blue component of light that passes through them. The light that leaves film layer No. 1 passes through the enlarger lens and falls on the printing paper.

The printing paper consists of three layers of silver-salt emulsion, each layer being sensitive to only one of the three additive primary colors. (There are also two thin layers of clear gelatin separating the emulsion layers; they have been omitted from the illustration for clarity.)

The first emulsion layer on the printing paper is sensitive to red light. Where layer No. 1 is struck by light containing a red component, silver salts begin to be reduced to metallic silver. Thus, the red latent image will be recorded, while the intensity of the red component of the impinging light will be diminished as its energy is consumed in the photochemical reaction. Figure 2–18 illustrates this effect in the first, third, and fourth sections of paper layer No. 1.

Paper layer No. 2 will record a latent image of any green light that strikes it, while diminishing the intensity of the green light causing the latent image to be formed. This effect will be noted in the first, second, and fourth sections of paper layer No. 2. Now, with all of the red light absorbed in paper layer No. 1, and all of the green light absorbed in paper layer No. 2, only the blue light remains to fall on paper layer No. 3.

Paper layer No. 3 records a latent image of the blue component in its first, second, and third sections.

The process of development of color paper is essentially the same as that of color negative film: cyan dye is deposited where the latent image of red was formed, magenta dye is deposited where the latent image of red was formed, magenta dye is deposited where the latent image of green was formed, and yellow dye is deposited where the latent image of blue was formed. The brilliant white color of the paper base, paper layer No. 4, is not affected by development.

The bottom sections of the illustration show the appearance of the printing paper after development. It must be understood that a developed color print is viewed by observing light that is first transmitted through the three dye layers, then reflected back from the white paper base through the three dye layers to the eye. With this in mind, let's view the developed print of the multicolored fence.

White light enters section one and passes through dyes of the three subtractive primary colors (cyan, magenta, and yellow). You will recall that three subtractive primaries form neutral density; therefore, little light will reach the paper base in this section to be reflected, and that which does will be absorbed. Section one will appear black.

In section two, white light must pass through magenta and yellow dye layers, then be reflected back through these dye layers on the way to the eye. Therefore, red is the color that this section will appear to be.

In section three, the white light must traverse yellow and cyan dye layers twice on the way to the eye, losing its blue and red components. This section will then appear to be green.

In section four, white light must make two passes through cyan and magenta dye, losing its red and green components, before being seen as blue.

Finally, in section five, you will see that since no light at all fell in this section of the printing paper under the enlarger, no latent image was formed, and no dyes were deposited in development. Therefore, the light reaching the eye from this section of the developed paper is only that which is reflected unfiltered from the paper base. It will appear white.

Now, let's go back to those asterisks — you remember, the ones which I did not stop to explain.

Reference to Figure 2–18 (see color section) will show that I have indicated small losses of blue and green light to all of the light component arrows that have passed through film layer No. 5, the cyan dye layer. These losses are brought about by the deliberate incorporation of a coupler that remains in this layer after development and colors the layer red wherever cyan dye is not formed. This is done by the film manufacturers to compensate for unwanted green and blue absorption by the cyan dye. In the same manner, small blue losses caused by unwanted absorption by the magenta dye are compensated for by incorporating a coupler in film layer No. 3 that colors this layer yellow wherever magenta dye is not formed in development. Therefore, asterisks indicate small, but equal, blue losses to all of the light passing through film layer No. 3. The combination of the red and yellow masks is responsible for the overall orange appearance of color negatives.

How the Positive-to-Positive Chromogenic System Works

How a Latent Image Is Recorded on Film

The strangeness of the color reversal process won't phase the dedicated reader, but if you have only been randomly reading…good luck from here.

The structure of a color reversal film is, for all intents and purposes, identical to that of a color negative film, with one or two important differences. The first, and most obvious difference between color negative and color positive film, is that the color positive material (transparency film — the film for slides) doesn't incorporate the color couplers that result in an orange printing mask after processing. Transparencies are intended for direct viewing over a white light source. It is this direct-viewing requirement that brings me to describe the second major difference between the negative and positive materials. The dye density of positive material must be twice as great as that of negative material. This is so because a print is viewed by white light that has two passes through the dyes (not a single pass as is the case with all positive materials), once on its way to the paper base and once on its way from the white paper base to the viewer's eye. A dye density change in a negative will yield twice the effect in a print.

Aside from these differences, most color negative and color transparency films are very much alike. The exceptions are the Kodachromes, which are different because they do not have any couplers incorporated in their emulsion layers. Instead, both the couplers and the dyes are added to the Kodachromes during processing. (The processing of the Kodachromes is also quite different from that used for other films. I will get to it shortly.)

If Figure 2–19 (see color section) looks strangely familiar it is because the upper portion of the diagram is very similar to the drawing used to illustrate how the latent image of a multicolored board fence is recorded on color negative film. The latent image is formed identically for both color negative and color positive materials. It's the next part that is so tricky. If you have read through the explanation of how a color negative is formed you know that the color developer reduces the exposed grains of silver halide to metallic silver. In so doing, the developer is oxidized and color dyes are formed in proportion to the amount of oxidized developer. The dyes are then attracted and held by couplers incorporated in the emulsion layers. You also know that the result of this process, once the remaining silver is removed and the film washed, is a negative image. Where the subject was red the negative will be cyan, where the subject was green the negative will be magenta, and where the subject was blue the negative will be yellow. That's fine for a negative, whose colors are again reversed during printing, but it doesn't quite suffice for an image that must be viewed directly.

How the Latent Image Is Developed to a Positive Transparency

To solve this difficult problem, let's consider what would happen if I simply developed a piece of color positive film with a latent image of the black, red, green, blue, and white boards of a wooden fence, in a simple black-and-white developer. I would have metallic silver wherever the emulsion's silver-halide particles had been exposed to the color of light that they were sensitive to, and unaffected silver halide wherever there had been no exposure. In essence, I would have a metallic-silver negative image and a silver-halide positive one. Now, here is where things get devious. Suppose that after producing this metallic-silver negative, I now

reexpose the piece of film to strong white light. If you will think about if for a moment, you will see that what I am doing can be likened to making a sort of "contact print" using the metallic silver as the negative and the previously unexposed silver halide as the "printing paper." Now I have a metallic-silver negative and a latent positive image. Continuing down this path, I put the film into a color developer which reduces the silver halide of the latent positive image to metallic silver, and forms dye, which is coupled wherever such a reaction is taking place. In this way I will produce a color positive *only* in the reexposed areas. This is so because the negative image was reduced to metallic silver in the black-and-white developer, so the color developer has no effect on it and no dyes at all are deposited in the metallic-silver negative portion of the image. After the color-development step, the film is further processed to remove all of the metallic silver, both that of the negative image and that which was formed while developing the positive image; all that remains to be seen are the dyes forming a proper, positive image.

The white light reexposure prior to color development is still a feature of such processes as Kodak's E-3, Unicolor's Unichrome, and others; however, the reexposure step can conveniently be carried out chemically with a strong fogging agent, as it is in Kodak's E-4 process.

The Kodachromes are not simply reexposed to white light, or chemically fogged, after the initial black-and-white development as are other color reversal films. Instead, two of the three emulsion layers must be separately reexposed to the color of light they were designed to respond to in the camera. After each reexposure, the reexposed layer must be separately processed in a bath containing both the necessary couplers and the dye required for that layer. The entire operation is carried out automatically in a processing machine.

First the bottom, red-sensitive layer is reexposed to red light. This layer is then color developed in cyan-coupled dye. The film then continues on through the automatic machine, where the top blue-sensitive layer is reexposed to blue light then processed in yellow-coupled dye. Finally, the machine carries the film to a bath containing magenta-coupled dye which reacts directly with the remaining silver halides in the middle green-sensitive layer.

After all three layers have been selectively reexposed and/or processed, all the remaining metallic silver is removed, and the film is dried and cut. This is hardly the sort of operation that can be carried out in a simple home darkroom. It takes a very complicated setup to handle the physical and mechanical requirements, and the chemical and temperature controls involved are too demanding for anything but fully automated equipment.

How the Transparency Is Printed on Color Reversal Paper

There is very little difference between making a color transparency in the camera and making a reversal color print on the enlarger easel. Figure 2-20 (see color section) does, however, show one physical difference in the finished products of each process quite clearly. The densities of the dyes in the print are only half that of the dye densities of the transparency. You will recall that a slide is viewed by light that makes only one pass through the dyes—from behind the transparency, through the dyes and to the eye—while a print is viewed by light that enters from above, passes through the dye layers, bounces off the white paper base, passes through the dyes again, and finally emerges from the surface of the print and travels to the eye.

Figure 2-20 (see color section) shows our slide of the black, red, green, blue, and white board fence placed emulsion side down in an enlarger. White light from the enlarger's lamp shines through the transparency and is modified by the dyes in it.

There is no dye at all in the section carrying the image of the white board, so white light shines right through that section and emerges as unaffected white light on the other side of the transparency.

The section of the transparency carrying the image of the blue board contains highly saturated cyan and magenta dye. The white light loses its red and green components passing through these dye layers, so that only blue light emerges.

The section of the transparency carrying the image of the green board contains saturated cyan and yellow dye layers. These layers absorb the red and blue components of the white light from the enlarger lamp, allowing only the green to pass through the transparency.

The section of the transparency carrying the image of the red board contains saturated magenta and yellow dye layers. These layers absorb the green and blue components of the enlarger lamp's white light and allow only red light to emerge.

The section of the transparency carrying the image of the black board contains saturated cyan, yellow, and magenta dye layers. These layers absorb all of the white light from the enlarger lamp and allow no light at all to pass through.

The focused image of the board fence is projected onto a sheet of reversal printing paper, where the several colors expose the emulsion layers sensitive to them to form a latent image of the fence.

How the Latent Image on the Color Reversal Printing Paper Is Developed to a Positive Print

Once again, as in the case of producing a positive color transparency, the processing involves two separate development stages. First, the negative image is produced by developing the reversal color printing paper in a black-and-white developer. This renders the negative image in metallic silver and leaves the silver halides unaffected wherever no image is formed.

This step is followed by a reexposure of the paper to white light (or to chemical fogging) and then color development. The reexposure, as in the case of a positive color transparency, acts to sort of "contact print" the negative metallic-silver image, using the remaining silver halide as the "printing paper." The latent positive image formed in the remaining silver halides is then reduced to metallic silver by the color developer. The color developer is oxidized by the process and its oxidation causes dyes to be formed and to attach to the couplers incorporated in the paper's emulsion layers. Each layer's coupler will attract and hold only dye of the color appropriate to that layer.

At the end of the color development process all of the silver halide in all three emulsion layers has been reduced to metallic silver, either by the first black-and-white developer or by the color developer, and the transparent dyes are formed and are coupled in place.

The paper is now bleached and fixed (usually in a single step) to remove all of the silver. This leaves only the dye image of the multicolored board fence.

How the Positive-to-Positive Dye-Bleach System Works

How the Dye-Bleach Process Differs from the Chromogenic System

Until now all of the film and paper I have discussed have been of the chromogenic type; that is, the materials themselves contained only silver salts and couplers. The dyes were formed in the processing of these materials. There is, however, another process, called dye-bleach, which is used in the widely available Cibachrome materials. All of Cibachrome's products are reversal materials, that is, they are all used for making positive-to-positive images. Ilford, the company which markets these materials, offers both transmission and reflection media for making transparencies and prints, respectively. Both types of materials work essentially the same way, utilizing the dye-bleach technique.

Cibachrome printing materials leave the factory with all the dye they will ever have— three layers of it, in cyan, magenta, and yellow, arranged in the same order as the dye layers that form in the processing of the chromogenic materials. But, unlike the chromogenic materials, where you add dye in processing, when you process Cibachrome you actually remove dye from the printing materials.

How Cibachrome Paper Is Designed

Figure 2-22 (see color section) illustrates the construction of Cibachrome's CCP-D 182 professional printing "paper." (There is actually no paper at all in Cibachrome's reflection printing material, as the base of it is entirely made of cellulose triacetate.) Cibachrome has even more layers than the chromogenic materials do. Starting from the top, there's the anti-abrasion layer, which serves no image-forming function at all. It is there only to protect the paper from mechanical abrasion and is removed in processing. The layer below it, labeled SH-Y, contains silver halide that is sensitive to blue light. The YD layer contains fully saturated yellow dye and additional blue-sensitive silver halide. The YF layer is yellow-dyed gelatin, which serves as a filter to absorb any blue light that penetrates this far. The SH-M layer contains silver halides that are sensitive to green and blue light. The MD layer contains fully saturated magenta dye and additional green/blue-sensitive silver halides. The G layer is a simple gelatin layer that serves to

separate the MD and CD layers. The CD layer (no, I haven't made a mistake, the CD layer is above the SH-C layer in spite of the opposite arrangement used for the other two-dye/halide-layer pairs) contains fully saturated cyan dye and some red/blue-sensitive silver halides. The SH-C layer contains silver halides that are sensitive to red and blue light. Finally, the B layer is the white, opaque, triacetate base upon which this entire edifice rests.

How the Cibachrome Dye-Bleach Process Works

While the structure of Cibachrome's printing material looks quite complicated, the procedure used for processing it is, in essence, delightfully simple.

To illustrate it (see color section, Fig. 2-21), I have put my slide of the black, red, green, blue, and white board fence in the enlarger's negative carrier and put a sheet of Cibachrome's CCP-D 182 printing material on the easel to make a printing exposure. The dyes in the slide remove the various components of the enlarger's white light, as illustrated, and latent images of the fence's boards are duly recorded in the appropriate emulsion and dye layers. The white board's portion of the slide leaves a latent image in all of the silver-halide layers and in the silver halide dispersed in all three of the dye layers. The blue board's image is recorded in the blue-sensitive silver-halide layer above the yellow dye layer, and it is also recorded in the silver-halide grains within the yellow dye. The green board's image is recorded in the green-sensitive silver-halide layer immediately above the magenta dye layer and it also leaves a latent image in the silver-halide particles in the magenta dye layer. The red light, carrying the red board's image, manages to leave a latent image in the red-sensitive silver-halide grains in the cyan dye layer and get through the cyan dye to be recorded by the silver-halide particles in the red-sensitive emulsion layer immediately below it. I know that up until now I have categorically stated that cyan absorbs red, and accordingly, that no red light should be able to get through the fully saturated cyan dye layer to reach the silver-halide layer below, but those clever Swiss (Ilford is owned by Ciba-Geigy, a Swiss concern) have deliberately mismatched the peak spectral absorption characteristics of their cyan dye and their red-sensitive emulsion, to make this seemingly impossible feat into an everyday occurrence. (In case you are wondering why the cyan dye layer and the red-sensitive silver-halide layer are reversed when compared to the other two-dye/halide-layer pairs, it is to allow the makers to keep the total emulsion coating thickness to a minimum and thereby increase the resolving capabilities of the material.)

These latent images are reduced to metallic silver in a black-and-white type of developer. Then, in a dye-bleach processing step, the dye stuff adjacent to the metallic silver particles is removed. Subsequent processing removes all residual silver-halide and metallic-silver particles, leaving only three layers of dye.

Since the dye was *removed* wherever a *negative* image had been formed in the first development step, the dyes remaining form a positive image of the multicolored board fence.

Positive-to-Negative-to-Positive Color Printing

Internegatives

In the days before Kodak introduced their Ektachrome RC brand Type 1993 reversal color-printing paper, and before Ilford had their Cibachrome materials widely available on the market, there was good reason to make color prints from color transparencies via an intermediate image on a color negative. Today, such a procedure is an unnecessary waste of time and will probably result in a print of lower overall quality than can be obtained by printing directly from the slide onto one of the new direct-reversal materials.

In the earlier days of color printing, if you had a slide you really wanted to make a high-quality print of, you really did have to make an internegative because the reversal printing materials then available for working directly from the transparency, positive-to-positive, were not capable of delivering any real image quality. (An alternative procedure was to prepare three color-separation negatives and use the dye-transfer process to make reflection copies. I will not go into detail here, however, since this procedure is beyond the scope of this book.)

There is still another, if somewhat dubious, advantage to going this route to get from slide to print, and that is the fact that black-and-white conversions are more readily and directly available from a color internegative than they are from a transparency. Black-and-white prints can be made directly from color negatives on special panchromatic black-and-white printing papers such as Kodak's Panalure.

An internegative is made by photographing the positive image on the transparency, on special internegative film stock, such as Kodak's 6008 or 6110, using a tungsten (3200 K) source of illumination. The internegative film is then processed in modified C-22 chemistry. Once processed, it is printed as any other color negative would be. The special film and developer are needed to prevent excessive contrast in the internegative. Color problems, and to some extent, density problems, in the original transparency can be corrected by the use of color correcting filters between the source of illumination and the slide, and by regulating the exposure of the internegative film. However, it is probably easier and more effective to do this kind of problem correction in the printing rather than in the making of the internegative.

Since the 6008 roll film is sold only in bulk (the shortest 35mm roll is 80 feet) most photographers leave their internegative making to professional labs, which use the 6110 sheet film (4″ × 5″, 5″ × 7″, and 8″ × 10″) or have Kodak make their internegative for them. (This is an inexpensive, but somehow little-known service that Kodak provides and is available through any corner drugstore dealing with them. Kodak-made internegatives from 35mm full- and half-frame slides are 2¼″ × 3¼″. They are 2¼″ × 2¼″ for most roll film sizes.)

Once in hand, an internegative is dealt with just as any color negative would be. Figure 2–16 (see color section) illustrates the exposure of internegative film in the camera. Figure 2–18 (see color section) illustrates how a print is generated from an internegative.

Chapter 3

What You Need To Have: Color Darkroom Materials

Hardware for the Dry Side of the Color Darkroom

This chapter is meant only as a brief introduction to the crowded (and awfully expensive, if you let it get out of hand) collection of photographic materials available to the color printer. I'll deal with these things generically here, and more specifically in the following chapters which describe the use of these devices or offer manufacturer's specifications for them.

Enlargers

Condenser /Diffuser Enlargers

There are two basic types of enlarger available on the amateur market. They are the condenser and diffuser machines. The condenser-type enlarger is designed to focus the light from the enlarger lamp strongly on its way to the negative. This type of machine is particularly effective for printing small-format (35mm) black-and-white negatives, particularly dense ones. Unlike silverless color negatives, black-and-white negatives carry their images in metallic-silver particles (the black portions of black-and-white negatives are black with silver grains). Because metallic-silver grains have the ability to not only absorb, but also to scatter light rays trying to pass through them, the black-and-white printer may need the extra intensity a condenser machine can supply. The strongly focused light of a condenser enlarger has a better chance of getting through the silver thicket without undue diffusion. Stated simply: You can get more contrast, in black-and-white printing, from a condenser machine than you can from any other type. It should also be noted that condenser enlargers are more efficient than other types because they make the best use of the enlarger lamp output, concentrating it all directly on an area a bit larger than the format of the negative being printed.

Some condenser enlargers are designed to handle only one negative format. These machines employ fixed condensers. Other enlargers are adjustable to efficiently handle several different size negatives. These enlargers employ movable condensers, or provide for condenser interchangeability, to bring the diameter of the illuminating cone of light to the proper size for the negative being printed. Because condenser enlargers make such efficient use of their lamp's output, they are able to use low-power incandescent bulbs (designed for operation at a color temperature of between 2900–3200 K) and still provide fast printing speed. Because low-power bulbs (typically 75–150 watts) are employed, condenser enlargers are adequately cooled by means of conduction, convection, and radiation, without any need to resort to power-consuming, vibration-inducing, fan-forced air cooling.

So far, so good, but now we come to the one huge drawback that condenser enlargers have— their strongly focused light source faithfully reproduces every minute speck of dust and dirt, every negative blemish and every water mark. The careful black-and-white printer must make very sure that his negatives are pristine before they are printed with a condenser machine. But even with the most elaborate precautions, if there is only one single speck of dust in the darkroom it always seems to wind up on the negative being printed. While this sort of problem is tolerable in black-and-white printing, where spotting involves only a 00-size sable brush and a bottle of Spotone, it can become a nightmare in color printing, where spotting may often involve a half-dozen different dyes, several brushes, and cotton balls galore. This is where the diffusion-type enlarger has a big advantage over the condenser type. Diffusers tend to minimize all of the problems that condensers tend to oftentimes exaggerate.

Most contemporary condenser enlargers provide a drawer, usually located between the condensers or between the lamp and the condensers, that will accept the various filters (I'll get to them shortly) required for color printing. Very old condenser enlargers do not have such filter drawers, though some of them do have provisions for swinging filters below the lens. These machines are only marginally suitable for color printing work, unless it is possible, with modification, to add a filter drawer above the negative stage. (I'll explain that statement too, when I get to the subject of filters.)

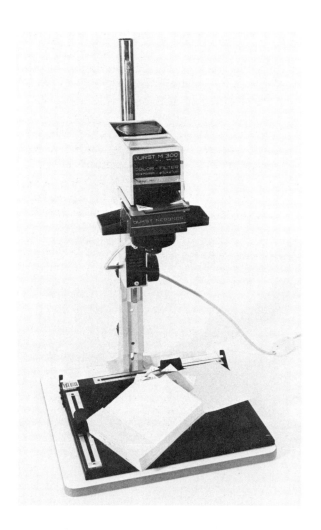

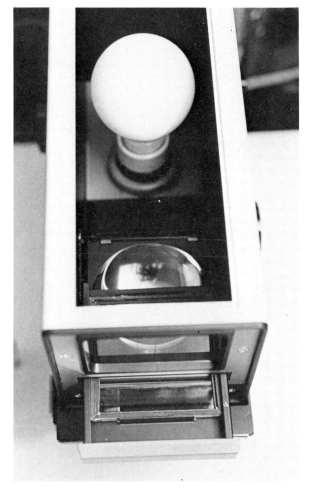

This little Durst 300 condenser-type enlarger is typical of light, amateur equipment that can be used to make color prints with a single, subtractively filtered exposure. Because this 35mm enlarger is provided with a filter drawer located above the image-forming light path, it can be used with acetate color printing (CP) filters (several of which can be seen hanging out of its drawer).

A reflex condenser enlarger employs a mirror at a 45° angle to both the lamp and the condensers to direct the light down through the filter drawer, through the condensers, and to the negative stage. I've removed the heat-sink top and the 45° mirror from this machine to illustrate the component arrangement. The filter drawer is pulled halfway out to reveal the condensers below it.

Diffusion Enlargers

The diffusion enlarger is an inefficient machine that is very well suited to the requirements of color printing. These enlargers make only poor use of their lamp's light output, but this low-efficiency lamp utilization is quite intentional on the part of the designers. Diffusion enlargers, designed specifically for color printing, employ light-mixing chambers between their lamp/filter compartment and the negative stage. These chambers are designed to insure that all of the portions of the enlarger lamp's output that have been modified through filtration (usually dichroic—I'll explain that term shortly in the section on filters) are thoroughly "mixed" on their way from the filter section to the negative stage. Some diffusion enlargers employ mirror chambers to do this mixing, while others rely on rough-surfaced white plastic panels to do the job. At the bottom of the mixing chamber just above the negative stage, such enlargers universally employ a diffusion plate which takes the already multidirectional light and scatters it still further, insuring that whatever illumination does finally fall on the material loaded in the negative stage will be highly diffused (coming from all directions at once). Some diffusion plates also perform as built-in ultraviolet (UV) filters.

While this kind of arrangement provides for the least efficient utilization of the lamp's output possible, it also provides a type of illumination that goes a very long way toward suppressing the imaging of all the dust, dirt, water marks, blemishes, scratches, and other horrors that are often found on even the most pampered negatives and slides.

If all of these imperfections fail to leave an image on the print, it follows that you won't have to go through the often tedious process of spotting your color prints. Anything that reduces this requirement is desirable, and if this reduction has to be brought about through the inefficient use of the enlarger lamp, well, so be it.

But, in this world you seldom get something for nothing, so you will note that many diffusion enlargers have had to go to the extreme of using high-powered (typically 150 to 300 watts) quartz-halogen (typical color temperature of 3200 K) bulbs and vibration-prone fan-forced cooling systems. The diffusion enlargers that rely on convection/conduction/radiation cooling and lower-wattage bulbs often have considerably reduced printing speeds.

I should mention that the reason that this highly diffused light is able to get through color negatives or color transparencies with relative ease is that these color images have no silver in them at all, just transparent dyes (as explained in the previous chapter). Diffusion enlargers can be used to print black-and white material, but it is necessary to develop black-and-white negatives somewhat longer than is thought of as normal so as to increase their contrast or, alternatively, to use standard negative development but print on a harder grade of paper than would be called for by a condenser enlarger in order to get the proper printing contrast.

It is helpful when using a diffusion enlarger with the capability of printing rather large negatives (say 4″ × 5″ for example) to print small-format negatives (typically 35mm) using special light-concentrating mixing chambers designed to provide the most efficient utilization of

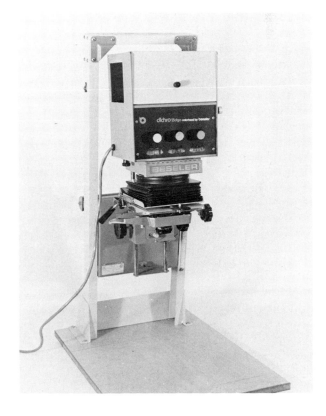

This Beseler enlarger started out in life as a model 23C condenser-type machine. It was converted to a diffusion-type enlarger, featuring built-in dichroic filtration, by purchasing the 23dga conversion head (seen on this enlarger) and using it to replace the original enlarger's lamp housing and condensers.

The bottom of this diffusion enlarger's lamp house has been removed to show the mirrored light-mixing chamber. The white diffusion plate and a circular CP2B filter fit inside the bottom cap.

the enlarger lamp's output under the circumstances. Otherwise, these large format machines often provide prohibitively slow printing speeds when used to do small-format work.

Condenser/Diffuser Conversions

Perhaps the cheapest way to convert a condenser-type enlarger to a diffusion-type enlarger is to remove one or both of the condensers and add a diffusion sheet just above the negative stage. While this is an inexpensive and simple way to get from a focused to a diffused light source, it is also a method that will cut the enlarger's printing speed way down.

A considerably more expensive alternative is to purchase a conversion head for your enlarger. These devices are often offered by the firm that built the machine, and are also widely available from several independent sources (see Chapter 9). All of the condenser/diffuser conversion heads that I am familiar with provide a set of dichroic filters as a built-in feature. They allow you to simply turn one or two knobs and dial in the amount of filtration desired, rather than having to manually open a filter drawer and remove and/or insert filters to make a change. These conversion heads also have their own source of illumination (always a quartz-halogen bulb in my experience) of sufficient wattage so that little, if any, printing speed is lost by making the change from condenser illumination.

A condenser/diffuser conversion has been made on this enlarger. It began life as a Beseler 23C with its original condensers and lamphouse shown lying on the easel. The conversion was made by removing these components and slipping the rather large Dichro 23dga color head onto the machine. The entire procedure took less than 5 minutes the first time, and now reconversion each way takes about 2 minutes.

Other Types Of Enlargers and Enlarging Equipment

One piece of enlarger hardware that gained some notoriety before it ceased to be produced, was the Sable I Color Printing Machine. This peculiar device was essentially a diffusion enlarger with programmable, below-the-lens, subtractive, cutoff filters. It offered the advantages of printing with a diffused light source and the disadvantages of below-the-lens filtration and a great deal of electromechanical complication necessary to make the system function. I will explain the cutoff filtration scheme elsewhere in the text.

Another device, which so far as I know, had a similar marketing history, was the Janpol color enlarging lens. This device consisted of an enlarging lens with several CC filters built into its barrel. These filters could be swung into or out of the light path at will. While it might seem to some that such a device would be useful to aspiring color printers who owned older enlargers without filter drawers, such an impression would be incorrect. The device suffered from a lack of adequate filter availability because it offered very limited densities in the subtractive primaries.

Cold Light Heads

One final piece of enlarging equipment that should be mentioned here is the cold light head. Enlargers that have noninterchangeable cold light heads are inappropriate for use in color printing. Their fluorescent, or gas discharge, tubes provide a diffuse source of illumination that some workers (I am not among them) feel is useful for printing black-and-white negatives. However, the color temperature of these light sources is rather hard to define (some tubes are filled with mixed gases, others are coated with mixed phosphors) and all but impossible to properly filter for color printing purposes.

The Sable I Color Printing Machine uses a cutoff filtration scheme, with subtractive filters being swung in under the lens in response to the settings of an electronic control panel below the baseboard.

Filters—What They Do and Why They're Needed

Do you remember my explanation, in Chapter 2, that the dyes in a color negative or a color slide, when placed in the enlarger's negative carrier, would absorb portions of the enlarger lamp's white-light output? I lied. The light output of an enlarger lamp is anything but "white." Most enlarger lamps have a color temperature of about 3000 K when they are new. This means that the color of the light they radiate is closer to a candle (1930 K) than to noon sunlight (5400 K) or the international standard (D_{65}) for "white" light, which is 6504 K. After they have burned for a while, their color temperature often drops further. In addition to the lamp's not being "white," each box of printing paper has its very own peculiarities. The response of the paper's emulsion layers to the additive primaries will most often vary widely from layer to layer and from emulsion batch to emulsion batch. There are other variables to contend with as well, but these two will do here as an illustration. To bring the light reaching the color printing paper to a proper color balance, in order to produce an accurate rendition of the material contained in the image being projected, it is most often necessary to alter the properties of the light coming from the enlarger lamp with color printing (CP) filters. These filters are used to absorb or reflect some of the unwanted components of the visible portion of the spectrum.

Acetate Color Printing CP Filters

Acetate CP filters are made from thin sheets of acetate plastic containing dyes of several colors and densities. They are the type most widely used by color printers. This is not because they have any magical properties but simply because they are the cheapest and most convenient type of filters available for what is probably the majority of color printers. And the majority of color printers are using the type of enlarger that features a filter drawer somewhere in the light path between the enlarger lamp and the negative stage. Acetate CP filters are fine for use in situations such as this, but because of their rather poor optical properties they should not be used under the lens. That location calls for CC filters. I'll get to them shortly.

When used in a filter drawer above the image-forming light path, acetate CP filters perform their color temperature-modification task by absorbing specific portions of the spectrum. The most common types of CP filters are those in the colors cyan, magenta, and yellow. However, red CP filters are also available. The CP filters in the subtractive primary colors are used to absorb their complementary colors from the enlarger lamp's output—cyan absorbs red, magenta absorbs green, yellow absorbs blue—while the red filters (red being an additive primary), are used to absorb the two other additive primaries (blue and green) simultaneously. CP filters are available in several different dye densities (deepness of color) ranging from 2.5 to 40 (80 in yellow) from Kodak, and in several other density values from various other sources.

Those density values may be a bit hard to appreciate all by themselves, so it may help to explain them in terms of the amount of light the filters will absorb. A 5 density filter in any of the three subtractive primaries will absorb about 20 percent of the light of (the spectral peak of) its complementary color, while a 40 density filter in any of the subtractive primaries will absorb about 70 percent of the light of (the spectral peak of) its complementary color, which tries to pass through it. These same absorption figures apply approximately for the red CP filters as well, but, of course, in the case of this additive primary color it is the two other additive primaries which are being absorbed rather than the complementary color. Just to confuse matters a bit, there is another type of CP filter, which Kodak recommends for printing color negatives, called cyan-2. The cyan-2 filters are designed to absorb more of the far-red and infrared than the standard cyan filters (which Kodak suggests for use with their papers designed for printing color slides). The

There are many manufacturers' products to fill your filtration needs. Shown here are a set of unicolor 3″ × 3″ acetate CP filters, a CP2B made by Kodak (and cut down, with a pair of scissors, to the 3″ × 3″ size of the filter drawer), and a heat-absorbing glass (HAG) made for this enlarger by its manufacturer, Durst.

cyan-2 filters in a 5 density have a peak absoption of about 30 percent. The cyan-2 filters of 40 density absorb about 70 percent of their peak complementary.

Now that you have some idea of what's available, what function each of the CP filters performs, and how much capacity each of them has, it might be useful if I let you know how many of them you will need for normal color printing requirements. I suggest a set consisting of the following densities in cyan (or cyan-2), magenta, and yellow: one each at 5, 10, 20, and 40. In addition, you will also need one more 40 magenta filter and one additional 80 yellow filter.

If your enlarger has an odd-sized filter drawer, and your enlarger's manufacturer doesn't make a set of color printing filters specifically for it, you can purchase larger acetate filters and simply trim them to the required dimensions with a razor blade or a pair of scissors.

The densities of acetate CP filters are additive; that is, if you need to make a filtration

change of 55 density in yellow, you can make the change by adding a 40 yellow, a 10 yellow, and a 5 yellow filter together to get the 55 density required.

Ultraviolet and Infrared Filters

There is another acetate filter called a CP2B, which I haven't mentioned as yet. This filter is used, when printing color negatives or color slides on Cibachrome, to cut off radiation beyond about 390 nanometers at the ultraviolet end of the spectrum. This filter can simply be left in the enlarger's filter drawer at all times (it won't hurt your black-and-white prints and, as a matter of fact, it may help them a bit), unless you are printing color slides on Kodak materials when it should be replaced with a 2E filter. The 2E filter also cuts off the ultraviolet end of the spectrum, but it is designed to cut off everything below about 415 nanometers. The 2E filter is only made (by Kodak) in gelatin and is not available in sizes larger than 5″ × 5″ at this writing. For all

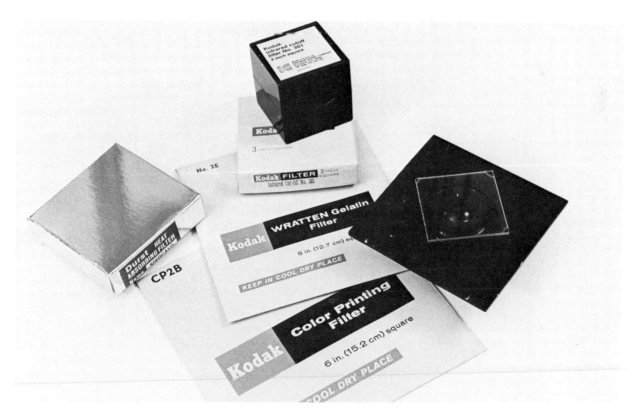

Filters designed to remove infrared and ultraviolet come in a wide variety of sizes and materials, and with various spectral absorption/transmission characteristics. The small, two-inch-square glass filter seen balanced on the back flange of an enlarger lens is a 301A. This location is not the best one possible, but it allows the use of a small, and therefore less expensive, filter.

practical purposes, a CP2B will do in place of a 2E. The 2E can also be left in place when printing black-and-white, if it is convenient to do so.

The ultraviolet end of the spectrum is not the only one that has to be cut off if you expect to get first-rate color prints. You will have to cut the infrared end (beyond 700 nanometers), as well. The cheapest way to accomplish this is to add a heat-absorbing glass (HAG) to your filter drawer. HAGs are usually available through the manufacturer of your enlarger, in a size appropriate to the model you own, as well as being available from independent suppliers. It is a good idea to leave a HAG in the enlarger at *all* times. They can't be anything but beneficial. In addition to the HAG, Kodak recommends a 301A (the successor to the 301) dichroic infrared cutoff filter for use in printing certain types of transparencies directly onto Kodak Type 1993 paper. This filter is very expensive and its size availability is rather limited. Here again, for most practical purposes, the 301A can be substituted for by a HAG without any overly serious consequences. If, however, you do purchase this filter, be sure that you find some place in the lightpath to put it where it will be parallel to the negative stage. Dichroic filters such as this one work improperly when they are not correctly oriented in relation to the source of illumination.

Dichroic Filters

Dichroic filters consist of a microscopically thin film of material that has been vapor deposited on a glass substrate. They are quite different from the acetate CP filters I have been discussing. The acetate filters work by absorbing the unwanted portion of the spectrum. Dichroics work by reflecting the part of the spectrum you don't want to hit the printing paper. It is necessary with the acetate filters to have a number of them in each of the subtractive primary colors, so that pack changes can be made by substituting filters of different densities. Only one dichroic filter in each of the subtractive primary colors is required. In order to vary the amount of filtration achieved with a dichroic filter, one simply puts more of the dichroic filter into the enlarger lamp's light path.

That concept may be a bit hard to grasp, so perhaps a bit more explanation of how the dichroic filter's density is varied, is in order here.

Let's say that a magenta dichroic filter 1 inch square in size is placed so that its entire 1 inch square area is completely illuminated by the enlarger lamp. Placed in such a manner, it will reflect as much green light as a 150 magenta acetate CP filter will absorb. It shouldn't be too hard to decide to call that setting of the dichroic filter 150M. Now, if I begin to retract the dichroic filter (remove it from the enlarger lamp's light path) until I am able to determine that the amount of dichroic filter remaining in the light path is reflecting an amount of green light equal to the amount that two 40 magenta acetate CPs will absorb, I can mark that position of the dichroic filter in the light path as 80M. Similarly, I can keep on removing more of the dichroic filter's area from the light path so that it will reflect less green light, until I reach a point that is equal in reflection of green light to the absorption of green light by a 20M acetate CP. And on, and on, until I have removed *all* of the area of the dichroic magenta filter from the light path, at which point I will have 00M filtration.

This is exactly how dichroic filters are used. They are mechanically moved into and out of the light path in accordance with the amount of control-dial movement the operator elects to use. The control dials of most dichroic enlarger heads are usually calibrated in very fine increments, many as fine as 1 density, so that very precise filtration changes can be very conveniently achieved. The control dials are accessible at the front of the enlarger and are, of course, mechanically linked to precise nonlinear cams used to position the dichroic filters in the light path.

While it is possible to use dichroic filters in exactly the same way that acetate filters are used (by stacking them in several specific density values to obtain the amount of reflection required), this is never done, for several reasons, the biggest being money. Dichroic filters are very expensive. Size and fragility are other factors. The glass substrate of a dichroic filter is many times thicker than a typical acetate filter, as it must be for mechanical reasons. You would have to have an awfully large filter drawer to accommodate more than a few dichroic filters in a stack. It is easy to damage the thin coating of dichroic filters, and they break when they are dropped.

So you can see why you can't run out to your neighborhood camera store and buy a set of dichroic filters. Even if you could, you would need to have a rather large machine shop at your disposal to modify your enlarger in order to put the filters to work. The only practical way to obtain dichroic filters is to buy a set that is already incorporated in an enlarger, or an enlarger conversion head that is optically and mechanically designed to use them. Such enlargers (or conversions) provide a special quartz-halogen lamp plus all of the mechanical linkage needed, in addition to the filters themselves. And they incorporate light-integrating (mixing) chambers to insure that the light which has been modified by portions of one or two dichroic filters is thoroughly mixed with the unmodified white light which has bypassed them. This thorough mixing is absolutely essential to proper dichroic-filtration enlarger operation. (The 301A dichroic, infrared cutoff filter is an example of a partial exception to the previous statements. But, while it is available for use much like an acetate CP filter, there are very few printers who can afford one, or who are willing to spend the amount of money required to buy one.)

At this time, the maximum dichroic filter density that can be directly dialed on an enlarger (as far as I know), is 200Y. This density may, in some rare cases, be insufficient for color printing needs. However, there is no reason why acetate filters can't be combined with dichroics when and if you run out of dichroic filtration. Of course, to be able to combine these two types of filters, the enlarger head itself will have to be able to accommodate both types. There are several that will and several that won't. It is something to consider when shopping for an enlarger with built-in dichroic filtration.

Gelatin Color Correcting Filters

It is *possible* to do single-exposure subtractive color printing using an enlarger that, because of its ancient design, must have its color printing filters located under the lens; however, it is not a very practical sort of activity.

Gelatin filters are manufactured in both the additive and the subtractive primary colors in a wide range of densities. You can use gelatin color correcting (CC) filters anywhere in the image-forming path, but doing so involves a good deal of ingenuity, a good stock of CC filters, and very clean fingers. Unlike people who use acetate filters, who can be rather sloppy about keeping

Dichroic filters are expensive and they must be accurately positioned in the enlarger lamp's path. Small dichroic filters are attached to each of the three cam-follower plates shown. The plates are positioned, by knobs external to the enlarger head, to bring the filters into the small square opening directly below the lamp. A cooling fan is often required to dissipate the heat produced by the high-powered tungsten-halogen lamp.

their CP filters clean since they are placed above the image-forming light path, the user of CC filters must be a fanatic about filter cleanliness and must keep his filters scrupulously free of scratches. Any dirt, dust, or optical imperfections in the image-forming light path will degrade the image being printed. The below-the-lens CC filter user must also be quite sure that all of his filters are parallel to one another and that they are all perpendicular to the optical axis of the lens, or he may also end up with degraded images. As a matter of fact, it is advisable to keep the number of below-the-lens filters down to an absolute minimum to reduce optical problems to manageable proportions.

Using CC filters below the lens does not eliminate the need for both IR and UV cutoff filters. If they can't be accommodated somewhere above the lens, they too will have to be located below it, increasing the number of surfaces the image-forming light path must cross and increasing the probablility of producing degraded images. Both the 2B and 2E UV cutoff filters are supplied in gelatin.

The HAG and 301A filters are glass. One possible way to accommodate them is to simply place either or both (when printing on Kodak Type 1993 paper) of these glass filters right on the rear flange of the enlarging lens. This assumes, of course, that the enlarging lens you are using has a rear flange, and, if it does, that the rear element doesn't protrude out beyond it. There is still another alternative open to you diehards who insist on using below-the-lens filtration, and that is to use tri-color printing (which I will mention in the following section and then promptly forget for the remainder of this book). This procedure is possible because gelatin-type separation filters in the additive primary colors are readily available.

Tri-Color Printing Filters

Most auxiliary tricolor filter hardware available to the amateur color printer is designed for the person who has nothing—not a filter drawer somewhere above the image-forming light path, not a filter holder that can be swung in below the lens—nothing!

I am presently aware of several such devices that simply clamp onto the barrel of an enlarging

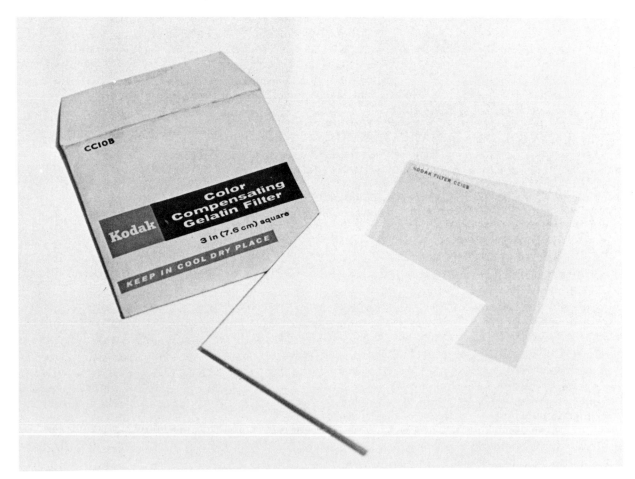

Gelatin color correcting (CC) filters, which are widely available in a large variety of dye colors and densities, are easily mechanically damaged.

This Uniwheel tri-color printing filter was designed to be clamped to the barrel of an enlarger lens by means of the ring and three screws at the lower right. The turret contains not only three filter windows (one in each of the additive primaries: red, green and blue), but also a diffuser window and an open (non-filtered) window. The open window is used for focusing. The diffuser is used with a calculator device sold with the Uniwheel. When printing with the Uniwheel, the user makes three separate exposures, one through each of the additive-primary filter windows in the turret. After each exposure, the turret is rotated to bring the next filter window under the enlarger lens.

lens (assuming, of course, that the barrel design is compatible with the clamping arrangement—not all of them are). Once in place these units provide filter windows arranged on a rotating turret or a sliding platform, each of which may be individually located directly beneath the lens' front element. There is little likelihood that the user will be able to mount either of these devices so that the filters they contain will be perfectly perpendicular to the lens' optical axis, but this wlll not be too critical so far as image degradation goes, as only one filter is beneath the lens at any time, and all the filters will be plane-parallel when in position under the lens.

The filter windows contain gelatin separation filters, one in each of the additive primary colors, red, green, and blue (typical Kodak filter numbers would be 29, 61, and 47B).

In use, the printer must move each one of the filters into position under the lens and make a separate exposure through them. Each complete image gets three individual exposures. You will remember that color printing materials have three layers of emulsion, each one sensitive to one of the additive primary colors. With the tri-color system the printer actually exposes each of these layers separately, one at a time. It is a very easy system to understand but a very clumsy one to use, especially with light, amateur-type enlargers, because it is so easy to cause mechanical movement during or between exposures, thereby grossly degrading the image that is being produced.

Tri-color printing is also a time-consuming process because the dye density of the three separation filters is rather high and the three exposures required for each print can take a considerable amount of time. However, where there is a will there is a way. If you really have the patience and mechanical dexterity required by this process, there is no reason why you can't use

it. Just bear in mind that subtractive, single-exposure color printing is much faster and much more convenient to do.

It may be of interest to note that an automated version of the tri-color printing system is used commercially to make prints of motion pictures, so it is hardly an unknown procedure—just one which is poorly suited to amateur use.

Subtractive Cutoff Filters

I mentioned earlier in the text that I would explain the system of subtractive cutoff filters used in the shortlived Sable I enlarger; so I will, right now.

With ordinary subtractive filtration, the printer chooses his printing filter pack so as to remove unwanted components of the enlarger lamp's output as the light passes through all of the filters in the pack at the same time. If, for the sake of example, I want to get rid of about 20 percent of the lamp's blue content and about 70 percent of its green component, I will use a printing pack consisting of a 5 yellow filter, a 40 magenta filter, a heat-absorbing glass, and a CP2B filter (the latter two filters to get rid of UV and IR, respectively). Using this pack, and a single white-light exposure, I can get a properly exposed print.

However, the same effect can be obtained by using nothing more than the IR and UV filters in the light path for most of the exposure. Then, after 30 percent of the exposure time has elapsed, I can swing a strong magenta filter under the lens to terminate any further green light exposure of the paper, while permitting red and blue light exposure to continue undiminished. Then, after 80 percent of the exposure time has elapsed, I can swing a strong yellow filter under the lens to terminate all further blue light exposure. The effect of making the exposure this peculiar way would be just the same as the exposure I made through the 5Y + 40M pack. This exposure technique is useful for automatically controlled printing hardware such as that which is used by some large commercial photo finishers, but it has no real application in an amateur or small volume darkroom.

The Sable I Color Printing Machine uses a system of electronic programming to control its two subtractive cutoff filters, which are swung in under the lens by solenoids to terminate blue and green exposure. The third below-the-lens filter is a diffuser disk used to initially establish the built-in analyzer's program.

Miscellaneous Hardware Items

As I begin to write this section, I do so knowing full well that every time I think I've completed it, I will remember, or worse yet, be made aware of, still some other bit or piece of gear designed to make the color printer's lot an easier one. I'm sure that this section is one which will be supplemented many times over in the future. But since I have to start somewhere ...

Safelights

The negative-to-positive color printer has two choices of safelight filter—both of them from Kodak—the No.10 and the No.13. Both are of a dark amber color. The No.10 gives off very little light with a 15 watt bulb behind it. The No. 13 filter will allow you a bit more illumination and may be considered as a luxury item when printing color negatives. Essentially though, I would suggest that you put a color printing safelight at the very end of your list of items needed to fit out your color darkroom. If you decide to process color prints in a rational manner, that is, in daylight print-processing drums, you will have virtually no need for a safelight at all, because the only time you will have to turn out the darkroom's white light will be for the few seconds during which you make your printing exposure and then, subsequently, load the exposed sheet of paper into the drum. However, if you opt for working with the Kodak Model 11 or Model 16 processors, or trays, you will have a definite need for one of these two Kodak safelight filters.

The materials used for making color prints directly from transparencies are even fussier about their safelight requirements. Kodak's Ektachrome RC Paper, Type 1993 must be worked in total darkness. Ciba's several direct-positive materials can be worked under an Ilford GB-908D filter (over a 15 watt bulb), but it is hardly worth the effort for all of the illumination you will get out of it.

If you do decide to use a safelight of any kind in your color darkroom, be sure that it is at least four feet from the surface of your sensitized materials. Or, better yet, bounce it off the ceiling or walls.

Easels

There is only one thing you need to know about enlarger easels and that is that the only easel color suitable for use with color materials, is black—matte black. If you already own an easel and it is yellow, white, or gray, paint it matte black. If you think I'm nuts, try putting a few strips of black tape on the surface of your other-than-black easel and then use it to make a few color prints. Don't be surprised to find the tape pattern clearly reproduced on the print. A yellow easel surface bounces red and green light right back up through the paper, reexposing it from the bottom up. A white easel reexposes all three emulsion layers, and a gray easel acts like a white one, but to a lesser degree.

If you can't (and you probably won't) find a matte-black easel available, buy a can of matte-black paint and do it yourself. In case I seem to be overly emphatic about this, it is because I learned about it the hard way, by ruining a number of exhibition, mural-size prints making them on an easel that was not black—a lesson I will not easily forget.

Timers

Darkroom timers serve two principal purposes. On the dry side of the darkroom they monitor or control the time during which the enlarger lamp burns, during print exposure; on the wet side of the darkroom they monitor or control the amount of time elapsed during any of the numerous processing steps. Some darkroom timers resemble clocks, others look like leftover props from a Buck Rogers movie, and still others don't look like much of anything at all, as they aren't meant to be observed. These devices keep track of time audibly by clicking like a metronome, or, perish the thought, by talking to you from the loudspeaker of a tape player. I have some very strong feelings about darkroom timers and I will make them known here. Essentially, I feel that 99 percent of them don't belong in a darkroom. I will try to amplify and explain this statement as I go along.

Some timers are nothing more than timekeeping devices. They perform no electrical switching functions at all. This type of device is usually spring-powered and is usually, but not always, cheaper then the switching-type timer. If you can afford to purchase an electrically-powered timer capable of performing electrical switching it will save you a good deal of trouble to do so.

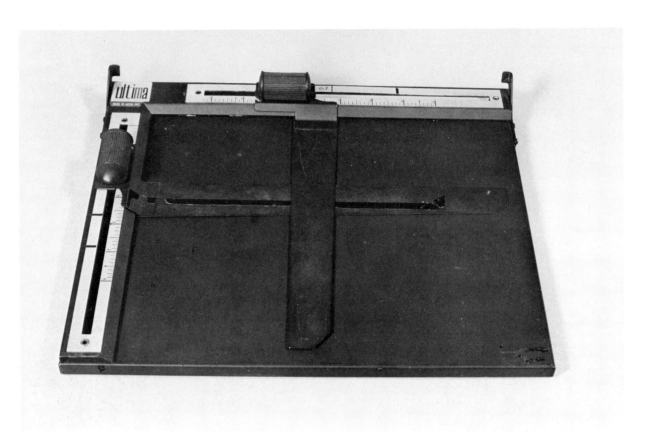

Regardless of what kind of easel you may have, if it isn't already black, paint it matte black to make it suitable for use with color materials.

Most switching timers allow you to manually turn the enlarger lamp on and off, or to select an automatic mode of operation that turns the enlarger lamp on at the beginning of the timer-controlled print exposure, and off at the end of the preset length of exposure time. Such timers provide an outlet into which your enlarger's line cord may be plugged. Many such timers also provide a second receptacle into which a safelight may be plugged. The timer's switch is so arranged that the safelight will go out when the printing exposure is started and back on again at the end of the exposure. This isn't much of a consideration in color printing, but it can be useful in black-and-white work, where the level of safelight illumination is much higher.

Some switching timers provide for operation by foot pedal as well as their normal hand-operated mode. This feature can be useful for burning and dodging operations.

Switching timers with sufficiently long controlled time periods are also very useful in processing color prints. Print-processing drum agitators can be plugged directly into their enlarger outlets and will run for the predetermined length of time set on the timer. At the end of this period, some timers will sound an alarm. This feature allows you to do other things while your print is being processed.

There seems to be a good deal of confusion among printers about just what kind of timer is suitable for color printing use. I have seen an incredible array of extremely sophisticated, incredibly accurate timing devices being touted for color printing application. My students are often amazed to find that they are expected to work with timing devices which won't split the second into tenths. I can think of nothing more useless than the ability to set my timer at 47.3 seconds.

Consider, if you will, that most amateur, and many professional, enlargers provide a level of illumination, which, when focused on an easel through an $f/4$ of $f/5.6$ lens opening, will produce a color print of average size (say between 3× and

6×) in the neighborhood of between 10 and 30 seconds. Even if you have an enlarger that is appreciably faster, the chances are that you will stop down your lens to increase the exposure time to give you sufficient time to do a bit of dodging or burning. If your minimum exposure time is ten seconds, then a one second change in exposure will provide a 10 percent exposure time difference. A 10 percent exposure change is a very small one indeed. As a matter of fact, it is so small that the thought of bothering with anything much smaller seems to me to be pretty much a waste of time and effort. But suppose you decide that you really have to make a 5 percent exposure time change, for whatever reason. If you have a timer calibrated in one second increments of an electromechanical (clock movement) type, you will be able to set the timer to a spot between the 10 and the 11 second marks to get your barely perceivable 5 percent change. (I would like to meet the printer who can distinguish between two prints exposed and processed identically in all respects except one; that one being that one print got 10 seconds of exposure while the second got 10.1 seconds. No way!) And, of course, this splitting of seconds into minute parts becomes even more ridiculous when it is done for longer exposures. The exposure difference between a print exposed for 30.3 seconds and one exposed for 30 seconds is one percent. It is undetectable.

The properties I have found to be absolutely essential in a darkroom timer are: the ability to count time down (as it is in a rocket launch) and be easily readable in the dark while so doing; repeatability, if not accuracy; good visibility in the dark; that it can be easily set in one second increments; that a switch be provided which will allow you to shut the enlarger lamp off during the automatically-timed period. My own secondary considerations include the timer's ability to: make a series of exposures of identical duration with no need for resetting; function over a rather long (about one hour) time span; sound an audible alarm at the end of a preset time span.

I've tried almost every timer ever offered for darkroom application but I've always returned to using my favorite, the GraLab. (This is an unsolicited testimonial.) It provides for all of my primary considerations and all but one of my secondary ones. It is a little peculiar to operate, but then, most of these devices are.

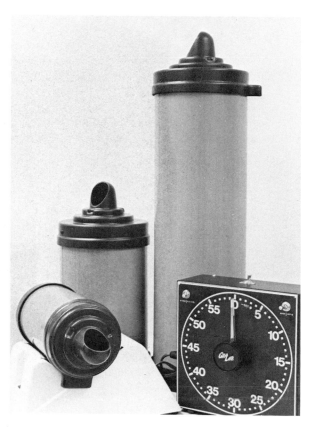

Because the GraLab timer offers up to one hour of controlled-interval timing and its huge luminous dial is easily readable in the dark as it counts time backwards, it is a favorite with many darkroom workers. Here it is shown with a motor base plugged into its switched enlarger receptacle.

Some solid-state timers are an anathema to me because they don't tell me how much time I have remaining to do what I want to do. The ones with big enough digital displays to show me how much time has elapsed are very expensive, and I suspect will fog paper under the right circumstances unless a dimmer switch is provided. Actually, the luminous dials of all darkroom clocks will fog printing paper if you bring it very close to them.

Both metronomes and cassette tape instructions may be useful to some people but they are not for me. I can tolerate, and sometimes even enjoy, music in the darkroom. No other audible inputs need apply.

I hope that you will pardon me for ranting on so about darkroom timers. But do take the properties I have mentioned as being desirable into account when you choose one, if you don't want to find yourself confused in the dark.

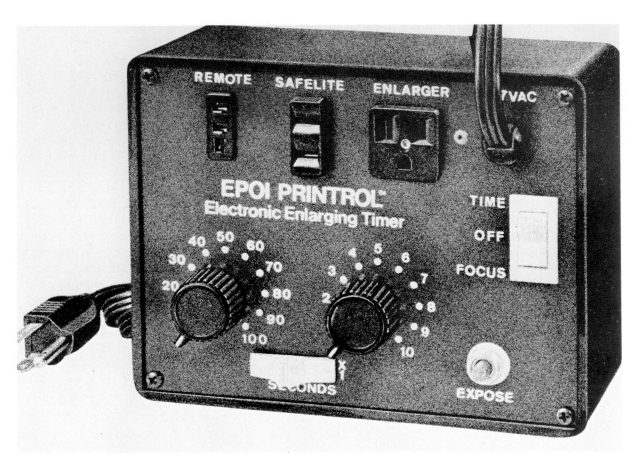

This electronic enlarging timer provides excellent accuracy and control, but doesn't provide the user with any means of knowing how much time is left before his enlarger lamp will switch off (absolutely essential information to a printer who may want to burn or dodge an image).

Constant Voltage Transformers

The stuff your power company sells you is anything but constant in quantity. Sometimes the juice you get from your wall outlet is at 97.3 volts and at other times its 117.4 volts. The most awful thing about the nature of the electrical energy you purchase is the unpredictability of just what voltage will be delivered at the moment you decide to make your printing exposure. If you make a print you like while your line voltage is at 110 volts, and then make an exact duplicate, but this time with only 105 volts across the enlarger lamp's filament, you will find that the second print is of a considerably different color from the first, perhaps off by as much as 10 blue. The lower the line voltage, the lower your enlarger lamp's color temperature.

There are several ways you can fight this problem. You can stay away from the darkroom except during the hours of 1 A.M.–4 A.M; you

can buy your own power generating equipment; you can buy a variable transformer and a voltmeter and monitor the line and correct the voltage manually; or you can buy a constant voltage transformer (or solid-state device).

My first alternative solution has some obvious drawbacks, and even if you do work only in the very late hours, you may still find that there is a factory on your power distribution line that starts throwing heavy loads on and off the line about the same time you begin to work. It's tough to beat line-voltage variation by regulating your working hours. And I seriously doubt that many color printers will be in a situation where owning and operating their own power supply systems will make much sense. So it seems as if there are two real choices, both of them involving one kind of a transformer or another.

The cheapest of the transformer routes is the manually-adjustable variable transformer.

These devices, available from any electrical or electronic supply house, will, with the twist of a knob, bring your voltage either up or down, compared to what is coming out of your wall outlet, but you won't know by how much unless you also buy a voltmeter and hook it across the output line. Now all you have to do is keep your eye on the voltmeter to make sure that you have the voltage level you want just before you push your timer's start button. The big problem with this solution is that it is a pain in the neck to implement. Chances are that you will remember to check your line voltage for the first exposure and forget to do so thereafter. If the power company's product comes in at a different voltage between your first and third exposures, and you don't notice it, you will have a couple of off-color prints.

Then there is the problem of line transients which I haven't mentioned yet. A line transient, for our purposes here, is a very short time variation of line voltage caused by the surge of power required to start heavy motors, etc. If you live in an old and inadequately wired building you can see these transients occur as your lights dim when the building's elevator starts up, or when a heavy appliance such as a powerful vacuum cleaner or a washing machine starts up. These short-duration line-voltage transients may not affect you too badly if you are making long exposures, but they can play havoc with short ones. A variable transformer won't take these little spikes out of your line voltage.

Having exhausted all of my cheap alternatives, I have finally reached the one that provides the best, if the most expensive, solution, the constant voltage transformer (CVT). A CVT will automatically keep the voltage across your

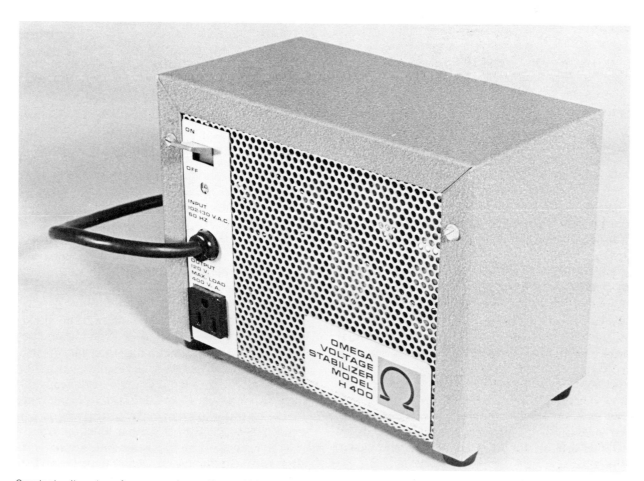

Constant voltage transformers are heavy, they get hot, and worst of all, they emit a 60-cycle hum that can be annoying in a quiet darkroom. But, in spite of these features, and especially where printing color negatives is concerned, they are very often a darkroom necessity.

enlarger lamp's filament at a constant level, plus or minus about 1 percent, for an input line variation of about ±10–15 percent, depending on the unit. It will also go a long way toward ironing out line transients. The problems with CVTs are that they cost a lot of money, they emit an annoying 60-cycle hum, and they are large and heavy. In spite of all their problems they are an excellent investment for the serious color printer.

There are several constant voltage devices on the market that do not use the massive iron core of a CVT for regulation, but instead substitute some clever solid-state circuitry. These units are small, quiet, and light, but I don't recommend them to you, because those I'm familiar with suffer from several other shortcomings. Their output is usually chopped DC as opposed to a true AC waveform. This makes such devices inappropriate for use with anything but a resistive load. If you use them to drive an incandescent enlarger lamp directly, they will work, but if there is a transformer between the solid-state regulator and the lamp, forget it, you may damage your transformer. That means that you had better not try to hook up any enlarger that uses a low-voltage, quartz-halogen bulb to such a device. Another nasty problem with these solid-state devices is that, in all of the units I have seen, the designers chose to solve some of their problems by providing a rather low output voltage. While they do manage, through clever circuitry, to hold that output voltage rather constant, I have found that most enlargers using normal incandescent type bulbs lose about a full stop of printing speed when connected to these devices. I would strongly recommend that you avoid the solid-state voltage controllers in favor of the CVT.

One interesting recent development along these lines is that several manufacturers are offering CVTs built in to their color enlarger's power supplies. This kind of design is a natural with any color enlarger that uses a low-voltage, quartz-halogen bulb, as the CVT can be economically designed right into the power transformer required for the enlarger lamp. If such an option is available for enlarging equipment you may be considering purchasing, I would strongly suggest it to you.

Just one final note on CVTs; if you purchase a unit rated for an output wattage considerably higher than the load you intend to put across it, in most cases you will find that its regulation will not be quite as tight as it will with a load equal to its rated capacity. Typically, a 400 watt CVT will deliver about ±1 percent regulation to a 400 watt load, but will provide only about ±2 percent regulation to a 75 watt load. Your best bet then will be to use a CVT of a rated output not appreciably higher than your enlarger's lamp load.

Focusing Aids

Focusing aids are devices designed to help you to bring your composed image into sharp focus on the enlarging easel. They are a virtual necessity in color printing, because it is usually considerably harder to focus a color image than it is to get a black-and-white image sharp. By the time you get all the filtration you need into the enlarger lamp's light path and then pass what is left of that light through the dyes of the image itself, there isn't that much left to focus by. That's a long way to say that a color image is most often rather dim on the easel. It is for this reason that very fast enlarging lenses are a boon to color printing. Even if they are never used to print wide open, they can certainly be used for composition and for initial focusing at their widest stop. Of course, the focus should be rechecked when the enlarging lens is stopped down to its exposing opening, but with a quality lens there should be very little or no focus shift from the wide-open down to the middle-aperture settings.

To my way of thinking and seeing there is only one type of focusing aid even worth mentioning, and that is the grain focuser. However, some people can't use grain-focusing devices, therefore I will also mention screen- and parallax-type focusing devices here.

Grain Focusers. Incorporated within a grain focuser is a mirror, at a fixed angle and a precisely regulated distance from the surface upon which you are focusing, which reflects a tiny portion of the image being focused up into a tube containing a reticle and an eyepiece. The eyepiece, most often, provides an image magnification of between 10× and 20×. If you are looking through a 15× eyepiece at an image being projected at 8×, you see the image at an effective 120× magnification. The reticle is provided to give your eye something to focus on as grain focusers provide an aerial image at the plane of the reticle.

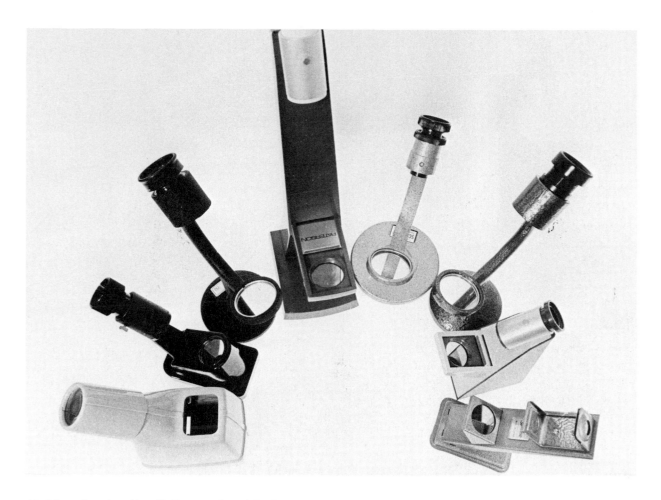

All of these focusing aids, with the exception of the first one on the left, operate by showing the printer an aerial image of the negative's or slide's "grain." The cost of these grain focusers ranges from under $5 to over $30. The tallest one (now replaced by a later model) is designed for work at high magnifications. The one exception (at the extreme left) is a B & L parallax focusing device.

With your eye focused on a $120 \times$ magnification of the image, it is quite easy to see the individual silver grains that comprise a black-and-white image. If you read Chapter 2 you know that there are no silver grains in a color image, but when you look at a color image through a grain focuser you can see the places where the silver grains used to be. (I know that sounds silly, but it is true because of the way that the dyes form in the immediate vicinity of metallic-silver particles and coupler globules.) The biggest problem most grain focusers suffer, because of their optical design, is that they can't be used very far away from the center of the projected image. Because of this it is impossible to check the corners and edges of the projected image for critical focus. There is only one grain-focusing device I know

of, at present, which has been able to overcome this problem. It is Chromega's Micromega. The problem with this unit is its high price.

Screen Focusers. Screen-focusing devices operate very much the same way that grain focusers do except for two characteristics: Their images are focused on a ground-glass screen and their eyepiece magnifications are considerably lower than those of the grain focusers. It is impossible to use a screen-focusing device to focus on the grain (or where the grain used to be), because the texture of the focusing screen itself obscures the grain. These devices are best used on an area of the image that contains a great deal of fine, high-contrast detail, such as printed material, ruled lines, etc. One of the most unusual of the screen-focusing devices I have

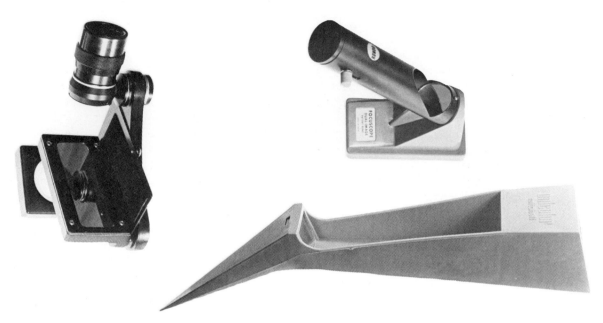

A focusing aid is a necessity in the darkroom. The arrow-shaped unit in the foreground is a Unicolor-Mitchel screen-focusing device that permits sharp focusing of details at the extreme edges of the image. The object at the top is a Rondo Dual-Image Focuscope, which is both a screen-focusing and a grain-focusing device. The unit at the left is the Micromega, which will focus grain anywhere on an image.

come across is the Unicolor-Mitchel Focusing Aid. Because of its very peculiar design it is sort of a poor man's Micromega. It can be used to get the most remote corner of an image into focus, if that corner provides sufficient image detail to focus on. Used with a specially prepared black-and-white negative, it can help in aligning an enlarger. And, because this unit is physically quite long, it makes focusing mural size-, wall-, or floor-projected images less of a problem than it would otherwise be.

There is one inexpensive focusing aid, which I must admit I use constantly in preference to several others of considerably higher quality (and price). It combines the properties of both a grain-focusing and a screen-focusing device. It is the Rondo Dual-Image Focus Scope. This unit incorporates a thin ground-glass screen with a hole cut out of its center. The image can be brought into coarse focus on the screen quite easily and quickly, and then can be finely focused on the grain, which is clearly visible in the aerial image seen in the hole in the center of the screen. The edge of the hole serves as the unit's reticle.

Parallax-type Focusers. Finally there are parallax-type focusing aids available. These are similar in construction and eyepiece magnification to most screen focusers. They differ in that they offer a clear glass or plastic screen at the plane in which the image is brought to focus. There are markings on the clear screen. To focus with such a device, one first brings the image to the best focus possible by simply observing fine image details on the screen, then by moving the head from side to side the user observes if the focused image moves relative to the markings on the screen. If it does, it is out of focus and a focusing adjustment must be made. These devices can afford great focusing accuracy, but they are difficult to use.

A final note before leaving this subject—it is essential, because you now have a matte-black easel (remember), to use a focusing sheet. For maximum focusing accuracy use the back of a piece of the exact same printing paper you are about to expose to compose and focus your image on. In this way you will insure that the surface of your sheet of printing paper is exactly the same distance from the enlarging lens as your focusing sheet was. This is especially critical if you have a slow enlarging lens, and you must use it wide open where it has an extremely shallow depth of focus.

Printing Aids

If there is any one area of color printing in which there is a maximum of confusion and a minimum of concrete information, this is it. Devices in this category constitute color printing's "catch 22."

All too many people decide, on the basis of half-understood ad copy, hearsay, and advice from a photo-shop clerk, that they will go into color printing. They think the whole process can be handled automatically, without a real need for any skill or comprehension of what the process is all about. Many people are convinced that all they have to do is push a button or two on the wonderful machines they can buy, and the prints will automatically be exposed, processed, and pop out dry and ready for mounting. There are a few somewhat useful printing aids, but none of them even remotely fit that description. In color printing, as in basket weaving or belly dancing, either you know what you are doing, or your results will show it.

Printing Calculators

Printing calculators are relatively uncomplicated little devices that are, under the best of circumstances, able to tell their users what printing filter pack and what exposure time are required to print a specific negative or slide, at some definite magnification on paper from a specific emulsion batch with a specific batch of chemicals, under a particular set of processing circumstances in a room at some specific temperature. If that sounds a bit more complicated than the way you may have thought of printing calculators up until now, what can I say but that you will have to change your thinking. Every condition I just mentioned that was preceded by the word specific or particular is a color printing variable. If you use a printing calculator on a Monday and get a good result, and then return to your darkroom on Friday and try to duplicate the print you got on Monday but fail miserably, it will probably be because you changed one of these variables. If you don't know what the variables are, and you don't know how to control them, you will have to use a printing calculator to make a test print just prior to every print you make. That means that you will have to make *at least* two prints for every one you hope to keep. This can be a very expensive, annoying, and time-consuming process. If you have read and understood Chapter 2 there is very little reason why you should entertain the idea of using a calculator. These devices are little more than crutches to get timid printers to start printing. They are simply not needed once you understand what you are doing. However, after all of that, it might be a good idea if I describe what these devices are, how they operate, and what they can do.

Most color printing calculators are a collection of many tiny acetate CP filter segments, in a wide range of densities of all of the subtractive primary colors, arranged so as to provide a large number of filter combinations. These are all bound together in a frame, about 4" X 5" in size. In addition to the collection of subtractive filter segments, most calculators also feature a set of red filter windows of graded density or graded neutral-density filter windows. Almost without exception these units are designed to be placed on a small piece of the paper you wish to make a print on and be contact printed onto that paper by diffused light coming from your enlarger lens. This contact print is usually made with the negative or slide you wish to print placed in the enlarger's negative carrier and with the enlarger's head height set to get the magnification you need to make the final print. The image you wish to print is first focused and composed on the focusing sheet on your easel. Then the enlarger lens is set to a stop recommended by the calculator's manufacturer. The calculator is then placed on a sheet of unexposed printing paper, a diffuser is placed somewhere in the image-forming light path, and the contact print of the calculator is made under the diffused light of your composed and focused image. Of course a filter pack, as recommended by the maker of the calculator, is placed in the enlarger's filter drawer or dialed into its head, prior to making the exposure. All of this done, the contact print must then be completely processed and then dried. Once dry, the color image of the many filter segments is visually scanned and compared to a series of gray patches supplied with the calculator to find a tiny segment of gray on the contact print. Once that is found the calculator user can determine what corrections are necessary to the filter pack he made the contact print of the calculator with, to make an acceptable print of his negative or slide. The process of translating the position of the gray segment on the contact print to a filter-pack change is either very simple and direct or very complicated and confusing, depending on which calculator you use and how your head works. The contact print is then again examined to determine which of the several red or neutral density filters was the last to leave an image on it. That data must also be translated, with varying degrees of difficulty depending on whose calculator you use, into the proper printing exposure time for an acceptable image.

Now, with all of this done you can make the pack change recommended and set your timer as determined to make your print per the calculator's instructions. The chances are fairly good, perhaps as high as 75 percent in your favor, that you will come up with an acceptable print—if you have done everything exactly the right way while making the test contact print, and if you do all of your processing exactly the same way on both the test contact print and on the actual print itself. If you don't meet these requirements and you don't really understand the precesses involved, you will come up with a weird looking print and not have the foggiest idea of why, or of what you ought to do about it, except, perhaps, to go all the way back to the beginning of this long and complicated process and start all over again by making another test contact print. The most a calculator will ever do, under the best of circumstances, is get you to a filter pack which is about 5 or 10 density, in one of the subtractive primary colors, away from the perfect one. So you will most likely have to reprint after your second print, in any event, if you really want to get the color balance right on the money. That means that you will have to make three prints (counting the initial test contact print) before you reach a final print.

This is where the "catch 22" of color printing comes in. If all you know is how to use a

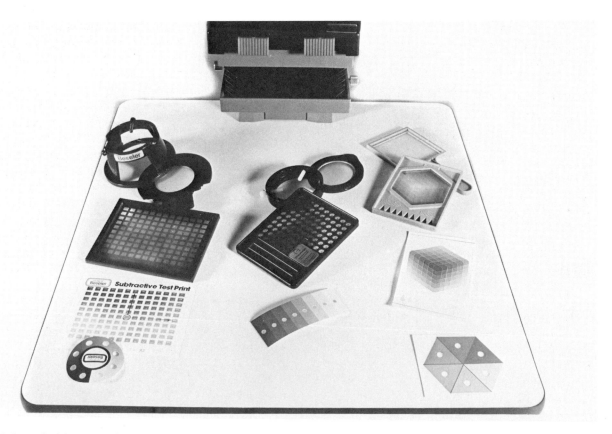

Printing calculators come in several shapes, sizes, and makes, three of which are shown here. These devices are contact printed to determine the correct printing filter pack and exposure for a given negative. The units shown are designed for use with negative-to-positive printing only; however, positive-to-positive calculators are also available.

printing calculator to determine your printing filter packs and printing exposure times, you simply won't be smart enough to know to correct your slightly off-color print. And if you do learn how to make the correction needed to get from, say 10 magenta away from the perfect printing filter pack, you will be smart enough so that you really won't need a printing calculator in the first place.

One further note on printing calculators is pertinent here. These devices are all based on a simple, and most often valid, assumption that any image you may want to print with their help will contain equal amounts of the colors red, green, and blue, and will be neither extremely high nor extremely low key. If you are into shooting monochromes, or even images that have one very predominant color (a fire engine for example) among others, these devices won't be of any great use to you. They will be equally unhelpful if you tend to do much high- or low-key work.

Electronic Analyzers

Electronic color analyzers are impressive looking machines. Most of them have a number of switches, knobs and dials, and a large illuminated meter to read. They are also expensive.

With such an array of technological "goodies" staring at a color printer it is easy to understand why he might easily be awed into believing that if only he had such a wondrous device his thinking days would be over—that he could leave all his color printing problems to his electronic marvel. Once again, friends, I'm afraid it just isn't so, particularly for the beginning color printer.

Consider the one basic requirement that all analyzers, off-easel or on, share in common; it is that the users of these devices must be sufficiently expert to make perfect color prints all by themselves (or with a little help from their friends, or a calculator) *before* they can even *begin* to use an electronic analyzer—another "catch 22."

Now consider the fact that every one of the color printing variables (plus a few additional electronic ones) that could cause a color printer to come to grief with a calculator is also as great a problem to the user of an electronic analyzer. If after all that considering you still think that such a machine will relieve you from the necessity of understanding what you are doing when you make a color print, then you need help. I'll try to offer it.

Electronic color analyzers do not require that you make a test print to determine the proper filter pack and exposure time to print a particular negative or slide. Instead, these devices look directly at the light from your enlarger lamp, which has passed through the image you wish to print. They compare the color balance of that light to what you have told the machine the proper color balance should be, and tell you if the light's color balance matches the information you provided. If there is no match, the analyzer tells you how to change your color printing filters to achieve one. Color analyzers also compare the overall amount of the light falling on their probes to the level of light you found you needed to make a properly exposed print and tell you if a match is achieved, or if not, what your proper printing time and lens opening ought to be to achieve one.

In order to tell the analyzer what proper color balance and exposure light level to look for, you must, before ever turning the machine on, make an absolutely perfect color print of a negative or transparency which you know has been properly exposed and processed, and which contains certain other very specific information. If you are unable to make this flawlessly perfect calibration print you will be unable to program your analyzer. If you can't program your analyzer, it will simply sit on its shelf, totally useless. If you think that you can establish a program for the device from data obtained by making a print that is less than perfect, you are right, you can. But, as with all computational devices—you get out of it what you put into it. Every print you make, using a less than perfect program will be less perfect than the less than perfect one.

Assuming you are able to somehow make a perfect print, you are now faced with a dilemma with regard to programming your expensive analyzer. You must decide what to program it for. Of course, there are some analyzers that do not cause you this kind of grief. I am referring to the type that reads the diffused-light output of your enlarger lens, just as its far less expensive cousins, the calculators, do. These electronic analyzers are designed to believe that all color images contain the same amounts of red, green, and blue that your calibration print did. This, as I pointed out in the section on calculators, is often simply not the case.

But getting back to the analyzers which do cause a programming dilemma.... The more flexible analyzers can operate on the assumption just outlined, or they can be used with a spot-reading probe to analyze a particular type of color situation. The most popular of these special color-situation programs is called "flesh tone." Once you have made your perfect print, if the image it contains has, for example, the face of a human being somewhere in it, you can insert a program into your analyzer that will make all succeeding prints you make of human beings come out so that their flesh tones will match the flesh tones of your perfect calibration print.

I won't belabor the obvious flaws in this kind of programming—what if your calibration print showed a Caucasian but you want to print a shot of an Oriental or a Black person, etc.—I'll just mention that I've never seen any two people with identical flesh tones, and leave it at that. It is also possible to establish a program for any specific color, but here again it is rather doubtful that any future shot will ever have that specific color included in it, unless you put it there.

Perhaps the most useful of the programs you can load into an electronic analyzer is the data on how you printed a perfect reproduction of an 18 percent gray card. It is not too farfetched to include a gray card in the corner of a frame of a subject you are shooting, or to shoot a full frame of an 18 percent gray card when you are working under the constant lighting of a studio strobe or hot-light setup.

At any rate, the choice of how you program your analyzer is yours. Some of these machines will store several programs internally. Whatever program or programs you do insert into your analyzer's memory will be applicable to prints made on paper from the same emulsion batch as the paper you made your calibration print on, processed in the same batch of chemicals under identical conditions of temperature, time, and

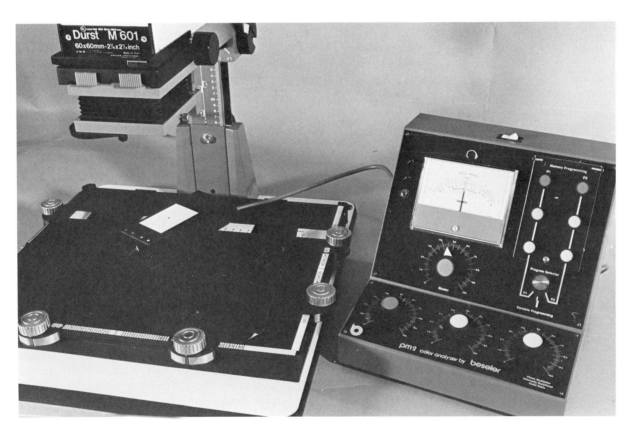

Electronic analyzers, such as this unit, are capable of determining the correct printing filter pack and exposure by checking the color balance of light projected through a negative or slide against what you have determined the light should be. The analyzer's results can only be as good as the data you have stored in it. This Beseler unit will store three separate programs internally.

agitation. If you change any of these factors, you will have to make a brand new calibration print with the new materials or processing conditions or your analyzer will be providing you with inappropriate data. As a matter of fact, if you decide to change the type of color negative film you use from the one originally used to make the calibration print with which you programmed your electronic analyzer, you will have to make a new calibration print from a new negative on the new film and reprogram your analyzer with the data so obtained.

I certainly do hope that the material above has gone a long way toward dispelling the myth that surrounds electronic color analyzers. These devices do work, and they do work well, but they don't eliminate skill or knowledge as requirements of color printing. They are simply another type of tool that is available to the color printer, but one that has no magical power at all.

Hardware for the Wet Side of the Color Printing Darkroom

Film Processing Equipment

Processing color film of almost all types is not really very much more difficult than processing black-and-white film. However, there are several good reasons why most amateur printers would probably do well to avoid it. The most convincing one I can think of is cost. Unless you shoot a lot of color film, or you save the film you've shot in the freezer until you have at least a half-dozen rolls to be processed at the same time, you will come out ahead by letting Kodak, or some independent lab you really trust, process your color film for you. But if you do have sufficient volume or money is no object, and you have the free time and the inclination to control your images from latent to mounted, there is absolutely no reason why you can't process your own color film.

I don't bother processing my own color film for several reasons, the prime one being that the bulk of the color material I shoot is on Koda-chrome, and I've already explained why processing that material is impossible without special automatic equipment and large quantities of special chemistry. Other reasons, aside from cost, are simply time, convenience, and control. If I set up to do a half-dozen rolls of Ektachrome myself, I will be at it for at *least* three quarters of an hour and my results won't be any better than Kodak's.

The articles shown at left—a gallon pitcher, a few small graduates, a turkish towel, a dishpan, an accurate thermometer, and an 8″ × 10″ daylight print-processing drum—are all you absolutely need for color print processing; however, there's no limit to the number of goodies you can acquire. The small sample at right includes both an 11″ × 14″ and a 16″ × 20″ daylight print-processing drum, a remote, water bath–temperature controller, a motor base to automatically agitate the processing drums, and a dial and an armored glass-rod, mercury-type thermometer.

And, if I process my own Vericolor II rolls with process C-41, I'm going to be tied up for almost half an hour, and once again my own processing results won't be any better or any different than Kodak's.

There is only one way to process color film, and that is accurately. It isn't like black-and-white materials where you can exercise a great deal of control over everything from grain size to contrast. With color film either you do it exactly the way the book tells you to or you get an image of lower quality than you would have if you followed the book. So, since I haven't the time to spend over a sink doing something I can't really do any better than Kodak I leave all of my color film processing to Kodak. The one big exception to this is when I am up against a deadline that even a custom lab on 200 percent rush can't meet, or at 2 A.M. on a Sunday when a custom lab isn't even open for business.

Tanks and Reels

If you already own film tanks and reels that have served satisfactorily for black-and-white work, and which you are used to working with, chances are that this same equipment will serve you well for your color film-processing chores.

In general I would suggest film tanks that are designed to be agitated by inversion and to be used with stainless-steel wire film reels. I prefer all PVC-type tanks for the smaller tank sizes and stainless-steel tank bodies with PVC lids and caps for the larger tank sizes. Under no circumstances (in my opinion) should you consider an *all*-stainless tank. They are notorious for their sticking covers and caps, which, when they aren't refusing to come off, are dripping and leaking during agitation.

Unicolor manufactures some unique and very ingenious equipment, designed specifically for amateur use. It simplifies film processing by effectively eliminating the need for a temperature-controlling water bath and a precise schedule of manual tank agitation. This equipment, called the Unicolor Film Drum II System consists of a special double-walled film tank with a movable piston where most film tanks have their bottoms. The tank's double wall construction cuts down on heat transference through the tank walls to a considerable extent, and allows the tank to be used for film processing outside of a temperature-controlling water bath. Because of the piston, which can be moved within the tank bore, the user can effectively control the reel capacity of the tank, changing it from a tank having room enough for only a single 35mm film reel to one that will hold six 35mm reels. The tank is designed to be used in a horizontal

While it is possible to use any of these tanks and reels to process color negative or positive film, I can only personally recommend the all PVC tank (far right), the stainless-steel tank with PVC lid and cap (rear left), and stainless-steel wire reels to fit them. All-stainless tanks often leak or suffer sticking caps or lids. Some plastic tank bodies are easily broken when dropped.

The Unicolor film drum features a movable piston that permits varying the unit's internal volume to suit the number of reels to be processed. A system of hollow rods pipes chemicals to the tank bottom to prevent splashing during filling.

This is a photo of the Unicolor film drum with lid, cap, and piston removed. The thick drum walls are hollow to reduce thermal conduction.

position while being agitated by Unicolor's motor base, called a Uniroller. Because of this combination of features, a considerably lesser volume of processing chemicals can be used for a given quantity of film than is usually used in more conventional film tanks.

This same system employs a rather complicated but effective system of light-baffled center-filling tubes of various lengths, or interlocking hollow reel cores, to insure, that when the tank is first loaded with film and then filled with chemicals that the chemicals will fill the tank evenly from the bottom up rather than from the top down. This is to prevent the splashing of chemicals over portions of the film in the drum during filling operations thereby preventing uneven development, stains, or mottle. This same effect can also be obtained by filling a conventional tank with chemicals first and then gently lowering the film reels into the tank.

The motor base used to agitate this tank/reel system is also unique and particularly effective for film-development work because it reverses the direction of rotation of the film drum periodically to minimize the possibility of streaking. Needless to say, this Unicolor film-processing hardware system can hardly be classified as inexpensive.

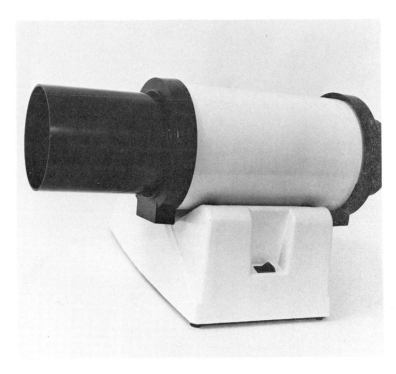

The Unicolor film drum is intended for use with that same company's motor base; however, it can be used as an inversion tank if so desired. Since both ends of the tank are sealed, it is also capable of being used in a temperature-controlled bath.

Temperature Controllers

One of the hard-to-kill myths about color printing concerns the impossibility of undertaking it successfully unless you are able to maintain the temperature of your chemicals and your processor to within $\pm\frac{1}{4}$ F ($\pm\frac{1}{8}$ C). That myth is, of course, absolutely ridiculous. It is perfectly simple to make excellent color prints with absolutely no temperature control whatsoever by working at whatever temperature your darkroom happens to be. I won't, however, go quite so far as to say that the same is true for processing color negative or positive film.

When you are making color prints, mistakes are correctable. But when you are processing color film, if you make an error, you've had it. You don't get a second chance. So if you do intend to do your own color film processing, I would strongly recommend that you do work with carefully regulated and controlled chemical and processing temperatures.

Temperature controllers fall into two main categories: automatic or manually-controlled temperature-regulating faucets and water-bath temperature controllers. The units in the former

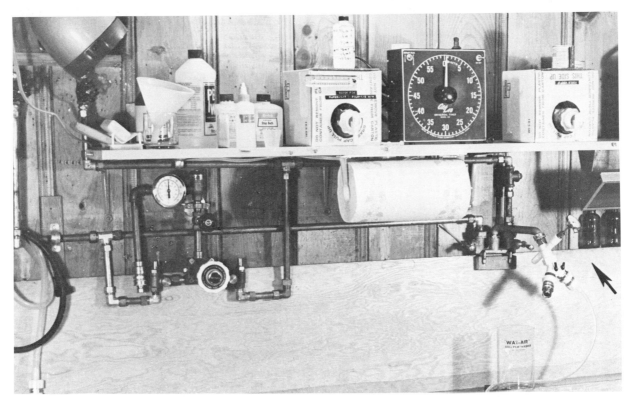

This homemade plywood sink features an automatic, thermostatically controlled, pressure compensated–water flow regulator on the left, and a Flo-Temp thermometer well on the ordinary laundry-type faucet on the right.

category are, most often, part of the plumbing of a well-equipped darkroom sink. One of the simplest of these devices is the Flo-Temp unit market by Pfefer. It is nothing more than a thermometer well that is designed to fit at the end of a standard laundry-tub faucet by means of a female hose fitting. The Flo-Temp's well accommodates most standard dial thermometers. Its purpose is to allow you to monitor the temperature of water flowing from the faucet. The Flo-Temp does no controlling whatsoever. That's your job when employing it. It just helps you to keep track of how well you are regulating the running water's temperature by adjusting the tap handles.

Next in order of expensiveness is a simple single-handle shower-type mixing valve or, for that matter, any single-handle faucet. These pieces of plumbing must be combined with a Flo-Temp if you are to know how well the single handle of such a valve has done to get your initial water-temperature setting accurately established. While many people think that these single-

handle devices somehow automatically control the temperature of the water they allow to flow through them, the fact is that none of them do any such thing. They do nothing more than the separate tap handles of a common sink faucet do; that is, they regulate the size of the passages through which the hot and the cold water passes on its way to the sink. If the temperature of either the hot or the cold water varies, the output water temperature from such a unit will vary right along with it. The same thing is true for water pressure. If it varies on either line, the output water temperature from a shower valve or a single-handle faucet will also vary. The dial thermometer you put in a Flo-Temp will happily reflect any of these changes but none of the equipment I have mentioned so far has even the slightest power to *automatically* regulate the temperature of a flow of water from a faucet. However, it is possible to add a pressure compensator across the lines feeding a shower valve or single-handle faucet, to reduce or eliminate pressure as a factor of output water-temperature

The Flo-Temp thermometer well doesn't control water temperature but does allow you to quickly determine the temperature of water flowing from a faucet. The flow of water is controlled by regulating the tap handles. When the unit is combined with the snap fittings and Y-valve shown here, the entire assembly can be quickly snapped on or off a faucet, and a single stream of water is handily converted to two.

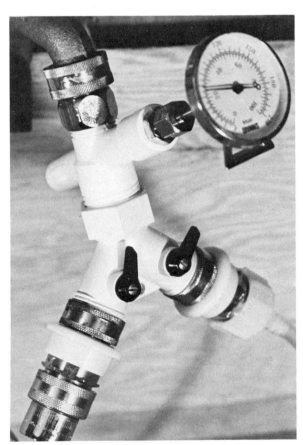

This Flo-Temp is mounted directly on the end of a laundry faucet by means of its female hose connector. The dial thermometer, mounted in the unit's well, quickly indicates the temperature of the water flowing through both valve-controlled legs of the Y-value fitting. An aerator and a hose line are snapped onto the legs of the Y-valve with quick-disconnect snap fittings.

variation. But pressure compensators cost about as much as shower valves or single-handle faucets, and hot-water input temperatures are notoriously inconsistent.

At from two to three times the cost of such devices a thermostatically-controlled water-temperature flow regulator can be obtained. These thermostatically-controlled regulators go directly into the plumbing of a darkroom sink. They will maintain the output water temperature you initially establish, on a large, built-in thermometer dial, to within rather close limits, most often to $\pm \frac{1}{2}$ F ($\pm \frac{1}{4}$ C), quite automatically, *if* the temperature and the pressure of the input water doesn't vary *too* drastically. Some of these regulators have built-in pressure-compensator devices and most of the others can be ordered with them as optional external plumbing. Most such equipment is designed with the commercial user in mind, however, and provides minimum controllable flow capacities grossly in excess of anything an amateur would even dream of using (if that amateur is paying to heat his own hot water or is at all concerned with conserving fuel). I have used one thermostatically-controlled temperature regulator, called the Meynell Photomix, which, in addition to having a built-in line-pressure compensator and good accuracy, also provides output water-temperature control down to a flow rate of one half gallon per minute. I've not been able to find one with a lower controllable flow rate, but I would certainly like to.

For just a bit less than the cost of a

This thermostatically controlled, water temperature–flow regulator is installed in the darkroom plumbing. The large white knob regulates the temperature of the output water, which is indicated on the thermometer dial at the top-left of the unit. The small dark knob above the large white one regulates the flow rate of the output water. This Meynell Photomix Model 155 is capable of controlling flow rates as small as one-half gallon per minute. Most such units require higher flow rates for proper operation. This unit also features a built-in pressure compensator to accommodate line-pressure fluctuations.

thermostatically-controlled, water-temperature flow regulator, a water-bath temperature controller can be obtained. These devices have nothing at all to do with the plumbing and, for the most part, can be used to control the temperature of a container of several gallons of water to very close limits, typically well within $\pm \frac{1}{4}$ F ($\pm \frac{1}{8}$ C), anywhere a source of 110 volt AC power is available. The ones I favor consist of a housing containing a pump, a temperature sensor, and one or more heaters. Long hoses are attached to the housing so that water may be pumped out of a separate container and into the unit's housing, where it flows over the temperature sensor, over the heater coils, and then back through a hose to the remote container. One such unit I'm partial to is the Supertemp.

I prefer these units over others that are permanently mounted, without hoses, directly to the container holding the temperature-controlled water. I feel that such units lack flexibility. The remote-type water-bath temperature controller can also be used (with a bit of ingenuity) to supply a constant-temperature stream of water to a Kodak Model II processor, should you be inclined to use one. I know of some color printers who have adapted large fish-tank pumps and heaters to serve this purpose.

One thing to avoid is a water-bath temperature controller that does not provide a pump, paddle or some other device to provide good agitation of the controlled bath. Without good bath agitation it is impossible to get even water-temperature distribution throughout the bath. And if the heater's temperature sensor, in such a nonagitated bath, happens to lie in a particular spot that is either atypically hot or cold, it will have the heater doing all sorts of awful things. In case you may be wondering what you are to do with a flowing, automatically temperature-controlled water bath or with the water contained in a constant-temperature bath, it is most often used to store chemical bottles in. Doing so brings the chemicals within the bottles to the exact temperature specified for processing. These baths are also used to control the temperatures of some processing tanks and drums.

Finally, I should point out that such a temperature-controlled bath can be maintained with very good accuracy with nothing more than your devoted attention, a thermometer, and a pitcher of very hot water. If you bring several gallons of water in a controlled bath to the temperature you need and then periodically monitor the temperature of the water with a thermometer left immersed in it, you will find that it is really quite simple to keep the bath temperature closely regulated by simply adding hot water and stirring from time to time.

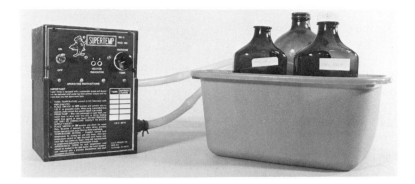

This remote water bath–temperature controller pumps water from the deep dishpan, holding several bottles of processing chemistry, and circulates it over its temperature sensor to determine if the water is at the proper temperature. From the sensor, the water is circulated over a pair of heating coils and then returned to the temperature-controlled bath. This continuous circulation and sampling insures that all of the water will be well mixed and, therefore, of uniform temperature.

Thermometers

A decent thermometer is a bedrock item on any color-darkroom hardware "must" list. Many color darkrooms have several, but, when it comes right down to it, just one reliable unit is all that is absolutely necessary. I would recommend, for the one-thermometer darkroom, that a glass rod-type unit be selected. This type of thermometer can double as a stirring rod (but *do not* use it as a pestle for dissolving powders), and that feature is very desirable when you measure the temperature of a processing presoak bath. The thermometer you do choose should cover a range of at least 60–120 F (15–50 C) and be readable down to ½ F (¼ C). For a thermometer to be dependably readable to ½ F (¼ C) it must be calibrated in 1 F (½ C) increments.

Kodak produces an inexpensive alcohol-filled, glass-rod unit called, appropriately enough, Color Thermometer. That same firm produces a much more expensive, mercury-filled, stainless-steel-sheathed, glass rod-type unit that they call the Process Thermometer. Either one is all a color printer really needs.

The biggest disadvantage that glass-rod thermometers suffer is that they are easily broken. Metal-armored types are more durable than the unprotected glass rod. Another problem these units suffer is that they can be slow and annoying to read. These thermometers must be properly oriented for their calibrations to be visible at all and sometimes, even when their calibrations are readable, their alcohol or mercury columns aren't.

Dial thermometers are often very useful luxuries in a color darkroom. They are easy to read and are designed to be placed over the lip of a deep, temperature-controlled bath container. The drawback to dial thermometers is that they

A metal-sheathed, mercury-filled, glass rod-type thermometer is being used here to recalibrate a dial-type thermometer. Both types have their advantages and disadvantages, and both are very useful to the color printer.

eventually go out of calibration and, with many of them, it is impossible to recalibrate them yourself. Beseler, Bogen and some other companies have overcome this problem with a user-readjust unit. Another drawback of the dial thermometer is that while they are easy to read at a glance, from a distance, when the precision of the reading is not a greater factor, they can be very difficult to read down to ½ F (¼ C) because of parallax problems. If you don't read a dial thermometer from directly in front of the dial, chances are that you will read it incorrectly. Some dial-type units are equipped with a mirror inset into their dials so that the user can check the mirror to insure that no image of the needle is visible from the reading position. Such a mirror scale is almost a necessity for this type of thermometer.

Whichever type you may choose, make sure that the unit you select has a very low thermal inertia and, therefore, a very rapid response time. There is nothing as annoying as having to wait while you watch the reading on a thermometer slowly creep up or down. Part of this annoyance is brought about by the uncertainty you feel over trying to determine whether, at any given moment, the reading of a long-response time-type of instrument reflects the actual temperature of the solution you are trying to measure, or if the reading is still changing.

Paper Processors

There is, in my mind, only one reasonable method for an amateur or a small-volume professional color printer to use, to process prints in sizes up to 16″ × 20″, and that method involves a very simple type of device called a daylight drum processor.

However, there are several other ways to process prints, and I would be remiss if I didn't at least mention them here (and, in the case of several of them, in much greater detail later in the text). The most obvious but least practical of the available methods involves trays or baskets. I'll skip over baskets because they are not really applicable pieces of gear for use with less than a few dozen prints at a time. These costly devices require the use of large volumes of chemicals, and most often rely on expensive gas-burst equipment for agitation.

While it is *possible* to process color prints in trays, it is hardly *practical* to do so. Color print processing is nothing like black-and-white work. You can't watch a color print come up in the tray—the safelight is too dim to let you see anything worthwhile and there's not that much worth seeing until after most of the processing is over. You can't pull the print during development to do a bit of hotsouping or local stopping—there is no hotsoup (concentrated developer) procedure

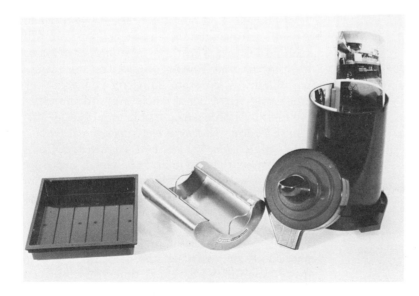

At first all amateurs used the same set of trays to process color prints that they had used for their black-and-white chores for years. Trays must be used under safelight conditions and may contaminate chemistry, lungs, and hands. The invention of the canoe was a big improvement that allowed a tiny puddle of chemistry to be rocked back and forth over a print and then dumped, but canoes still had to be worked under safelights. The daylight print-processing drum lets you work in the daylight, uses a tiny amount of chemistry, and keeps your contact with processing chemicals to a bare minimum. Drums also permit the processing of several smaller-sized prints at the same time.

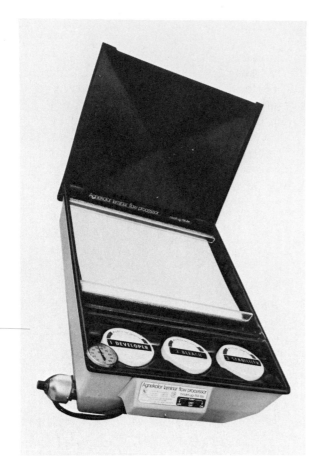

Each of these color print-processing devices costs about ten times more than a daylight drum of equal or greater capacity and capability. The Agnekolor processor incorporates a non-circulating type, thermostatically controlled heater (in this deluxe model) to regulate the temperature of its replenished chemistry; however, it provides no temperature regulation for wash water. The Kodak Model 11 Rapid Color Processor requires the user to work under safelight conditions, consumes large quantities of chemistry, and puts a good deal of chemical vapor into the darkroom air. No temperature control is supplied with the basic machine. Temperature-controlled water can be user supplied via the black hose.

applicable and even if there was, the dim glow of a No. 13 safelight wouldn't give you enough illumination to let you know what you were doing. Color print processing is much like black-and-white film processing, in that it is best done by time and temperature methods. Trays offer a huge surface area for cooling their contents through contact with the surrounding air, so they must be placed in a water bath for temperature control, and that can get messy. The large surface area of color chemistry left exposed to the darkroom atmosphere also releases a large amount of chemical vapors which are hardly the most benign things you can inhale. As a matter of fact, using *any* method of print processing a reasonable and prudent printer will make certain that the room or area in which the processing is taking place is more than adequately ventilated (by a complete change of air every several minutes).

If the thought of breathing large quantities of less-than-benign chemical vapors doesn't faze you, perhaps contact dermatitis will. Processing prints in trays, particularly if you want to do more than one print at a time, involves using your fingers to grab and move the prints for interleaf agitation. Color chemicals can irritate your skin. You can, of course, wear rubber gloves while you do your processing, but if you have worn rubber gloves for any length of time you will vividly remember just how unpleasant that can be.

If you don't care about your health, how about some concern for your pocketbook? Processing in trays involves the maximum possible contamination and oxidation of chemicals per print processed. While it may seem like a cheap way of getting started, I suspect that you will soon find that it is costing you more per print, to tray process, than it will if you process in a drum.

Finally, I do want to warn you that tray processing is the least repeatable and therefore the least desirable way possible to process prints. I have found *the single most important control a color printer has is his own consistency.* Color printing materials are tolerant of a lot of exposure and processing errors and because of this you can get good results *if you do everything exactly the same way every time.* If you do things consistently it will be possible to pin down problems and thereby correct certain things you are doing to predictably achieve a desired effect. But, if you do everything differently every time you do it, you might as well give up on the idea of ever becoming a good color printer. You won't have a chance. Since trays add considerably to the unpredictability of processing for even the most careful worker, they really ought to be avoided at all cost. As a matter of fact, I feel so strongly that trays are a tool of the devil where color printing is concerned, that *I am going to drop them right here, never to mention them again.* If you want to know more about tray processing color prints, you will have to look for the information elsewhere; you won't find it in this book.

There are several print-processing machines on the market, and the one thing all of these machines have in common is high cost. The cheapest of them sells for at least $200. High cost would be understandable in machines that provided the color printer with print-processing quality, speed, simplicity, and economy of operation otherwise unobtainable, but none of these machines have such exclusive abilities or features. All of them will process prints satisfactorily, if not uniformly well or easily, but none of them offer anything more than you can get for a lot less money from a daylight print processing drum. As a matter of fact, the Kodak machines, which begin in price at very close to $400, must be used under safelight conditions during the first part of the processing procedure, and their chemical consumption rate is two to three times as high as that of the much cheaper daylight drum. Other high-priced devices are designed around the use of chemical replenishment, a system that I am convinced has absolutely no place in the amateur color darkroom.

Now, after having damned all print processing tools and techniques but one, I suppose I had better make a pretty good case for daylight color print-processing drums, or risk raising your ire.

Daylight color print-processing drums are essentially nothing more than hollow tubes with a removable light-baffled pouring spout at one or at both ends. An exposed piece of printing paper is shaped into a tube and inserted into a drum immediately after the exposure has been made. The cap then is put back on the drum and the white lights may be turned on again in the darkroom. So, the first advantage of using such a device is the fact that they allow you to work in broad daylight.

The drums are, in my opinion, most properly used with one-shot processing. With one-shot

This daylight print-processing-drum original was manufactured by Simmard, in Canada, and sold in the U.S. by Unicolor. The cam-shaped end caps, a patented feature of Simmard drums, provide agitation of the chemical puddle inside of the drum by causing a wave of chemistry to move from one end of the drum to the other.

The cam-shaped caps are easily visible in this head-on view of a new Simmard drum (now marketed by Chromega).

processing you use a bare minimum of chemicals to process each print, or group of prints, and then immediately discard the chemicals once they have been used. While this may seem like a wasteful procedure to some printers, it really isn't too uneconomical when you consider that many drums require only 1½ to 2 ounces (40–60ml) of each processing solution (per 8″ × 10″) and you gain a huge advantage in the consistency with which you are able to process. However, for die-hard replenishment freaks, daylight drums are quite easy to use with replenishment techniques (but *I* certainly don't recommend doing so).

My favorite drum processing method involves only the most rudimentary temperature control. I use all the processing chemicals at whatever temperature my darkroom happens to be, but I warm the drum and the print inside it with presoak water, poured into the drum, before I begin processing. Many drum manufacturers provide a simple, printed graph-type device, called a nomograph, which will, for a known room temperature and a chemical manufacturer's recommended processing temperature, automatically provide the drum user with the proper presoak water temperature to use.

Once the drum and paper have been brought to operating temperature, the presoak water is discarded and the drum is drained through its pouring spout. Then a small quantity of developer is added through that same spout and the developer puddle, formed inside the drum, is agitated over the print surface by rolling the drum about its longitudinal axis. This rolling agitation may be accomplished either manually, by rolling the drum on a level, padded surface (a turkish towel or a foam-rubber pad will provide sufficient friction to insure that the drum will roll rather than slip), or the drum may be rolled by an electromechanical agitator. The electromechanical device is the better choice because it is more consistent than manual agitation, but either method will work. When development is complete the drum is tilted to pour off the developer, then the drum is drained for a few seconds; the

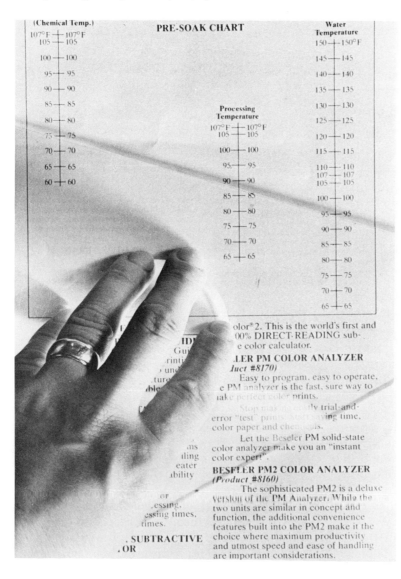

This is a nomograph. If you place a straightedge across the two known temperature values—the processing-chemical temperature, which is most often the room temperature, and the processing temperature, which is recommended by the chemistry's manufacturer—the point where the straightedge crosses the third scale will indicate the temperature needed for presoak processing water. In this case, the Beseler nomograph suggests that for room-temperature chemistry at 75F (24C) and a manufacturer's recommended processing temperature of 88F (32C), presoak water at 95F (35C) will be required.

next processing solution is poured in through the pouring spout and the drum is agitated with this new solution for some specified length of time. Then this solution is poured off and another one is added to the drum. And so on and so forth, until the completely processed print is removed from the drum to be dried.

Since all of this activity goes on in broad daylight, or white room light, there is never any fumbling in the near darkness of a No. 13 safelight's glow. If the chemistry is used in the one-shot manner I recommend there is never any bother about collecting it after use and about how much replenishment is needed, and about how much of a time or temperature increase is necesary for the next print processed in the recycled soup. When you work one-shot you always do everything the exact same way. That helps you to become and to remain a consistent worker.

Typical processing times, using a daylight drum, run between eight and ten minutes. If volume production becomes necessary, several prints can be processed simultaneously in a daylight processing drum. Typically, a 16″ × 20″ drum will process four 8″ × 10″ prints or two 11″ × 14″ prints or a single 16″ × 20″ print at the same time. Using a 16″ × 20″ drum you can get an effective 8″ × 10″ print-processing time of one print every two minutes. That's not too much

slower than a black-and-white stablilization printer will process black-and-white prints.

Another big advantage of drum processors is that when you become used to them, you will find that you really don't even have to get your hands wet while you are processing prints. And since the tiny puddles of solution are contained within the drum, and they can be poured directly into the sink drain, the drum user gets to breath a lot less chemically-contaminated air than users of other processing devices.

A motor base is, by far, the best possible way to agitate a daylight drum processor, if only because it agitates more consistently than is possible by hand. In all cases, without exception, the drum must make one complete revolution before changing direction.

Always roll a daylight processing drum on an old towel or on a sponge-rubber pad. These high-friction surfaces prevent the drum from slipping and insure proper agitation when the drum is being rolled by hand.

The Cibachrome daylight processing drum is typical of the vertical type. Note the funnel shape of its pour-in cap.

There are two basic types of drums; the vertical and the horizontal type. Vertical drums usually, but not always, have pouring spouts at both ends. These are so arranged that when the drum is placed vertically, with its pour-out end down, any liquid within the drum will pour out; but while this is going on, you may pour the next solution into the drum without worrying about its mixing with what's already in the drum or simply pouring out with the rest of the drum's contents. The pour-in caps have a reservoir device that stores the fresh charge of chemical until the drum is deliberately placed in a horizontal position. When such drums are positioned horizontally nothing further will pour out

Notice the pour-out end of the Cibachrome drum in the top photo. If this drum is placed in a puddle in a sink during the pour in–pour out operation, it may air lock. Its smooth walls, as seen in the bottom photo, make loading quite simple, but require that washing and stabilizing be done in separate trays. Note that the reservoirs built into the end caps permit simultaneous filling and emptying of the drum.

of the drum, and whatever chemical has been added during the pour-in/pour-out operation will spill out of the reservoir and into the drum to process the print.

Almost all such vertical drums have smooth walls inside the drum. One disadvantage with this type of drum is that it will not hold very much presoak water. Another is that their smooth walls make it impossible to carry out all of the processing steps required for a color print, inside of the drum. With smooth-walled, vertical-type drums the wash and stabilization steps must often be carried out in a separate tray.

My own preference is for the horizontal, ribbed-wall type of drum. These units have only a single pouring spout at one end of the drum that is used to first pour the contents of the drum out and then to receive the next processing solution. These drums can be filled with presoak water when desirable, and they allow all of the necessary processing steps to be carried out within the drum, as the ribs, which run the length of the drum, allow processing solutions, and more importantly, the wash water, to get behind the prints in the drum.

There are several variations on these basic daylight drum types. Kodak (London, England; not Rochester) markets a vertical type that can be completely sealed and floated in a temperature-controlled water bath. Beseler makes a horizontal-type drum with smooth walls. Paterson makes a smooth-walled horizontal-type drum that has a helical slot in one end that engages a pin in a special stand (which is sold as an integral part of the drum system) and allows the drum to be agitated, in two planes at once, by means of a built-in hand crank. Simmard builds a cam shape into the end caps of their drums (which are marketed in the U.S. under the Chromega label), which causes their drums to be agitated in two planes simultaneously when they are manually rolled on a flat surface.

Essentially, all of the available color print-processing drums work fairly well. My own preference is for the Simmard or the Unicolor, horizontal-type, ribbed drums or for the Kodak vertical one; but I have used just about all of the units marketed in the U.S. and some of those available only abroad, and I have been able to obtain good print processing from all of them.

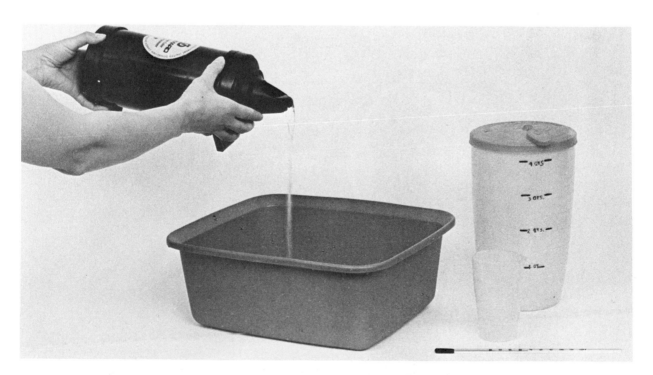

Horizontal-type processing drums use the same spout for pouring chemistry both out of and into the drum. Proper draining and flicking the drops off the end of the spout prevent undue chemical contamination. To process with a drum you can do without a sink and use, instead, a simple dishpan as your laboratory.

These Chromega (Simmard) drums are typical of the horizontal type. The ribbed walls, which permit the processing solutions to get to the back of the print, allow washes to be carried out in the drum. The round rods are removable for easy cleaning and may be installed in several positions to accommodate a number of different print sizes. The wing-like print separators permit several prints to be processed simultaneously.

The Unicolor drums also feature ribbed walls, but their print-retaining flanges are fixed and no print separators are provided. This drum has the best cap-closure system presently available. The end cap mounts in much the same way that an SLR's interchangeable lens does—via a fractional-turn bayonet system.

The Beseler drum is somewhat of a hybrid. It has smooth walls for the most part, but does provide tiny ribs to locate the print in the drum and carry a separator. While both caps are removable, only one carries a spout. The long trough will easily break off its small attachment area on the back cap if accidentally dropped. This drum is designed to use an absolute minimum amount of processing chemistry.

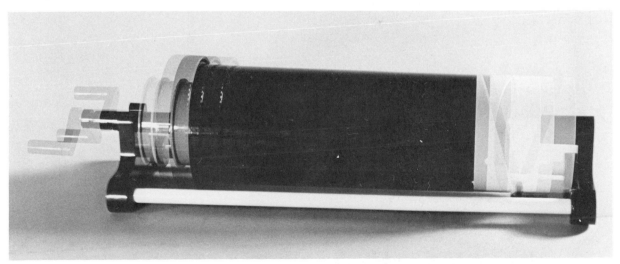

The Paterson processing drum is agitated by means of a small crank handle. The handle causes the drum to rotate about its longitudinal axis, and, at the same time, moves it rapidly back and forth, causing a similar movement in the puddle of chemistry within the drum.

Motor Bases

The electromechanical devices I praised as the most consistent means of agitating a daylight color print-processing drum, are most often referred to as motor bases by their manufacturers. I'm presently aware of three different makes of these devices available on the U.S. market. The Beseler motor base simply turns a drum on its drive wheels quite rapidly about its longitudinal axis. The Simmard motor base (marketed in the U.S. as the Chromega motor base) performs the same function, but additionally, it rocks the drum to cause a transverse wave of chemicals to form in the puddle inside the drum and to move from one end of the drum to the other. This feature, patented by Simmard, is said to provide superior chemical agitation. The Unicolor motor base is unique in that it turns any drum on its drive wheels at a much slower rate than the other two units, but after about three and one half seconds of rolling a drum one way, the unit emits a loud click and immediately reverses itself and begins to roll the drum in the opposite direction.

Both the Beseler and the Chromega units require that restraining devices be placed on the drum being agitated to prevent it from being walked off its drive wheels by the unidirectional rotation, vibration, or any incline the motor base may be operating on. The Unicolor motor base does not suffer from this problem as its constantly reversed, low rotational rate never seems to cause any shift in even the long, poorly balanced 16″ × 20″ drums. The Unicolor base is also useful with the Unicolor film processing tank.

For semiautomatic paper processing, any of these motor-base drum rollers can be plugged into a switching darkroom timer, such as the GraLab. The period during which agitation with a particular chemical is required can then be set on the clock, the drum placed on the agitator, and the clock started. The motor base will continuously agitate the drum for the proper period and then automatically stop, sounding an audible signal (on the GraLab) as it does so. This kind of operation frees the printer to do something other than watch his print-processing drum roll.

While motor bases are not an absolute necessity for color print processing, they certainly can make a color printer's life a lot easier, and more enjoyable. If you can afford one, buy one.

Both the Beseler and the Chromega (Simmard) motor bases rotate the drum in a single direction. Both require that a means of retaining the drum be used to prevent the drum from walking off the motor base. The ring around the center of this drum acts as the retainer for the Chromega unit.

The Chromega motor base uses eccentrically mounted idler wheels to cause its rotating tank to rock each end moving slightly up and down as the tank turns. This end-for-end movement in the puddle of chemistry inside the drum causes better agitation.

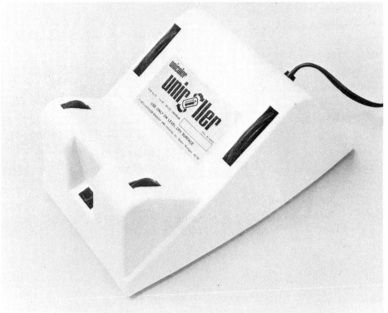

Unicolor's Uniroller motor base is unique in that it reverses the direction of drum rotation every three and one-half seconds. This unit provides much lower rotational speed than either the Beseler or Chromega (Simmard) units.

Because of its low rotational speed and its reversal-rolling direction, the Uniroller will accommodate any drum without any restraints required to keep the drum from walking off the machine.

Print Drying Equipment

Drying black-and-white prints never presents too much of a problem. Only the most super-critical black-and-white printers will bother to dry a print completely to see the changes drying will bring before deciding that the print is perfect.

The color printer does not have the luxury of choices. If you print on type-A paper you will have no idea of what a newly processed print will look like until after that print has been *completely* dried. While type-B color printing paper can be evaluated for color balance when wet, it really isn't too advisable to do so. There will be some changes in type-B paper's color balance between its wet and dry states, often as much as a 5 viewing filter's worth.

So the low-volume color printer is faced with a problem; we have to dry each new print as soon as it is processed in order to determine whether we have printed it properly or if filter pack and/or exposure modifications must be made to get the print we want. It is this requirement, more than any other, that has caused plastic-coated color printing papers to all but entirely drive barytabase papers off the market. It takes only about a minute to dry a plastic-coated print while it often takes several times as long to get a paper print dry. There is nothing as dull or as unproductive as sitting and watching a print dry. So, in spite of the fact that I really like the surface of glossy, air-dried baryta-base paper much more than any surface I have been able to find on the many plastic-coated papers I've tried thus far, I use plastic papers almost exclusively because of their fast washing and drying properties.

In addition to washing and drying fast, plastic papers dry flat (or nearly flat). It is possible to "cook" a baryta-base paper on a roaring hot dryer, to get it dry almost as fast as the plastic-coated prints do, but the baryta-base print so dried will be warped, curled, and buckled in when you take it off the dryer.

I suspect that all of the comparison offered is really rather academic. I won't be at all surprised to see all of the world's color-printing-materials manufacturers simply stop making baryta-base printing paper in the very near future, because the new environmental-protection laws and the need to conserve water will force them to do so.

The equipment I have found the most practical for this instant print-drying requirement consists of either a Falcon Resin-coated Print Dryer (which looks and operates like an old-fashioned miniature clothes wringer) or a large 20" × 24" sheet of 3/16" thick glass and a rubber squeegee; a chamois and a hair dryer or a flatbed print dryer for the fastest results. For data on the use of this equipment, see Chapter 4.

Software for the Color Darkroom

I'll use the term software throughout this book, referring to the materials consumed in the processes of color photography—film, paper chemistry, drymounting tissue, retouching dyes, etc. By now I'm sure that my use of the term hardware is understood to mean all of those items useful to the color printer which are not consumed in the process of making color images—enlargers, processors, focusing aids, etc. Considerably more detailed information will be provided, for many of the products mentioned here, in later chapters.

Film

There are a large number of film types available and useful to the color printer. The major categories of such products include; color negative film, color positive film (slide film), special internegative and duping films, and specialty films such as infrared, aero, and special photomicrography types.

The color negative films presently available all fall into about the same speed category, between ASA 80 and 400. Some of the old standard emulsions are being phased out of production; Ektacolor S and L films will not be with us much longer. These color negative films have been superseded by new, finer-grained emulsions such as those found in Vericolor II and Kodacolor II. These newer films provide better color quality and saturation, better resolution, and very different printing characteristics. The newer color negative films have considerably lighter printing masks and are, therefore, considerably easier to evaluate by eye prior to printing than the older materials were; however, they do call for very heavy magenta and yellow filtration when being printed. Printing filter packs containing 60–80 magenta and 100 yellow or more are not uncommon with Vericolor II film. One negative feature of the new Kodak films, however, is their decreased stability. Vericolor II negatives should be stored in sealed, foil-lined envelopes at low temperature if a life expectancy in excess of two years is desirable.

Things are in a similar state of flux in color transparency films. Perhaps the most heartbreaking event in the history of photography took place when Kodak announced that they would discontinue their Kodachrome II and Kodachrome-X films and replace them with newer and "better" ones called Kodachrome 25 and Kodachrome 64. I stocked my freezer full of Kodachrome II and I'm not sorry I did. The new Kodachromes got off to an awful start when Kodak shipped large quantities of them "green" (unseasoned) and thereby got involved in a major photographic-industry product recall.

Film Processing Chemicals

Any color film except Kodachrome (old and new) can be processed in even a rudimentary darkroom. But I really can't, in good conscience, recommend the practice to you, for reasons I've already outlined in this chapter's section on film-processing hardware. However, if you do decide to do it yourself, Kodak, Unicolor and Beseler all offer negative film-processing chemical kits for small-volume users.

Be sure that you purchase the type of chemicals appropriate to your particular type of color film and that you don't mix incompatible film types in processing baths. There are two major processes for color negative film these days; C-22, for the Kodacolor-X, Ektacolor S and L, as well as Eastman 5254 film; and C-41, for Kodacolor II, Kodacolor 400, Vericolor II, Eastman 5247, Fujicolor F-II, etc.

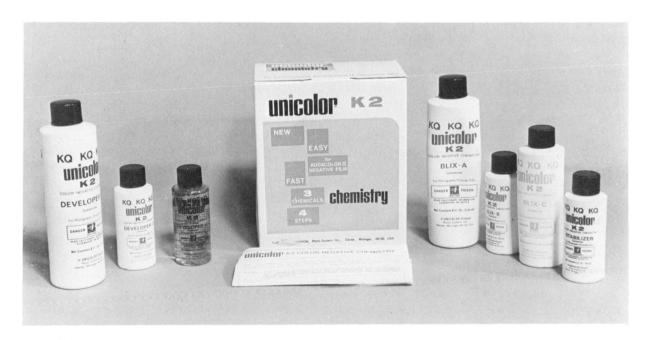

This Unicolor negative film-type processing kit is typical of the small, amateur kits available. This one is designed to process the newer color negative films which use the C-41 process.

Kodak, as well as Unicolor, make small-size kits to process any of the color reversal (slide) films, except, as explained earlier, the Kodachromes. Among these kits, I find the Unicolor-Unichrome material to be the most flexible of the processing chemicals. Rather extensive instructions are provided with the Unichrome materials that cover processing most of the commonly used reversal films, as well as such unusual films as Ferrania, 3M, bulk-loaded Ektachromes, special-purpose duping films, Fujichrome, etc. At present, a new group of Ektachrome films is being introduced by Kodak which requires the use of a new Kodak process called E-6. Both Kodak and Unicolor offer small size E-6 chemical kits.

Unicolor and Photo Technology Ltd., offer kits of chemicals (Total Color 1 and 2 and Photocolor II, respectively) which are designed for use in developing C-41 type color negative films and subsequent reuse, with the addition of several of the chemical kits' components, for processing negative-to-positive printing paper. While I normally lack enthusiasm for amateur color film processing, and recommend against the reuse or replenishment of color processing chemicals, the economies made possible by the proper use of these kits for *both* film and paper processing are just too significant to be overlooked. They should be considered for this dual-purpose processing, however, when they are used for *either* film *or* paper processing alone, these materials lose their economic advantage and my normal prejudices apply.

Negative-to-Positive Color Printing Papers

I'm afraid that I have said about everything that ought to appear in this section earlier in the text, so please bear with me in my redundancy or simply skip this and the next section if you have a low pain threshold.

There are two basically different types of negative-to-positive printing paper, simply called, type-A and type-B. The essential difference between them lies in the way their couplers are incorporated in their emulsion layers. Type-A encapsulates the couplers in oil globules; type-B uses molecular structure to hold the couplers in place in the gelatin matrix. All of which is of no importance to the printer whatsoever, except as it affects the characteristics of the paper in printing. The principal difference between the two types, for all practical purposes, is that each one requires a different type of developer and that type-A paper can't be evaluated for color balance until it is dry. Type-B can be evaluated for color balance when it is wet, but frankly, I would advise drying it before evaluation.

Another area of difference between the two types of paper is that, to the best of my knowledge, there are no type-B plastic-coated color printing papers available in the U.S., though Agfa has one on the European market.

Since all of the type-B paper you can buy is baryta-base paper, it will be harder for you to dry it quickly and keep it flat. I like the way type-B papers look, but I don't like the problems I encounter drying them, so I must admit that I allow practical processing considerations to outweigh my aesthetic sensibilities and I use type-A paper almost exclusively. (Beneath every artist's exterior there lies the soul of a Philistine.)

There are several brands of negative-to-positive printing paper—Colourtronic, Unicolor (Mitsubishi), Kodak, Agfa, Luminos, etc.—all of which can be obtained in several cut sizes, usually ranging from 5" × 7" to 16" × 20". If you are financially able to do so, it is always best to purchase the largest quantity of paper from the same emulsion batch that you are able to store under refrigeration. I suggest this because each emulsion batch of color printing

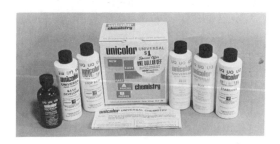

There's an exception to prove every rule. In Chapter 2 I mentioned that type-A paper requires a different developer than type-B paper, and to be sure not to confuse the two. This set of chemicals from Unicolor, however, provides the proper processing for either type.

paper (just as each emulsion batch of color film), will have different printing characteristics. So each time you begin to print with paper from a new emulsion batch you will first have to make several calibration prints to find out how the new paper differs from the last batch you were using.

Positive-to-Positive Color Printing Paper *

At present there are only two different types of positive-to-positive paper that are widely available and they are as different from one another as day is to night. Kodak's material is called Ektachrome RC paper, Type 1993. Ilford's material is called Cibachrome, Type-A, or CCP-D 182U. The Kodak material is very similar in construction and in processing characteristics to the Ektachrome films. The Cibachrome material is unique, at present, in that it uses dye-bleach processing. Cibachrome leaves the factory with all the dye it will ever have. You *remove* dye when you process it. The Kodak material is of the conventional chromogenic type, containing no dyes whatsoever (except for a yellow filter layer and whatever additional filter layers are added to correct the printing balance—all of which wash out during processing). The dyes are *formed* when you process Kodak's Type 1993 paper.

Perhaps the most important difference between the two materials is in the nature of the dyes used and the reasonable life expectancy of the prints. The azo dyes in Cibachrome material are said to have considerably more resistance to fading than the azomethine and indoaniline class dyes used in the chromogenic materials.

The exposure latitude and exposure procedures of both materials are quite similar. It is far easier to print positive-to-positive than it is to print negative-to-positive.

The Cibachrome material is not a paper in the strict sense of the word, because its base is entirely made of triacetate plastic. The Kodak Type 1993 is on a resin-coated paper base. Both materials are quite simple to process. Both air dry to a very high gloss.

I find that Cibachrome is capable of providing extremely high color saturation, but I am not overly fond of its high contrast and, in my experience, its tendency towards thin and off-color blacks. I've found that the Kodak material can't match the color saturation of Cibachrome, but it is far less contrasty and therefore better able to more closely reproduce the subtleties of color gradation found in high-quality transparencies. I also find the Type 1993 to provide better, cleaner blacks.

The biggest difference between the two types of materials, however, is their cost. A finished Cibachrome print in any size can cost almost twice as much as the same size print on Type 1993. Because of that I use more of the Kodak material. I'll probably be sorry when my reversal prints fade to mere pastels.

Paper Processing Chemicals

Negative-to-Positive

Every manufacturer of color printing paper, with a few minor exceptions, produces and markets chemicals specifically designed to process their own paper. In addition, several other firms manufacture and market chemicals to process the more popular brands of paper. For example, Beseler and Unicolor both produce kits of chemicals designed to process Kodak's very highly regarded 74 and 37 RC paper. All of these materials will, if used with a modicum of care, give you very high-quality prints. Aside from, or because of, the several chemical differences (I suppose there are) among the processing chemicals, each manufacturer or marketer of such materials has his own recommendations for the procedure to be used with their products. I consider some of these instructions to be a lot less then useful, while others offer the color printer procedures that are easy to use and yield consistently good results. Among those instructions I consider to be less useful than others are the ones that call for print-processing times shorter than five minutes, or demand large volumes of processing chemicals, or call for very high processing temperatures, or insist on iron-

---

*As this book goes to press, Kodak has just announced replacement of Ektachrome Type 1993 and Ektaprint R-500 with materials called Ektachrome Type 2203 and Ektaprint R-1000 not yet available for experimentation. They will be covered in the supplements as soon as possible.

clad extremely narrow processing-chemistry temperature limits. The instructions I feel are most useful are those which give a printer sufficient time to comfortably carry out the whole processing procedure and sufficient latitude so that small timing and temperature errors become uncritical. Some marketers of chemicals cover all bases, offering several sets of instructions with their materials, some of which fit both of my categories. I'll go into this whole area in greater detail later in the book.

Positive-to-Positive

Here too, the makers of the printing materials also manufacture and market their own processing chemicals. Independents such as Beseler and Unicolor also make processing chemicals for the Kodak material, but, to date, only Ilford makes and markets Cibachrome processing chemicals.

Both Kodak and Unicolor Total 3 and 2 chemicals allow the user of Type 1993 paper to process prints without a white-light reexposure step. Processing times for the several available kits range from about 8 to 15 minutes. There are about a half dozen chemical processing steps and about five separate washes involved in making a print on Kodak Type 1993, but in spite of the number of steps, the process goes quickly—but not so quickly that a printer is rushed—and is not at all complicated. In my own experience I have found it to be virtually impossible to make a bad print on Type 1993 due to processing problems.

There are several types of Cibachrome processing chemicals available, P-10, P-12, and P-18, but the only one sold in small enough quantities to be of interest to the low-volume user is the P-12. This is a three-solution, four-step, 12-minute process, which can, at times, give off some peculiar odors, but is quite simple to use.

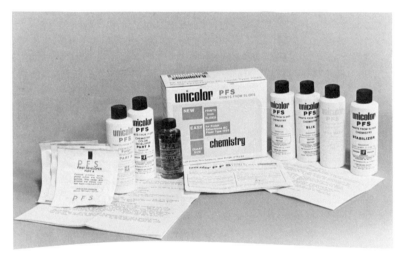

This Unicolor PFS chemistry will process Kodak's Type 1993 paper but, as in the use of Beseler's RP 5 materials, the paper must be physically reexposed to white light between developers. Kodak R-500 and Unicolor Total 3 and 2 materials perform this step chemically.

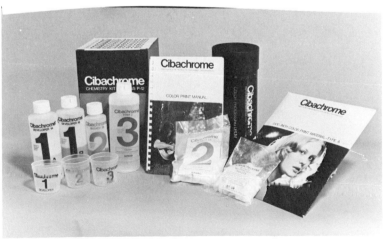

Pictured here are the various components of the Cibachrome process type A paper P-12 chemistry, and the Cibachrome processing drum and manual.

Chapter 4

Getting Started: Making Your First Color Prints

Before You Begin to Print

If you are the eager reader who I advised in Chapter 1 to skip directly to this chapter, please be further advised that I do not feel responsible for the confusion about to befall you. If, on the other hand, you have read the preceding chapters, what follows should not present any difficulties. Now, with that little warning out of the way, let's see just what you will need before you make your first print.

Standard Negatives

The color negative system is an incredibly clever one. It is designed to allow high-quality color positive prints and transparencies and black-and-white prints as well, to be made at reasonable cost from the same negative. In theory, the color negative system is terrific. In practice, particularly in amateur practice, it is a gigantic headache. The principal problem with color negatives is that they are virtually impossible to interpret directly. This is true to a far greater extent than it is for black-and-white negatives. Even the latest types of color negative film, with their very pale masks, are still impossible to deal with on the basis of an accurately previsualized print. And, to make matters a bit more confusing, given some kind of average subject material—let's take a portrait, for example—it will be all but impossible for the inexperienced printer to examine a processed negative and determine if the exposure used to make the shot was the proper one, or if the processing used to prepare the negative was done correctly. Even if we assume that you are an expert and experienced photographer and that you have

processed your own film in the most meticulous manner, the colors in the prints that you make from your properly exposed and processed negative may (but more likely may not) match very closely the colors of your original subject. While it is quite possible to use color negative film to produce images that very closely approximate the colors of the subject, the only accurate way you will be able to do this is to have your subject close at hand so that you can compare it with the prints you are making. In the case of a portrait, you will need your model positioned close to the darkroom door for reference while you print. If your model happens to get a suntan, a case of yellow jaundice or even a bad hangover, your reference material will have vanished, even if your subject camps on your darkroom doorstep throughout your printing session.

Now, if you had included a bit of additional material somewhere in the portrait that was essentially an unchanging and easily available reference, you could send your model off to cure the hangover and compare the reference material with the image appearing on your prints. And, if the reference material you select to put somewhere in the portrait frame is designed to provide you with information on both the initial camera exposure and the subsequent film processing, so much the better.

Needless to say, that is exactly what I am proposing that you do before you try to get started making color prints from color negatives. I want you to be sure that you have a printable negative and to be sure that you will have an accurate idea of what the subject portrayed on that negative should look like on the finished print, before you waste a lot of time and money trying to print something unprintable. The item I am going to suggest you acquire, before we go any further, is called a standard negative. It can be obtained two ways. You can buy one or you can make one. I suggest you buy one first and make more later.

The Kodak Dataguide's "Shirley." Kodak publishes something which, for want of a better word, I will call a book, entitled the Kodak *Color Dataguide*. I hesitated to call it a book because it is really much more than a collection of printed pages. It is also a collection of color printing "hardware" produced and packaged in book form for the sake of convenience. For instance, included between its covers are a complete set of viewing filters, an 18 percent gray card, a set of density wedges, a set of color bars, a circular-slide rule type of color printing computer (about which I will have a good deal more to say later in this book), a ring-around and, more directly pertinent to the business at hand, a 35mm standard negative, and a color print made from it. Copies of the Kodak *Color Dataguide* printed prior to mid-1975 contain standard negatives made on the now discontinued Ektacolor Professional type-S film (perhaps more commonly known as CPS). Copies of the book printed after the latter part of 1975 contain standard negatives made on Vericolor II Professional S film.

These Kodak standard negatives are called "Shirlies." They always contain a portrait of a pretty woman and a set of color bars (or the equivalent in color cushions or drapes on some of the CPS negatives). The newer Shirlies also contain a set of density wedges, but somehow Kodak eliminated the density wedges from many (but not all) of the CPS Shirlies.

If you will contain yourself for long enough to make your first prints from these Kodak-produced negatives, you will be doing yourself a very large favor. You will be printing a negative that has been properly exposed and processed, and you will be able to compare your printing results with a standard print that Kodak has already cleverly made from that negative to prove to you that it really can be done. Of course, by doing things this way you won't be able to blame your off-color prints on the quality of the negatives you are working with. The blame will have to fall where it belongs, on you, the printer.

But that is really a small price to pay for such a valuable printing aid as this one.

I should also point out, for those of you who may have some sort of aversion to working with 35mm negatives, or who, for one reason or another, do not wish to work with a Vericolor II negative, that Kodak also produces standard negatives on Kodacolor-X, Kodacolor II and 6008 (internegative stock) in various sizes ranging from 110 to 120. These are all listed in their product catalog and each of them will cost more to individually acquire than a copy of the entire *Color Dataguide*.

Shooting Your Own Standard Negative. If you insist on doing things the hard way, you will ignore my advice and rush off and make your own standard negative rather than buy your first one from Kodak. In my opinion you will be doing yourself a considerable disservice; however, that's your prerogative. I suggest that beginning printers skip this section and return to it much later. First learn to print fairly well, using Kodak's standard negative to get started, and then when you are more familiar with the process, shoot your own set of standards.

Unless you are prepared to store your standard color negatives in accordance with Kodak's recommendations for color-negative preservation (wrapped in vapor-tight foil containers and stored in darkness inside a freezer), it will be a very good idea to prepare your own fresh standard negatives at about two-year intervals (photographic color-product dye stability being what it is, two years is about the serviceable life of a standard color negative).

Shooting standard negatives need not present any particular problems. A set of standards shot with different light sources will be very handy to you in preparing calibrated contact sheets, which I will discuss later. I would suggest that you use a living, breathing person of any sexual persuasion as part of your subject material, and that you include an 18 percent gray card, a set of density wedges, and a set of color bars as prominent in the frame as the model's face. Be sure to place your camera and lights so as to avoid any hot spots, reflections, shadows, or glare, on the model or the reference material. Bracket your exposures around a very carefully obtained meter reading. Film and film processing are cheap when compared to paper and paper processing, so it will be a good idea to bracket in half-stop intervals perhaps as much as plus or minus two stops on either side of the metered exposure value. Keep an accurate shot record. Among the several light sources you may want to produce standard negatives for are. 3200 K tungsten, 3400 K tungsten, electronic flash, and daylight. You may want to make standard negatives with one or more of these light sources on any or all of the color negative films you normally shoot. When you have completed shooting your standard negatives, I strongly suggest that you send the exposed film to its manufacturer for processing rather than processing it yourself. After all, these are standard negatives you are making. However, if you do your own film processing, make sure to treat these standard shots with great care, and, if possible, fresh chemicals. These are *tools* you are making as you will see shortly.

While this may sound like a very crude way of doing things, perhaps the easiest (and acceptably accurate) way of determining which of the bracketed negatives is the most properly exposed one is to make a careful visual comparison of the portions of these negatives containing an image of the full set of density wedges. Use a loupe to compare the frames closely. Select a frame that seems to offer the fullest tonal range and the best separation between each of the wedges as your standard for each of the conditions and film stocks you shot.

Standard Transparencies

While the color negative system looks wonderful in theory, it turns out to be much less than wonderful to deal with in practice. Just the opposite is true for printing directly from color transparencies. A pretty good case can be made against the theoretical problems inherent in this process, but in practice it turns out that printing directly from slides is quite simple and easy to do. To begin with, you know exactly what the print you are trying to make should look like because you can examine it, by a common light source, side by side with the positive image on the transparency being printed. And, unlike the color negative printing process, which often needs gross changes of printing filter pack when going from one negative to the next, the process of directly printing color transparencies seldom involves any significant pack changes from one slide to the next, unless some specific special effect is desired. And, just to sweeten the slide-

printing pot still further, the exposure and filtration latitude involved in the process is at least twice that found in the color negative printing process.

It is really not necessary to buy or make a standard color transparency for all of the reasons just mentioned. However, standard transparencies can be very useful at times. A standard transparency is useful when it is necessary to accurately determine the printing characteristics of a new supply of reversal printing materials, or when you want to determine the effects of varying certain procedures, products, or processing methods.

In general, the subject material and process for making standard transparencies is the same as that which was suggested for making standard color negatives. You can make standard slides with different light sources and on different films; however, the name of the game with slides is to get the proper color balance in the transparency, rather than filter for it during printing.

I would suggest using the same bracketing procedure recommended for making a standard color negative for each of the different transparency films you normally shoot. But I further suggest that you shoot only under the lighting conditions for which the slide films were designed. Examples are: Ektachrome B and High Speed Ektachrome (Tungsten) with 3200 K tungsten illumination; Kodachrome II Professional A with 3400 K tungsten illumination; Kodachrome 25 and 64, Ektachrome, Fujichrome, etc., with sunny sky, midday, outdoors, diffused daylight, or with electronic-flash illumination indoors or outdoors.

If the process of making a standard transparency does not appeal to you, you can buy them ready made from Kodak. They list several types in their Kodak *Photographic Products* catalog.

Essential Hardware and Software to Have on Hand

Now that you have a standard negative or a standard transparency (or any properly color-balanced, properly exposed transparency), it's time to consider which of the various hardware and software items, discussed in Chapter 3, you must have as a bare operating minimum.

Obviously, you will need an enlarger. If you use a condenser enlarger you will also need a set of CP acetate filters (see Chapter 3 for details). If your first print is to be made from a negative, you will also need a CP2B filter and a heat-absorbing glass. If your first print is to be made from a transparency, you can get away with those filters too, but for the recommended Kodak materials I suggest that you substitute a Wratten 2E filter for the CP2B.

If your enlarger is a diffusion type with built-in dichroic filters, you can probably do well enough without additional filtration; however, for the best results in printing slides, a Wratten 2E filter should be introduced into the light path above the transparency.

Of course, you will also need an area big enough for you and your enlarger that is entirely free of white light.

You will need an enlarging easel. Any kind will be all right so long as it is painted matte black. The best kind will be one that, while remaining stationary, can make several individual exposures on a single sheet of 8″ × 10″ paper. The worst kind, for our purposes here, will be a borderless type of easel.

While it isn't an absolutely essential item, an enlarger timer will certainly be a very useful thing to have your enlarger plugged into when you make your first print. However, you can always time exposures by counting one-thousand-and-one, one-thousand-and-two, etc., if you can't afford one.

A focusing device is also not an absolute must, but you will need one eventually, so why not go first class and buy one for your maiden printing session.

In the event that you think I have forgotten to mention a safelight, you are wrong. They are not usable at all with reversal printing (printing from slides) and they are strictly a luxury, not at all a necessity, for printing from negatives.

If you own a voltage stabilizer, that's fine; use it. If not, don't worry about the lack for now.

One item you most definitely must have to process your prints with the method I will describe here, is an 8″ × 10″ daylight drum processor (see Chapter 3) of any make. For those of you who are affluent, a motor-base drum agitator is another must. For the impecunious, your own two arms and a Turkish towel will have to substitute for the motor base.

You will need one-quart air-tight containers that can be sealed. If your druggist is a coopera-tive type of person, he or she can obtain brown glass bottles with screw caps for you; buy a half dozen. If you can't get brown glass bottles, you can usually find brown, high-density plastic ones for sale (usually at outrageous prices) in the darkroom department of large camera shops.

Among the other miscellaneous bits and pieces of equipment you will have on hand are a one-quart and half-pint graduate (or any graduate that can be conveniently used to measure to half-ounce accuracy); a one-ounce graduate measuring cup (again, check with your druggist) will also be a godsend at times; and, strange as it may seem, a dime-store one-gallon plastic pitcher or its equivalent is also a must.

You will need a thermometer (see Chapter 3) that can double as a stirring rod.

While they aren't strictly necessary for experienced printers, I would recommend that first-time printers also buy a half-dozen four-ounce dime-store drinking glasses and use small strips of electrician's tape to mark them at the two, three, and four ounce levels.

If you are able to work at a sink you won't need a container to hold your spent chemicals. If you can't use a sink or toilet, a bucket or plastic dishpan will do nicely instead.

One 11″ × 14″ and one 8″ × 10″ tray may also be useful to have.

So far, everything that I have mentioned as being necessary before you can begin to print has fallen into the hardware category—materials which are not expended in the process of printing. You will, of course, also need some software before you can begin. The materials I'm going to recommend here are the ones I feel can give an amateur printer the best results, the greatest latitude of operation and of printing characteristics, and the lowest possible price per print compatible with these characteristics. There are several other excellent software systems available, but the ones I've selected for use here seem to me, as this is being written, to be those best suited to the first-time printer's needs.

If you intend to make your first print from a color negative, I suggest using Unicolor's Resin Base Type A paper and their R-2 chemicals. If you can afford it, I suggest that you purchase a 100 sheet box of paper and several one-quart kits of chemistry (as opposed to one-gallon kits).

If you intend to make your first prints from a color transparency, I suggest that you purchase a

100 sheet quantity of Kodak's Ektachrome Type 1993 paper and several one-quart kits of their R-500 chemicals (as opposed to the one-gallon components).

All of the instructions provided in this chapter will be based on the use of these materials. If you wish to use other materials for your early efforts, you will find information on many alternative products elsewhere in this book.

Before you enter the darkroom to make your first print, you should prepare all of the working-strength solutions of the processing chemicals you intend to use. In the kits I've recommended, all of the chemicals are supplied in concentrated liquid form. These must be diluted to the proper working strength. I have recommended that you begin your printing with quart-size kits because the concentrates contained in these small kits can be easily and conveniently mixed all at one time to make up a very useful quantity of processing chemicals. One quart, generally speaking, is sufficient to process 16 sheets of 8″ × 10″ paper, using the one-shot (the chemicals are used once and then discarded) method. You will most likely consume all of this quantity of working-strength chemicals way before the manufacturer's stated shelf life for working-strength materials (usually several weeks to several months, depending on storage conditions) has passed. These small kits are much more expensive than either the larger kits or larger quantities of the individual chemical components needed. Therefore, once you begin to feel comfortable with all of the processes involved and you feel able to handle yet another variable, I suggest that you switch from the small kits to the larger quantities of materials needed and dilute only the quantity of working-strength chemicals you need at any given time. The remaining concentrates will have a longer shelf life than the working-strength solutions, and you will save yourself a lot of money in the bargain.

The actual dilution processes are quite simple and directions for them are provided by the manufacturers and packaged with their products. You will have no difficulty following the directions. Do so carefully. Your first printing session is no time to improvise. Try to mix your working-strength chemicals about one day prior to the time you intend to use them and then store all of the working strength solutions in the room in which you will do your processing, so that they can come to the room (ambient) temperature at which you will work. If this is not practical, and you find that you have to mix your chemicals immediately prior to processing, first determine the ambient temperature of the room in which you will do your processing and, if it is above 70 F (21 C), use water at room (ambient) temperature to dilute the concentrated chemicals contained in the kit.

As each of the concentrated components of the processing chemicals is diluted to a one-quart volume at its working strength, it should be stored in one of the brown glass (or plastic) bottles, and snugly capped. Label each bottle clearly to indicate its contents (developer, bleach fix, stabilizer, etc., etc.) and the date on which the working-strength chemicals were mixed and stored. Make sure that both the labels and the ink used to make them are waterproof.

Once you have assembled all of the materials mentioned here, you are almost (but not quite) ready to make your first color prints.

Making Multiple Test Prints on a Simple Easel

Before you make your first color print, you will need to know how to make that print give you as much useful information as possible. This is so for two very good reasons; the first being that color printing is an expensive process and the second being that it is a time-consuming one. If you begin to print by making an 8″ × 10″ of your standard negative, and your first print comes out of the processing drum anything less than perfect, you will have to remake it to get it right. It is an excellent bet that no one will get the first or second prints to come out perfectly. As a matter of fact, most thoroughly experienced and competent color printers need at *least* three tries to get a truly good color print from a color negative even with the most sophisticated lab equipment to help them. Color prints from slides are easier for experienced printers to make properly, but they are just as tough for beginners to make as prints from color negatives are.

A beginning color printer shouldn't be at all surprised at having to make 10 to 15 trial exposures before getting a perfectly color-balanced print with just the right density. Oh, you will get color images all right. And most likely, by the second or third one you will be so enthused about your newfound skill that you will consider mounting and framing your work. But when calm returns, you will realize that the Shirley you have printed looks very pale and wan, or mysteriously oriental, or perhaps even a bit seasick-green.

I'm not going into all of this to discourage you about color printing, but to emphasize the importance of making test prints that will quickly provide you with a maximum of information at a minimum cost. The way this is most conveniently done is by making multiple images on a single sheet of paper. If it takes 12 different exposures to make your first print perfectly, and your choice lies between making twelve 8″ × 10″ prints or three 8″ × 10″ prints with four images on each one, to be able to do it, it seems to me that only the very perverse would opt for the dozen separate prints.

So, before you turn out the lights to make your first exposure, take a few minutes to set up your easel to allow you to make four separate images with four separate printing conditions on a single sheet of 8″ × 10″ printing paper, without any need to move the easel during the print exposure process.

The most commonly found enlarging easel is the adjustable, two-bladed type. Most such easels, even those which are very inexpensive, allow the printer to vary the image size by changing the position of two movable blades and also to adjust the width of the print borders. The first thing to do with such an easel is to adjust the border width to its minimum setting. Next, set the moveable blades to give you a 3″ × 4½″ image area. Now, take an 8″ × 10″ sheet of paper and cut off a small portion of one corner of the sheet. Put the cut corner into the easel's paper gripper and close the easel. Run a pencil around the inside of the easel blades to define the number-one image area, and mark a No. 1 in the middle of the area. Open the easel and rotate the sheet of paper 90° clockwise. Close the easel again and mark the No. 2 image area. Open the easel, rotate the paper 90° clockwise, close the easel, and mark the No. 3 image area. Do the same thing to establish the borders of the No. 4 image area. Open the easel and remove the sheet of paper. Check to see that there is no overlap of the image-area borders. If all of this has been less than clean, then perhaps the accompanying illustrations will help to show you what I have been trying to explain. The only thing that remains to be done is to tape some black paper skirts to the blades of your easel to cover the portions of the paper that are not being printed. If you are making an exposure on image area no. 1, you certainly don't want stray light from the enlarger to fog image areas 2, 3, and 4, so it will be necessary to protect the three-quarters of the sheet not being exposed from the light that is exposing the remaining quarter. Just make sure that when you attach the skirts to your easel's blades you make them big enough to cover *all* of the paper in *both* the horizontal *and* the vertical positions it will assume on the easel. Once again, I suspect the accompanying illustrations will go a long way toward clarifying the explanation used above.

Those of you who may already own easels that can make multiple images on the same sheet, without moving the easel, can disregard the information just given and use your step-and-repeat easels to make test prints.

If you own a borderless easel, a Speed-Ez-El, or some other similar type, it will be a bit difficult for you to conveniently make multiple images on a single sheet of paper. It can be done, but doing so involves using a black cardboard mask that covers three-quarters of the paper at a time and then flipping the mask, first top-to-bottom, then end-for-end, then bottom-to-top, to enable four separate exposures to be made on the same sheet. The biggest problem with this procedure is that the image area being exposed is never in the same place for any two exposures, but must be centered under the enlarger lens four separate times. This is not a usable procedure in color test printing. Four-bladed easels can be set in a manner very similar to that described for two-bladed easels.

In case all of this discussion about easels is confusing to you, I think it will make much more sense as I get into the procedures to use when making your test prints. But, if even then you can't quite get the hang of making four exposures on a single sheet of paper, don't worry! Just make single exposures and keep working until you begin to get the hang of it. I haven't recommended that you use four separate 4″ × 5″ pieces of paper and process them all together in the same daylight processing drum at the same time, because while it is reasonably easy for an experienced printer to do, it will probably not be very easy for a beginner to do. However, if the idea appeals to you more than putting four small images on one sheet of paper, try it.

PREPARING A SIMPLE EASEL
TO MAKE MULTIPLE TEST EXPOSURES

Cut off one corner of an 8″ × 10″ sheet.

Put the cutoff corner into the easel's paper gripper (if there is one).

Close the easel and, using a marker pen to define the image area (3″ × 4½″), mark it No. 1

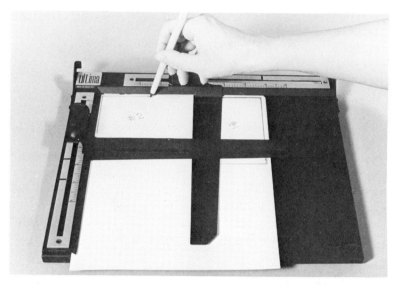

Open the easel. Remove the sheet of paper, rotate the sheet of paper 90°, reinsert the paper in the easel, close the easel, and mark the second image area.

Continue this same process, marking all the image areas, and check to see that they don't overlap.

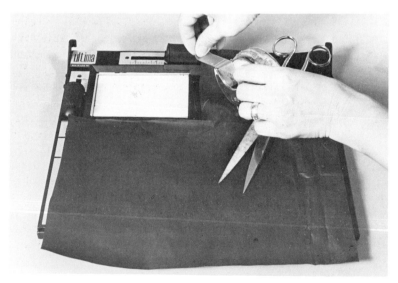

Attach black, lightproof paper skirts to the easel blades, large enough to shield the portions of the paper not being printed.

And, finally, for those of you who may be wondering why I'm going to such great lengths to describe a process of making several images under several different printing conditions on one sheet of paper when I could just as easily make test strips or use a projection print scale, I can only say that I feel that test stripping is not as useful a process as the one I will eventually recommend. Test stripping, for those of you who, mercifully, may be unacquainted with the procedure, is the process of exposing different portions of the same image being projected on your enlarger's easel for differing periods of time. Then, when the print has been processed, the densities of these sections are compared, one to another, to see which one looks best for the image being printed.

Since the most convenient way to carry out this process is by moving a straight-edged dodge in timed stages across the full length or width of the print, the resulting unequally exposed sections are in the form of strips across the image.

Such a process may be useful for a full-frame image of an 18 percent gray card, where every strip will contain the identical image information, but for real images of real subjects, I consider test strips to be just a bit better than useless. And I don't confine my opinion to the use of test strips for color images. I think they are just as useless for black-and-white work as well.

Making Your First Negative-to-Positive Print

Exposure

It is difficult enough to try to anticipate the characteristics of the printing hardware and software you will be using without the added complications involved with your initial efforts at printing some very peculiar and totally unknown (to both of us) type negatives. So I will simplify my own task here by assuming you are a reasonable person and will follow my advice by restricting your first-time printing activities to the use of a Kodak-produced standard negative and the other materials referred to earlier.

Remove the standard negative and the print made from it from the envelope bound into the Kodak *Color Dataguide*. Put the negative into your enlarger's carrier with its emulsion side down (facing the lens). Use a soft, sable brush to remove any dust from the negative. If the brush doesn't get the dust off, try blowing it off with the blast from an infant's ear syringe. Don't use canned aerosol products for this dust-blasting process, or the freon propellant will probably ruin your health, one way or another.

In case you can't figure out which side of the negative is the emulsion side, the easiest way I know of to do so is to look at the frame numbers. If they appear as normal, legible numbers you know that you are looking at the film-base side. If the numbers are the wrong way around, you are looking at the emulsion side. Kodak suggests that if the arrows along the film top edge point to the right you are looking at the emulsion side of the film. Unfortunately, I can never remember which way the arrow is supposed to point to indicate what side of the negative is facing in a particular direction—but that's my problem.

Put the negative carrier in the enlarger. If your enlarger is a condenser type, open its filter drawer and insert a heat-absorbing glass and a CP2B filter. If your standard negative is on Vericolor II (or Kodacolor II) insert an acetate CP filter pack consisting of 80 magenta plus 100 yellow (80M + 100Y). The values of CP filters are additive so that your pack can consist of two 40M filters plus an 80Y and a 20Y. If you are using a diffusion-type enlarger, with built-in dichroic filtration, dial in 60M + 110Y.

If your standard negative is on CPS or Kodacolor-X and you are using a condenser enlarger, try a starting pack consisting of a heat-absorbing glass, a CP2B and 50M + 30Y. Try 25M + 75Y for a diffusion-type enlarger with dichroic filters, but with many diffusion machines you can leave out the heat absorbing glass and the CP2B, as the manufacturer has built them in. If you are in doubt, put them in.

Set your enlarger lens to its widest opening; now, set your enlarger's head height to get a focused image on the baseboard of about 3½× magnification. If you don't know how to determine magnification, it is as simple as being able to use a ruler. Just measure the short dimension of the image projected on the baseboard. When it equals three and one-half inches you are at about 3½× magnification. This is so because the short dimension of a 35mm negative carrier is just under one inch. If you insist on absolute exactness, measure your carrier's opening and multiply its short dimension by 3.5; then adjust the head height until the projected image's short dimension is equal to the product of your multiplication.

Place your preset, multiple image-making easel (see p. 4-7) on the enlarger's baseboard and put a sheet of printing paper (any black-and-white print on medium-weight (MW) resin-coated paper will be ideal; otherwise load a sheet of single-weight SW or double-weight (DW) paper into the easel so that the back of the print is facing up (emulsion down). Turn on the enlarger lamp and, without changing the head-height setting, refocus the image on the printing paper on the easel. Move the easel on the baseboard to center the image in the image area, and make sure that it overlaps the borders just slightly. Turn off the enlarger.

Set ten seconds on your enlarger timer (if you are so equipped). Place your unopened package of color printing paper and a pair of scissors near the enlarger.

Get your daylight processing drum and, following the manufacturer's instructions, remove its paper-loading end cap. Remove the focusing sheet from the easel and use it to practice loading the drum with the lights on and your eyes open. The drum's manufacturer will supply loading instructions to follow. When you get to be very good at loading the drum with your eyes open, shut them and keep on practicing. When that is no longer a challenge, turn off the lights and practice loading the drum in the dark. When you have mastered that simple trick, try to remember where you put the end cap and, without turning on the lights, put the end cap back on the drum. As soon as you can load the paper (remember, the paper's emulsion faces the center of the drum) and cap the drum in total darkness with never a fumble, you will be ready to proceed.

With all of the darkroom lights out, wait a few moments, until your eyes accommodate themselves to the gloom, then carefully check to insure that there are no light leaks. If you find any, take whatever steps are needed to get rid of them. When you are sure that there is no white light entering your working area (turn on a No. 13 safelight if you are leery of the dark), you can open your box of color printing paper, open the

inner wrapper, and remove one sheet of paper. (Remember, this procedure is based on the use of Unicolor's Resin Base Type-A color printing paper.)

Handle the paper only by the edges as far as you find it possible to do so. Most type-A resin-coated paper has an emulsion that will accurately reproduce fingerprints, so careful handling of this material is a must.

I must admit that what I am about to say neatly contradicts what I just said, but still I have to tell you that in the dark, or even four feet from a No. 13 safelight, it can be very confusing for the first-time printer to determine which side of a sheet of this kind of color printing paper is the emulsion side and which side is the back. About the only way you can tell is to run your fingers over an area near the edge of both sides and determine which side offers the most resistance to the movement. That side will be the emulsion side. If you are careful and hold the sheet just the way it came out of the box, you will know if the inner envelope is packed with sheets with their emulsion facing the bottom of the box or the top of the box. Once you have determined this bit of useful data you will no longer have to run your fingers over the surface of the paper, as you will know the orientation of the emulsion surface when you remove sheets from the box. If you use a paper safe remove the paper, which is still inside its inner wrapper, and place the package in the safe so that the emulsion side is down.

Search around in the vicinity of your enlarger until you locate the pair of scissors. Use it to cut off a tiny portion of the corner of your sheet of unexposed printing paper, just as you did when you set your easel up to make multiple exposures. Now insert the cut corner of the sheet into the paper gripper of your easel. The cut corner will identify the No. 1 image area for you later. Be sure that you put the printing paper into the easel with its emulsion side facing up (toward the enlarger lens). Close the easel.

If you have followed all of the previous instructions, at this point all you need to do to make the first ten-second exposure is to start the timer. After the enlarger lamp goes off, locate the aperture-control ring of the lens and twist it until you feel it reach its first click stop (one stop down from wide open). Now, open the easel and rotate the sheet of printing paper through 90 degrees to its No. 2 image position, close the easel, and start the enlarger timer to make your second ten-second exposure.

After the enlarger lamp goes off, close the lens down another stop and rotate the paper on the easel to the No. 3 printing position. Make your third ten-second printing exposure.

And, finally, after the enlarger lamp is extinguished, close the lens diaphragm down still another stop, rotate the printing paper to the No. 4 printing position and make your fourth ten-second printing exposure.

Congratulations, you have just made four full-frame test exposures, all on the same sheet of 8″ × 10″ color printing paper. Now all you have to do is remove the paper from the easel, load it into the drum, put the cap on the drum, check to see that your box of paper is completely closed (with the remaining paper inside and wrapped in its inner wrapper, of course), and then turn on the normal white lights. Your time in the dark is all over. If you do everything you have to without a hitch, your total elapsed time in darkness, to produce four separate images, should be about one minute. That's not too frightening a prospect, is it?

Processing

The following procedures are based on two basic assumptions. The first being that you are using the recommended chemistry/paper combination (Unicolor's R-2 chemistry and Unicolor's Resin Base Type-A paper) and the second being that the room (and therefore the chemicals) in which you will do your processing is at some temperature between 75 and 80 F (24—27 C). For other materials simply disregard this section and see the appropriate sections of this book or follow the manufacturer's instructions. For other temperatures either refer to Chapter 9 for further data, follow the instructions supplied with the chemicals, or use the modified nomograph on p. 4-14 to determine the appropriate presoak water temperature to use to replace the range of 105-110 F (41-43 C) recommended.

Take your loaded drum to the area in which you will do your wet processing. If you can use a kitchen, laundry, or bathroom sink, so much the better. If you can't have immediate access to a source of running hot and cold water or to a drain, you needn't be overly concerned. It will be easier to have these conveniences, but lacking

them won't be much of a handicap.

If you are going to use a motor base to agitate your drum, place the drum on the motor base in accordance with the manufacturer's instructions, then use a spirit level to check if the drum is level, or close to it, from end to end. If necessary use shims or adjustments under the legs of the motor base to level the drum.

If you are going to agitate the drum by hand, first spread a Turkish towel over the area in which you intend to roll the drum (in accordance with the drum manufacturer's instructions) and place the drum on top of the towel-covered surface in the position it will be in during agitation. Use a spirit level to determine if the drum is level from end to end. If it isn't try to level it by shimming the supports of the surface upon which the drum rests. (If you can't manage to level the drum, never fear, just use four ounces of chemicals where I call for two. Collect and reuse each four ounces to make a second print, but do not expect the same consistency as you get working with the one-shot method.)

In case you wondered, the Turkish towel is not placed below the drum for any decorative purposes, but to provide a surface with considerably more friction than a Formica or varnished counter top or table would. Friction between the drum and its supporting surface is necessary to prevent the drum from slipping rather than rolling. A daylight processing drum relies on a near-uniform rolling motion to provide agitation and distribution of the small amount of liquid processing chemicals it contains. So much for Turkish towels. Oh yes, if you want to use a similar material for a rolling pad, feel free to do so, just as long as the surface you select provides enough friction to prevent the drum from slipping during agitation, even when wet.

Use your waterproof marking pen (Dri-Mark's Medium Line Nylon Tip Marker is the best one I know of) to label each of three of your four-ounce drinking glasses: "developer," "stop," "blix." This done, fill each one with two ounces of the working-strength chemical called for by its label. Set the glasses down in a convenient place, near where the drum will be agitated, but out of harm's way. Originally, R-2 chemical kits were supplied with a stabilizer solution. New kits may omit this chemical, though it can be purchased separately. Unstabilized prints must be washed twice as long as stabilized prints. I have always found stabilization to be a worthwhile, time-saving process and I advise its use. If your chemicals are supplied with stabilizer, or if you purchase it separately, proceed as follows.

Either spill the one quart of stabilizer into an 8″ × 10″ tray and then place an 11″ × 14″ tray over the 8″ × 10″ tray to keep the stabilizer from evaporating into the air of your working environment; *or* plan to do your stabilizing right in the drum. If you choose the former option you will be following the chemistry manufacturer's recommendations and you will eliminate a separate drum-washing procedure at the end of the print-processing step. If you decide to do your stabilizing in the drum, you will keep the amount of noxious fumes you have to breathe to a minimum, and keep your working environment as simple and uncluttered as possible. *But you will have to take pains to clean out your drum when you are finished processing the print.* I recommend the latter course, but the former will be fine if you have a good ventilation system and lots of room in which to work. If you decide to do your stabilizing in the drum, as I suggest, you will need to use the waterproof ink to label a fourth four-ounce drinking-glass "stabilizer," then fill it with two ounces of stabilizer, and set it alongside the other three glasses already filled. If you decide to eliminate the stabilization step, simply double all of the agitation times called for in the final water-wash steps from 20 to 40 seconds each.

Remove the lid from a one-gallon plastic pitcher and put your thermometer into it. Fill the pitcher from a hot-water tap while watching the thermometer. If your hot-water heater is anything like the ones I've worked with, you will soon be getting water from the tap that is hotter than the highest temperature on the thermometer. Add cold water to keep the thermometer from breaking. By alternately adding hot and cold water, while stirring with the thermometer at the same time, you should have little trouble quickly obtaining a pitcher full of presoak water at some temperature between 105 and 110 F (41–43 C). Try to hit 107 or 108 F (42 C) right on the money. It's really quite easy to do.

For wet-processing area-ambient temperature outside of the 75–80 F (24–27 C) range, use the following nomograph on page 4-14 to determine the presoak water temperature required. Simply place a ruler so that its edge connects the dot between the two temperature scales and the ambient temperature of the room in which you are working. The point where the edge of the ruler intersects the Presoak Water Temperature scale will determine the temperature of the presoak water that you should use. For example, if your wet processing area (and, therefore, the liquid chemicals you have stored in that area) is at 70 F (21 C), you will need presoak water at 115 F (46 C). Make sure that your chemicals are at the same temperature as your room if you use this method.

Once the pitcher is filled, remove the thermometer and put the pitcher's cover back in place. Pour one pint of the presoak water from the pitcher into the processing drum, agitate the drum (on the motor base or by rolling it on the Turkish towel) for 30 seconds, then pour the water from the drum down the drain or into a bucket or dishpan. Pour another pint of presoak water from the pitcher into the drum and agitate the drum for another 30 seconds. Pour the water out of the drum and drain the drum for another ten seconds. Gently shake the drum during this drain period to help to get all of the presoak water possible out of the drum. Now you have brought the print and the drum up to the temperature required by the Unicolor chemistry that we are using, and you are ready to begin the print processing.

Place the drum on its legs (or with the pouring spout up if you are using a vertical drum), pour two ounces of developer into the drum, and begin to agitate the chemical over the surface of the print by rolling the drum back and forth on the Turkish towel (or start the motor base and let it do the agitation for you). Continue to agitate the drum (if agitated manually, it should be done at about one revolution per second or faster) for four minutes, then pour the developer down the drain or into a bucket, etc., and continue to allow the drum to drain for 10 seconds. Gently shake the drum during the drain period to help to get all of the developer out of it.

Place the drum in a position to receive two ounces of stop bath. Pour the stop bath into the drum and agitate for 30 seconds. At the end of this period drain the drum, while gently shaking it, for 10 seconds.

Place the drum in a position to receive two ounces of blix (a combination of bleach and fix). Pour the blix into the drum, agitate for two minutes, then pour the blix away and drain the drum, while gently shaking it, for another 10 seconds.

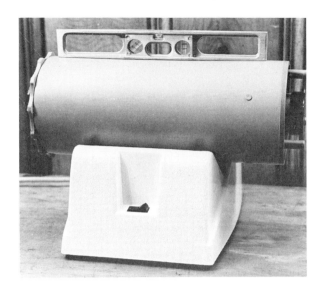

Place the drum in a position to receive the wash water. Pour about eight ounces of the remaining presoak water from the pitcher into the drum. Agitate the drum for 20 seconds (40 seconds if stabilization is omitted) then drain the water off, while gently shaking the drum, for 10 seconds more. Repeat this procedure four more times.

Now, if you elect to stabilize your print and you want to do your stabilizing in a tray, you can open the drum, remove the print (gently, holding it only by the edges), and slide it, emulsion side up, into the stabilizer tray. Agitate the print in the tray for 45 seconds. If you decide to do your stabilizing in the drum, simply leave the print in

If the drum is to be agitated by a motor base (top photo), place the drum on the motor base and then place a spirit level on the drum to determine if the drum is level. If it isn't, try to level it by putting shims under the motor-base legs; or, if the motor base is so equipped, by changing the setting of the leveling leg. If you intend to agitate your drum manually by rolling it across a towel-covered surface (middle photo), first orient the drum to the position it will be in during agitation. Then place a spirit level on it, as shown, to determine if the drum is level. If it isn't, try to adjust the supports of the surface upon which the drum rests to center the bubble. The English Kodak drum (bottom photo), which is not available in the U.S., is designed to float in a tank of water. No leveling is required for floating-type tanks.

the drum at the end of the drain after the last wash step, add two ounces of stabilizer to the drum, and agitate it for 45 seconds. At the end of that period you can open the drum, dump the stabilizer out, and remove the print.

No further chemical processing is carried out, but if you did stabilize your print in the drum, be sure to thoroughly wash the drum and its cap with warm water once the print has been removed. If you have been collecting used chemicals and wash water in a container of some sort, now is the time to dump it all down the drain.

At this point you most likely have some fairly awful looking images on your wet sheet of paper; however, take heart. Drying the images will change them a great deal for the better. Skip over the next two sections to the print-drying instructions which begin on page 4-22.

MODIFIED NOMOGRAPH
FOR USE WITH UNICOLOR R-2 CHEMISTRY

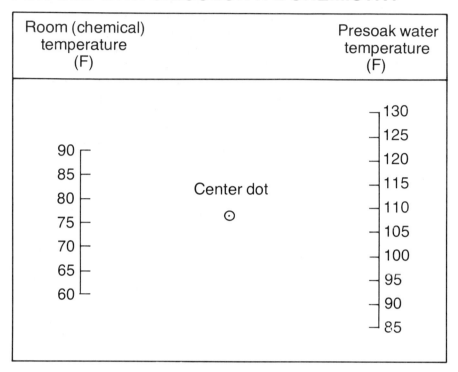

Room (chemical) temperature (F)	Presoak water temperature (F)

This modified nomograph is for use with Unicolor Resin Base Type-A paper and R-2 chemistry in areas with ambient temperatures outside of the 75–80F ambient temperature range.

Table 4-1   DAYLIGHT DRUM PROCESSING INSTRUCTIONS FOR UNICOLOR R-2 CHEMICALS

STEP	SOLUTION*	VOLUME†	DURATION OF AGITATION	DRAIN PERIOD	TIME AT END OF STEP
1	Water at 108 F	16 oz.	30 sec.	dump	30 sec.
2	Water at 108 F	16 oz.	30 sec.	10 sec.	1 min. 10 sec.
3	Developer	2 oz.	4 min.	10 sec.	5 min. 20 sec.
4	Stop	2 oz.	30 sec.	10 sec.	6 min.
5	Blix	2 oz.	2 min.	10 sec.	8 min. 10 sec.
6	Water (70-100 F)	8 oz.	20 sec. ●	10 sec.	8 min. 40 sec.
7	Water (70-100 F)	8 oz.	20 sec. ●	10 sec.	9 min. 10 sec.
8	Water (70-100 F)	8 oz.	20 sec. ●	10 sec.	9 min. 40 sec.
9	Water (70-100 F)	8 oz.	20 sec. ●	10 sec.	10 min. 10 sec.
10	Water (70-100 F)	8 oz.	20 sec. ●	10 sec.	10 min. 40 sec.
11	Stablizer	2 oz.‡	45 sec.	dump	11 min. 25 sec.

*All chemical solutions are used at room ambient temperatures between 75–80F.

†Volumes given are for use with a typical level 8″ × 10″ drum.

‡If stabilizing is done in an 8″ × 10″ tray, use 32 ounces in the tray and process 16 prints in the chemical before discarding it.

●Agitate for 40 seconds if you do not intend to stabilize the print. The water used for steps 6 through 10 is the remainder of the original one gallon of presoak water.

Making Your First Positive-to-Positive Print

Exposure

As I did with the preceding *"Negative-to-Positive"* print exposure section, I will begin this one with a disclaimer. I am proceeding on the basis of your being a reasonable person and your understanding that the procedures called for involve the use of Kodak's Ektachrome Type 1993 paper and their R-500 chemistry. If you choose to use any of the several proprietary chemicals designed to process Type 1993 (Beseler's, Unicolor's, etc.) other than R-500, or if you prefer to use Cibachrome Printing Material Type-A and their P-12 chemicals, simply disregard the section dealing with processing that follows and refer to Chaper 9 or to the manufacturer's instructions for processing data. When using Cibachrome materials, it will also be useful to follow the starting filter-pack recommendations on the label of the envelope the printing material is packaged in.

I needn't insist that you start your positive-to-positive printing career with a standard slide. You can use any properly exposed slide you want. However, if you do elect to make or purchase a standard transparency and use it for your maiden run, you will probably find the whole process to be a bit simpler and easier to understand. Now, with all of that out of the way, let's get to work.

There are several ways to put a 35mm transparency into an enlarger. You can remove the slide from its cardboard mount and use any standard glassless (or glass if you prefer) carrier. This is, without a doubt, the best way to go, but it involves having to remount the slide when you remove it from the enlarger. This, too, is a simple task. If your enlarger's manufacturer makes a 2 inch-square cardboard slide-mount carrier, you can buy one and simply drop your mounted slide into it. This isn't as good an idea as the first suggestion because it involves yet another piece of hardware and because most cardboard-mounted transparencies are buckled and can't be brought into sharp overall focus. Or, you can modify a 2¼ inch-square carrier, with a couple of pieces of black cardboard and some black vinyl tape, to accept mounted slides. This is the least good idea for all of the reasons mentioned plus the fact that the cardboard insert probably won't be exactly parallel to the rest of the carrier; but I must admit that I use such a carrier myself when I'm in a hurry.

In any event, put your transparency into whatever type of carrier you choose, with its emulsion side down. Use a soft sable brush to remove any dust from the slide. If the brush doesn't get the dust off, try blowing it off with a blast from an infant's ear syringe. If you don't care about the earth's ozone layer or the state of your health, you can use one of the several canned aerosol products to do this job. Put the negative carrier in the enlarger. If you can't figure out which side of the slide is the emulsion side, there are three ways to tell. If you remember to check before you remove the slide from its mount, the side of the mount that has all of the printing on it is the slide's emulsion side. Once the slide is out of the mount you can check the edge numbering to see if it reads correctly. If it does, you are looking at the back of the film. If it doesn't, you are looking at the emulsion side. And, finally, if you are still in doubt, and the slide is on Kodak material, turn the slide so that the arrows on one edge are at the top of the image and check to see which way they are pointing; if to the right, you are looking at the emulsion side, if to the left, you are looking at the back of the film.

If you are *very* wealthy, put a 301A filter and a Wratten 2E filter into your enlarger's filter drawer, regardless of whether it is a condenser- or a diffusion-type machine. Make sure the 301A, which is a dichroic-type filter, is parallel to the negative (or perpendicular to the light path) and as close to the enlarger lamp as possible. If there isn't any place you can put a 2 inch-square or a 3 inch-square filter up close to the lamp, then, as a last resort, you can put the 301A right on top of the back flange of the enlarger lens and very carefully reinstall the lens in the enlarger.

If you aren't very wealthy and you can't be bothered with trying to accommodate the very expensive 301A filter, you can do quite well by inserting a heat-absorbing glass and a CP2B into the filter drawer of a condenser-type enlarger or any diffusion-type machine which is not already equipped with these filters.

You won't find it necessary to use any other filters to make your first positive-to-positive printing exposures.

Set your enlarger's lens to its widest opening. Now, set the enlarger's head height to get a focused image on the baseboard of about 3½ ×

A 2¼″ × 2¼″ carrier can easily be modified to accommodate a 2″ × 2″ mounted slide by taping a simple cardboard frame into the carrier. Make sure that the opening in the cardboard is larger than the opening in the slide mount. Try to keep the cardboard insert flat and parallel to the carrier. You are looking at the bottom of a modified Beseler carrier.

This is what the top of the cardboard-modified carrier looks like. A narrow, black cardboard rim is cemented to the bottom layer of cardboard, serving to keep the 2″ × 2″ mounted slide centered in the opening.

The mounted slide is simply dropped into the cardboard insert, the carrier is closed and placed in the negative stage of the enlarger, and the slide is printed without being removed from its mount. This is a cheap and handy way to do things when you are in a hurry, but it's not an advisable way to obtain top-quality work. For best results, always remove the slide from its mount and use it in a normal carrier.

magnification. If you don't already know how to determine the magnification, learning to do it is a cinch. Just measure the short dimension of the image focused on the baseboard. This dimension, in inches, will determine the number of times the approximately one-inch dimension of the negative carrier has been enlarged. (A focused image of a 35mm transparency, measuring 3½″ × 5¼″ on the baseboard, would indicate that the enlarger's head height was set to provide 3½ × magnification.)

Place your preset, multiple image-making easel (p. 4-7) on the baseboard. Insert a sheet of resin-coated middle-weight printing paper in the easel, with the back of the sheet facing up (toward the enlarger lens). Turn on the enlarger lamp, leave the head height as set, and refocus the image on the printing paper on the easel. Move the easel to center the image in the image area, and make sure it overlaps the black easel blades just slightly. Turn off the enlarger lamp.

Set ten seconds on your enlarger timer (if you are so equipped). Place your unopened package of color printing paper and a pair of scissors near the enlarger.

Get your daylight processing drum and, following the manufacturer's instructions, remove its paper-loading cap. Remove the focusing sheet from the easel and use it to practice loading the drum, with the lights on and your eyes open. The drum's manufacturer will supply loading instructions to follow. When you get to be quite good at loading the drum with your eyes open, close them and keep on practicing. When that is no longer a challenge, turn off the lights and practice loading the drum in the dark. When you have mastered that, try to remember where you put the end cap and, without turning the lights on, find it and put it back on the drum.

As soon as you can flawlessly load the paper (remember the paper's emulsion side is always loaded so that it is facing the center of the drum)

A 301A filter (worth about $68 in early 1976) is shown sitting on the back flange of a lense. This workable, although undesirable, location for the filter is often used because Kodak doesn't make this filter in sizes large enough to fit many enlarger filter drawers. If they did, the prices of the filters would be astronomical.

into the drum and get the drum's end cap back on, all in total darkness, you will be ready to proceed.

Turn off all lights in your darkroom (or closet, bathroom, or what have you). Wait a few moments, until your eyes accommodate themselves to the gloom, then carefully check to insure that there are no light leaks. If you find any, take whatever steps are necessary to get rid of them. When you are sure that there is no white light entering your working area, you can open your box of printing paper. (Remember, this procedure is based on the use of Kodak's Ektachrome Type 1993 resin-coated, reversal printing paper.) *No safelight whatever is usable with this material.*

Handle the paper only by the edges, as far as you find it possible to do so. Most resin-coated papers have emulsions that take great pride in accurately reproducing fingerprints, so be sure to handle the paper as carefully as you can. One of

the nasty problems with resin-coated printing paper is how to tell the emulsion side from the back of the sheet. The only practical way I know of to perform this in total darkness is to run your fingers over both surfaces to determine which one offers the greatest resistance to movement. I know that this method neatly contradicts what I just warned you not to do, but I simply don't know of any other good way to do this job. I suggest that you do this just once per box of paper. After you determine if the sheet came out of the box with its emulsion side either up or down, you can rest assured that the other sheets in the box will be oriented the same way. Simply make a mental note to mark the paper box "emulsion up" or "emulsion down" (whichever is appropriate) the next time you turn the lights back on again.

Now, with your sheet of fingerprinted paper in hand, search around in the dark until you find the scissors. (You put them in an easy to find spot,

MODIFIED NOMOGRAPH
FOR USE WITH EKTAPRINT R-500 CHEMISTRY

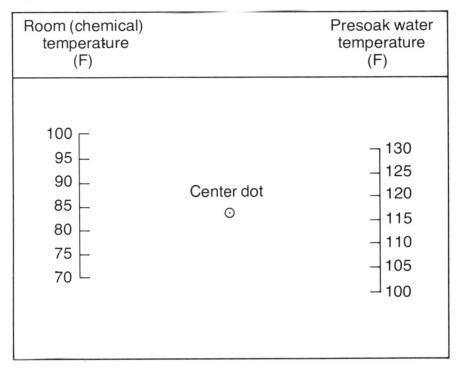

Room (chemical) temperature (F)	Presoak water temperature (F)

This modified nomograph is for use with Ektachrome Type 1993 paper and Ektaprint R-500 chemistry in areas with ambient temperatures outside of the 75–80F ambient temperature range.

Table 4-2   **DAYLIGHT DRUM PROCESSING INSTRUCTIONS FOR EKTAPRINT R-500 CHEMICALS**

STEP	SOLUTION*	VOLUME†	DURATION OF AGITATION	DRAIN PERIOD	TIME AT END OF STEP
1	Water at 123 F	16 oz.	30 sec.	dump	30 sec.
2	Water at 123 F	16 oz.	30 sec.	10 sec.	1 min. 10 sec.
3	1st Dev.	2 oz.	1 min. 30 sec.	10 sec.	2 min. 50 sec.
4	Stop	2 oz.	30 sec.	10 sec.	3 min. 30 sec.
5	Water‡	16 oz.	30 sec.	10 sec.	4 min. 10 sec.
6	Water‡	16 oz.	30 sec.	10 sec.	4 min. 50 sec.
7	Color Dev.	2 oz.	2 min.	10 sec.	7 min.
8	Rinse	4 oz.	20 sec.	10 sec.	7 min. 30 sec.
9	Blix	2 oz.	1 min. 20 sec.	10 sec.	9 min.
10	Water‡	16 oz.	30 sec.	10 sec.	9 min. 40 sec.
11	Water‡	16 oz.	30 sec.	10 sec.	10 min. 20 sec.
12	Stabilizer	2 oz.	30 sec.	10 sec.	11 min.
13	Water‡	16 oz.	15 sec.	dump	11 min. 15 sec.

*All chemical solutions are used at room ambient temperatures between 75–80 F.
†Volumes given are for a typical, level, 8″ × 10″ drum.
‡Water from the remainder of the one gallon of presoak water.

remember?) Use them to cut off a tiny portion of the corner of your sheet of unexposed printing paper, just as you did when you set your easel up to make multiple exposures. Now, insert the cut corner of the sheet into your easel's paper gripper. The cut corner will identify the No. 1 image area for you later. Be sure that you put the printing paper into the easel with its emulsion side facing up (toward the enlarger lens). Close the easel.

If you have followed all of the previous instructions, at this point all you need to do is start the timer to make the first of your four ten-second exposures.

After the enlarger lamp goes off, locate the len's aperture-control ring and twist it until you feel it reach its first click-stop (one stop down from wide open). Now open the easel and rotate the sheet of printing paper through 90 degrees to its No. 2 image position. Close the easel. Make your second ten-second exposure.

As soon as the enlarger lamp goes off close the lens down another stop, open the easel, rotate the paper 90° to its No. 3 printing position, close the easel, and make your third ten-second exposure.

Finally, after the enlarger lamp is extinguished, close the lens down yet another stop (you are now four stops down from wide open), open the easel, rotate the paper 90° to the No. 4 printing position, close the easel, and make your fourth ten-second exposure.

That's it. You have just completed making four full-frame test exposures, all on the same sheet of 8″ × 10″ printing paper. Now all you have to do is remove the paper from the easel, load it into the drum (remember the emulsion side faces the center of the drum), put the drum's cap back on, check to see that your box of paper is properly closed (with the remaining sheets all tightly wrapped in the inner wrapper), and turn the white lights back on again. Your time in total darkness has come to an end. If you do it all the way I told you to and you don't fumble somewhere in the middle, your total elapsed time in the dark, to produce four separate images, should be about one minute. That's not too terrible is it?

I must apologize to those of you who have had the misfortune to read both the negative-to-positive printing exposure and the positive-to-positive printing exposure sections. There is a great deal of redundancy between them. I'll apologize in advance for the same kind of redundancy which, of necessity, occurs in the following section on processing.

Processing

The procedures that follow are based on two basic assumptions. The first being that you are using the recommended chemical/paper combination (Kodak's R-500/Ektachrome Type 1993), and the second being that you are working in a room which has an ambient temperature between 75 and 80 F (24–27 C). For other materials see the appropriate sections of this book or follow the manufacturer's instructions. For other temperatures either refer to Chapter 9 for further data or follow the instructions supplied with the chemicals, or use the modified nomograph on page 4-19 to determine the appropriate presoak water temperature to replace the 120–125 F (49–52 C) recommended for the general procedure.

If you work in an unheated area and process at very low ambient temperatures in the wintertime, you can use the general procedure recommended here if you first bring your chemicals up to 80 F (27 C) and keep them at that temperature, with a water bath or some other means, throughout the processing steps.

You begin by taking your loaded drum to the area in which you will do your wet processing. If you can use a kitchen, laundry, or bathroom sink, so much the better. If you can't have immediate access to a source of running hot and cold water, or to a drain, you needn't be overly concerned. It will be easier to have these conveniences of course, but lacking them won't be much of a real hardship.

If you are going to use a motor base to agitate your drum, place the drum on the motor base, in accordance with the manufacturer's instructions, and use a spirit level to check if the drum is level (or reasonably close to level) from end to end. Use shims or adjustments under the legs of the motor base to level the drum.

If you are going to agitate the drum by hand, first spread a Turkish towel over the area in which you intend to roll the drum (in accordance with the drum manufacturer's instructions) and then place the drum on top of the towel-covered surface in the position it will be in during agitation. Use a spirit level to determine if the drum is level from end to end. If it isn't, level it by shimming the supports of the surface upon which the drum rests.

If you can't manage to level the drum, never fear. Just use four ounces of chemicals wherever I call for two, and then collect and reuse the four ounces of each solution to make a second print.

In case you wondered, the Turkish towel is not placed below the drum for any decorative purposes, but to provide a surface with considerably more friction than a plastic or varnished counter top or table will. Friction between the drum and its supporting surface is necessary to prevent the drum from slipping rather than rolling. A daylight processing drum relies on a near-uniform rolling motion to provide agitation and distribution of the small amount of liquid processing chemicals it contains. So much for Turkish towels. If, by the way, you want to use some other similar material for a rolling pad, feel free to do so, just so long as its surface provides enough friction to prevent the drum from slipping during agitation, even when both the drum and the pad are wet.

Use a waterproof marking pen (DriMark's Medium Line, Nylon Tip Marker is the best one I know of) to label each of six of your four-ounce drinking glasses: "1st developer," "stop," "color developer," "rinse," "blix," and "stabilizer." When this is done, fill each one with two ounces of the working-strength chemical called for by its label, with the exception of the "rinse" container, which should be filled with four ounces of a potassium iodide working-strength solution. Set the half-dozen glasses down in a convenient place near where the drum will be agitated, but well out of harm's way.

Remove the lid from a one-gallon plastic pitcher and put your thermometer into it. Fill the pitcher from a hot-water tap while watching the thermometer. If your hot-water heater is anything like the ones I've worked with, you will soon be getting water from the tap that is hotter than the highest temperature on the thermometer. Add cold water to keep the thermometer from breaking. By alternating hot and cold water from the taps, and by stirring constantly with the thermometer while doing so, you should have little trouble with quickly obtaining a pitcher full of presoak water at some temperature between 120 and 125 F (49–52 C). Try to hit 122 or 123 F (50–51 C) right on the money.

For wet-processing area-ambient temperatures outside of the 75–80 F (24–27 C) range, use the accompanying nomograph to obtain the presoak water temperature required. Simply place a ruler so that its edge connects the dot between the two temperature scales, and the ambient temperature of the room in which you are working. The point where the edge of the ruler intersects the Presoak Water Temperature scale will determine the temperature of the presoak water you should use. For example, if your wet-processing area (and therefore the liquid chemistry you have stored in that area) is at 70 F (21 C) you will need presoak water at 130 F (54 C). Make sure that your chemicals are at the same temperature your room is if you use this method.

Once the pitcher is filled, remove the thermometer and put the pitcher's cover back in place. Pour one pint of the presoak water from the pitcher into the processing drum, agitate the drum (on the motor base or by rolling it back and fourth on the Turkish towel) for 30 seconds, then pour the water out of the drum and down the drain (or into a bucket, dishpan, etc.). Pour another pint of presoak water from the pitcher into the drum, agitate the drum for 30 seconds, then pour the water out of the drum and continue to drain it, while gently shaking it to help to get all of the presoak water possible out of the drum, for another 10 seconds.

Now you have brought both the print and the drum up to a sufficiently high temperature to transfer the necessary amount of heat to the first developer, and you are ready to begin the print processing.

Place the drum on its legs (or with the pouring spout up, if you are using a vertical type of drum). Next, pour two ounces of the first developer into the drum and begin to agitate the chemical over the surface of the print by rolling the drum back and forth on the Turkish towel (or start the motor base and let it do the agitation for you). Continue to agitate the drum (if manually, at about one revolution per second or faster) for one minute and 30 seconds, then pour the developer out of the drum and continue to allow the drum to drain, while gently shaking it, for another 10 seconds.

Place the drum in a position to receive two ounces of stop bath. Pour the stop bath into the drum, agitate the drum for 30 seconds then drain the drum, while gently shaking it, for 10 seconds.

Place the drum in a position to receive wash water. Add a pint of the presoak water remaining in the pitcher to the drum, agitate for 30 seconds, drain, while gently shaking the drum, for 10 seconds. Repeat this whole washing process again. These two wash steps will also serve to bring the print and the processing drum back up to a sufficiently high temperature to transfer the required amount of heat to the color developer.

Place the drum in a position to receive the color developer. Pour two ounces of color developer into the drum, agitate for two minutes, then drain the drum, while gently shaking it, for another 10 seconds.

Add four ounces of the rinse solution to the drum, agitate for 20 seconds, then pour it out and drain the drum, while gently shaking it for another 10 seconds.

Place the drum in a position to receive the blix. Add the blix to the drum, agitate for one minute and 20 seconds, then pour the blix out of the drum and continue to drain the drum, while gently shaking it, for another 10 seconds.

Place the drum in a position to receive wash water. Pour a pint of the remaining presoak water from the pitcher into the drum. Agitate for 30 seconds then dump the wash water and drain the drum for 10 seconds more, while gently shaking it. Repeat this wash step with another pint of water.

Place the drum in a position to receive the stabilizer. Pour two ounces of stabilizer into the drum, agitate for 30 seconds, then spill the stabilizer out of the drum and continue to drain the drum, with some gentle shaking, for another 10 seconds.

Finally, place the drum in a position to receive the final water wash. Add a pint from the pitcher of the remaining presoak water to the drum. Agitate for 15 seconds then remove the drum's end cap and, gripping it only by the edges, carefully remove the print from the drum.

You've done it! The chemical processing part of making your first reversal print has come to an end. Just be sure to thoroughly rinse out the processing drum and its cap with warm water once the print has been removed. And, if you have been collecting used chemicals and wash water in a container of some sort, now is the time to dump it all down the drain.

At this point you will have some fairly peculiar looking images on your wet sheet of paper. However, don't let it worry you. Drying will do a great deal to improve them.

Print Drying

Now that you have your first exposed, processed, and very damp 8″ × 10″ sheet of resin-coated color printing paper in hand, it would be a fine idea if I gave you some clue as to how to get it dry. Actually there are several ways to go about it, but for the most part color printers, be they expert or beginner, are confronted by one paramount requirement where print drying is concerned; and that requirement is *speed*. With virtually all of the contemporary color printing papers, and with all of those which are resin-coated (and imported into this country), you must get the print bone dry before any kind of color-balance or density judgement can be made. So while it is entirely possible to lay a color print flat down (emulsion side up) on a piece of plastic screen and wait for nature to take its course and dry it, it is far more practical and much faster to run the print through the soft rubber-covered rollers of a Falcon RC Print Dryer, or to lay the wet print, emulsion side down, on a smooth, clean sheet of glass, and use a good, heavy squeegee with considerable muscle behind it, to get as much moisture off both sides of the print as is possible in just a few swipes. Most squeegees will leave a black deposit on the print back when you do this, so it is a good idea to clean this black rubber residue off the back of the print with a piece of paper towel before you put a fingernail or a knife blade between the print and the glass and remove the now much-less-damp print from it. While holding the print in the air, you can take a few wiping swipes at the glass with a piece of paper towel to get it dry too, before you put the print back down on it, this time with its emulsion side up. I never use a squeegee on the emulsion side of any kind of a print, black-and-white or color, and most particularly not on any kind of a plastic-coated print. Instead I use a squeezed-dry Kodak Photo Chamois to quickly remove any last traces of surface moisture from the print's emulsion. However, there are times when I am too lazy to get my piece of chamois cloth from its water-and-sodium bicarbonate bath, rinse it out thoroughly in running cold water, and then press as much of the rinse water out of it as I can. It is at such times that I simply unroll still another sheet of paper towel and gently dry the surface of my print with it. Some brands of paper towels shed lint, so check before using them on your print. It's not the best idea to use paper towel on tender emulsion, but if you're reasonably careful, it does work.

Once you have squeegeed the back and chamoised (or toweled) the front of your print, it will be rather dry. Plastic-coated prints can't absorb much water into their paper fibers, because the only place those fibers come in contact with water is at the extreme edges of the print (where the plastic coating has been cut when the paper was sliced from roll stock into sheets). The only significant amount of water left will be that which is still in the emulsion layers themselves, which can now be gotten out very quickly indeed.

My favorite tool for drying prints from this stage onward is a 1000 watt hair dryer. I simply turn the blower speed up to high, turn the temperature up to maximum, and let it blast hot air at the print lying, emulsion side up, on the sheet of glass. It takes me about 90 seconds to get the emulsion side of the print bone dry that way, and about another 30 seconds to lift the print up off the glass and blast any traces of moisture off the back of the print.

When I am really in a hurry, I turn a flatbed dryer up to high, pull the canvas apron over it, lay the print (after first squeegeeing and chamoising it) on top of the apron (never on top of the metal bed of the dryer itself, for fear of melting the plastic coating of the print), emulsion side up, and blast the emulsion side with my hair dryer while the flatbed dryer cooks the back of the

print. Drying prints this way, I can go from a sopping wet one to bone dry one in under 90 seconds total time.

There are as many variations on these basic techniques as there are color printers. Other commonly used techniques include: squeegeeing the emulsion surface, wiping the back and then putting the print, emulsion side up, on the apron of a very hot flatbed dryer until both sides are cooked dry; hanging the soaking-wet print up with a pair of clothespins and letting it drip and air dry; squeegeeing the print and putting it into an RC paper-drying tunnel; putting the prints in very close proximity to a photoflood lamp; and, in a pinch, I have even known printers to use the hot top-platen surface of a dry-mounting press as a print dryer. I have even, on very rare occasions, used a 200 F oven and a large cookie sheet to do the job.

You can choose from these various techniques, but be forewarned that if you do decide to squeegee the emulsion side of your prints, do so with extreme care because RC papers have very tender emulsions. And, what's more, those black rubber residue marks I spoke of earlier are much harder to deal with on the emulsion side of a print than they are on its unimportant and unseen back side. If you can buy, beg, borrow, or steal a blower-type hair dryer, I recommend that you do so as it is the best print-drying tool I know of.

A final note here: Never try to ferrotype glossy resin-coated paper. The moisture in the emulsion won't be able to escape through the plastic-coated rear surface of the print and the results you obtain will often be catastrophic, and will always be unsatisfactory. Glossy-surface paper should, if at all possible, be dried with heat or heated air to achieve the best appearance.

How to Evaluate Your First Prints Without Really Knowing What You Are Doing— Programs for Impatient Printers

The Negative-to-Positive Print Evaluation Program

Now that you have in hand one dried 8″ × 10″ sheet of color printing paper with four differently exposed images of your standard negative on it, it is time to discover just how close you were able to come to getting an acceptable image in the four tries you had, and if need be,

how to straighten things out to get a considerably better set of four test images the next time you make a print. You will be able to do this without any real knowledge of the processes involved, by making use of a few tools, including the Negative-to-Positive Color Print Evaluation Flow Chart, the Negative-to-Positive Ring-Around (see color section, Fig. 4–2), the Exposure-Time

Correction Table that also follows, and the standard print which is in the little white envelope bound into the Kodak *Color Dataguide*.

Let's begin by looking at the Negative-to-Positive Color Print Evaluation Flow Chart. You start, naturally enough, at the top. The uppermost circle refers to your 8″ × 10″ sheet of paper with four images on it. Follow the arrow from the circle down to the first instruction box. It tells you to *USE RING-AROUND TO CHECK PRINT DENSITY* (see color section, Fig. 4-1).

The ring-around is nothing more than a collection of prints made from a Kodak standard negative, much the same as the ones you have made, displayed so as to best illustrate increasing degrees of print problems. The image at the center of the ring-around has the best density and color balance obtainable from the standard negative used to make it, with the materials and processes used (Unicolor's Resin Base Type-A paper and their R-2 chemistry used with the manufacturer's rapid process). The three images directly above the one in the center represent overexposure through the correct printing filter pack. The three images directly under the center one represent underexposure through the correct printing filter pack. The six other lines of three images each represent the proper exposure through increasingly incorrect printing filter

Table 4-3

EXPOSURE TIME CORRECTIONS FOR ACETATE (CP) FILTER PACK CHANGES TO BE APPLIED TO ORIGINAL PRINTING TIMES*

FILTER TYPE		EXPOSURE TIME CORRECTION	
Color	Density	For Each Filter Added	For Each Filter Subtracted
Yellow	5 thru 80	+10%	−10%
Magenta	5 and 10	+25%	−25%
	20	+50%	−50%
	40	+90%	−90%
Cyan	5	+10%	−10%
	10 and 20	+25%	−25%
	40	+90%	−90%

*These time-change values do not apply to dichroic filters. Exposure time corrections required for such filters may vary from enlarger to enlarger. I would suggest, as a starting point, that you try to use between one-third to one-half the corrections called for here.

packs. These images are all labeled according to the problem color seen in the print. For example, the image in the uppermost right-hand corner is labeled *+40 YELLOW*. This indicates that it was made with a printing filter pack that resulted in a print having 40 density too much yellow dye in it.

Similarly, the print appearing in the lower left-hand corner of the ring-around labeled *+40 BLUE* appears to be considerably too blue; the print closest to it, labeled *+20 BLUE* seems to be somewhat less too blue; and the print labeled *+10 BLUE* next to it, has even less excess blue color when compared to the *PERFECT* print at the very center of the ring-around.

Now you know everything you need to know, for the moment, about how a ring-around is laid out, and you are ready to follow the arrow down into the first decision box which asks you *IS PRINT EXPOSURE OK?* The way you answer this question is to determine if one of your four test images has the proper image density. To make this check compare them to the seven prints that make up the ring-around's vertical column. Disregard any consideration of color-balance problems here. Just do as the instruction box told you to do and check which one of your four test images comes closest to the overall density shown by any of the prints in the ring-around's vertical display. Hopefully, at least one of your four images will fit at least somewhere into the density range covered by the vertical column.

Let's suppose for the moment that the densest of the four images on your sheet, your No. 1 image, is about as dark as the *−1 STOP* example on the ring-around. That would indicate that you did not get enough exposure, even with your enlarger lens wide open. In this case you would leave the decision box along the *UNDER* line and repeat the original exposure and processing steps, but this time using more exposure. Follow all of the procedures previously outlined exactly, except this time use 25 seconds of exposure time. When the new print containing four more heavily exposed images is processed and dried, you start the evaluation procedure all over again.

Now, let's look at the other side of the coin. Let's suppose your initial effort contains four images, the lightest of which, image No. 4, is about as dark as the *+1 STOP* example on the ring-around. In that case you would have overexposed everything on your first sheet. Make a

NEGATIVE-TO-POSITIVE PRINT EVALUATION CHART

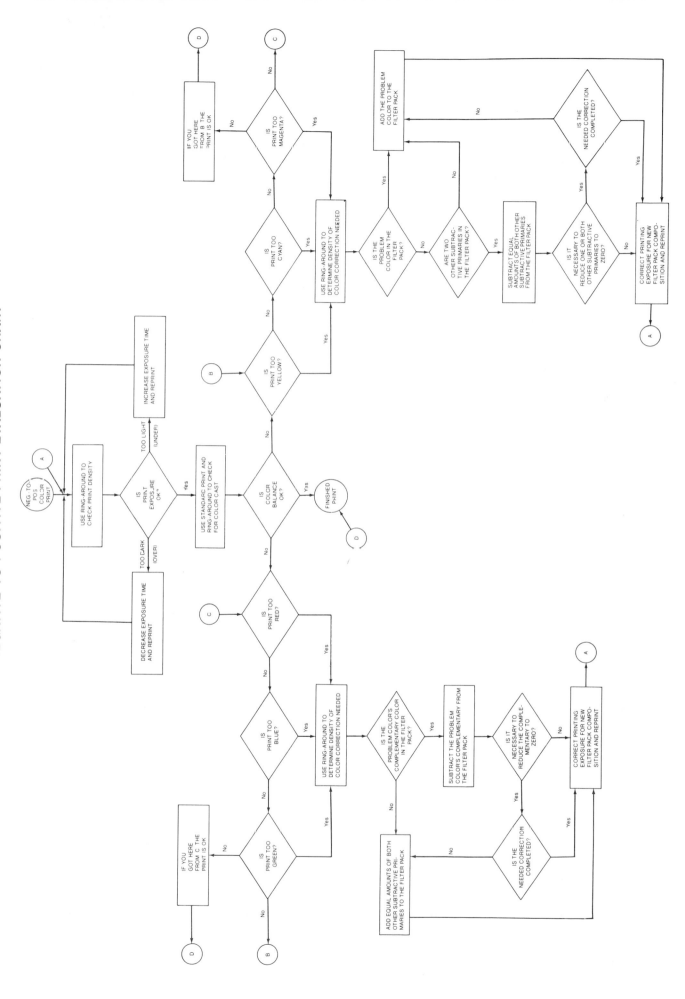

second set of four images on a single 8″ × 10″ sheet, but this time cut your exposure time down to 2 seconds. When the new print is processed and dried, you begin the print evaluation procedure from the top of the chart again.

If your sheet of paper is totally black, brown, or gray, chances are you somehow managed to fog it with white light somewhere along the way. Repeat the original printing, processing, and drying steps again, but be more careful to avoid the white light this time.

If your sheet of color printing paper is completely blank (white), chances are that you mistook the back of the paper for the emulsion side when you first put it on the easel. Repeat the original printing, processing, and drying procedures again, but this time make sure you get the paper's emulsion side facing the enlarger's lens during the printing steps.

If any one of your four images has a density (overall print darkness) that falls somewhere between the +½ STOP and the −½ STOP examples in the ring-around, you can disregard all of the others on the sheet and continue your print evaluation. You leave the decision box along the YES arrow which brings you to an instruction box that tells you USE STANDARD PRINT AND RING-AROUND TO CHECK FOR COLOR CAST. To follow this instruction, make a side-by-side comparison of the image under consideration and the standard print enclosed in the little white envelope in Kodak's Color Dataguide. Your own eyes will quickly tell you if the two images are a close color match. Be sure that you use the same light source to illuminate the two images. Flourescent lamps or photoflood lamps are fine, but even a 100 watt incandescent bulb will do for our initial purposes here.

It is a virtual certainty that your image and the standard print won't be a close color match. You can confirm this by looking at the 18 different off-color examples shown on the ring-around. It is, however, a remote possibility that you have gotten lucky.

This brings you to the next decision box, which asks you IS COLOR BALANCE OK? If it is (as I just mentioned), you have somehow, (with the benefit of the starting filter-pack and printing-time instructions), managed to make a perfect print on your first try. Congratulations! You get to leave this decision box by way of the YES arrow to discover that you have a FINISHED

PRINT. Now all you have to do is read the rest of the book to find out how to keep up the good work.

Okay, the rest of you follow me. We'll leave the decision box by way of the left NO arrow and compare our prints to those on the ring-around which offer examples that are too red, too blue, and too green. Did you find anything that looked like your off-color print? If you did, just follow the appropriate YES arrow and do your best to follow the instructions you encounter. Or better yet, why not wait for the rest of us? If you did not find that any of those ring-around images looked like your print, you have managed to reach the leftmost NO arrow that points to a circle with a B in it.

Check the chart and you will find another circle with a B in it. An arrow leads out of that circle and it brings you into the decision box that asks you to compare your print to the too-yellow ones shown in the ring-around. If your print isn't too yellow, following the NO arrows you will be asked to determine if it is too cyan or too magenta, once again by comparing it to the examples shown in the ring-around.

If, by the time you have checked the print against the TOO MAGENTA examples, you still have not found a color that resembles the one that is adversely affecting your print, you have two ways to proceed: either up the top NO arrow to the box that tells you IF YOU GOT HERE FROM THE CIRCLED B YOUR PRINT IS OK, or out the rightmost NO arrow to an encircled C. Don't take the upper route if your eyes tell you there is an overall color cast present in your print that shouldn't be there. If you follow the C route, you will find yourself back in the decision boxes that ask you if the print is too red, too blue, or too green again. This time through be more careful and see if one of these three additive primaries isn't your problem color. Just keep on trying until you find out which of the six options offered you is the one that comes closest to looking like your problem color. You probably won't find any exact match. All you have to do is find one of the problem colors that looks similar to the one you have in your print.

If you can't perform this task, there are two sad possibilities to consider. Perhaps you missed the part that said not to try to check any of your prints unless at least one of them was no more than ½ stop away from having the proper density. If you thought you would try to get through the maze with a print outside of this density range, you have wasted your time. Go back to the top of the chart and follow all of the density instructions before you start back through the color evaluations again. The other possibility is that you are color blind. No, I'm not kidding. See your family doctor to determine if perhaps this isn't the problem. Many people are color blind, you know.

Let's run through a few examples of how to use the remainder of the evaluation chart. But, before I can offer any examples, I will have to provide you with some rules which I'll present here without any further explanation. They are all amply covered elsewhere in this book, but this section has been provided for people who can't wait to read the book and want to race right into the darkroom and print.

1) There are two basic types of colors in photography: the additive primaries, red, green, and blue and the subtractive primaries, yellow, cyan, and magenta.

2) For our purpose here, red is made up of yellow and magenta, blue consists of magenta and cyan, and green consists of cyan and yellow.

3) Each of these six colors has an exact opposite color, called its complementary color. Cyan is red's complementary color, yellow is blue's complementary color, and magenta is green's complementary color.

4) Never have filters of all three of the subtractive primary colors in the printing filter pack at one time.

5) Always try to use only yellow and magenta filters in the printing filter pack whenever possible.

6) Filter density values are additive. If you need 25M filtration you can get it by adding a 20M filter and a 5M filter. Similarly, 40R filtration is obtained by using a 40Y filter in combination with a 40M filter.

Now on to the examples. Let's say that you have compared your prints to the vertical column of the ring-around for density and found that your No. 4 image was very close in density to the *PERFECT* print at the center of the ring-around. Your enlarger lens' largest opening is *f*/4, so you know that your No. 4 image was made at *f*/11 and the exposure time was ten seconds. You used a

Kodak Vericolor II standard negative in your condenser enlarger and printed with my recommended printing filter pack, consisting of a heat-absorbing glass, a CP2B, and 80M + 100Y. You have compared your No. 4 image to the standard print and to the various examples of color problems in the ring-around and decided that your No. 4 image looks like it has the same kind of color cast as the ones in the ring-around showing *+Cyan* values do.

You follow the *YES* arrow down from the *TOO CYAN?* decision box, to the instruction box below it, which tells you to *USE RING-AROUND TO DETERMINE DENSITY OF COLOR CORRECTION NEEDED.* To follow this instruction you simply compare your No. 4 image to the *+10, +20,* and *+40 CYAN* illustrations to decide which one its overall cyan cast resembles most closely. Let's say that you find your No. 4 image looks pretty much the way the *+20 CYAN* one does. Follow the arrow from the instruction box down into the next decision box, which asks you *IS THE PROBLEM COLOR IN THE FILTER PACK?* You had only magenta and yellow in your printing filter pack, so you will have to leave this box along the *NO* line, to enter the next decision box, which asks *ARE TWO OTHER SUBTRACTIVE PRIMARIES IN THE FILTER PACK?* Your answer to that question is yes, so you leave the decision box along the *YES* arrow to arrive at an instruction box that tells you to *SUBTRACT EQUAL AMOUNTS OF BOTH OTHER SUBTRACTIVE PRIMARIES FROM THE FILTER PACK.* You open up your enlarger's filter drawer and remove a 20M and a 20Y filter to comply with this instruction, then you proceed down the arrow to the next decision box, which asks *IS IT NECESSARY TO REDUCE ONE OR BOTH COLORS TO ZERO?* Since you took 20M and 20Y away from an 80M + 100Y pack, your new printing filter pack is 60M + 80Y, and your answer to that question is no. Therefore, you leave the decision box along the *NO* line and enter an instruction box that tells you to *CORRECT PRINTING EXPOSURE FOR NEW FILTER PACK COMPOSITION AND REPRINT.* In order to comply with this instruction you will first have to refer to table 4-3 on p. 4-24. It tells you that you should decrease the exposure time by 10 percent for the yellow filter removed and by 50 percent for the magenta filter you pulled from the pack. That means that you need to make a 60 percent adjustment to your printing time, so your new, hopefully perfect, exposure will be made at f/11 for four seconds rather than for the ten seconds originally used. Now, to finish complying with the instructions in this box you will have to make a new set of four exposures through the new filter pack. Since table 4–3 gives only approximate values of exposure changes required, it will be best if your next four test images bracket the four-second recommended exposure. You might set your timer at four seconds and make image No.1 with a f/5.6 lens opening, No. 2 at f/8, No. 3 at f/11 and No. 4 at f/16. Now you have all of the information you need to reprint, reprocess, and dry the new print, and return to the top of the chart to begin to evaluate your corrected images. You just keep on going around and around like this until you do manage to make a perfect print.

Note that you can also use the multiple-image test procedure to bracket color changes as well as density changes. For example, you may want to print a set of four test images, each one with 5 more magenta filtration than the last, to accurately determine the effect of small filtration changes. You can even combine filter and exposure variation both, in the same set of four test images, but make sure to keep an accurate data sheet (see typical data sheet example below) if you do this type of test image making.

Once you do manage to make a perfect print you most likely will have gotten over your anxiety about your ability to do so, and hopefully, will be inclined to read the rest of the book before you move on to greater exploits of color printing. However, for those of you who just can't wait, instructions for a simple procedure that will allow you to make the exposure time adjustments necessary for changing the enlarger's magnification are offered in the *"Magnification and Exposure Time"* section of this chapter.

As much as I would like to leave this whole sordid mess right here, I can't because I feel obligated to take you through some of the other loops possible to keep you from getting lost. But from here on in we will go a lot faster.

Suppose that your initial print had looked too

COLOR PRINTING DATA   Negative File No. _____

DATE	FRAME	MAGNIFI-CATION	F/STOP	TIME	M	Y	C	NO. PLASTIC FILTERS	PAPER/CHEMICALS	REMARKS

magenta. Then you would have left the *IS THE PROBLEM COLOR IN THE FILTER PACK?* box via the *YES* arrow, added magenta filtration to the pack, and added time to the exposure. Right? Right!

Suppose that you had originally printed with a 20Y + 50M pack and you decided that the result obtained looked like the *+40 CYAN* example. When you reached the *SUBTRACT EQUAL AMOUNTS OF BOTH OTHER SUBTRACTIVE PRIMARIES FROM THE PACK* instruction you would only be able to get 20Y and 20M out of the pack. Then you would have to leave the *IS IT NECESSARY TO REDUCE ONE OR BOTH OTHER SUBTRACTIVE PRIMARIES TO ZERO?* decision box along the *YES* line because your pack would consist of only 30M after the subtraction. Leaving this way would bring you to the *IS THE NEEDED CORRECTION COMPLETED?* decision box. You would have to answer this one no, because you have so far only been able to make a 20 correction where you need a 40 correction. Following the *NO* arrow brings you to the instruction to *ADD THE PROBLEM COLOR TO THE FILTER PACK*. You complete your correction then by adding 20C to the pack. Your new pack is 20C + 30M. Now, correct your printing time by subtracting 10 percent for the yellow filter removed and 50 percent for the magenta filter pulled, and add 25 percent for the cyan filter added. This yields a net change of minus 35 percent of exposure time. Okay, let's get over into the additive primary problems.

Suppose that you found your print was green and it looked like the *+20 GREEN* example. Your original printing filter pack was 80M + 100Y. Green is the problem color and its complementary color, magenta, is certainly in the pack. Removing 20M from the pack does not reduce the pack's magenta content to zero. An exposure correction calling for a 50 percent reduction in the printing time is called for.

If the problem color had been red, then because cyan, red's complementary color, is not in the pack, the correction called for would be the addition of both magenta and yellow filtration to the pack and an appropriate increase in the printing exposure time.

If the problem had looked like a *+40 BLUE* one and the original printing filter pack had been a 30Y + 70M, you would be able to correct most of the problem by removing 30Y, but doing so would reduce the yellow content of the pack to zero. However, this would not quite correct the color imbalance. To finish the job you would have to add 10M and 10C to come up with a final pack of 80M + 10C. The exposure time correction would be minus 10 percent for each of the two yellow filters removed and plus 25 percent each for the magenta and cyan filters added. This would yield a net increase to exposure time of plus 30 percent.

The Positive-to-Positive Print Evaluation Program

Just so that you won't feel that I am cheating, I want to admit, out front, that if you just finished reading the preceding section, you will experience a serious feeling of deja vu when you start reading this one. I have quite deliberately made the sections on negative-to-positive evaluation and positive-to-positive evaluation as identical as possible. I used this procedure not *only* because I am lazy, but also because once you have made something perfect there is little room for improvement. But don't be fooled by the near identical language of the two sections into thinking that the processes are at all alike. They very emphatically aren't. As a matter of fact, you will soon note that they are exactly opposite. Needless to say then, you will have to read through this section also if you want to follow my simplified procedure for positive-to-positive print evaluation.

I have every reason to expect that you now have a fully dried 8" × 10" sheet of Ektachrome Type 1993 reversal color printing paper, containing four differently exposed images of the slide you chose to print. Now it's time to find out just how close to producing an acceptable image you were able to get in the four tries you had, and, if need be, to make whatever corrections to your exposure time or printing filter pack may be required to get you a better set of four images the next time you try.

You can accomplish all of this, with no particular understanding of what you are doing, by following the step-by-step instructions provided by the accompanying Positive-to-Positive Color Print Evaluation Flow Chart, by making use of the Positive-to-Positive Ring-Around (see color section, Fig. 4–2), and by referring to the Exposure Time Correction Chart on p. 4-24.

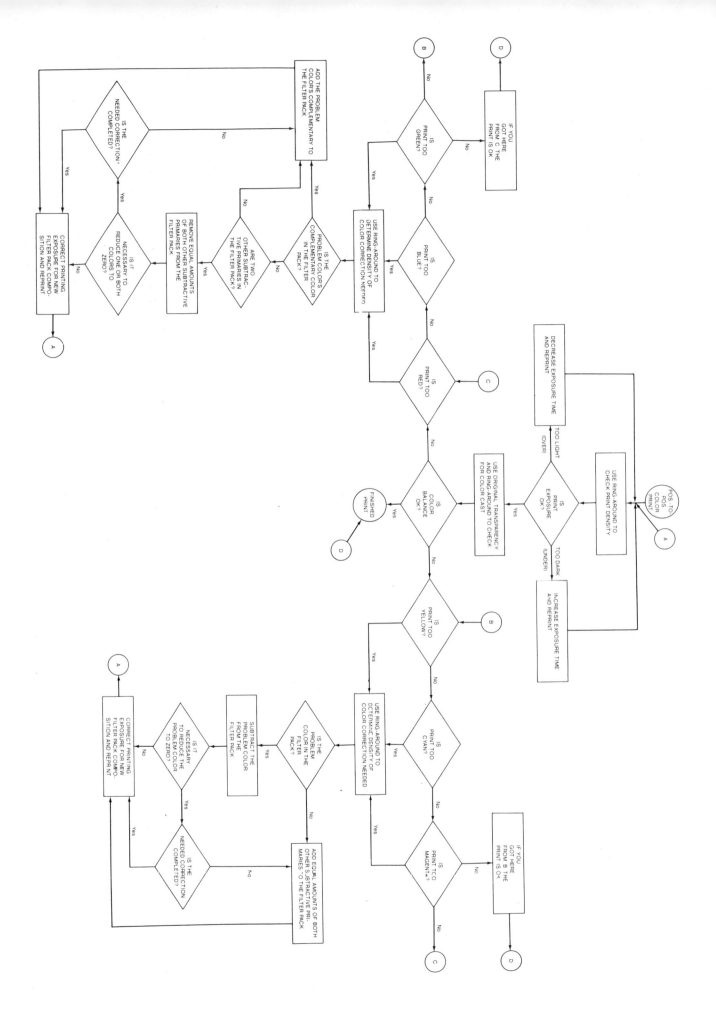

POSITIVE-TO-POSITIVE PRINT EVALUATION CHART

The evaluation chart just looks confusing, but in reality it isn't. All you need to do is follow the arrows, comply with its simple instructions, answer easy questions, and in a very short time you will find that you have mastered the maze and simultaneously produced a fine looking print.

You start to determine just how good those four images you are holding are by entering the chart at the circle at the very top and traveling down the first arrow out of the circle to a rectangular instruction box which tells you to *USE RING-AROUND TO CHECK PRINT DENSITY* (see color section, Fig. 4–3). The ring-around is nothing more than a collection of prints made from a Kodak standard transparency, displayed so as to best illustrate increasing degrees of print problems. The image at the center of the ring-around has the best density and color balance I could obtain from the transparency I used, and the materials and processes I used to make it (Kodak's Ektachrome Type 1993 resin-coated reversal paper and Ektaprint R-500 chemistry). The three images directly above the one in the center represent overexposure through the correct printing filter pack. The three images directly under the center one represent underexposure through the correct printing filter pack. The six other lines of three images each represent the proper exposure through increasingly incorrect printing filter packs. These images are all labeled according to the problem color seen in the print. For example, the image in the upper-most left-hand corner is labeled *+40 RED*. This indicates that it was made with a printing filter pack which resulted in a print having 40 density too much yellow and magenta dye in it (yellow and magenta combined are seen as red).

Similarly, the print appearing in the lower right-hand corner of the ring-around, labeled *+40 CYAN*, appears to be too cyan; the print closest to it, labeled *+20 CYAN*, seems to be somewhat less too much cyan; and the print next in line to it, labeled *+10 CYAN*, has even less of an excess overall cyan color cast when it is compared to the *PERFECT* print at the center of the ring around.

Now, armed with this knowledge of how a ring-around is laid out and what it is intended to show you, you are ready to follow the arrow down into the evaluation chart's first diamond-shaped decision box, which asks you *IS PRINT EXPOSURE OK?* The way you answer this question is to determine if one of your four test images has the proper density. To make this check, compare them with the seven images that make up the ring-around's vertical column. Disregard any consideration of color-balance problems here. Just do as the instruction box tells you to do and check which one of your four test images comes closest to the overall density shown by any of the images in the ring-around's central vertical display. Hopefully, at least one of your four test images will fit somewhere into the density range covered by the vertical column. Now, let's suppose for the moment that the densest (darkest) of the four images on your sheet, your No. 4 image, is about as light as the *+1 STOP* example on the ring-around. That would indicate that your image had gotten too much exposure, even with your lens closed down four stops from its widest opening. In this case you would leave the decision box along the *TOO LIGHT (OVER)* line and repeat the original exposure and processing steps, except that this time you would use less exposure time. Follow all of the procedures previously outlined exactly, except this time around use only two seconds of exposure time. When the new print, containing four more lightly exposed (therefore darker) images is processed and dried, you start the evaluation procedure all over again.

Now, suppose that your initial effort contains four images, the lightest of which, your No. 1 image, is as dark as the *−1 STOP* example on the ring-around. In this case you would have under-exposed everything on your first sheet. Make a second set of four images on a single 8″ × 10″ sheet, but this time increase your exposure time to 25 seconds. When the new, more heavily exposed (and therefore lighter) print is processed and dried, you begin the print evaluation all over again, from the top of the chart.

If your sheet of color printing paper is totally brown, gray, or white, you have probably managed to fog it with white light somewhere along the way. Repeat the original printing, processing, and drying steps again, but be much more careful of white light this time.

If your sheet of color printing paper is completely black, chances are that you mistook the back of the paper for the emulsion side when you first put it on the easel. Repeat the original printing, processing, and drying procedures, but this time make sure that you get the paper's emulsion side facing the enlarger's lens during the printing steps.

If any one of your four images has a density (overall darkness) that falls somewhere between the +½ STOP and the −½ STOP examples in the ring-around, you can disregard all of the others on the sheet and continue your print evaluation. If you are in this fortunate group, you leave the exposure decision box along the YES line which brings you to an instruction box that tells you to USE THE ORIGINAL TRANSPARENCY AND RING-AROUND TO CHECK FOR COLOR CAST. To follow this instruction, first compare the image under consideration to the transparency, side by side. Your own eyes will quickly tell you if the two images are a close color match. Be sure that you use the same light source to illuminate both the printed image under examination and the transparency. Flourescent lamps or photo-flood lamps are okay, but even a 100 watt incandescent bulb will do for our purposes here.

It is a virtual certainty that your image and the original slide won't be a close color match. You will probably be able to confirm this by looking at the 18 different off-color examples shown on the ring-around. It is, however, a remote possibility that you have gotten lucky.

In any event, it's time to move along down the next arrow to the next decision box which asks IS COLOR BALANCE OK? If you did get lucky, your answer is yes and you exit this box along the YES arrow to discover that you have a FINISHED PRINT. You are a lucky person all right—now you have finished your introduction to positive-to-positive color printing and you will have to read the rest of the book now that you are no longer a novice. If only to avoid having to read anything more taxing, I suggest that you stay with the rest of us for the time being, though, and continue to explore the remainder of the chart. Or, you can simply rejoin us at the end of this section and I'll give you a clue as to how to get from those little 3″ × 4½″ images to larger print sizes.

As far as the rest of you are concerned, you will all have to leave the decision box by way of one NO arrow or the other. Let's try going along the NO arrow that points to the left, and compare our prints to the ones on the ring-around which offer awful examples of prints that are too red, too blue, and too green. See if you can find anything that looks like your off-color print. If you can, just

follow the appropriate YES arrow and do your best to follow the instructions you encounter, or better yet, why not wait for the rest of us?

If you don't find that any of these ring-around images look like your print, you will manage to reach the left-most NO arrow which points to a circle with a B in it. Check the chart and you will find another circle with a B in it. An arrow leads out of that circle and following it brings you into a decision box which asks you to compare your image to the too yellow ones shown in the ring-around. If your print isn't too yellow, follow the NO arrow to the right where you will be asked to determine if it is too cyan or too magenta, once again, by comparing it to the example shown in the ring-around.

If, by the time you have checked the print against the TOO MAGENTA examples, you have still not found a color which resembles the one that is adversely affecting your print, you have two ways to go: either up the top NO arrow to the box that tells you IF YOU GOT HERE FROM THE CIRCLED B YOUR PRINT IS OK, or out the rightmost NO arrow to an encircled C. Don't take the upper route if your eyes tell you that there is an overall color cast present in your print which you know shouldn't be there. If you follow the C route you will find yourself back in the decision boxes that ask if the print is too red, too blue, or too green again. This time through be more careful and see if one of these three additive primaries isn't your problem color. Just keep going through the decision boxes until you decide which of the six options offered you is the one that comes closest to looking like your problem color. You probably won't find any exact match. But all you really have to do is find one of the problem colors that looks similar to the color cast you have in your print.

If you can't perform this task there are two possibilities to consider. Perhaps you missed the part that said not to try to check any of your prints unless they were no more than ½ stop away from having the proper density. If you thought you would get through this maze with a print outside of this density range, you have wasted your time. Go back to the top of the chart and follow all of the density instructions before you start through the color evaluations again. The other possibility is that you are color blind. No, I'm not kidding. See your family doctor to determine if this isn't the problem.

All right, let's run through a few examples of how to use the remainder of the chart. But, before we can do that I will have to provide you with some rules which I shall simply present here, without offering any explanations for them. They are all amply explained elsewhere in the book, but this section has been provided for people who can't wait to read the book and want to race right into the darkroom and make prints. The rules are as follows:

1) There are two basic types of colors in photography: the additive primaries, red, green, and blue and the subtractive primaries, yellow, cyan, and magenta.

2) Never have all three subtractive primary colors in the printing filter pack at the same time.

3) For our purpose here, red is made up of yellow and magenta, blue consists of magenta and cyan, and green is made up of equal parts of cyan and yellow.

4) Each of these six colors has an exact opposite color called its complementary color. Cyan's complementary color is red, yellow's complementary is blue, and magenta's complementary is green.

5) Always try to use only yellow and magenta filters in the printing filter pack whenever possible.

6) Filter density values are additive. If you need 25M filtration you can get it by adding a 20M filter and a 5M filter. Similarly, a 40R filtration is obtained by using a 40Y filter in combination with a 40M filter.

Now on to the examples. Let's say that you have compared your print to the ring-around and found that your No. 2 image is very close in density to the *perfect* print at the center of the ring-around. Your enlarger lens' largest opening is *f*/2.8 so you know that the No. 2 image was made at *f*/4 with a ten-second exposure. You used no filters other than a heat-absorbing glass and a CP2B (or alternatively, a 301A and a Wratten 2E). You have compared your No. 2 image to the original transparency and to the examples of color cast problems in the ring-around and decided that your No. 2 image looks as if it has the same kind of color cast as those in the ring-around which illustrate +*MAGENTA* values do. You follow the *YES* arrow down from the *IS PRINT TOO MAGENTA?* decision box to the

instruction box below it, which tells you to *USE RING-AROUND TO DETERMINE DENSITY OF COLOR CORRECTION NEEDED*. To follow this instruction you simply compare your No. 2 image with +*10*, +*20*, and +*40 MAGENTA* illustrations to decide which one its overall magenta cast most closely resembles. Let's say that you find that your No. 2 image looks pretty much the way the +*40 MAGENTA* one does. Follow the arrow from the instruction box down into the next decision box which asks you *IS THE PROBLEM COLOR IN THE PACK?* You had no color filters whatsoever in the pack, so you answer to this query is no. Leaving the decision box by the *NO* arrow brings you to an instruction box which tells you to *ADD EQUAL AMOUNTS OF BOTH OTHER SUBTRACTIVE PRIMARIES TO THE FILTER PACK*. To comply you simply add 40C and 40Y to the printing filter pack and move on to the next instruction box which tells you to *CORRECT PRINTING EXPOSURE FOR THE NEW FILTER PACK COMPOSITION AND REPRINT*. To comply with this instruction you refer to table 4-3 on p. 4-24, where you find that adding a 40C filter calls for a 90 percent increase in printing exposure and adding a 40Y filter calls for an additional 10 percent exposure time. Now you know everything you need to know to be able to reprint another four images with the color-corrected printing filter pack. Your new pack will still have the heat-absorbing glass and CP2B (or 301A and 2E) but now you will also include 40C +40Y. Your new approximate printing exposure will be at *f*/4 with 100 percent more time than your original exposure, or 20 seconds instead of 10 seconds. Use the four exposures on the reprinted sheet to bracket the one that you determined from the approximate values shown in table 4-3. Make all of your exposures at 20 seconds but make No. 1 with an *f*/2.8 lens opening, No. 2 with *f*/4, No. 3 with *f*/5.6 and No. 4 with *f*/8. Process and dry the resulting test print and reenter the evaluation chart at *A* to determine how good a correction job you did. If your second set of test images is still not right, just run through the appropriate sections of the chart again and make a third test. Keep on going until you make a perfect print.

You should note that you can also use the multiple image test procedure to bracket color changes as well as density changes. You may, for example, want to print a set of four test images, each one with 5 more yellow filtration than the last, to accurately determine the effect of small filtration changes. You can even combine filter and exposure variation both in the same set of four test images, but make sure to keep an accurate data sheet if you do this type of test image making, (a sample data sheet is shown on p. 4-28).

Let's look at another hypothetical printing situation. Suppose you had made your print with a 10C + 15Y pack and found that one of your four test images had the right density but looked as if it was 20 too yellow. You have to exit the *IS THE PROBLEM COLOR IN THE PACK?* decision box along the *YES* arrow to the instruction box which tells you to *SUBTRACT THE PROBLEM COLOR FROM THE FILTER PACK.* But since you only have 15Y in the pack and the needed correction is 20Y, you find that you have to exit from the next decision box, which asks *IS IT NECESSARY TO REDUCE THE PROBLEM COLOR TO ZERO?* along the *YES* arrow. You are then confronted by another decision box which asks *IS THE NEEDED CORRECTION COMPLETE?* The answer to that, of course, is no, and following the *NO* arrow you reach an instruction box that tells you to *ADD EQUAL AMOUNTS OF BOTH OTHER SUBTRACTIVE PRIMARIES TO THE FILTER PACK.* Completing the needed correction calls for another 5M and 5C to be added to make the new printing pack 15C + 5M.

It is interesting to note that the printing exposure time correction called for by this pack change would be minus 20 percent for the yellow filters subtracted (minus 10 percent for each filter removed from the pack), plus 25 percent for the magenta filter added and plus 10 percent for the cyan filter added, for a net change of plus 15 percent of the original exposure time.

If you find that your print exhibits a color cast resembling one of three additive primary colors, the rules for filter-pack corrections differ somewhat. Once you determine what the problem color is, the first decision box you encounter asks you *IS PROBLEM COLOR'S COMPLEMENTARY IN THE PACK?* Suppose that you had printed with a 10C + 10Y pack and found that your print was 20 too blue. You would leave the

decision box along the *YES* line to enter an instruction box telling you to *ADD THE PROBLEM COLOR'S COMPLEMENTARY TO THE FILTER PACK.* Your new pack then would be 10C + 30Y, and you would have to increase your printing time by ten percent to accommodate the change.

If you had printed with a 10C + 20Y pack, and found that your print was 40 too green you would have to leave the *IS THE PROBLEM COLOR'S COMPLEMENTARY IN THE PACK?* along the *NO* line to enter another decision box asking *ARE BOTH OTHER SUBTRACTIVE PRIMARIES IN THE PACK?* You would leave this box by way of the *YES* line to an instruction box telling you to *REMOVE EQUAL AMOUNTS OF BOTH OTHER SUBTRACTIVE PRIMARIES FROM THE FILTER PACK.* All you can get out of this particular pack in equal amounts is 10C and 10Y so that when you leave the next decision box which asks *IS IT NECESSARY TO REDUCE ONE OR BOTH COLORS TO ZERO?* you would exit along the *YES* arrow to be asked *IS THE NEEDED CORRECTION COMPLETE?* The answer to that is obviously no, and following the *NO* arrow brings you to an instruction box that tells you to *ADD THE PROBLEM COLOR'S COMPLEMENTARY TO THE FILTER PACK.* You complete the needed correction by adding 30M to the pack which makes your new printing filter pack 10Y + 30M. The exposure correction called for is minus 25 percent for the 10C filter pulled, minus 10 percent for the 10Y filter pulled, plus 50 percent for a 20M filter added, and plus another 25 percent for a 10M filter added to bring the pack to the requisite 30 density. The net change in printing exposure time is plus 40 percent of exposure time.

I'm sure that you are as dizzy from going around the evaluation chart's loops as I am, and since we have followed almost every possible path, it is time to move on to greater things. I mentioned earlier in this section that you would need more information to be able to go from the small 3″ × 4½″ test-image size to greater magnifications. You will find a simple method for doing so in the *"Magnification and Exposure Time"* section of this chapter.

Magnification and Exposure Time

If you go into your darkroom, turn on your enlarger lamp, open the lens diaphragm to its

widest setting, and focus the machine to get an unfiltered image of your empty 35mm negative carrier that measures 3½″ × 5¼″ on the baseboard, that little 18⅜ square-inch rectangle of light is going to be rather bright. Now, if you change the enlarger's head height so that the focused image on the baseboard of the empty carrier is 8″ × 12″, but leave the lens opening just as it was, you will be able to see that the 96″ square-inch rectangle of light on the baseboard is considerably dimmer than the 18⅜ square-inch one was. There should really be no mystery about why this is so. Just consider that the same enlarger lamp has its light output concentrated on 18⅜ square inches in the first case, and then has that identical amount of light output spread out over 96 square inches in the second. The amount of light available from the lamp doesn't change. It is just that it has to be spread a lot more "thinly" to cover 96 square inches than it does to cover 18⅜ square inches. The "thinner" the light is spread, the dimmer it appears.

Now, if you can see that the light intensity decreases as you raise the enlarger's head height to spread the light out more, it should come as no shock to you to learn that you will have to give more exposure time to a print made at 8× than one made at 3½×.

You can compare these two different printing exposures under the enlarger's lens to filling up two different size containers with water from a garden hose. If the hose nozzle is left at the same setting, maintaining a constant water flow, it will obviously take more time to fill a gallon container than it will to fill a quart bottle. So it is with the enlarger. If you have a fixed amount of light coming from the enlarger lens it will take longer for that light to expose 96 square inches than it will to expose 18⅜ square inches both to the same level of exposure.

It isn't difficult to determine how much of a time increase is required for any particular change in magnification that you may choose. All it will take is a pencil and paper and a moment or two. However, all of you who have electronic pocket calculators will be delighted to learn that, here at last, is something you can use the machine for.

You can determine the change in printing exposure time required for a change in enlarger head height, either up or down, by using the following formula to approximate the data available from the Kodak Color-Printing Computer:

$$T_2 = T_1 \times \frac{(X_2)^2}{(X_1)^2}$$

$T_2 =$ the new printing exposure time for the same lens opening as was used for the properly exposed print.

$T_1 =$ the exposure time used to make the properly exposed print.

$X_2 =$ the magnification used for the new print.

$X_1 =$ the magnification used for the properly exposed print.

In case you don't know what the figure two is doing at the top of the right side of the parentheses surrounding the X's, it simply means that the number inside the parenthesis is to be squared. To square a number, you multiply it by itself. For example:

$$(9)^2 = 9 \times 9 = 81.$$

That's all there is to it.

Okay, now let's look at a few practical examples that can be expected to occur if you decide to make a larger print of the standard negative or slide you have been working with. Up until now you have worked with a focused image size of 3½″ × 5¼″ measured on the enlarger's baseboard. As I explained earlier, because a 35mm negative carrier has an opening the dimensions of which are approximately 1″ × 1½″, the magnification you have been using is equal to approximately 3½×. Now you know the value of X_1 in the equation. Let's assume that you have decided to fill up an 8″ × 10″ sheet of printing paper with the image. The first thing to do is to set your easel for an 8″ × 10″ print, less whatever border you intend to use, of course. Then with your negative or slide in the enlarger, raise the head height and focus the image until you get the cropping and composition you want within the easel's borders. Since you have painted your easel black, you will have to use a focusing sheet on the easel in order to be able to see what you are doing. Once you have the image sized and accurately focused, lock the enlarger's head and lens stage, if your enlarger offers provisions to do so, and remove your easel from the enlarger's baseboard. Use a ruler to measure the short dimension of the image being projected on the baseboard. Let's say in this case it is 8¾ inches. Turn off the enlarger lamp, turn on the darkroom lights, get your pencil and paper, or your calculator, and you can now determine what exposure time is needed to make the larger print. Only one more piece of information is needed, though, before you can begin the calculation, that is the original printing time. Let's say that after three trips through the print evaluation chart your No. 3 image came out perfectly with an exposure time of six seconds through an $f/8$ lens opening. Now you have all the data you need to calculate your new printing time. You know that T_1 is equal to six seconds, that X_1 is equal to 3½, and that X_2 equals 8¾. Plug all of these values into our simple formula as follows:

$$T_2 = 6 \times \frac{(8.75)^2}{(3.5)^2}$$

and calculate to determine that:

$$T_2 = 6 \times \frac{8.75 \times 8.75}{3.5 \times 3.5} = 6 \times \frac{76.56}{12.25} = 37.5 \text{ sec.}$$

There now, that wasn't too bad was it?

This simple formula is satisfactory for situations where the same lens opening will be maintained for the second exposure and where the ratio of X_2 to X_1 does not exceed about three (for example if X_1 is 4×, then this simple formula will be satisfactory to use with an X_2 of up to 12×, etc.).

Beyond this size ratio, the effects of refocusing and of reciprocity (nonlinear response of the paper's emulsion to varying levels of light intensity) will introduce an unacceptably high margin of error into this simple calculation. To calculate new exposure times for gross size changes you will have to use the Kodak Color-Printing Computer (the use of the device for this purpose is covered elsewhere in the book).

Before leaving this subject I do want to point out one additional pitfall. Let's assume you have made a test print at 3½× and you want to make a 10× enlargement. If your initial printing time at $f/11$ was 13 seconds, your new printing time, according to the formula, will be 106 seconds. That is an awfully long exposure and it is one that includes an error of about 12 percent (an exposure of about 119 seconds is called for to account for reciprocity) which is easily tolerable. But if the exposure time is reduced by the simple old black-and-white darkroom rule of thumb that says that for each stop you open up the lens you can decrease the exposure time by one half, you will find that if you go much further than one stop with it you will pick up even greater and, therefore, unacceptable exposure time errors. For example, if you choose to reduce the printing time from 106 seconds at $f/11$ to 26.5 seconds at $f/5.6$ by that handy rule of thumb, you would introduce an exposure error of about 26 percent (the reciprocity-adjusted exposure called for at $f/5.6$ is 21 seconds) and that level of exposure error will show up in a print. However, if you do limit the use of this old rule of thumb to one stop, you will remain within an acceptable margin of exposure time error. In this case rule of thumb calls for an exposure of 53 seconds at $f/8$ while the reciprocity-compensated exposure time called for is 50.5 seconds (in this instance the error is actually reduced from 12 percent to only 5 percent).

Chapter 5

Color Print Evaluation and Correction

Understanding Color Print Evaluation Problems

Being able to correct color-printing filter-pack problems by means of the Color Print Evaluation Charts in the previous chapter is in no way indicative of your understanding of the process you are engaged in. Those charts are designed to eliminate any need for comprehension and to allow anyone who is able to read to perform the required tasks just the way a computer would—with a total lack of appreciation for what is really involved in the process. The sole aim of this chapter is to finally convince you that a color print is made up of only three layers of dye, and that those dye layers are always made up of the same three subtractive primary colors, placed in the same order, and formed in response to the paper's exposure to the three additive primary colors. When you habitually think of all color prints as nothing more than collections of three layers of dye (aesthetics aside, of course), you will have no trouble analyzing and correcting color printing problems, with your own two eyes and the gray matter that lies behind them.

Light Sources For Viewing Color Prints Under Evaluation

When you have exposed, processed, and dried a color print you have reached one of the trickiest stages of the color printing process. Now you have to, somehow, determine if the print you have made has been made properly.

There are two basic ways to undertake that task. You can use the incredibly fine set of transducers and the unbelievably swift and accurate computer nature has provided you with—your eyes and your brain—or you can invest a great deal of money in a cranky kind of instrument called a reflection densitometer to perform the eyes' function; but, even with this instrument, in the end you will have to depend on your brain for guidance. Since this book is being written for amateur printers, and since I really dislike *all kinds* of instrumentation in the darkroom, I'm going to completely ignore the expensive reflection densitometer, and only discuss the use of human eyes and brains to evaluate color prints.

Before you can begin to evaluate any kind of color print you will have to be able to see it. You will need light, and that's where the fun starts. The colors you see in a color print depend on the color of your viewing light source, and light sources are most definitely not all the same. If you have ever bought clothing or a home furnishing in a shop equipped with flourescent lights, and then gotten home to where you burn incandescent lamps, looked at your purchase, and scratched your head in wonder over how you could have selected anything with such an awful color, you will appreciate just what I mean.

Flourescent light is *emotionally* "colder" than incandescent light. Things viewed under incandescent lamps also seem somehow "warmer" than things viewed by the light coming in through a window on the north side of a building (in North America). Confusing, isn't it? It is even more confusing to learn that the "cold" light of flourescent lamps and of the northern sky is, in reality, much hotter than the "warm" light coming from a relatively cool incandescent lamp.

The explanation for all of this confusing nomenclature is fairly simple. North American people like to think of "warm" colors as those they see in cozy (but not very hot) wood fires— yellows and reds. They also choose to think of "cold" colors in terms of the pale blues and blue-greens seen in ice and snow. Emotionally, this kind of human psychological color-temperature scale is easy to understand, but unfortunately, in the physical world, things are a mite different.

If you heat a piece of metal in a very hot fire, it will soon begin to glow—first a dull red, then as the temperature of the metal increases, the brightness of the glow also increases and changes in color to a pale yellow. As the temperature is increased still further, the color of the glowing metal our eyes perceive will change to blue. Your eyes will *perceive* the "warm" colors at much *lower* physical temperatures than they will the "cool" ones.

Now, with all of that out of the way, we can begin to decide on what kind of light source to use to view our color prints. There is no one answer. The best single answer is to use a light source to evaluate your prints that is identical to the one the prints will always be finally viewed by. For instance, if you are making color prints that will be displayed in the interior of a building and illuminated entirely by incandescent spot lights (not at all an unusual situation), then you should use one of the same spot lights to evaluate your prints.

Ah, but life is seldom so simple. Most of us make color prints that must be viewed under a wide variety of lighting conditions, ranging from a mixture of flourescent tubes (not all flourescent lamps are the same) to a mixture of flourescent and incandescent illumination, to a mixture of daylight and incandescent light. There is absolutely no way that you can duplicate any of these peculiar mixtures in your print evaluation area. So for prints that will be seen under a variety of circumstances, perhaps the best thing you can do is to pick one standard light source, essentially at random, and stick with it, if only to simplify your life.

Just bear in mind, however, that your finished prints will look very different in all of the several light sources mentioned. You may repeat the experience of finding out that you bought a suit that's a horrible color even though it looked just fine in the clothing store, when you finally emerge from your darkroom and hang your print up on your living room wall.

Kodak recommends, and I often use, flourescent lamps manufactured by General Electric, Westinghouse, or Sylvania under the designations of Deluxe Cool White. The former two manufacturers also produce a Living White-Type lamp that is satisfactory. All of these lamps have a color temperature of about 4000 K.

There are times, however, when I prefer to use a 3200 K floodlamp in a bowl reflector with a piece of white fiberglass cloth in front of it for my viewing light source. Prints viewed under the flourescent lamps will appear slightly "cooler" (bluer) than those seen under the "warmer" (redder) floodlight. In the unlikely, and very undesirable (color prints fade quickly in direct sunlight), event that your color prints will be viewed out of doors, you can obtain 5600 K flourescent lamps, which approximate the color temperature of daylight, from Macbeth Color & Photometry, P.O. Box 950, Little Britain Rd., Newburg, New York 12550.

And, finally, depending on just how your eyes and your mind perceive color, you may decide to use some mixture of all of the above, or to add one or more standard household incandescent lamps to any of the above, or simply to ignore everything mentioned and use an ordinary 100 watt incandescent bulb to do the job. It is really up to you; but just as in everything else you do in color printing, always try to be consistent. Try to use the same light source the same way to do as much of your print evaluation as possible.

Determining Print Density

Density is the very first quality to be judged in a color print. There are several factors that enter into this judgement. At first thought, it might seem as if it would always be best to produce a print with an overall density as closely approximating the subject's original illumination level as possible, but actually this is often not the case. Color prints, just like black-and-white ones have certain aesthetic properties all their own. This is rather difficult to illustrate, but perhaps the following example will help. Experienced photographers often deliberately overrate their color transparency film's speed by about ½ stop to get more density and color saturation into a scene. Similarly, experienced color printers will often deliberately underexpose a reversal image or overexpose a negative-to-positive image on the enlarger's easel to achieve similar effects.

One problem with the aforementioned example is that not all color printers are experienced. Another is that even the most experienced color printers often have a hard time previsualizing the effects of varying print densities. If you fall into either of these categories perhaps your best bet will be to make several different test exposures for each image to be printed, and then compare them side by side. ("The Making Multiple Test Prints On A Simple Easel" section of Chapter 4 offers a relatively simple and painless procedure for making four full-frame—from 35mm size negatives or positives—images on the same sheet of 8" × 10" printing paper.)

Where aesthetics aren't the main consideration, but technical accuracy of a negative-to-positive print is, you will have to make sure that some easily evaluated item is included in the frame to be printed, along with the rest of the subject matter. The most useful single such item would be a gray scale, but the combination of a gray scale, an 18 percent gray card, and a set of color bars, will go a long way toward helping you get the print density to be as close a representation of the original scene as it is possible to produce. Print density can most easily be judged by observing how closely the density wedges reproduced on the print match the corresponding densities of the wedges on the gray scale you photographed.

For initial gross print-density evaluation, ignore color casts. Printing exposure time should be adjusted to the minimum level that will produce a solid black at one end of the gray scale and a barely textured white at the other, with the wedges in between these two extremes clearly differentiated from each other.

When technical accuracy is the most important criterion of a positive-to-positive print, keep in mind that you can't, under any circumstances, obtain a *perfect* match between a print, which is illuminated by reflection, and a slide, which is transilluminated. Really, it just can't be done, so don't knock yourself out trying.

And, while it may seem painfully obvious to many, I'm sure it is not uncalled for here to remind all the rest of you forgetful color printers that when printing from a negative, you increase printing exposure (open up the lens diaphragm, or increase the exposure time, or both) to increase the resulting print's density. But, when printing directly from a slide, you do just the opposite (close down the lens diaphragm, or decrease the exposure time, or both) to increase print density.

It's important that you decide on the print density you need before going on to evaluate the print from the standpoint of color balance, because the color balance of the print will be effected in the process of adjusting its density. *Get the print to at least within ½ stop of the density you consider to be appropriate for it before you go on to make any color-balance corrections.* Gross initial print-density changes will be entirely controlled by printing exposure, either through changing the lens aperture or adjusting the printing time. Such changes won't involve any modification of the printing filter pack at all.

A Graphic Method of Print Color-Balance Notation

Before going further into color print evaluation, I have constructed a simple notation system to help define, analyze, and correct color-balance problems in prints (see page 5–4, first graphic).

The leftmost column of the accompanying graphic provides the additive primary colors to which the paper's three emulsion layers, represented by the four horizontal lines at the right, are sensitive during the printing exposure on the enlarger's easel. The middle column of information provides the subtractive primary colors of the dyes that will form in these layers after the exposed paper is processed and dried.

COLOR PRINTING PAPER		
Sensitive to (on easel)	**Dye Color (after development)**	
Red	Cyan	_____
Green	Magenta	_____
Blue	Yellow	_____

That arrangement is a bit clumsy for repetitive use, so I've shortened it to this:

Sen.	Dye	
R	C	_____
G	M	_____
B	Y	_____

Now that we have a simple graphic outline to draw, let's begin by illustrating a section of a print that should appear medium gray:

Sen.	Dye	Medium Gray
R	C	///////////////////////////
G	M	///////////////////////////
B	Y	///////////////////////////

The slashes in each of the three dye layers indicates that there are equal amounts of a moderate density of dye in each of the three dye layers on the paper. All three subtractive primaries, viewed over a single source of white light, will yield neutral density (shades of gray).

If white light passes through equal amounts of only a very low density of all three of the subtractive primary color dyes, then only a small amount of neutral density will result and we will see a very light gray. This situation is illustrated as follows:

Sen.	Dye	Light Gray
R	C	///////////////////////
G	M	///////////////////////
B	Y	///////////////////////

Using the same system, dark gray is shown as follows:

Sen.	Dye	Dark Gray
R	C	XXXXXXXXXXXXXXXXXXXX /
G	M	XXXXXXXXXXXXXXXXXXXX /
B	Y	XXXXXXXXXXXXXXXXXXXX /

And, finally, if white light passes through equal amounts of a high density of all three of the subtractive primaries, a great deal of neutral density will result and we will see black. This situation is illustrated by the following:

Sen.	Dye	Black
R	C	XXXXXXXXXXXXXXXXXXXX XXXXXXXXXXXXXXXXXXXX
G	M	XXXXXXXXXXXXXXXXXXXX XXXXXXXXXXXXXXXXXXXX
B	Y	XXXXXXXXXXXXXXXXXXXX XXXXXXXXXXXXXXXXXXXX

By now you should have a good idea of how this little system of notation works. The slashes in each of the paper layers graphically represents the density of the dye in each layer.

Just as an aside, for those of you who may have forgotten why neutral density is formed when white light is passed through all three subtractive primaries, it is because each of the subtractive primaries does just what its name implies, it subtracts its complementary color from the white light. White light is composed of equal parts of red, green, and blue light. Since cyan subtracts red, magenta subtracts green, and yellow subtracts blue, it shouldn't take too much imagination to visualize the white light growing progressively dimmer and seen as darker and darker shades of gray, as it has to pass through more and more dense layers of the three subtractive primary color dyes. Finally, when the subtractive primary dye layers reach sufficient density, they will manage to absorb all of the additive primary components of the white light and the surface of the print will appear to be black; black of course, being the total absence of light.

All of that is well and good, but what I haven't yet gotten into is how you can use this simple graphic to help you to evaluate what is wrong with your color prints. To do that I will have to provide you with a few more examples of off-color prints. But before I do I want to point out that all of the color-evaluation data offered here will be based on gray. By that I mean that the area of a print to be evaluated will always be that which should reproduce a clean, repeatable gray color. I fully realize that many subjects do not include anything that is gray in color, and that this can cause a problem at times, but I will offer ways out of that dilemma later. As for any instructions you may have ever read for the evaluation of color prints by observation of "flesh tones," I can only wish you well in following them. Perhaps the best way to convince you that it is literally impossible to balance a print around flesh tones is to suggest that you take a walk along a crowded street and observe the colors seen in different people's faces. Forget the obvious differences, such as those which black, brown, yellow, and red people provide, and just regard the multitude of differences found among Caucasian complexions. After you have observed for about five minutes I believe you will agree with me that all procedures of color print evaluation based on the color of human flesh are very subjective.

Okay, now back to good old basic gray. It is very usable because almost every photographer owns an 18 percent gray card. There is one in the Kodak *Color Dataguide,* and also one in their Kodak *Professional Photoguide,* or 18 percent gray cards can be purchased individually in any camera store worthy of the name. If you take a picture of your own 18 percent gray card and then compare a print of that shot to the card

itself, you may notice some of the following problems:

Sen.	Dye	Cyanish Gray
R	C	
G	M	
B	Y	

The cyanish-gray print appears so because more of the red component of white light is absorbed, by the more abundant cyan dye, than the green or blue components are by the magenta and yellow dye layers, respectively. Reference to Chaper 2 will remind you that green and blue are seen as the color cyan.

Sen.	Dye	Magentaish Gray
R	C	
G	M	
B	Y	

Similarly, magentaish gray is seen here because more of the green component is being removed from the white viewing light than are its red and blue components. Red and blue, of course, are seen as magenta.

Sen.	Dye	Yellowish Gray
R	C	
G	M	
B	Y	

A yellowish-gray color is seen where an overabundance of yellow dye absorbs more blue light than the balanced magenta and cyan dye layers absorb of the green and red components of white light. Strange as it may seem, your eyes (and brain) are fooled into seeing a mixture of green and red light as yellow.

Sen.	Dye	Bluish Gray
R	C	XXXXXXXXXXXXXXXXXXXXXX ////////////////////////
G	M	XXXXXXXXXXXXXXXXXXXX ////////////////////////
B	Y	/////////////////////////// ////////////////////////

Sen.	Dye	Reddish Gray
R	C	////////////////////////// ////////////////////////
G	M	XXXXXXXXXXXXXXXXXXXX '////////////////////////
B	Y	<XXXXXXXXXXXXXXXXXXX> ////////////////////////

Bluish gray is seen here because the more abundant cyan and magenta dyes remove more of the red and green components of white light than the weaker yellow dye does of the blue light. Since there is more blue light left to reach your eye, your view will be of blue-tinted gray.

Sen.	Dye	Greenish Gray
R	C	XXXXXXXXXXXXXXXXXXXXXXX ////////////////////////
G	M	//////////////////////// ////////////////////////
B	Y	<XXXXXXXXXXXXXXXXXXXX. '////////////////////////

In this situation the yellow and cyan dye layers are stronger than the magenta layer. This results in more green reaching your eye than red and blue, so that a greenish gray is seen.

In this example of a problem color cast we can see that the magenta and yellow dye layers are stronger than the cyan dye layer. This means that more green and blue than red light will be subtracted from the white viewing light, and this will cause you to see a reddish-gray print.

These several simple black-and-white graphics have clearly depicted most of the color printing problems you can reasonably expect to encounter. When you are confronted with a color-balance situation that confuses you, simply sit down and draw a simple graphic representation of just what it is that you are looking at. Once you do, you should have no further difficulty in understanding the nature of your problem. I will make use of these graphics in later sections where specific examples of how to solve various color printing problems are offered.

How Viewing Filters Work and How to Use Them

We've just been discussing color prints in the best of all possible terms—as images formed on a collection of three separate dye layers. If you had no difficulty dealing with that, you will have no problem in understanding that *a viewing filter is nothing more than a fourth layer of dye, external to the print.*

Let's go back to our simple graphic representing a bluish-gray print:

Sen.	Dye	
R	C	XXXXXXXXXXXXXXXXXXXXX ////////////////////////
G	M	XXXXXXXXXXXXXXXXXX ////////////////////////
B	Y	//////////////////////// ////////////////////////

It shows that there is greater dye density in the cyan and magenta dye layers than there is in the yellow one. If you are a sufficiently experienced printer you may be able to tell, just by looking at such a print, that an area which you know should be a clean gray has, instead, a bluish-gray appearance. If you are able to do that by eye and memory alone, you should also be able to remember that this particular color imbalance is brought about by the presence of too little dye in the print's yellow dye layer (or, conversely, too much dye in its magenta and cyan dye layers). However, until you do reach the point where you are able to make such determinations based on long and hard experience, you will only be able to look at such a print and realize that *something* is wrong with it. But, chances are, you won't really have the foggiest notion of what the color imbalance that's troubling you is, or what to do about it. This is where viewing filters can come to your rescue.

Suppose that you were looking at the troublesome bluish-gray print when, lo and behold, a yellow viewing filter popped up between your eye and the print. Using the graphic helper, the scene might be represented as follows:

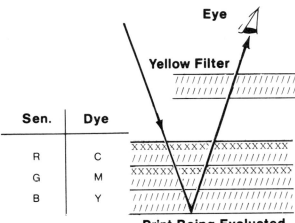

Print Being Evaluated

The arrow entering from above and to the left of the print represents a single ray of white light. The light ray passes through each of the print's three dye layers once on its way to the paper's white reflective base (which I have omitted from this little drawing for the sake of clarity). Then it bounces off the paper base and makes a second pass through each of the three dye layers as it emerges from the print (looking very bluish because of the lack of dye in the print's yellow dye layer). However, the light ray now encounters yet another layer of yellow dye, which it must traverse on its way to your strategically placed eye. What a wonder to behold! Our little bluish light ray is bluish no more. Passing through the extra layer of yellow dye has brought our little ray of light back to a nice, clean, gray color, by absorbing the extra blue from it. So now we all know exactly how a viewing filter works. Right? Right!

The proper way to use viewing filters is to flick them quickly into and out of your line of sight, between your eye and the surface of the print, until you notice that one seems to remove or reduce the problem color cast. When so used, a viewing filter of the proper color to correct your problem will cause the area of your print that you know should appear to be a clean gray to, indeed, begin to appear that way. All bets are off, though, if you decide to just interpose a viewing filter

between your eyes and the print and then just hold it there motionless for a while. The problem with this procedure is that the brain, given sufficient uninterrupted time to perform, will cause you to perceive whatever color it is that you really want to see, regardless of the color of the viewing filter you are looking through. Your mind doesn't do this sort of thing because it has anything against viewing filters. It does it because it is trying to keep you from being uncomfortable. The flicking motion, then, is used to prevent your brain from having enough time to provide its well meant, but hard to deal with, accommodation.

If you can avoid it, you shouldn't just start flicking viewing filters at random. Instead, you should have a plan of attack. Before you even pick up viewing filter number one, you should *try* to identify, by memory, guess, or comparison to a ring-around (we'll get to ring-arounds a little later), just what the color imbalance is. Once you *think* you know what the problem color is, draw the same kind of a sketch that I have been using to graphically represent it. If you are able to do this, your selection of viewing filters will be greatly simplified, because you will be able to *see* exactly which layers of dye need reinforcement with external viewing filters.

However, if you can't figure out what the problem color in your print is before you reach for the viewing filters, don't feel in the least bit embarrassed. It happens all the time to the best of us. In that case you just run through the flicking procedure with all six of the primary colored filters, until you note some color improvement. Then, once you know what the color problem is, you can begin to get a line on how dye density is involved. But I'm getting a little bit ahead of myself here.

Let's take a look at another possible way to use a viewing filter. Supposing we take a look at a portion of a print that should be gray, but instead seems to have a very strong color cast. It looks like the following:

Sen.	Dye	
R	C	`'/////////////////////////////` `'/////////////////////////////`
G	M	`X X X X X X X X X X X X X X X X X X X` `X X X X X X X X X X X X X X X X X X X`
B	Y	`/////////////////////////////` `/////////////////////////////`

This time the filter won't just pop up, though. We'll have to find out for ourselves what the problem color is. The way we do this is easy, but not quite simple. The first thing you will need is a set of viewing filters. One is to be found bound right into the Kodak *Color Dataguide*. Another set is right in your darkroom. You can use your printing filters to view through. To make filters in the three additive primaries this way you will have to use two subtractive primary color filters held together (red = yellow + magenta, green = cyan + yellow, blue = cyan + magenta), which is a bother, but it's a lot cheaper than going out and buying a special set of viewing filters, such as the excellent one that's sold by Kodak.

In the example under consideration you know that the print has two dye layers that have a normal dye density (cyan and yellow) and one dye layer that is abnormally strong (magenta). You also know that the complementary color of magenta is green. Let's assume, just for the hell of it, that you are using your acetate color printing (CP) filters as viewing filters. This being the case you won't have any green viewing filter, but instead, you will have two equally dense filters that will yield the working equivalent of a green filter. Let's, therefore, take a 20Y and a 20C filter and hold them above our magentaish print to see if they are able to correct the problem. Doing so would look like the graphic below.

Since this is my example, I've decided that the 20G filter equivalent you've made is just not strong enough to get rid of the light ray's magenta cast entirely with the light ray making only one pass through the viewing filter. But, I'm not really a cruel person, so I'll show you how to use that same 20G equivalent filter to fully correct the print. Just lay it down on the print surface so the little light ray has to make two passes through it. That way the light ray loses some red and some blue on its way into the print and some more on its way out. You double the effectiveness of the viewing filter by placing it flat down on the print as shown in the graphic on the following page.

Now you know everything you need to know about the mechanics of how viewing filters are used to evaluate prints, but you haven't got the foggiest idea of what to do with the information because I haven't as yet discussed printing filter packs. This then, would seem like a logical place to start; but before I can, I will have to leave the subject of viewing filters momentarily to describe how printing filters operate. Once I've gotten that chore out of the way, I can tie the two subjects together and explain how you can use viewing filters not only to analyze what is wrong with color prints, but also to produce specific instructions on how to arrive at a new printing filter pack that will eliminate the problems.

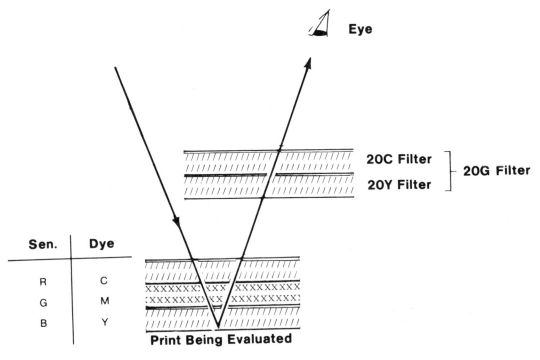

Sen.	Dye
R	C
G	M
B	Y

Print Being Evaluated

20C Filter
20Y Filter
20G Filter

Eye

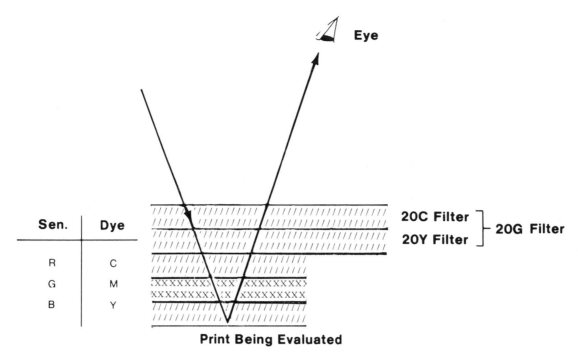

Eye

Sen.	Dye
R	C
G	M
B	Y

20C Filter
20Y Filter ⎤ **20G Filter**

Print Being Evaluated

How Color Printing Filters Work

All color printing filters modify the properties of the light used to expose color printing paper. It makes no difference if your filters are dichroic, acetate (CP's), gelatin (CC's), subtractive (cyan, magenta, and yellow), or additive (red, blue, and green); their purpose is simply to adjust the spectral energy content of the enlarger lamp's output to suit the requirements of the negative or positive you intend to print and the particular sheet of paper you intend to expose.

Negative-to-Positive Printing Filtration

Let's take a look at a typical negative-to-positive printing situation to begin to understand how these pieces of colored plastic or coated glass do their jobs. In order to do so, I am going to use the same sort of simple graphic presentation that I did when I explained how viewing filters work. The illustration that follows consists of two sections: the upper one representing the color printing filters used in the enlarger; the lower one depicting a portion of the print that should have been a clean gray as a result of the exposure.

Note that I have omitted the IR and UV filters from the illustration. While these filters serve the same purposes as the others, they are never varied during printing but, instead, always

remain in the enlarger lamp's light path. Since they would always appear the same way in every diagram, and only add to the clutter and confusion, I won't bother to show them in any of the illustrations that follow. To further simplify all the following illustrative filter-pack diagrams, I have shown only two filters in the printing filter pack. By representing the pack this way, I don't mean to imply that only two filters (plus the IR and UV filters, of course) can ever be physically present in the pack, but only that it is a lot easier to draw the pack as shown on the next page.

This drawing illustrates a situation in which a color-printing filter pack consisting of 50M and 80Y was used to produce a color print that shows a definite cyan color cast. For the purpose of this example, the print has been made from a color negative and the area under evaluation should have been a clean middle gray. (The printing filter pack was made up of a 40M + 10M + 40Y + 40Y, but was shown as only two filters for clarity.)

Looking at the bottom section of the illustration, it is simple to see that the print's color-cast problem lies with an excess of cyan dye density. The diagram also shows that the color of light, which the problem dye layer is sensitive to during exposure, is red. The top section of the diagram tells us that neither of the filters in the

COLORS CONTROLLED

Exposure Light	Print Dye		Filter Densities	
G	M	/////////////	50M	**Printing Filter Pack**
B	Y	XXXXXXXXXXX	80Y	

Sensitive To	Dye Color			
R	C	XXXXXXXXXXXX		**Printing Paper**
G	M	/////////////		
B	Y	/////////////		

pack controls red light. Since having more than two of the subtractive primary colors in the printing filter pack is to be avoided, (doing so just creates neutral density in the pack and slows down the printing), the only way we can correct the color balance of this print is to increase the dye density of the print's magenta and yellow layers. Since we lack cyan filters in the pack, and are working with a pack that already contains two subtractive primaries, we can't reduce the density of the cyan dye layer. Let's also say we have determined that the amount of excess dye density in the print's cyan dye layer is 20. That being the case, it will be necessary to increase the density of the magenta and yellow dye layers by 20 to bring all three layers of dye back into balance, so that they will produce a clean gray color. Achieving that is really quite simple to do.

If you check the top section of the diagram you will see that the magenta filters in the printing filter pack control the enlarger's output of green light, and that the yellow filters control its blue light output. Reference to the bottom section of the diagram shows that the more green light the print gets during exposure, the more magenta dye it will have after processing. Similarly, the more blue light the print gets during exposure, the more yellow dye will be formed after processing. To get more magenta and yellow dye into the print, therefore, we will have to provide the print with more green and blue light during exposure. To get more green and blue

light out of the enlarger, we will have to remove magenta and yellow filters from the printing filter pack. If we want to increase the yellow and magenta dye density in the print by 20, we have to remove 20Y and 20M from the printing filter pack. If we do so, our new printing filter pack will be 30M + 60Y. That's all there is to it. The new pack and the resulting print will look like the drawing at the top of the following page.

Positive-to-Positive Printing Filtration

The effects of varying the printing filter pack in reversal printing are somewhat harder to illustrate than they are in the negative-to-positive process. To show these effects in reversal printing, I will have to represent the printing paper at two stages: one showing the effects of exposure on the three emulsion layers; the second illustrating the dye formed in those layers after all reversal processing has been completed and the print is dry and ready to be viewed

Let's look at a situation in which a reversal print is made with a 10M + 10C printing filter pack; a section of the print that should appear as a clean gray shows a definite yellow color cast. This situation can be depicted as shown in the drawing at the bottom of the next page.

Hopefully, this rather cluttered illustration will show that while the red and green sensitive layers of the paper's emulsion were more heavily exposed than the blue sensitive layer, the result, after reversal processing, is a print which has

COLORS CONTROLLED

Exposure Light	Print Dye		Filter Densities	
G	M		30M	**Printing Filter Pack**
B	Y		60Y	

Sensitive To	Dye Color			
R	C			**Printing Paper**
G	M			
B	Y			

more dye in the yellow dye layer than in either the magenta or the cyan layers. Always bear in mind that the name of this game is *reversal*.

While the illustration is a bit more complex than the negative-to-positive graphic, the solution to the problem of how to adjust this printing filter pack, to provide a print showing a balanced gray, is actually quite simple.

Let's say that we determine that the excess of yellow dye calls for a 15 density change to the filter pack. (I'll explain how that sort of determination is reached in the following section.) If we had yellow filters in the pack, the easiest way to straighten out the print's color balance would be to simply remove them. Doing so would allow more blue light to hit the paper so that, during reversal processing, less yellow dye would be formed. However, since there are no yellow filters in the pack, the alternative solution is to increase the magenta and cyan filtration by equal amounts, cutting down on the red and green light in the printing exposure and, during reversal processing, causing more dye to form in the cyan and magenta layers. The corrected printing situation is shown in drawing on the next page. (Note that I show only two filters in the printing filter pack, for the sake of clarity; however, if CP filters were being used, the typical makeup of the new filter pack would be: 20M + 5M + 20C + 5 C.)

10M
10C

Printing Filter Pack

R
G
B

Printing Paper as Exposed on the Easel

C
M
Y

Printing Paper after Reversal Processing

```
/////////////////////////////////    25M
/////////////////////////////
/////////////////////////////////    25C
/////////////////////////////
```

**Printing
Filter Pack**

- - - - - - - - - - - - - - - - - - - -

```
/////////////////////////////////
/////////////////////////////
/////////////////////////////////
'/////////////////////////////
/////////////////////////////////
/////////////////////////////
```

**Printing Paper as
Exposed on the Easel**

```
X X X X X X X X X X X X X X X X X X X X X:
/////////////////////////////,
<X X X X X X X X X X X X X X X X X X X X
'/////////////////////////////
X X X X X X X X X X X X X X X X X X X X X:
/////////////////////////////
```

**Printing Paper after
Reversal Processing**

By now, I'm sure you have noted that I omitted the IR and UV cutoff filters from my illustrations. I did so for the sake of simplifying the drawing and because these filters are not changed during printing. They simply remain in the enlarger at all times.

One reason to be of good cheer in the face of all of these confusing diagrams, is that with reversal color printing, essentially, what you see is what you get. If the print has too much yellow in it, just change the printing filters to make the image projected on the easel look less yellow, and you will be okay. If you think about it, that is just what I did in the preceding example. I added magenta and cyan filtration. Cyan and magenta yield blue; blue is yellow's complimentary color. Adding blue made the projected image look less yellow.

Of course, the same prohibition on having all three subtractive primaries in the filter pack at one time applies to reversal printing just as it does to negative-to-positive printing, and for exactly the same reason. Having all three subtractive primaries in the pack at the same time simply produces neutral density and requires longer exposure times. The exposure times needed for

**Table 5-1   GENERAL PROCEDURES FOR PRINTING FILTER-PACK ADJUSTMENTS
IN NEGATIVE-TO-POSITIVE PRINTING**

IF THE PRINT IS TOO ...	INCREASE THE PRINTING PAPER'S EXPOSURE TO ...	BY REMOVING THESE FILTERS FROM THE PACK	OR DECREASE THE PRINTING PAPER'S EXPOSURE TO ...	BY ADDING THESE FILTERS TO THE PACK
Red	Red	Cyan	Green & Blue	Magenta & Yellow
Green	Green	Magenta	Red & Blue	Cyan & Yellow
Blue	Blue	Yellow	Red & Green	Cyan & Magenta
Cyan	Green & Blue	Magenta & Yellow	Red	Cyan
Magenta	Red & Blue	Cyan & Yellow	Green	Magenta
Yellow	Red & Green	Cyan & Magenta	Blue	Yellow

**Table 5-2   GENERAL PROCEDURES FOR PRINTING FILTER-PACK ADJUSTMENTS
IN POSITIVE-TO-POSITIVE PRINTING**

IF THE PRINT IS TOO ...	INCREASE THE PRINTING PAPER'S EXPOSURE TO ...	BY REMOVING THESE FILTERS FROM THE PACK	OR DECREASE THE PRINTING PAPER'S EXPOSURE TO ...	BY ADDING THESE FILTERS TO THE PACK
Red	Green & Blue	Magenta & Yellow	Red	Cyan
Green	Red & Blue	Cyan & Yellow	Green	Magenta
Blue	Green & Red	Magenta & Cyan	Blue	Yellow
Cyan	Red	Cyan	Green & Blue	Magenta & Yellow
Magenta	Green	Magenta	Red & Blue	Cyan & Yellow
Yellow	Blue	Yellow	Green & Red	Magenta & Cyan

positive-to-positive prints are long enough without this added problem.

Tables 5–1, 5–2 offer a full list of printing filter-pack changes required by both printing processes, to cover any normally encountered color-cast situation. If you want to know how to take care of some of the more peculiar situations you may encounter with regard to printing filter packs, review the appropriate sections of Chapter 2.

If all else fails, reference can also be made to the Negative-to-Positive Print Evaluation Chart on page 4-25 and to the Positive-to-Positive Evaluation Chart on page 4-30 for foolproof programmed procedures for making printing filter-pack changes for any printing circumstances.

Using Viewing Filters To Determine Printing Filter-Pack Corrections

The way you use your viewing filters to determine the amount of printing filter-pack filtration changes necessary to bring any given print into perfect color balance will, to a very large extent, depend on the type of viewing filters you use. However, some general rules apply to all of the several types you may use, so we'll look at those first.

When you place a viewing filter between your eye and the print being checked, and the filter allows you to view the print without seeing a problem color cast, you are part way to knowing how to adjust your printing filter pack; but there is still a lot more you will need to know before you can open the enlarger's filter drawer and change any of the filters inside for others (or twist the dials to regulate your dichroic filtration). The first thing you must realize is that the color of the viewing filter you are looking through is the complementary color of the one which is causing you your grief: a blue viewing filter will make a too-yellow print look like it's in color balance; a magenta viewing filter will help a too-green print, etc.

The next thing you will need to know is if you are able to make the needed correction with the filter you are using, or if you can only get close. For instance, you may place a 10C filter between your eye and a print that has a red color cast, only to find that the filter does not provide enough correction (the print still looks a little too red) when the viewing filter is held in a position where the viewing light makes only a single pass through the filter on its way to your eye. But you may also find that the same 10C filter provides too much correction (the print now looks a little bit too cyan) when it is placed flat down on the print so that the viewing light has to make two passes through it on its way to your eye. Don't worry! There is an easy way out of such peculiar situations.

First, however, let's see what you would have learned if the 10C filter held away from the print, so that the viewing light made one pass through it on its way to your eye, had caused the print to look properly balanced. First of all, you would know that your print had more dye density in the yellow and magenta dye layers than it did in the cyan layer. Knowing that, you would realize that the reason the print lacked sufficient cyan dye was that it was getting an insufficient amount of red light during the printing exposure, and that this could be remedied most simply by removing cyan filtration from the enlarger's printing filter pack to allow more red light to get to the paper. Let's assume that you made the print from a color negative with a 20C + 60Y printing filter pack. What change would you make to the pack to correct your print based on your use of the viewing filter? If you said remove 10C from the pack, you're wrong. The correct answer is that you would remove 5 cyan from the pack. The reason for this strange state of affairs is as follows: The density of cyan dye needed to correct the too-red appearance of the print is 10, *when the viewing light makes only a single pass through the viewing filter,* but you will recall that light has to make *two passes* through each dye layer of a color print—one on its way into the print and one on its way back out—before it reaches your eye. This being the case, a dye-density change of only 5 is called for, *in the cyan dye layer of the print,* in order to provide the same effect as is shown by a 10C viewing filter external to the print and in a position where the viewing light makes only a single pass through it.

The proper way to use viewing filters to correct printing filter packs in *negative-to-positive* printing, is as follows:

- If the viewing filter overcorrects when held away from the print, so that the viewing light makes one pass through it, use a printing filter-pack correction equal to one-fourth of the density of the viewing filter.
- If the viewing filter is held away from the print, in a position in which the viewing light makes one pass through it, and it corrects the print properly, use a printing filter-pack correction equal to one-half of the density of the viewing filter.
- If the viewing filter undercorrects when it is held away from the print with the viewing light making a single pass through it, but overcorrects when it is placed flat down on the print so that the viewing light makes two passes through it, use three-fourths of the density of the viewing filter for your printing filter-pack correction.
- If the viewing filter provides the proper correction when placed flat down on the print with the viewing light making two passes through it, use the full value of the viewing filter's density as the correction to the printing filter pack.
- Finally, if the viewing filter undercorrects when placed flat down on the print, so that the viewing light makes two passes through it, use one and one-half times the value of the viewing filter's density as the printing filter-pack correction.

For *positive-to-positive* printing, double all of the suggested correction values just offered. For instance: If the viewing filter used provides proper correction when held away from a reversal print so that the viewing light makes only one pass through the viewing filter, use the full value of the viewing filter's density as the correction to be applied to your printing filter pack (rather than half the viewing filter's density as is proper for negative-to-positive printing). The reason that this strange doubling is called for in reversal printing is implicit in the name of the process. The exposure made on the easel is, quite literally, reversed during the processing of the print. This reversal effectively brings the *final* amount of dye-density change, in the processed and dried print, right back into line with the general rules offered for negative-to-positive printing.

All of the examples I have used to illustrate print color-imbalance problems and the use of viewing filters have been based on an examination of a portion of the print known to contain an image of a gray object. I have done this, as previously explained, because gray is the best possible color to deal with when printing, since the paper must have equal dye density in all three dye layers to render it cleanly. While I strongly recommend that you do use gray as your evaluating color wherever possible, it obviously won't be possible to do so in all cases. Where a gray area of the print is not available for evaluation with viewing filters, you will simply have to do the best you can with some color in the print which you can remember accurately (good luck!); or, better yet, one that you can physically compare to a sample of the original. If you do have to go this route, or worse yet, you have to evaluate a print on "flesh tones," try to avoid using the viewing filters to check highlight or shadow areas. Wherever possible, stick to checking the middle tones and try to apply common sense.

Once you have developed a degree of skill using a single color of viewing filter, you will begin to see that not all color-cast situations lend themselves to a simple solution with a single complementary color. Once it becomes apparent to you that a single color is able to remove most, but not all, of the problem color cast from a print, that is the time to begin stacking different colors together. As an example, let's look at a portion of a print which should be gray but instead has a peculiar somewhat reddish/magentaish-gray look. Such a print can be represented as follows:

```
/////////////////////////////.    C
XXXXXXXXXXXX XX XXXXXXXX.          M
///////////////////////////·
///////////////////////////·      Y
///////////////////////////·
```

It would look better through a strong cyan filter, but through such a filter the print's appearance would change to bluish-gray. The obvious solution then would be to stack a weak yellow filter over the cyan one.

Let's, for the sake of example, assume the print was made from a negative with a 60M +

125Y printing filter pack, and that the viewing filters found to bring the portion of the print under examination back into color balance were a 40C and a 20Y held away from the print so that the viewing light made only one pass through the filters, as is shown in the following:

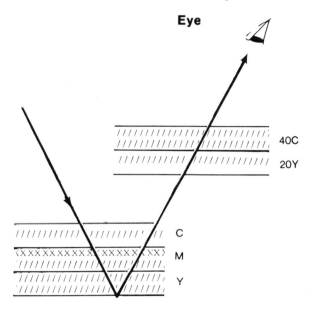

Then the most obvious change to the printing filter pack would be to remove one half of each of the viewing filter's values from the printing filter pack. That would be easy, if only we had some cyan filters in the pack to remove, but, alas, we don't. This being the case the solution gets a bit trickier. First, remove the 10Y from the

pack to bring the magenta and yellow layers into balance, so the resulting print will look like this:

```
/////////////////////////////   C
<XXXXXXXXXXXXXXXXXXXX>
////////////////////////////,   M
\XXXXXXXXXXXXXXXXXXXXX
'////////////////////////////   Y
```

Now, since you can't boost the cyan dye-layer's density, you will have to add 20 density to both the magenta and the yellow components of the printing filter pack. This will weaken both these dye layers in the print equally and bring them into balance with the cyan layer. The new printing filter pack will be 80M + 135Y and the resulting print will look like this:

```
////////////////////////////   C
/////////////////////////////   M
/////////////////////////////   Y
```

All you have to do is think a bit about what you are doing, and draw a few little sketches like those shown, and you'll be able to solve any off-color print problem with relative ease.

Using a Ring-Around to Determine Printing Filter-Pack Correction

A ring-around is not the sort of color printing tool that most workers will use long after they have gained a bit of experience. But until then, ring-arounds can sometimes be useful. Two ring-arounds appear in this text. One shows 25 prints made from a standard Kodak negative. Each of 18 of these prints illustrates a different printing filter-pack color-imbalance problem. Another six of the prints offer examples of incorrect print density. All of these prints are arranged around one central print, which shows both the correct color balance and the proper print density.

The other ring-around contains the same number of prints showing the same types of problems, but each of the prints used to make it

was printed directly from a standard Kodak transparency using reversal processing.

Both the Negative-to-Positive Ring-Around on page C4-2 and the Positive-to-Positive Ring-Around on page C4-3 are arranged to show properly color-balanced prints, with increasing degrees of over and underexposure, in a vertical column above and below the central "perfect" (the quotation marks are there because nothing is really ever perfect) print. Prints showing the various color imbalances are arranged like six spokes of a wheel, radiating out from the "perfect" print at the hub. The three spokes showing prints with too much of the additive primary colors appear on the left of the hub and the three spokes showing prints with too much of the subtractive primary colors are to the right of the hub. The spokes directly opposite one another show complementary color problems.

It may be of interest to note that I very carefully made each of the prints that went into these two ring-arounds with a diffusion-type enlarger, using dichroic printing filtration, by deliberately dialing exactly the amount of color error indicated into the printing filter pack. However, if you elect to compare your off-color prints against these rings-arounds, don't expect to find a high level of color correspondence between them and the images you see on the printed pages of this book. The many complicated processes necessary to get the color photographs that I made onto these pages, in ink, have rendered some very definite changes in both the color and the density of the images. About all you can hope to get from any printed (on a printing press) ring-around is an *approximate* idea of the nature of the color imbalance you are trying to evaluate. Viewing filters are a far more accurate tool for color print evaluation and correction.

The proper method to use when evaluating a print with a ring-around is to first compare it to the images in the vertical column to insure that your print's density is within about ½ stop from the correct one, or is approximately the density you want to have in the final print. If your density is further off than this, it will be necessary to correct it with more or less printing exposure as required, before bothering to check the print for color balance. This is so because the density correction itself will cause some color shifting in the print.

When you have the print density where you want it, the print can then be compared with the various awful examples of color imbalances shown in the ring-around. If the reproduction in this book isn't too far off, you will probably be able to find that one or two of the images on one of the six spokes will show something that looks at least approximately like the peculiar color cast that you want to get rid of in your print. Once you get this far you have sufficient information to correct your printing filter pack.

Let's say, for example, that you made a reversal print that seemed to be about right in density but had an overall greenish appearance that came fairly close to matching the bilious look of the 40 too-green example in the Positive-

to-Positive Ring-Around. Let's go even further and specify that you made the print with a 20C + 15Y printing filter pack. You know all you need to adjust the filter pack, but you may have to think a bit about just how you are going to be able to do it. The situation looks like this in your original, too-green print:

The Paper as Exposed

The Paper after Reversal Processing and Drying

40 TOO GREEN

The Paper as Exposed

The Paper after Reversal Processing and Drying

CORRECTED

It would be easy to correct this situation if there was magenta in the original printing filter pack, or no more than one other subtractive primary in it, but unfortunately this is not the case. Therefore, the first step in correcting the pack is to take the maximum *equal* amount of *both* yellow and cyan from the pack in order to reduce one to zero. You can get only 15 density out of each of the pack components (increasing the print's exposure equally to red and blue accordingly), but the correction called for is 40 not 15. That means that you must still reduce the print's greenish cast by 25 density. That will now be simple because by removing 15 density from both components of the original filter pack you have reduced the pack to a single component, 5C. Now all you need to do is add 25M to that and your printing filter pack will yield a print that is 40 less green than the one you liked so little. The print you make with the corrected 5C + 25M pack can be represented as shown in the bottom drawing on the previous page.

Understanding Exposure Compensation

Every time you decide to change the density, the color balance, or the magnification of an image you have already printed, you will also, almost invariably, have to make some change to your original printing exposure.

Just for the sake of definition, printing exposure is the product of the overall brightness (intensity) of the image projected by your enlarger (onto the paper on the easel), multiplied by the amount of time during which the projection takes place.

Print Density

It is hardly very likely that, at this point in this book, I ought to have to go into the need for, or reasons behind, changing printing exposure to vary print density. But, just for the sake of completeness, I will mention here that when printing from negatives, print density is directly related to print exposure (if your print is too light more exposure will provide more print density); while when printing from transparencies, just the opposite is true. The density of a reversal print is inversely related to the amount of exposure it receives. (If your print is too dark, more exposure will make it lighter.) If this information comes as a shock to anyone, I strongly recommend that you go back to Chapter 2 and review both processes.

Magnification

To most printers, the reason for varying printing exposure with magnification is quite obvious. The light available for exposure is determined, essentially, by the enlarger's lens opening and by the enlarger lamp's output. For any given lens opening, the same amount of available light will have to cover more area as the enlarger head is raised, and less area as it is lowered. This is easily seen in the darkroom. As you raise your enlarger's head, keeping the lens at a constant aperture, the image projected on the easel or baseboard will be seen to grow dimmer and dimmer. The change in image brightness is directly proportional to the ratio of the original projected area to that of the new projected area. (This is not strictly true, as it doesn't take refocusing of the enlarger lens into account. But because of the reciprocity characteristics of most color printing materials, it is a better working approximation than the more commonly used, and technically accurate, statement that the change in illumination is proportional to the ratio $(1 + X_2)^2/1 + X_1)^2$ where X_1 is the original magnification and X_2 is the new magnification.)

For example, if your enlarger is set for $8\times$ and you have a 35mm negative carrier in the machine, the image area projected will be approximately 96 square inches (8×12). If you then raise the enlarger head to get an $11\times$ magnification, the area illuminated by the enlarger lamp is about twice what it was at $8\times$ ($11 \times 16.5 = 181.5$), and the image will be about half as bright as it was when the head was at the lower setting. It is, of course, quite simple to restore the original brightness to the projected $11\times$ image by simply opening the enlarger lens up one stop, thus doubling the area of the lens opening through which the enlarger lamp's light output may pass. But if your enlarger lens is wide open at $8\times$, you simply won't be able to get the same image brightness at $11\times$.

Reciprocity

Fortunately, printing paper responds not only to the brightness level (intensity) of the projected image, but also to the total quantity of light energy which the paper receives. To put it a bit more simply, for the most part, printing paper doesn't care very much if it gets a lot of light for a little time or a little light for a lot of time. In the example we just looked at, an enlarger with its lens wide open at 8× had its head raised to 11× causing the image it was projecting to dim by half. Since the lens couldn't be opened any further, we couldn't do anything to restore the projected image's brightness. Had we wanted to make an exposure at 11×, we wouldn't really have had to worry about the brightness of the projected image, as we could have gotten the amount of light energy the paper needed to yield an image at approximately the same density as the one made at 8× by doubling the amount of time the dimmer image was projected on the paper.

Please note that I said that the paper is *for the most part* indifferent to how it gets its exposure — at high intensity for a short duration or at low intensity for a longer time. Actually the paper *does* care, but, within limits; not to a very great extent. The way the paper acts, in this regard, is called it's reciprocity-failure characteristics. All printing papers, black-and-white or color, exhibit certain reciprocity-failure characteristics which careful printers always take into account when it is necessary to change projected image size, lens opening, print density, etc. To a considerable extent, the printing paper's overall reciprocity-failure characteristics are not too great a consideration; as an example, when doubling an image area from 5× to 7× at a constant lens opening, only about five percent more exposure is needed than a simple doubling of the original exposure time would indicate. This small difference will hardly be noticed in the print; but, if you make a 12.3× print (six times the original print's area) at the same lens opening, the exposure difference called for to compensate for reciprocity failure will be more than 35 percent greater than that found by simply multiplying the original exposure time by six.

The only simple way I know of to determine reciprocity-failure exposure-time compensation is to use the Kodak *Color-Printing Computer.* This little first-cousin to a circular slide rule is an integral part of each Kodak *Color Dataguide.* I have devoted a separate section of this chapter to its use.

Another type of reciprocity failure, which is not compensable, is often encountered when gross density changes are deliberately made to a print. In this case the problem is caused by unequal reciprocity-failure characteristics in each of the three emulsion layers. Think about the nasty implications of that awful situation for a few moments and, if they don't make you sick, you will soon realize why I have stressed the importance of first correcting your color prints for density; and only *then* , when you have the print's density where you want it, going on to evaluate and correct the print for color balance.

Printing Filtration Changes

The reason that changes to the color-printing filter pack may require exposure compensation is somewhat less obvious than the ones I've discussed so far. The villain here is reflection, and it only applies to CP or CC-type filters. Both filters have two surfaces, each of which reflects part of the enlarger lamp's white-light output that is trying to pass through them, right back up to the lamp house. Enlargers that use dichroic filters do not suffer much from this reflection problem as, most often, only a portion of the dichroic filters are ever introduced into the light path at any given time.

If you evaluate your prints layer-by-layer in the manner I've described in this chapter, exposure compensation for changes to the printing filter pack are, most often, quite small. If you stick to the simple approach to printing offered in the previous chapter, these exposure compensations for filter pack changes can get to be rather large.

Chapter 4 placed its emphasis on getting a person who had never made a color print into the darkroom and printing with a bare minimum of comprehension of what the printing process was all about. This chapter has been designed to emphasize that color prints are properly analyzed and corrected when the relative dye densities of the three separate dye layers in the print are taken into account. If you understand that you can reduce a print's color cast by changing the dye density in a single dye layer without affecting the two adjacent layers, then you'll probably need never bother to make more than a ten-percent correction to exposure for any single low-density CC or CP filter added or removed from a printing filter pack.

Determining Exposure Compensation Requirements

Among the four categories of print variables requiring exposure compensation—density, magnification, reciprocity failure, filtration—only magnification can be easily handled arithmetically. And even then, plugging the numbers into the simple formula (see Chapter 4) and running through the arithmetic necessary to determine the amount of exposure change required to compensate for changes to the projected image's size is really not the most useful procedure available to you, because the answer you get won't completely take refocusing and reciprocity failure into account.

Fortunately, Kodak has provided an excellent, simple, and quick way to determine needed exposure changes, which automatically accounts for all of the color printing variables except density. Since print density is largely a matter of taste, it is just as well that they skipped trying to accommodate that one. The device they came up with to do all this is a simple circular slide rule-type of calculator which they call a *Color-Printing Computer.* One is bound right into every copy of the Kodak *Color Dataguide.* The device consists of four concentric circular scales, the outermost two of which are fixed and the innermost two of which can be rotated relative to each other and relative to the fixed scales. Each of the scales (or dials) is colored differently from those adjacent to it for ease of identification in use. The outermost "magnification" scale is bright yellow and indicates values of image magnification ranging from 1× (a contact print) to 25× . The next fixed "exposure" scale is magenta in color and it offers printing exposure times in seconds, from 2–500 seconds. The outermost moving "density" scale is cyan in color and offers two types of data. Most of this scale is taken up with numerical information concerning densitometer readings taken through a red filter, which, for our purposes here, are of no value whatsoever. However, there is one small portion of this scale which offers an index arrow and offsets, from −2 through +2, to be applied for additions to or removals from the printing filter pack. This is the portion of the density dial we will use. (The other numerical density data on this cyan-colored scale can also be used with a table of computer numbers provided by Kodak for individual CP or CC printing filters, but this method of use is really

not compatible with an analysis of print problems on a dye layer-by-dye layer basis.) Finally, the innermost dial is yellow, movable, and offers *f*-stops ranging from *f*/4 to *f*/22. This description probably makes the device sound awesome, but in actuality it is really easy to work with, and not the slightest bit complicated or clumsy to use.

The best way to illustrate how to operate this incredibly simple device is to offer several examples of its use. To do so, let's take a look at a portion of a negative-to-positive print which we know should be middle gray but our eyes perceive as an awful yellowish/greenish-gray. Let's also say that the overall density of this awful looking print seems to be about right. The dye layers of our terrible muddy-colored print would look like this:

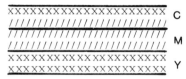

The viewing filters needed to make this awful color look gray could either be blue and red or magenta and cyan. Let's say that we find that a 40B filter combined with a 20R filter, held away from the print so that the viewing illumination makes only one pass through the filters, makes the print look gray. And, let's further specify that the original printing conditions used to create this color were a 5C + 95Y printing filter (CP acetate) pack, an *f*/5.6 lens opening, a 16 second exposure time, and an image magnification of 7.5× .

Since we decided earlier that the print density looks okay, the only thing we will have to do is to lower the dye densities in the yellow and the cyan dye layers. Fortunately, both the colors needed to do this are in the printing filter pack. To correct the pack, in accordance with our findings with the viewing filter, we must add 20Y and 10C to bring the new pack to 15C + 115Y. Each of these additions is made with a single filter. Now, let's see how the Kodak *Color-Printing Computer* is used to find the new exposure time

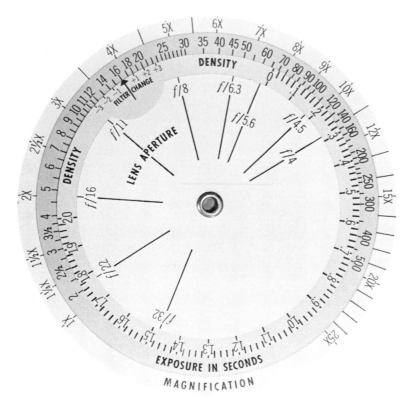

Initialize the Kodak Color Printing Computer by setting the Filter Change arrow to the original 16-second printing time and the original enlarger lens opening (f/5.6) to a magnification of 7.5×. If only two printing filters are added, read the new exposure time opposite the +2 Filter Change mark as 20 seconds.

required to compensate for the addition of these two CP filters. Doing that is simplicity itself. Just place the arrow on the cyan-colored density scale next to the original printing exposure time (16 seconds) on the magenta-colored exposure scale and read the new printing exposure time on the exposure scale opposite the +2 mark (for the two CP filters added to the pack) on the density scale. It turns out to be 20 seconds. Had you been using dichroic filters, rather than CP's, it is very likely that no exposure time correction would have been necessary. It would be equally simple to use this wonderful device to determine the proper exposure time for the color-corrected print made at a new magnification—let's say 12×—and a wider lens opening (to keep the exposure time down at this high magnification) of f/4.

To obtain all of these corrections from the computer at the same time, it is first necessary to initialize the dial settings. To do this, you simply set all of the dials to represent the conditions used to make the original print. First set the arrow on the cyan-colored density scale so that it points to the 16 second mark on the magenta-colored exposure scale. Then hold the density scale so that it can't move relative to the exposure scale, and rotate the innermost scale, moving the yellow-colored lens-aperture scale so that the original lens-aperture setting used (f/5.6) lines up with the original magnification setting (7.5×) on the outermost, fixed yellow-colored magnification scale. All of that should take you about 30 seconds to do if you are slow. Now you have initialized the *Color-Printing Computer*. To determine the exposure time necessary to compensate for the new printing conditions, simply lift the cyan-colored density dial just enough to get your forefinger under it, and hold it and the innermost yellow-colored lens aperture dial between your thumb and forefinger, so that neither dial can move relative to the other. Now rotate both these dials together until the f/4 indication on the lens aperture dial lines up with the 12× indication on the magnification scale. Now you read the new printing exposure time from the marking on the magenta-colored exposure dial which lines up

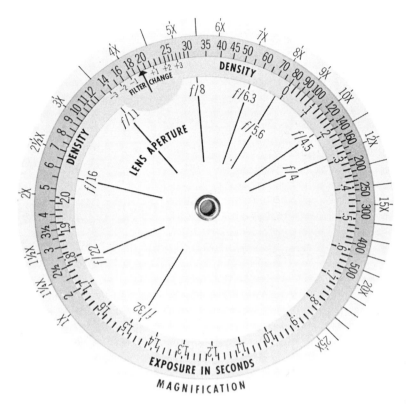

To determine a new printing exposure time at f/4 and 12×, set the f/4 line against the 12× magnification line, making sure that the Density and Lens Aperture scales move together. The new time read opposite the +2 Filter Change mark is 24 seconds.

with the number of filters changed (+2) on the cyan-colored density dial. The new time indicated is 24 seconds for a 12 × print made through an f/4 lens opening and using a 15C + 115Y filter pack.

In this case, had your enlarger been equipped with dichroic filters, rather than the CP acetate type, you would most likely find your correct new exposure time opposite the density scale's index arrow rather than opposite that scale's +2 offset. I'm sorry to have to be so vague as to use words like, "most likely," but different manufacturer's dichroic filters do tend to behave differently. In general, when using dichroic filtration, you can, to the greatest extent, simply ignore exposure corrections for filter density changes alone. However, if you find that doing so, particularly when making gross printing-filter changes, does result in significant print-density changes, you may do well to experiment with using about one-third to one-half the exposure correction you would if you were using acetate filters rather than dichroics. You should begin to

get a good solid feeling for the amount of correction you will need after you've made a few test prints of your standard negative following this procedure.

If you don't have one of Kodak's marvelous little devices in front of you as you are reading this, you will probably find it hard to believe that the entire procedure described above can easily be gone through in about 20 seconds once you have become familiar with the unit. As an added bonus, the exposure-time readout offered by the device is automatically compensated to account for the reciprocity characteristics of Kodak's printing materials (in practice, I find that the reciprocity compensation built into the *Color-Printing Computer* seems also to work quite well with other manufacturer's printing materials).

While the examples illustrating the use of the *Color-Printing Computer* offered have all involved only prints made from negatives, please be assured that the device works equally well to determine exposure compensation required when making prints directly from slides.

Calibrated Color Contact Sheets

I am not a fan of elaborate instrumentation in the darkroom, but I am enthusiastic about darkroom techniques that save money, time, and effort. Those are just some of the reasons I make calibrated color contact sheets.

A calibrated color contact sheet is nothing more than a single sheet of 8″ × 10″ (or 9″ × 12″, or whatever size you happen to prefer) color printing paper on which you have contact printed all of the images on a full roll of 35mm film (or a partial roll of a larger format) *along with the image of your standard color negative.* The reason I call this type of contact sheet "calibrated" is that it is contact printed with exactly the same printing filter pack, enlarger head height, enlarger lens opening, and exposure time necessary to make a *perfect* (calibrated) print of your standard negative. The printing data used to make the contact sheet is the sheet's calibration. Making a calibrated color contact sheet will always result in a perfect contact print of your standard negative (if you don't mess things up during exposure or processing) and a lot of imperfect prints of the negatives on the roll you have not previously printed. There is a very good reason for this strange way of doing things.

A calibrated color contact sheet will: allow you to see if you have any images worth printing (*before* you waste time and money printing them); allow you to accurately judge the printing exposure and filter pack required to print any individual frame in the roll, or all of them should you want to; tell you if your camera's lens was focused when you made the shots; let you know if your paper is aging; tell you if your processing technique is okay; let you know if your processing chemicals are still fresh enough to use; allow you to file your color negatives (or slides) in a way that makes the retrieval of specific frames, years after they have been shot, a simple matter; tell you exactly how to print a color negative on your current supply of printing paper, even years after you last printed it on an entirely different batch of paper, and even if the two different paper batches were made by entirely different manufacturers. How's that for performance? And, to make things even nicer, a calibrated color contact sheet will cost you well under a dollar to produce (as this is being written in mid-1976) and save you from ever having to consider spending

several hundred dollars on an electronic analyzer—a device that has almost all of the requirements associated with making a calibrated color contact sheet, but hardly any of its virtues.

Now, before I go any further, I want to warn all of you positive-to-positive-only printers that the last thing that you need is a color contact sheet. The biggest advantage gained from making prints directly from slides is that you work with positive images to begin with. All you need to know about the quality of those images is right there in front of you. You need only put a slide over a daylight illuminator, put a loupe over it, and use your eyes and brain to determine if you like the color balance, the color saturation, the contrast, the overall density, the aesthetic qualities of the image, and even the depth of field you used to make it. The second biggest advantage positive-to-positive printers have is that the process has far more latitude than the negative-to-positive process has. Once the right filter pack is found for a box of reversal printing paper, it is seldom necessary to change the printing filter pack very much to print any given transparency; unless, of course, you want to correct certain problems which are evident in the slide. Essentially, all you really have to do in reversal printing, once you've established your calibrated printing filter pack, is to keep track of the overall image density and make adjustments in the printing exposure to suit. About the only reasons positive-to-positive printers might want color contact sheets would be for purposes of filing, or storage, or to avoid the bother and expense of making duplicate transparencies. But, because 35mm transparencies most often arrive from the lab in 2 inch-square cardboard or plastic mounts, it can be a genuine pain to remove each individual frame from its mount and tape it into place to make a contact sheet. It is far simpler to put twenty 35mm slides into a 20-pocket plastic viewing sheet and file the sheet full of originals. Those positive-to-positive printers who process their own transparency film, or who instruct their processing labs not to cut their film, can indeed make calibrated color contact sheets in much the same way that I will describe for making them from color negatives. Just bear in mind that doing so you will get less returns for your efforts and expense then negative-to-positive printers do.

Making Negative-to-Positive Calibrated Color Contact Sheets

The procedure used to make a calibrated color contact sheet is quite simple. All you will need, in addition to your normal color printing hardware and software, is a contact frame (or a proof printer, a heavy piece of glass or plastic, etc.); assuming, of course, that you took my advice earlier in the book and obtained or made a standard negative.

The first thing you will have to do is make a perfect print of your standard 35mm negative at about 9× magnification (or at whatever magnification is appropriate to your film format and chosen size of contact sheet). And when I say perfect, I mean perfect—perfect density, perfect color balance, and perfect (consistent and repeatable) processing. Once you have done this—and as you know, it may take a fair number of test prints to do—leave your enlarger completely alone, except for taking the precaution to lock the head and lens stage if such locks are provided on your machine, and note the head height on the enlarger's logging scale if it is so equipped. Also, make a written record of the exact filter pack, lens opening, and exposure time you used to make your perfect print, and record the paper and chemistry types and the number of the emulsion batch of the paper. It will be best to keep a data sheet (see example) on which all of this information can be recorded as each trial calibration print is made. It will also be an excellent idea to mark all of this data right on the paper box; or if you keep your color printing paper in a papersafe, label the safe with the data. Retain the calibration print and mark all of its pertinent printing data on the back of the print.

With these preliminary steps out of the wa, you can proceed to make the calibrated color contact sheets themselves. To do so, simply place your previously unprinted negatives, in strips of six if you processed them yourself, or strips of four if you had them processed by Kodak or another commercial firm, emulsion side up, on the glass or plastic portion of your contact frame or proof printer. You can use whatever clips are provided on the device you decide to use to hold them in place, or you can easily tape the film to the glass with tiny strips of Scotch tape. When using the tape, be careful to keep the adhesive from touching the image area inside of the sprocket holes on the film margins. Once you have all of your negatives in place, put your standard negative right along with them, by clip or tape, with its emulsion also away from the glass. Now, under a No. 13 safelight (or in total darkness, if you are working with reversal materials), load a sheet of paper, from the same emulsion batch you just obtained the calibration data for, with its emulsion facing the film's emulsion, and expose it through the glass and through the empty negative carrier using the same head height, lens opening, focus, filter pack, and exposure time you did for the 9× calibration print. When the exposure has been made, process the sheet of paper exactly the same way you did those you used to get the calibration data. Dry the resulting contact print and check the 1× image of your standard negative against your 9× calibration print of that same negative to insure that both are of equal density and that both have the same color balance. If they match, you've made a successful calibrated color contact sheet. If they don't match, you made a mistake somewhere along the way. Try again until you get the hang of it, or isolate the problem which could be old chemicals, old paper, incorrect (not the same as the calibration data) pack, exposure, etc. You don't have to go through the making of a calibration print each time you want to make a calibrated contact sheet, so long as you have fresh paper available from the same emulsion batch you used to make your original calibration print. All you will have to do to make additional calibrated contact sheets, at any time, is to reestablish the enlarger's calibrated head height. Focus the projected image of the edge of the

Table 5-3   NEG. FILE #: STD. NEG. V II S

DATE	FRAME	MAG.	F-STOP	TIME	MAGTA	YELO	CYAN	FILT	PAPER/CHEM	REMARKS
10-10-75	Std. Neg.	9×	5.6	35 sec.	40	60		Dichroic	Uni. Resin/Uni R-2	Print is at least one stop over
10-10-75	Std. Neg.	9×	8	35 sec.	40	60		Dichroic	Uni. Resin/Uni R-2	20C viewing filter, 2 passes, under-corrects. Density about +½ stop
10-10-75	Std. Neg.	9×	8	27 sec.	65	85		Dichroic	Uni. Resin/Uni R-2	Too cyan. 20R, 1 pass, corrects. Density about −¼ stop
10-10-75	Std. Neg.	9×	8	33 sec.	55	75		Dichroic	Uni. Resin/Uni R-2	Ok—Use this data for calibration of emulsion batch #30226537E

empty carrier, reestablish the calibrated printing filter pack, set the enlarger lens for the same opening and the enlarger timer for the same exposure as were used to make the original calibration print. You won't be able to forget this data because, if you followed my instructions, you not only filed your data sheet away but you also wrote the data needed on the paper box or safe, and on the back of your calibration print.

You can go on using the same data to make additional calibrated contact sheets for as long as your standard negative and your supply of printing paper from the same emulsion batch last. You can expect your standard negative to begin to fade in about two years; however, you should run out of paper long before that. Every time you change standard negatives or purchase a new supply of paper, you will have to go through the same procedure for making a calibrated print again.

Using A Calibrated Color Contact Sheet

As mentioned earlier, the first thing you need to determine about any calibrated color contact sheet is if the image of your standard negative is correctly rendered. Assuming it is, you can proceed to use a loupe on each of the individual images on the sheet to determine which of them you find pleasing, technically and aesthetically. Don't concern yourself if some, or even all of the images, are obviously off-color, or even if they are over or underexposed. The wonderful thing about color printing is that you can fix many of the mistakes you make with your camera through your efforts in the darkroom. Only after you determine which of the images are worth the effort and expense of printing (two or three out of 36 frames is usually not an unreasonable number), do you begin to consider what you will have to do to print the selected frames properly.

The first thing to consider is the density of the selected images judged against the density of your standard negative's image. After you have a bit of color printing experience you will be able to tell with a fair degree of accuracy, just by looking at the contacted frame, to just what degree the frame is over or underexposed. It is important to bear in mind here that the reason you have gone to all of the trouble of making this a *calibrated* contact sheet as opposed to a simple

contact sheet is to allow you to make such judgments simply and with perfect confidence that the basis of your judgment is solid. The perfect image of your standard negative on each calibrated contact sheet is your assurance that the sheet has been properly exposed and processed to yield a perfect print of a perfect negative. If the contacted frames on your sheet are less then perfect in their density, you can blame it on your poor performance with your camera (or on your camera's poor performance), or on the film processor's poor performance with your film. You will know that it wasn't due to your poor performance in the darkroom, because that little perfect image of your standard negative will tell you so.

While the print density of the several images you may want to print may easily be attributed to your abilities with your camera, or your lab's ability to process your film, the color balance of the several images on your calibrated contact sheet most likely won't have anything to do with either of them. If the type of film you have contact printed is the same type as the film on which your standard negative was made, and both the standard negative and the images you want to print were made under average daylight conditions or by electronic flash illumination, chances are that the color balance of the frames being examined will be quite close to that of the image of your standard negative. However, if you use a standard negative on, let's say, Vericolor II S and you shoot Kodacolor II, you will most likely see a color-balance difference between such frames and the image of your standard negative. Of course, if you shot the frames you are checking under tungsten, flourescent, or candlelight, or you made them outdoors, but very early or very late in the day, you should also expect their color balance to be appreciably different from that of your standard negative's image. That's just fine. Don't worry! Being able to easily see that the images you want to print come up with a color cast when they are printed with your calibration printing conditions is exactly what a calibrated contact sheet is all about. All you have to do is use your viewing filters to determine what the particular color-cast problem with each of the frames under consideration may be. This done, and using your estimate of the proper density of any given frame, you should be able to plug this data right into your Kodak *Color-Printing Computer* and come up with a commercially acceptable print of each frame on your first attempt at printing it. That is about as good, or perhaps a lot better than even the best electronic color analyzers can do. And electronic analyzers require you to go through the same exact same calibration procedure that calibrated color contact sheets do, so they have no advantage there either.

An example of how all of these manipulations is done will, hopefully, serve to clarify the procedure. Let's assume that you have made a perfect calibration print, with your standard negative, using the following printing conditions: filter pack = 80M + 125Y; lens opening = *f*/8; exposure time = 27 seconds; number of CP acetate filters in the pack = 5; image magnification = 9×. You have made a calibrated color contact sheet of 36 frames of 35mm color negative film; plus, of course, your standard negative. After processing the contact sheet, you have dried it and determined that the image of your standard negative was a good match for the perfect calibration print you made when you did the original calibration run, on the particular emulsion batch of paper on which you have made this contact sheet, and on which you intend to print the frames contacted.

You have looked over the 36 printed images with a good-quality loupe, and found that, for now, you only want to print frame 14. You judge that the density of this frame is slightly greater, about ¼ stop, than that of the standard negative's frame. Frame 14 also has an odd color cast that looks purplish-blue. You sketch the color cast problem like this:

```
XXXXXXXXXXXXXXXXXXXX
/////////////////////////////   C
XXXXXXXXXXXXXXXXXXXX
XXXXXXXXXXXXXXXXXXXX        M
/////////////////////////////
/////////////////////////////   Y
```

You confirm your sketched solution to the imbalance with a green and a yellow viewing filter. You find that the combination of a 40G and a 20Y viewing filter, held away from the contact sheet so that the viewing light makes only one

pass through the filters, seems to make frame 14 look a lot better. That combination of viewing filters calls for removing 10Y and adding 20M to the printing filter pack to get a new pack consisting of 100M + 115Y. So far you have all of the data you need to make a 9× color-corrected print of frame 14 except for the printing exposure time modification required by the printing filter-pack change. You can find that by using the Kodak *Color-Printing Computer*. But while we're at it, let's make the next print of frame 14 at 5× so that it will be a 5″ × 7.5″ image centered on an 8″ × 10″ sheet. That change of magnification will call for still another exposure change that the computer will also be glad to determine.

But before you can even initialize the computer, you will have to determine, arithmetically, what the exposure time should have been to give frame 14 about ¼ stop less density than it got with the original 27 second calibration exposure. Use Table 5-4 and a pocket calculator to find that frame 14 would have looked better if it had gotten about 22.7 seconds of exposure. Round that off to 23 seconds since your estimate is really only an informed guess, and three-tenths of a second in 23 is really quite insignificant.

Table 5-4 FACTORS FOR ESTIMATING EXPOSURE CHANGES

STOPS OR FRACTIONS OF STOPS TO BE CHANGED	MULTIPLY ORIGINAL EXPOSURE BY
+2	4
+1½	2.83
+1	2
+¾	1.68
+⅔	1.59
+½	1.41
+⅓	1.26
+¼	1.19
−¼	0.84
−⅓	0.79
−½	0.71
−⅔	0.63
−¾	0.60
−1	0.50
−1½	0.35
−2	0.25

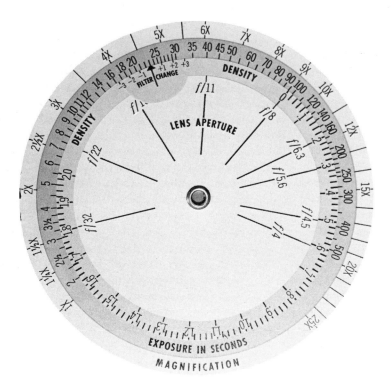

Initialize the Kodak Color Printing Computer by setting the Filter Change arrow to 23 seconds. Hold it in place while you set the f/8 mark to line up with the 9× Magnification indicator.

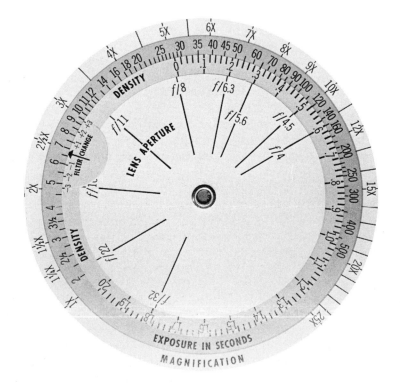

To find the new exposure time, lock the Lens Aperture and Density dials together and rotate them both until the f/8 mark lines up with the 5× Magnification indicator. Find the new printing time opposite the Filter Change's +2 mark to be 8.4 seconds. For all practical purposes, you can round this off to 8 seconds.

Now, set the arrow on the computer's density dial against the 23 second mark on the exposure dial. Hold the density dial so it can't move and set the aperture dial so that the original $f/8$ lens opening is opposite the $9 \times$ line on the magnification dial. You have now initialized the computer.

To find your new exposure data, lock the density and the aperture scales together and rotate them until the aperture scale's $f/8$ marking lines up with the magnification scale's $5 \times$ indicator. Put the computer aside for a moment and think about how many acetate filters you now have in your printing filter pack. You started out with five (two 40M's, one 80Y, one 40Y and one 5Y) to make up your original 80M + 125Y filter pack. Now your pack is 100M + 115Y and the way it is made up is with two 40M's, one 20M, one 80Y, one 20Y, one 10Y, and one 5Y, for a total of seven filters. The net change in the number of filters in the printing filter pack is, then, two. That being the case, you read your new exposure time for the $5 \times$ print from the computer's exposure dial opposite the +2 offset, to find that eight seconds will do the job well.

Believe it or not, that whole evaluation procedure can be gone through in about two minutes flat once you get the hang of it. I know it looks awesome the first time through, but once you've done it once or twice for yourself you will begin to see how elegantly simple the whole procedure really is.

If, by the way, you had been using a diffusion enlarger, with dichroic-type filters in the example we just went through, you wouldn't have bothered to make any compensation for the number of filters added to the pack, and you would have read your new exposure time, opposite the density scale's arrow, at 6½ seconds.

Filing, Retrieving, and Reprinting Images

The calibrated color contact sheet's applications are hardly limited to its use as an accurate and quick means of analyzing the images contained on entire rolls of color film. Contact sheets also provide you with an excellent image-filing and storage system; and, best of all, if you will keep just a few records, they will tell you how to reprint any given frame of any given roll of film long after you have printed it the first time. This book is hardly the place to begin to explore negative and positive image-filing systems, and I hardly consider myself to be an expert in the field. But I do have a simple system that involves my color contact sheets and I see no reason why it won't work well for anyone. In essence, all I do is number each contact sheet according to the day it was made (not the day the film was shot, but I see no reason why you couldn't do things that way if you were so inclined), and place each roll's strips of film into a glassine envelope that carries the same number as the one marked on the contact sheet. If more than one contact sheet is made on a given day, then the last hyphenated digit in that sheet's identifying number will separate it from the others made that day in the files. For example, the contact sheet shown in this chapter is labeled 10–1–75–C–1. All of that simply informs me that it was made on October 1, 1975, it is a calibrated color sheet, and that it was the first sheet I made that day. I also tend to make some notes on the subject of each roll of film on that roll's glassine envelope, but not on the contact sheet, where such information would be more easily seen by looking at the images. I don't bother to cross-file anything by subject, but I sure do try to keep clients straight. I find that I can mentally recall the image I need, when I need it; and, by simply leafing through my boxes of contacts, I can come up with the sheet containing that image in a reasonably short period of time. If you tend to have an awful memory, you will do well to devise a better system then the one I use.

I mark down something much more important than the filing data on each contact sheet; and that is the printing data. I make sure it gets noted on the back of each contact sheet. If I have printed frames 14, 8, and 32, I make sure to indicate the full set of printing data for those frames on the back of the contact sheet, right along with the data used for making the sheet itself. By doing this, I insure that I can reprint these frames in the future with virtually no effort whatsoever. I think the best way to illustrate the method of using calibrated color contact sheets, in this important manner, is by example.

Let's say that I've made a calibrated contact sheet with the following set of printing conditions: $9 \times$, $f/8$, 22 seconds, 60M + 95Y (on a dichroic-type machine), using 37 RC Ektacolor Paper and Ektaprint 3 chemistry—all of which I have dutifully noted on the back of the contact sheet. Let's also say that I printed frame 8 and found that I got a good print using the following set of printing data, also recorded on the back of the contact sheet: 6.5×, ƒ/8, 12 seconds, 50M + 100Y, also on 37 RC in Ektaprint 3. By looking at this data, I immediately know that frame 8 printed perfectly with a pack containing 10M less and 5Y more than my standard negative did.

Now, if I decide several months later to reprint that frame, all I need to do is check my current paper supply box to determine its calibration data with my standard negative. Let's say that I am now using Unicolor Resin Base paper with Unicolor's R-2 chemistry and that my standard negative has the following printing characteristics on this combination of materials: 9×, ƒ/8, 31 seconds, 40M + 50Y. I now know all I need to print frame 8 on the new material without a bit of fuss. Since frame 8 needs 10M less and 5Y more filtration than my standard negative, the printing filter pack for frame 8 on the Unicolor material will be 30M + 55Y. Since the Unicolor paper requires 31 seconds at the same magnification and lens opening that provided a perfect print of my standard negative on the Kodak material in 22 seconds, I know that the printing-speed ratio I will have to apply to frame 8 with the Unicolor materials is 31:22. That means that for a 6.5× print of frame 8, through a 30M + 55Y filter pack, on the same dichroic filter-type enlarger, I would need: 12 × 31/22 seconds or 17 seconds of exposure time through an ƒ/8 lens opening. Nothing could be simpler to do than to recompute these printing conditions long after you have made the original prints.

And the truly wondrous thing about the method is that it really works. That is considerably more than I can say for the several methods published by the manufacturers and marketers of color printing papers for converting old printing data for use with new materials.

Chapter 6

Image Manipulation and Enhancement

What This Chapter Is About

Anyone who has ever made a color print knows that it is a rare day indeed when a "straight" print can't be improved by a little creative manipulation during exposure, processing, or sometimes both. I'm sure that there is no one reading this book who feels that an unmounted, unspotted, unretouched, or unframed print looks better than one that has had the benefit of such enhancement. That, in a nutshell, is what this chapter deals with—not necessarily the making of silk purses out of sows' ears but, instead, making the most of what you've got.

Printing Exposure Controls

The same type of printing exposure controls that are widely used in black-and-white printing—burning, dodging, flashing, and contrast masking—are also available to the color printer. But the color printer can go the monochromatic printer one better. In color printing it is possible to not only modify local print density and overall print contrast with these techniques, but it is also often possible to modify print color simultaneously as well.

Basic Burning and Dodging

The basic techniques used to burn and dodge in negative-to-positive color printing are identical to those which black-and-white printers are familiar with. To dodge, you block part of the projected image from falling on the printing paper in areas where you want to open up shadows to show greater detail, accentuate highlights, generally lighten a portion of the print, or reduce the local color-saturation level. To burn, you selectively give extra exposure to only those print areas which you want to darken, or where you want to obliterate unwanted image detail, remove highlights, de-emphasize areas of the image, and increase local color saturation.

Techniques for burning and dodging are as numerous as printers. I personally almost never use anything but my hands to accomplish the necessary effects for the vast majority of my basic burning and dodging needs; however, there are always a few occasions when the task at hand is beyond my ability to perform with only ten fingers and five toes (on the one foot that operates my enlarger timer's foot switch). At these rare times I resort to using opaque paper or cutout cardboard masks to provide a specifically shaped area through which the image can be exposed. Some color printers prefer to always work with special dodging tools or even adjustable vignetting or burning devices. To each his own. The tool or technique that will work best for you is the one you find you are most comfortable with. If you like to do your dodging with a piece of opaque material stuck onto the end of a fine wire, more power to you. Whether you use tools or fingers and hands will make no difference whatever, so long as the shadows you are creating with these instruments fall where you want them to fall on your projected images.

There is no conceivable way that I will even dream of telling you what you ought to consider

I prefer to use my fingers and hands, but some printers like to use tools for burning and dodging. The black, cardboard tool on the left has ragged edges so that if kept in constant motion, the burned area it produces will not have sharply defined edges. The several opaque pieces of plastic can be interchanged with the small circular one at the end of the thin wire-dodging tool. The tool is held by its wooden handle and it, too, is kept in constant motion during the entire dodging operation to prevent the dodged area from being easily detected. CC filters can be placed over the hole in the burning tool or can be used to form the dodges at the end of the dodging tool for local color changes.

burning or dodging in an image. Such decisions are purely aesthetic ones to be arrived at only after the best possible straight print has been made and evaluated as to what can be done to improve the individual image. The best advice I can offer in this regard is *don't overdo it!* Nothing looks more awful than an image that has been badly manipulated in printing. Gray, washed out, smoky shadows; blank highlights; inky black undetailed shadows; or the overlapped effects of burning and dodging into areas where such image modification was never intended to show, are all, most often, more aesthetically undesirable than the unmanipulated image could ever have been. The only good dodging or burning job is an undetectable one. Toward this end, it is advisable to follow the normal black-and-white procedures of always avoiding sharp-edged dodges and always keeping the dodge moving to avoid any

clear evidence of a sharply delineated, manipulated area in the finished print. The same rule would also apply to a hole, between your fingers or pierced in a cardboard, used for burning. If possible, keep the edge of such a hole irregular and rough and keep it moving during the exposure.

It is very important to note, however, that in positive-to-positive printing the burning and dodging processes have exactly the opposite effects of those I have just described. *When you burn in an area in a reversal print, it gets lighter. When you dodge out a portion of a positive-to-positive image it gets darker.* Aside from these profound differences, the basic techniques of burning and dodging used in reversal printing are identical to those used for negative-to-positive printing; you just use them in the exact opposite way.

Color Modification During Burning and Dodging

If you use a piece of colored gelatin filter to do the job instead of casting a shadow with your fingers or a piece of cardboard, you will not only be able to modify print density through burning or dodging, but you will also be able to simultaneously modify print colors as well. Because I cautioned against overdoing straight burning or dodging earlier, I will urge you even more strongly here to use color-modifying burning and dodging procedures with even greater care. It is hard enough to do an undetectable job of straight, local-density modification, much less to modify both density and color without leaving some easily detectable evidence of your craft.

Please note that I have specified gelatin as the shadow-casting medium. You can use pieces of CC printing filters in the colors appropriate to your dodging and burning needs, but don't try to use the less expensive acetate CP filters for these purposes. The cheaper acetates will distort the image or degrade its fine detail because of their poor optical properties.

In negative-to-positive printing, where considerable local color correction is needed, it is possible to first dodge out an area with a dodge of one color of CC filter and then burn in the same area through a hole in a piece of opaque material covered with another color of CC filter. Alternatively, in less extreme cases, you may be able to modify the color of an area by dodging it with a CC filter directly. For example, you might try to change the color of a small area of a print from green to red by first dodging the area with a CC 50G dodge, then burning the same area in through a hole in a card covered with a CC 50C filter. However, in a less extreme case, it would be considerably easier to just dodge with a CC 50C filter.

In positive-to-positive printing, the same type of controlled area color manipulation is also possible but, of course, the procedure is just the opposite of the one used for negative-to-positive printing. For example, a pale grayish sky might be pepped up a bit by *dodging* with a CC 30B (or 30C, depending on your personal taste) filter. The sky could be both darkened and colored by first dodging with an opaque dodge for the entire exposure, then burning the same area in through an appropriately colored CC filter for only about two-thirds of the original exposure time. The permutations and combinations are without limit.

In color printing, one thing to be wary of when undertaking burning or dodging of any kind, is the color shifting that is likely to result *aside from any modification you may be trying to achieve through the use of gelatin filters.* Unfortunately, there is no way to accurately predict what will happen once you burn or dodge a portion of an image. You will simply have to make experimental prints until you are able to achieve the effects you want.

Printing Sandwiched Negatives and Transparencies

The whole bag of black-and-white printing tricks is essentially available to the color printer, though the ease of implementing many of them and the predictability and quality of the results obtained are probably considerably greater in positive-to-positive printing than they are for the negative-to-positive process.

An immediate example of this inequity comes to mind. I'm referring to the relative ease with which a sandwich of two transparencies can be printed, compared to the difficulty of printing color negative sandwiches. The difficulty with the negative sandwich is that doubling up on the layers of colored couplers causes all sorts of peculiar, and, most often, insurmountable printing problems. However, it is possible with either process to sandwich a black-and-white negative right along with your color material and achieve perfectly acceptable results. Using a color negative sandwiched with a black-and-white negative or positive, the best you can hope to achieve is the addition of white areas to the print. This might be just the thing for a large area of blank, blue sky, which seems to be just crying out for a big, brilliant, white sun or some fleecy white clouds (but watch out for the way the shadows lie, if you decide to plug a sun into your print). Just the opposite is true for sandwiching a slide and a black-and-white negative or positive. In this case, the best you will, in all likelihood, be able to achieve is to add solid black shapes to the image. While at first this may not seem like much of an advantage, if you think about it for a while, you may realize that being able to insert black silhouettes into a color image can sometimes be a very effective graphic device.

Whenever materials are sandwiched, they should be loaded into the enlarger's carrier, if possible, emulsion to emulsion, to enable the best possible focusing situation. Obviously, if three or more images are sandwiched, this will be an impossible procedure.

In positive-to-positive printing, sandwiching is an effective technique only when you want to place dark portions of one or more images in light areas of another. Of course, just the opposite is true when printing from negatives.

I have no idea if it is possible for one photographer to tell another how to go about picking combinations of images that will make effective prints when they are sandwiched and printed together. If it is possible to do so, I certainly don't know how.

One application for the sandwiching technique, in either direct or reversal printing, is to superimpose texture or pattern on your printed image. Screens that will enable you to achieve these effects are available from several sources, and may be sandwiched directly with the image in the enlarger's carrier. (One available source is: ByChrome Co., Inc., Box 1077, Columbus, Ohio 43216.)

Multiple Printing Techniques

There is no reason why only a single image from a single negative or slide can be printed on a single sheet of paper. With a modicum of care, it is relatively simple to print the images of several different negatives or slides all on the same sheet of paper, and, depending on what you may be attempting to achieve, there is no reason why you can't print the images contained on both negatives *and* positives on the same sheet of paper. About all you will need to do this is a thorough understanding of the processes involved, a bit of common sense, and all of the other equipment you use to make more normal types of images. The common sense comes in when you are deciding on what type of images you want to superimpose and in determining the printing order for the images. When working from slides, choose one for your primary exposure that has large enough black, or very dark, areas to provide you with sufficient space onto which you can print other images. When printing multiple reversal images, the superimposed images are added to these dark portions of the image on the previously exposed sheet of paper. In reversal printing, such areas receive little or no light during the first exposure, and images can be printed onto these unexposed or underexposed areas of the paper's emulsion as if original exposures were being made.

In printing from negatives, the opposite situation is true. Areas of the print that would be white after print processing, are those onto which other images may be projected during subsequent exposures. However, things are not quite as straightforward in combination printing from color negatives as they are in working with transparencies. Two different color negatives seldom require the same filter pack; while, in most cases, a single pack will do for a wide variety of transparencies. It's not impossible to make multiple exposures from color negatives, but it is a *lot* harder than working from slides. One way around this sort of difficulty is to project only silhouettes from black-and-white negatives into the highlight areas of color prints made from color negatives. Another is to use the time-consuming process of making several full-sized test prints under a variety of conditions until the desired effect is finally achieved.

It is also possible to simulate subject motion and a stroboscopic-image effect by moving the easel between successive exposures of the same image. Here again, this will only work effectively if your subject is shot against a black background for reversal printing, or against a white one in negative-to-positive printing. A rather contrasty subject will help a great deal in this sort of printing as well.

Contrast Controls

Frankly, I feel that this is a subject that is, to a considerable extent, inappropriate to this book. I feel this way because the color printer, lacking the availability of contrast-graded or variable-contrast papers — common items readily available to black-and-white printers — must rely on some very peculiar techniques to modify print contrast. The most effective methods for controlling the contrast of color prints involve the use of printing masks, and these call for procedures and materials that are not really very compatible with the small-format negatives or positives used by most amateur printers. There are, however, some simpler printing and processing techniques which can also affect print contrast in both reversal and direct printing, and I will begin with these more practical approaches.

Flashing

Excessive contrast in prints made either from negatives or positives can sometimes be reduced by flashing the printing paper, either before or after the printing exposure has been made. More care is required for flashing negative-to-positive materials than is needed for positive-to-positive prints.

When flashing negative-to-positive material, you will need a blank frame of developed film of the same type as that from which your image is being printed. Such frames can be easily obtained by simply leaving your lens cap in place, winding, and shooting a blank frame of film. The unexposed frame will be a uniform orange or yellowish-orange after processing; it will be the color of the film's built-in printing mask. You will also need neutral density (ND) filters, such as the glass type you use on your camera's lens, or a gelatin type, such as a Wratten No. 96 of 20 density.

Post-flashing is probably the most predictable technique. After making your normal exposure, leave the enlarger settings and printing filter pack as they are, remove the negative being printed from the negative carrier, and insert a blank, processed frame of the same kind of film you are printing into the carrier. Replace the carrier in the enlarger and either add the gelatin ND filter to the filter drawer, or use the glass ND filters below the lens. Try your initial post-flashing exposure at the same lens opening and exposure time which was used for the original printing exposure, then process the print and note the effect. If more or less flashing is required, vary the exposure time.

The effect here will be to add texture to highlights and some overall density to the entire print. If, in addition to excess contrast in the unflashed print, you also have a slight color-cast problem in the highlights, you can modify the

printing filter pack used for the post-flashing operation to reduce this problem. For example, if your unflashed print showed reddish highlights, you might want to try to subtract cyan from, or add magenta and yellow to, the pack during the post-flashing operation.

If preflashing is used, the process just described is simply reversed. First the light from the enlarger lamp (greatly attenuated by passing through the blank film frame, the printing filter pack, and the ND filter, or filters) is allowed to fall on the previously unexposed printing paper. Then the blank film frame is removed from the carrier, the negative inserted, and the image printed. The results of preflashing are more pronounced and harder to predict from both the standpoint of density and of color balance. Of the two procedures, post-flashing would be the one to try first.

Both pre- and post-flashing may also be effective in reducing the contrast of positive-to-positive prints. Once the slide has been removed, it isn't necessary to add anything to the negative carrier. Flashing is simply accomplished through the printing filter pack and the ND filter or filters. Flashing will tend to open up blocked shadow areas in a reversal print, and it will also lighten highlight areas. The flashing technique is generally most applicable to correcting overly contrasty low-key reversal images and high-key negative-to-positive ones.

Processing

While most suppliers of color software hardly recommend chemical procedures for contrast control, such controls do, nonetheless, work fairly effectively. The software manufacturers tend to shy away from the methods recommended here because these techniques are sometimes a bit on the unpredictable or temperamental side, and will often yield an image of lower technical quality (sometimes stained or mottled) as well as one of modified contrast. However, the most probable reason you may have for wanting to tamper with normal contrast in the first place is because the particular image you are printing really doesn't work all that well aesthetically. And, where aesthetics are concerned, technical quality takes a backseat.

Chemical contrast controls are the simplest to implement. To increase the contrast of a negative-to-positive print, increase the development time (try about a 30 percent increase and note the effect). Adjust the development-time increase, or the original printing exposure, or both, in accordance with the results obtained.

Conversely, you can decrease the contrast of a negative-to-positive print by decreasing the development time. In this case, your first trial print might be made with about a 25 percent reduction in development time. You can then make subsequent adjustments involving either more or less development time, or printing exposure, or both, as your results indicate which is necessary.

In either of the cases just mentioned you can also attempt to vary development, and therefore contrast, by increasing or decreasing the developer temperature, increasing or decreasing the developer dilution, or increasing or decreasing the agitation of the print in the developer.

Positive-to-positive prints can also undergo contrast change in accordance with your wishes and chemical manipulation. If you are using Cibachrome materials, you can use the same methods that were just outlined for negative-to-positive prints. If you are using Kodak Type 1993 paper and Kodak R-500 chemicals (or any of the several other manufacturer's chemical products designed to process this material), things get a bit more complicated, but the methods I'm about to outline should be of some assistance.

If you want to increase the contrast of a reversal print, try diluting the first developer by about 25 percent and then using deliberately oxidized color developer (leave it out in a tray overnight).

Chemical cures for excessive print contrast can be arrived at in several sneaky ways. You can deliberately overdevelop your print in the first developer (say, by about 20-30 percent), then process it in used, but unreplenished, color developer in the normal manner. If that doesn't seem to do it, try deliberately adding a few drops of blix to your color developer and otherwise processing normally. If you are still unsatisfied, try processing normally until you reach the color developer, then boost the chemical temperatures by about ten degrees for all of the remaining processing steps that follow.

I realize that all of the procedures just suggested will probably strike terror into the hearts of those readers who have been conditioned by some manufacturers to believe that one must never tamper with time, temperature, and chemistry in color processing; but they are, to varying degrees, effective, useful, and much simpler than any others for modifying print contrast.

Anyhow, if software vendors are so particular about the way their products are processed, why don't they offer color printing papers in contrast grades, or better yet, in controllable variable-contrast types, so that I wouldn't have to write chapter sections like this one?

Masking

If you are a masochist with unlimited time, patience, money, help, and facilities, you may want to try masking to raise or lower the contrast of images printed from negatives or transparencies. I don't fit that description, so the only conceivable reason I would ever dream of for undertaking the lengthy and demanding procedures and processes involved, would be to save a priceless image that otherwise could not be duplicated.

If I could reshoot the image from scratch, I would prefer to do so every time. If I couldn't reshoot the image, chances are I would give the job of mask-making and printing to a custom lab to save myself a lot of time and headaches.

How Masks Work. Masks are, for all practical purposes, dodges that are printed while bound in contact with a negative or slide, to modify printing characteristics of negative or slide. To reduce contrast of a print from a color negative through masking, you must make a thin, diffused, black-and-white negative of the color negative to serve as the mask. Just to keep our terminology straight, a negative of a negative is, obviously, a positive, so from here on we will call this a positive mask. The unsharp positive mask will, of course, have its maximum density in the image's shadow areas and its minimum density in the image's highlight areas. When the positive mask is placed in perfect register with the color negative, it will serve to decrease and diffuse the amount of light that can pass through the image's shadow areas, but it will have very little effect on the light passing through the pair to expose the highlights in the print. The net effect will be a print with decreased density in the shadows and an overall slightly softer quality in the middle tones and highlights.

To increase the contrast of a print made from

a color negative through masking, it is necessary to make two contact exposures on black-and-white film. The first exposure creates a sharp, positive black-and-white image of the color negative called an interpositive mask. The interpositive mask is then, in turn, contact printed onto the same type of (separation-negative) film that the interpositive itself was made on, to form the negative silver mask. When this process is properly carried out, the final negative mask will look rather thin and underexposed. It will have no density at all in the dark shadow areas. When this negative silver mask is bound in perfect register to the negative, and the pair is placed in an enlarger and printed, the mask will serve to hold back light in the highlight areas while not interfering with the transmission of light through the shadow areas at all. The net effect will be a print with normal shadows, but lighter middle tones and highlights than were obtained on the unmasked print.

The general processes and theory involved for controlling the contrast of color prints made directly from transparencies, through the use of printing masks, are exactly the same as those just described for controlling the contrast of color images printed from negatives through the use of masks. The only differences are the names of the masks used and the occasional requirement for an additional highlight mask.

In reversal printing, the unsharp mask used to reduce contrast is a negative mask, rather than a positive one, and the sharp silver mask used to increase print contrast is a positive one rather than a negative one. The general processes used to produce these masks are the same as those described for making the masks used for color negatives, with one notable exception. When transparencies containing important highlight detail print with excess contrast, it is necessary to produce a sharp, underexposed, overdeveloped, black-and-white highlight mask, and then to use this mask, bound in register with the original transparency, to produce the unsharp negative mask that will be used to lower overall print contrast. All of this may appeal to you, but I have better things to do with my time.

How Masks Are Made. What follows is only the most sketchy sort of outline of the kind of grief involved in the preparation and use of contrast-modifying printing masks. The information is not intended as a "how-to" presentation

by even the wildest stretch of the imagination. It is offered here only to give the reader a small appreciation of all of the trouble involved.

A mask, made on Kodak Pan Masking Film 4570, can be used to reduce excess contrast in prints made by either reversal or direct printing methods. To begin the process of making such a mask, first place the negative or transparency to be masked between a piece of ¼"-thick plate glass and a Kodak diffusion sheet (the former is available from any glazier, the latter from any professional camera shop). If the image to be masked is larger than 5" × 7", a second ¼"-thick piece of plate glass will be required between the sandwich just mentioned and the unexposed piece of Kodak Pan Masking Film 4570 on which the mask will be made. If the image being masked is smaller than 5" × 7" but larger than 2¼" × 2¼", this intermediate sheet of glass is to be only 1/8" thick. An intermediate piece of glass between diffusion sheet and film is not required for 35mm negatives or slides. Kodak offers no recommendations, however, for intermediate glass thickness appropriate to film formats between 35mm and 2¼" × 2¼". I suppose I would stick with the 1/8" thickness myself, were I ever confronted with such an unlikely choice.

All of the aforementioned—the top glass, the negative or transparency (emulsion side down), the diffusion sheet and the bottom glass—are placed on top of a piece of Kodak Pan Masking Film which itself is placed (emulsion side up) on your matte-black easel on your enlarger's baseboard. This has to be done in darkness as no safelight is permitted. The enlarger is used to expose the masking film. Prior to making the exposure, the enlarger lens is opened to its widest setting and the head height is adjusted to bring the level of illumination on the easel to 3 footcandles (or EV 3.6 at ASA 100 for those of you who use exposure meters to take this measurement).

If you were making your contrast-reducing mask for a color negative you would, at this stage, put four CC 10 blue filters into the enlarger's filter drawer or below the enlarger lens. Then the enlarger lens is closed down, four stops for transparencies or three stops for negatives, and the basic exposure is made at nine seconds. It's a good idea to make a few bracketing exposures as well. The mask is then developed for three minutes in Kodak HC 110 developer at dilution F at 68 F (20 C). A properly exposed mask will show very little image in the highlight areas.

Speaking of highlight areas, when masking contrasty transparencies with important ones, a special highlight mask on Kodalith Ortho Film 2556 Type 3 is required to be made *before* you can begin to make the contrast-reducing mask described above—a troublesome business—but I won't describe this special highlight mask here in a last ditch attempt to keep the few of you who are still awake with me.

When a satisfactory contrast-reducing mask has been made, it is taped in perfect register on the film-base side of the negative or transparency, and the masked negative or transparency is then put into the enlarger's carrier, emulsion side down, and printed. Printing exposure for such masked images is about 50 percent greater than that which is normally required.

Making a contrast-increasing mask, for either a negative or a transparency, is an even more complicated, two-stage affair. First, the negative or positive is placed (emulsion down) under a ¼"-thick piece of glass and these two are then put down on top of a piece of Kodak Separation Negative Film 4133 Type 2 (emulsion side up) on your matte-black easel, in the dark. The exposure of this film is identical in all respects to the exposure procedure described for the contrast-reducing mask. The exposed film is developed in DK-50 for four minutes at 68 F (20 C), and then fixed and dried. A proper exposure will yield an image with good detail in both highlight and shadow areas. The film you have just exposed and processed now replaces the negative or positive under the ¼"-thick glass, using the same enlarger illumination set up, and the same kind of Kodak Separation Negative Film 4133 Type 2; yet another exposure is made, this time for about 90 seconds. The film is processed the same as before. The result is the mask you will use. It has been properly exposed when it looks as if it had been underexposed, with no density in the highlight and middle-tone areas. Finally, this mask is taped, in register, to the film base of the negative or positive. The negative or positive is then placed in the enlarger carrier, emulsion side down, and an exposure is made through the pair to produce a print with increased contrast.

If all this information is a good deal less than perfectly clear, so be it. I have reduced the descriptions down to an absolute, bare minimum. But, if you do seriously want to pursue the matter of contrast-controlling masks further, and in more detail, I strongly suggest that you consult the latest Kodak literature specifically on this subject and the materials which are involved.

Creative Controls and Techniques

The number of ways that you can alter a perfectly good color image into some sort of gross graphic distortion of its former self are legion. Being essentially a plain old fashioned, straight-image man myself, I am not really fond of any of them. I can certainly understand why some darkroom workers do want to create new and unusual color graphics, but what really baffles me is why they want to bother using a camera and film to begin the process. Frankly, I think that manipulations requiring vast outlays of time, energy, materials, and cash, to arrive at some unknown and unknowable color-graphic end, are absurd in the extreme. It would be far better if the practitioners of these peculiar arts would simply learn to paint and thereby cut out all of the nonsense they have to go through in the darkroom.

There are, however, a few creative color printing processes that make a good deal of sense.

Such processes are easy, cheap, quick, and effective at rendering color-manipulated images which might otherwise be difficult or even impossible to produce.

Color Reversal Techniques

The color printer has a wide choice of simple ways to reverse the colors of the image contained on a transparency or a negative to obtain a print. Perhaps the simplest of these is to print positive images on negative materials and negative images on positive materials. This latter course is the less attractive one because the orange, or yellowish-orange printing mask incorporated in color negatives will be reproduced on a reversal print.

Perhaps a better way to reverse the colors of an image made from a color negative is simply to make use of that standard black-and-white manipulative technique, the Sabattier Effect. It works as well with negative-to-positive color images as it does with negative-to-positive black-and-white ones. All you need do to cause an image color reversal on a color print made from a negative is to remove the print from the drum in which it is being developed when its development is about one-third complete; then reexpose it to the light of a low-watt white or colored bulb located about three or four feet from its surface; then slip it back into the drum to complete the remaining two-thirds of the normal development period. When development is done, carry out the remaining processing steps normally. You can use anything from a candle to a 15 watt bulb for the reexposure. The duration of reexposure will have to be found experimentally for the source and source-distance you chose to use. You might try about one second for a 15 watt frosted bulb, four feet above the surface of the partially developed print. Remember, when using colored reexposure light sources, that the reexposure color will be reversed in the print. For example, reexposure to a red lamp will yield an overall cyan cast, to a green lamp will yield a magenta cast, and to a blue lamp will provide a yellow cast, etc.

There is no point in discussing the reexposure of reversal prints, since that is the very name of the game in reversal printing.

If you do want to reverse the colors of a transparency during printing and elect to go the route of printing the slide on ordinary (non-reversal) color printing paper and processing the print in negative-to-positive chemistry, it may be useful to include a frame of unexposed and normally processed color negative film above your transparency in the negative carrier. Doing so provides the printing mask lacking in the transparency and allows you to use normal printing filter packs.

Pseudo-Crystal Photomicrography

It is neither cheap nor easy to do good photomicrographic work with crystals. It requires a lot of special hardware and considerable skill to produce even mediocre results. However, if what you are really after are the beautiful, abstract color patterns that can be obtained by making excellent photomicrographs of many sorts of crystals, rather than accurate photographic reproductions of certain specific crystal patterns, it is possible to eliminate the need for a microscope entirely and do the entire job quickly and simply right in your enlarger.

What you will, indeed, obtain with the

TYPICAL SETUP FOR PSEUDO-CRYSTAL PHOTOMICROGRAPHY

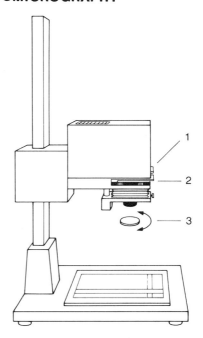

One polarizer, one sheet of birefringent material, and one piece of unexposed, normally processed color negative film can be located either: (1) in the filter drawer, (2) or bound into the glass slide in the negative carrier. (3) A second polarizer is rotated below the lens to vary the colors projected on the paper.

technique about to be described are sharp photographic reproductions of specific crystal patterns, but the colors produced in these images are strictly up to you. You can manipulate these crystal image colors in any way you choose.

Since the major difficulty and expense involved with crystal photomicrography is brought about by the need to make tiny crystals visible by means of a microscope, this technique employs the simple idea of using crystals of a size so large that no microscope is needed. Large crystals of organic compounds can be grown, or simpler still, be bought on clean 2″ × 2″ glass slides. These mounted crystal-bearing glass slides can be taped to a piece of cardboard, which can then be inserted directly into your enlarger's negative stage in place of your regular negative carrier, or they can be placed in any mounted-slide carrier. In order to be able to produce controllable color images of the crystals, you will also need two small sheets of polarizing material (or one sheet and one camera polarizer), and a sheet of birefringent material (Mylar or

Cellophane). All of these items, combined with several varieties of large crystals grown on glass slides, are available from Edmund Scientific, Barrington, N.J. 08007 (catalog 762, No. P-41,381 and P-41,382).

Pseudo-crystal photomicrographs can be made on either normal or reversal color printing papers. Printing exposures are not very different from normal exposures. They are easily determined by making a multiple-image test print. The enlarger setup must include, in addition to the printing filter pack, a sheet of polarizing material and a sheet of birefringent material located somewhere in the light path above the crystal-bearing slide glass in the negative stage. The crystals, sold by Edmund Scientific, have these materials bound directly to the slide glass; however, they can be located in the enlarger's filter drawer if that is more convenient.

The enlarger is brought to focus on the crystal with the aid of any sort of focusing device except a grain focuser. Then the second sheet of polarizing material is introduced below the enlarger lens. It is at this point that the focused projected image of the crystal on the slide glass will take on some incredible colors. If you don't like the colors you see at first, you can simply rotate the polarizer below the lens and watch the colors change. When you have a pleasing pattern and color arrangement composed on your easel, turn off the enlarger, load a sheet of paper on the easel, and make your printing exposure. Remember, when printing with the negative-to-positive type materials, the colors seen on the easel will be reversed; however, if you print on reversed paper, what you see is just about what you will get.

CRYSTAL SLIDE PACKAGE

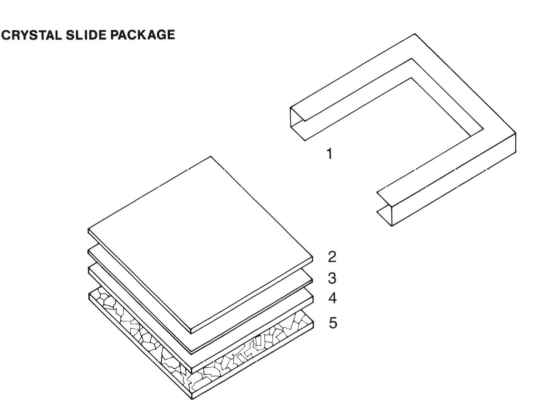

This sketch shows a typical 2″ × 2″ slide-glass package for use with the pseudo-crystal photomicrographic technique, available from Edmund Scientific Corp. If you wish, you can grow your own crystals, but it's a good deal simpler to buy them. You may also locate the polarizing material and the birefringent material (Mylar) in your enlarger's filter drawer.

(1) The assembled package is mounted in a metal frame or taped together. The layers of the slide-glass package include: (2) polarizing material; (3) birefringent material; (4) a top slide glass; (5) a bottom slide glass with a thin layer of crystallized organic compound on its upper surface.

Print Finishing

This area of color print making is, in my opinion, the least enjoyable but most rewarding part of the entire process. Let's face it, no matter how strong an image you may have been able to capture on film and subsequently print, it's going to look like less than it could unless you spot it, correct local color problems, mount, frame, and display it. It is very difficult to see and enjoy color images stored inside of cardboard boxes. (Sadly, I must admit that they do last a lot longer inside cardboard boxes. Color prints are not very stable and exposure to light does cause them to fade.)

Spotting and Area Color Modification

Nadler's first law of the darkroom states that if there is but a single speck of dust in the darkroom, it will, invariably, be on the negative you are printing. Even the most meticulous printers, working with diffusion-type enlargers, are still confronted with dust spots on prints.

There are two possible cures for dust spots on prints made from color negatives, and only one on prints made from slides. Dust spots on prints made from color negatives are white. They can be filled in with tiny dots of liquid dye, or you can remove the negative from the enlarger, thoroughly clean it, and then reprint it (hoping to beat Nadler's first law). Prints made from slides directly will show dust as black specks on the print. There is really no point in trying to bleach these black specks out and then fill them back in again with appropriately colored dyes. The print will, without exception, look worse for your efforts. The *only* real cure for dust-spotted reversal prints is to remove the slide from the enlarger's negative carrier, thoroughly clean it, return it to the carrier, clean it again, and reprint it. I find it very helpful, when doing my final cleaning of either negatives or slides, to work with a baby's ear syringe and an 8× loupe, with the material to be printed held firmly in its final printing position in the carrier.

There are several materials which I have found will do an excellent color-spotting job, if you have the patience, skill, and the steady hand required to use them. Not everyone does, and I must admit, I'm often not too happy with some of my own handiwork in this department. In any case, it is important to practice all the following techniques on scrap prints before trying to use

them on your hard-earned good prints. If the area surrounding a spot is black, dark brown, any shade of gray, or any really dark color at all, you may find that you can get rid of very tiny, white dust spots quite satisfactorily with plain ordinary Spotone No. 3, applied very carefully, in tiny dots, with the end of a top-quality 00 Sable brush.

If, however, your dust spots fall in an area that is both light and of some very definite and distinct color, look out — you've got good potential for grief. There are three materials I have used successfully to spot out such horrors. They are Kodak's Retouching Colors, Dr. Martin's Synchromatic Transparent Water Colors, and Marshall's Photo Retouch Colors. The latter two products are supplied as liquids, the former as cakes of solid dye. Of the three, the Kodak materials are the most flexible, but also the most costly, and require the greatest amount of skill. The Kodak Retouching Color Kit contains all six primaries, plus orange, brown, neutral (a warm gray), and reducer (which I'll get to in a while). Marshall's kit consists of colors labeled foliage green, primary yellow, primary blue, bright red, verona brown, and basic flesh. Dr. Martin, to the best of my knowledge, doesn't offer a special photographic retouching kit, but does provide a huge number of colors from which to choose.

Basically, the wet-brush spotting technique involves picking up some liquid dye (or dyes) on your brush, transferring it (or them) to a clean, white plastic, china or glass palette, and diluting it (or them) with a mixture of half water and half stabilizer. In the case of the solid Kodak dyes, the brush must first be dipped in the stabilizer solution and then worked over the appropriate dye cake or cakes to dissolve the dye. The dissolved dye or dyes are then transferred to and mixed on the palette. Once you have managed to achieve a color match for the area to be spotted on the palette, some of this proper shade of dye should be moved to a second clean, white palette and diluted again with more of the stabilizer solution. It is this very diluted dye of the proper color that should now be transferred from the second palette to the white spot on the print and deposited in minute dots well inside the borders of the spot. Avoid using too wet a brush by passing the brush tip over a blotter or a tissue before touching it to the print. Also, avoid getting

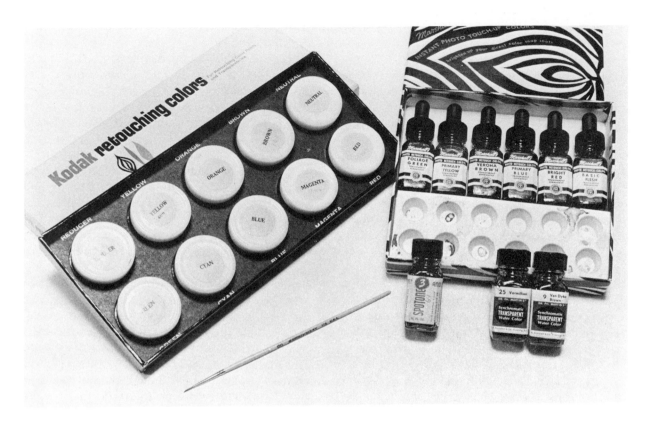

There are several excellent color print-spotting and retouching materials available. The Kodak retouching colors can be used wet or dry to spot or retouch large areas of prints. Marshall's Instant Photo Touch-Up Colors are liquid dyes suitable for spotting, but cannot be used instantly. Dr. Martin's Synchromatic dyes do the same job. Don't overlook Spotone No. 3 for spotting color prints. It is all you will need in many instances, and it works quite well. Another must is a good 00 Sable brush.

any of this dye over the edges of the spot like you would avoid a plague. Once you get any dye overlap you will also get a dark ring around the spot, and the dark ring will look a lot worse than the naked spot. Keep up this tedious procedure until the successive dots of low-density dye build up enough cumulative density to make the spot disappear. This will take time, patience, and a very steady hand, but if you persevere and do a good job, it will be well worth the effort.

It is actually a lot easier to change the overall color cast, or even add a good deal of original color to a large, relatively light area of the print, than it is to spot a color print. I would much prefer to color one four-square-inch area than to have to spot five little white specks with a total area of .001 of a square inch between them. Large area retouching is easy because of Kodak's solid dyes. The procedure is relatively simple. First, you clean the area on which you want to apply

dye with a cotton ball, then you simply breathe on a cake of the appropriate Kodak dye, pick a generous amount of it up from the cake with another cotton ball, and smear the dye on the print with a circular motion of the dye-bearing cotton ball. The dry dye, so applied, can be smoothed out so that the color laid down on the print is even and free of streaks and spots. This is done by lightly buffing the area with yet another cotton ball. As a matter of fact, if you look down at the print and discover that you really don't like it, there is no need for panic. You can actually buff most of the dry dye right off the print. If buffing still leaves some unwanted dye, you can use another cotton ball to apply some of the cake of reducer in the same way that you applied the dye, and remove anything left by the dry buffing. If you run out of reducer, anhydrous alcohol will do just as well. Once you have colored the area satisfactorily you can make the dye permanent by directing a jet of steam from a vaporizer or kettle against the dye-retouched area of the print. If you find that you can't build up sufficient density with just one application of dry dye, set the first application with steam and allow the area to dry thoroughly, or dry it with a stream of hot air from a hair dryer, before giving the area a second application of dry dye. Repeat, if necessary, until you get the density you need. Kodak's dyes can be manipulated just the way you manipulate the print with the printing filter pack. You can add the subtractive primary dyes to get a color match for anything seen in the print, assuming you have a great deal of patience and a reasonable amount of both skill and luck. One note of caution—Kodak's solid dyes, good as they are, can't be trusted to do *both* wet and dry-dye retouching. Once you get the cake dyes wet, they will not be suitable for use in dry-dye work. This is sad indeed, because it means that you need two sets of these very expensive dyes if you want to be able to work both ways with the Kodak materials.

Mounting

There are all sorts of wet or sticky adhesive mounting systems available for color printing materials these days, but, Scotch Brand Mounting Adhesive Sheets No. 567 is a product that I'll recommend here. I have also successfully used several different types of dry-mounting (tissue) systems which are designed to be used with a heated mounting press. But even dry mounting has gotten to be far less reliable and simple than it used to be.

Back in the good old days, when color printing paper was just that—paper—almost any dry-mounting tissue available, and any dry-mounting press that could have its thermostat reliably set to keep the platten temperature from exceeding about 220 F (104 C), would do the job with great ease. Now, however, ordinary paper-based color printing materials have all but disappeared. They have been replaced with all-plastic or plastic-coated color printing materials. It is the plastic bases or plastic coatings on the paper that make color prints so hard to mount. And, to confuse matters still further, each manufacturer of sensitized materials seems to be using a different type of plastic coating on their products, so that a mounting tissue developed to work satisfactorily with, let's say Kodak materials, may not work very well with Cibachrome's materials, for example. Add to this the fact that there are four major suppliers of dry-mounting tissue—Ademco, Bogen-Technal, Kodak, and Seal—and you can understand why it can be quite a chore to decide on what to use to keep your plastic-coated prints tightly adhered to a mounting board, and how to use it.

There is no one simple answer to these problems as this is being written. Since the materials involved are constantly undergoing change, it would be rather foolish to try to match specific tissues with specific color printing materials. However, it is possible to offer some general rules that will help with all of them including Cibachrome, which, with its mirror-like surface finish, is not well suited to being dry mounted at all.

Ademco, Bogen-Technal, Kodak, and Seal all make special dry-mounting tissue designed to hold plastic-coated printing paper. Not every tissue will work with every paper, and none of them will hold Cibachrome, which is an all-plastic material.

6-13

The best way I know of assuring that the thermostat of your press is set properly for any of the available tissues, except Ademco's, is to use Seal Temperature Indicator Strips. These little devices clearly tell you when your press is providing between 200–210F at the interface between the print being mounted and the mounting board. I strongly advise using them when mounting color prints.

The four major factors involved with achieving an acceptable dry-mounting bond between a color print on plastic-coated paper, and a mounting board are: temperature, pressure, moisture, and cooling. Each of them is very important but the first and last are, in most cases, absolutely critical.

Temperature. Temperature is critical for two reasons. If the dry mounting press is too cool, the mounting tissue won't melt and, of course, no bond will be achieved. If the press is too hot, not only will the mounting tissue melt, but so will the plastic-coated print. Obviously then, it is very important to make sure that the thermostat on your press is not only working, but that it is very accurately calibrated (most dry-mounting press thermostats do not fit this description). There are several ways to do this, but the most simple and accurate one I know of involves products called Seal Temperature-Indicator Strips and Release Papers (available from professional camera shops or on order from Seal Inc., Derby, Conn. 06418). These little strips contain two special colored wax patches: one that melts at 200 F (93 C) and another that melts at 210 F (99 C). In use, an indicator strip, wrapped in a release paper, is placed in the heated mounting press between a dummy print and a mounting board, and the press is closed and locked for some time judged appropriate to the thickness of the mount being used (between 30 seconds and one minute will probably be satisfactory in most cases).

The press is then opened and the wax patches are checked. If the low-temperature patch melts but the high-temperature patch doesn't, you know that your thermostat is properly set. If the thermostat is improperly set, both wax patches will either be unmelted or

melted. You should keep adjusting the thermostat setting, allowing the press' temperature to stabilize, and keep trying the press until you get exactly the temperature you need. (These strips are inappropriate for use with Ademco materials, which are specified as melting at 185 F (82 C).)

While all of this sounds like a lot of work, and it is, calibrating your press' thermostat needn't be done more than about once a year and doing so can save you untold grief. It is important that you practice mounting with scrap prints before trying to mount an important print. There are few things sadder to a color printer than having one of his, or her, prints melted.

Pressure. It is very difficult to recommend any specific dry-mounting press platten pressure. I will have to simply say that the press should neither be so tight that is is hard to close, nor so loose that it closes with very little effort at all. Each press manufacturer (Ademco, Bogen-Technal, Seal) has a different pressure-setting procedure. It would be wise to write to the manufacturer of your press for their specific pressure-setting recommendations for dry mounting plastic-coated paper.

The proper press platten pressure is necessary, of course, to insure that the heated press' upper platten maintains even and intimate contact over the entire surface of the print; thereby exerting constant pressure on the thermoplastic mounting tissue as the heat from the press' upper platten is conducted down through the cover sheet, the print, and the mounting tissue, and finally into the mounting board.

Moisture. Moisture was a big problem even in the halcyon days of real honest-to-goodness paper prints. Even then, if you loaded your press with a paper-based print, mounting board, or

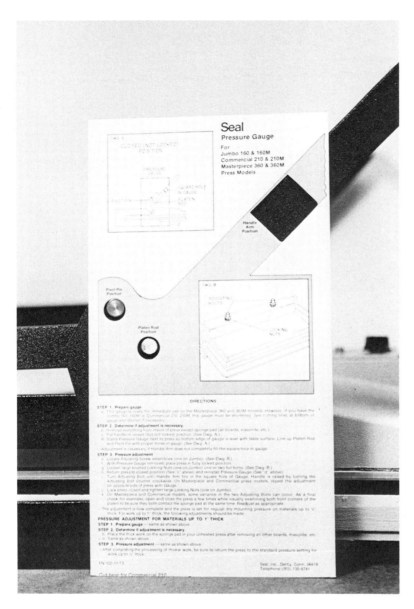

Dry-mounting press platten pressure is an important factor in obtaining a satisfactory bond between a plastic-coated color print and its mounting surface. Seal provides special templates for setting the platten pressure of their press to suit the needs of plastic-coated paper.

cover sheet that had traces of moisture absorbed in its fibers, and then proceeded to bond such a print to such a board, you would invariably remove a print that was firmly mounted, but had one or more easily seen water-vapor-filled bubbles in it. Prevention of this kind of problem was the same then as it is now — *thoroughly dry all of the materials that you are going to load into the press before you load them.* You can do this in a cool oven or you can use the press itself to heat up and thereby drive the moisture from these materials. You should also always open and close the press briefly several times before you finally lock it shut for the actual mounting. Opening and

closing the press a few times this way, immediately before mounting, will allow any last bit of moisture to escape before it is too late.

Cooling. It has been my recent experience that there is no bond at all between a plastic-coated print and the mounting board when a dry mounting press is opened. Even though the press has done all it should — heating the print, the mounting tissue, and the mounting board, and melting the thermoplastic tissue — when the press is opened the thermoplastic mounting tissue is still fluid and the print will be very happy to curl right off the mounting board and fall to the floor. I have found that the only way to avoid this is to remove the print-tissue mounting-board sandwich from the press as soon as all parts of the sandwich have been sufficiently heated, and then immediately put the sandwich down on a cool, flat, smooth surface and place a cool, clean, heavy, flat, smooth plate of metal or glass on top of the print. This procedure keeps even pressure on the sandwich while it sucks the heat out of it, causing the mounting tissue to solidify and complete the bond between the print and the mounting board. I can't stress the importance of this step enough; without it, I have never been able to get more than a very poor bond. As a matter of fact, when mounting Kodak's Type 1993 paper (something I find rather difficult to do), I place the hot sandwich on the floor, put a cold, 3/16″-thick plate of glass over the surface of the entire print, and then stand on the piece of plate glass for about 30 seconds to insure that the bond at the print edges is satisfactory. Even with this ungainly procedure, I often find that I have to reheat and then recool under pressure at least one or two of the edges of each print that I mount in this way.

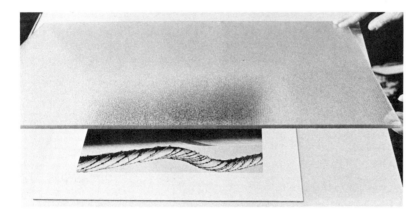

I have found that cooling is critical when dry-mounting color prints on plastic-coated paper. As soon as I open my press after mounting a print, I pull the mount and print from the press bed, lay them down on a cool, flat surface and immediately place a clean, cool, heavy sheet of glass on top of the print.

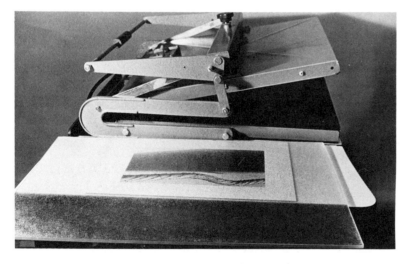

I leave the glass on the print for at least 30 seconds to 1 minute, depending on the material mounted. The pressure of the glass holds the print flat and in contact with the mounting board and the molten tissue between it and the board until the thermoplastic material of the mounting tissue has solidified.

Chapter 7

Processors and Processing

Throughout this book I have continually touted the combination of a daylight print-processing drum, a motor base, and a switching clock as the ideal for amateur use. This chapter in no way modifies my opinion. It does, however, give me an opportunity to present considerably more design and operational information about the several other color print-processing machines available, as well as to illustrate the typical use of a drum/motor base/clock combination. I hope that it will give you the opportunity to draw your own conclusion.

The Agnekolor Laminar Flow Processor
Model AG-1114-FM

This machine accomplishes color print processing by holding the printing paper stationary and moving the chemical solutions rapidly beneath its entire emulsion surface. For all practical purposes, the machine requires that the chemicals used in it be replenished (rather than dumped after a single use, as in one-shot operation) because of the large volume of each solution (11 ounces), which must be used for each of the processing steps.

The Agnekolor has several component sections and a fair number of parts. It has two wells, one holding water that is used to keep three containers of chemical solutions at some constant temperature. The other well serves as a pump reservoir. An electrically driven pump is incorporated in the machine to circulate the processing solutions. A flat, almost horizontal (there is a slight forward tilt) shelf is provided to support the print during processing. A pair of plastic bars hold the print in position on the shelf and regulate the flow of chemicals from the pump. A light-tight cover is provided for the shelf which allows the machine to be used in normal room light. Processing chemicals are stored in three canisters that are provided with floating as well as with screw-top lids. The canisters are normally kept in the temperature-

controlling well. An optional thermostatically controlled heater, available as an extra cost accessory, can also be placed in the temperature-controlling well. A dial thermometer is provided to monitor the temperature of the water in the well. The machine has two draincocks: one permits recovery of the processing solution from the pump well, while the other permits the water to be drained from the temperature-controlling well. A length of hose with a faucet coupling at one end is provided to bring water to the machine from a faucet or a thermostatically operated water-temperature controller.

The machine is sort of box shaped. It is made of a plastic material that is said to be highly resistant to staining or deteriorating through contact with color print-processing chemicals. Its dimensions are approximately 18″ × 24″ × 12″ and, when filled with chemicals and temperature-controlling water, it weighs about nine pounds. The pump (and accessory heater) requires 110 volt AC power. The dial thermometer is specified as being accurate to ±½ F (±¼ C).

The illustrations and text that follow will help to give you some idea of what processing with an Agnekolor machine is like. I'll describe processing with Kodak 37 RC paper and Kodak Ektaprint 3 chemicals, as these materials call for

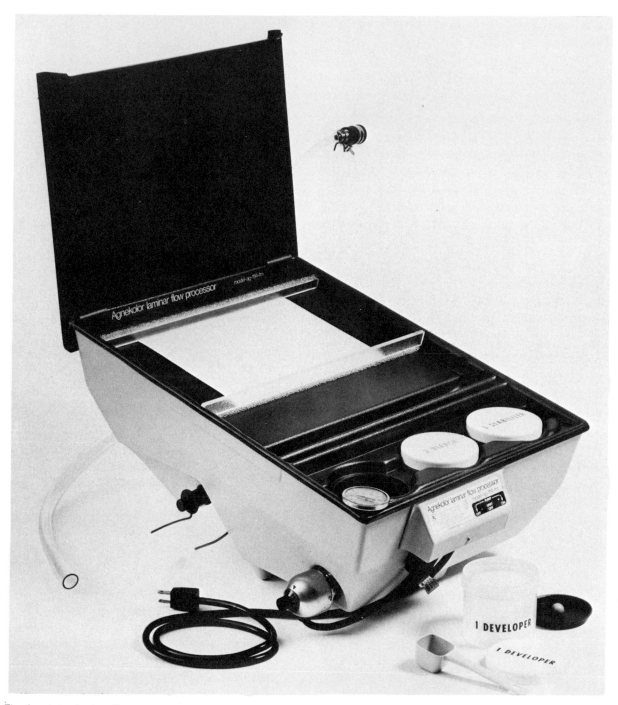

The Agnekolor laminar flow processor.

relatively simple and uncomplicated procedures.

Before the processing actually begins, 46 ounces of water at the selected processing temperature are poured into (step 1) the temperature-controlling well (or tub, as it is called in the Agnekolor literature). Room temperature chemicals are then poured from their storage containers into the three 11 ounce processing containers used with the machine. These 11 ounce containers are then placed in the tub and allowed to sit there for as long as it takes them to come to the desired processing temperature. The temperature of the water in the tub can be regulated by adding hot or cold water from time to time as the need for such alterations is indicated by the Agnekolor's dial thermometer. (The optional thermostatically controlled electric tub heater makes this job a lot easier, if initially more costly.)

Now the machine must be flushed out. You begin this procedure by installing both plastic positioning bars in the grooves they will occupy when holding the paper size you are processing. The maximum capacity of this Agnekolor machine is either a single 8″ × 10″ or a single 11″ × 14″ sheet of paper. (Note: There is also a 16″ × 20″ Agnekolor unit available.) Both of these bars have foam-plastic materials along one edge. This foam is positioned on the bottom edge of both bars during the flushing cycle. The actual flushing is carried out with clean water. Two very different procedures are used: one, if the flushing water is supplied to the Agnekolor from a temperature-controlled source of running water and allowed to drain from the machine directly into a sewer drain; the other, if the flushing water comes from a pitcher and is drained into a container and temporarily disposed of in a slop bucket.

If running water and a sewer drain are available, the pump's drain spigot is opened, the flushing-water supply source is turned on, the pump motor is turned on, and the machine is allowed to flush for one full minute before the supply water is turned off and the pump well allowed to drain. When the well is almost pumped dry, the pump is shut off and the water is allowed to continue to drain out of the machine by gravity flow.

If no temperature-controlled running water supply and no sewer drain are available, the pump's drain spigot is closed and 11 ounces of flushing water, at the processing temperature, is poured into the pump well from a pitcher. An 11 ounce container, available as an extra cost option, is placed under the pump's drain spigot, the pump is turned on and allowed to circulate the flushing water for ten seconds. Then, the pump's spigot is opened and all of the flushing water is drained and collected in the 11 ounce container. This water is then dumped into the slop bucket. This entire procedure is then repeated with another 11 ounces of water, and then the pump motor is turned off.

Now the Agnekolor is almost ready for the developing cycle. To complete its preparation, the choke bar, which is the uppermost of the two positioning bars, is removed. The machine's light-tight cover is put in it's vertical (open) position. The pump's drain spigot is closed. The temperature of the developer is checked and, if it is the one you've selected, all 11 ounces of it is poured into the pump well (step 2) and the pump is turned on. The machine is now ready to accept a sheet of paper for processing.

The exposed paper is loaded into the machine (step 3) emulsion-side down in darkness or under a No. 10 or No. 13 safelight. It is located against the foam edge of the lower position bar and then its top edge is released. The choke bar, foam-plastic edge up, is replaced to hold the top edge of the paper in place. At this point the paper is very gently moved to determine if all is well and if it is floating on a laminar flow of developer on the processing shelf, or if you have made an error in the loading procedure. Let's assume all is well and continue. Now the unit's light-tight cover is lowered and the normal room lights may be turned on. The amount of time the developing process requires is determined by the temperature you have selected to work at. Thirty seconds before that time is up (you supply the clock, set it, and watch it) the pump's drain spigot is opened and the developer is allowed to drain back into its container, which, hopefully, you have placed below the spigot prior to opening it (step 4).

At this juncture, you are ready for the first wash. If you have the Agnekolor's water hose connected to a temperature-controlled source of running water, that source is allowed to flow into the hose to fill up the pump well. However, care must be taken to keep the pump well from overflowing into the temperature-controlling well (something I always found difficult to prevent from happening). The unit's pump, which is left running throughout all of the processing steps and procedures, circulates the water under the print to remove the developer from its emulsion side. No washing of the back of the print takes place, however. The washing step is carried out for a total of 45 seconds, 30 of which are used to drain the wash water out of the machine (assuming, of course, that you have a sewer drain convenient).

In the event that neither a drain nor a source of temperature-controlled running water are available, the wash-water inlet and overflow pipes are clamped shut and 11 ounces of wash water, at the proper processing temperature, are added from a pitcher, circulated by the pump for 10 seconds, and then allowed to completely drain (about another 30 seconds) from the pump's spigot. The spigot is then closed and another 11 ounces of water are added to the pump well, allowed to circulate for 10 more seconds, and then drained completely. The draining is done into the 11 ounce accessory container or into a jar small enough to be conveniently placed beneath the pump's drain spigot. After each of the drains, the spigot is closed and the container full of contaminated wash water is removed and spilled into a slop bucket.

While the washing step is taking place, the developer container is replenished (step 5) with fresh developer. The Agnekolor instruction manual suggests 25 ml of fresh developer as a replenisher for Kodak Ektaprint 3, but does rather vaguely suggest that the age of the developer being replenished and the area of emulsion surface it has processed should be taken into account when determining the volume of replenisher used. Unfortunately the instruction manual goes no further to detail these important variables. (It is just this lack of uniformity and consistency which makes the replenishment technique totally inapplicable for amateur use, in my very strongly held opinion.)

Once all of the wash water has been drained from the processor and the spigot has been closed, the bleach-fix (blix) container is removed from the temperature-controlling well and its entire 11 ounce contents are spilled into the pump well and allowed to circulate under the print for the amount of time appropriate to the processing temperature being used. Thirty seconds prior to the end of that time period the blix container is placed under the pump's drain spigot, the spigot is opened, and the blix is allowed to drain back into its container. The blix is then replenished to bring the contents of the container back up to the 11 ounce level.

Now a somewhat more complicated washing step is begun. If running, temperature-controlled water and a sewer drain are available, the wash water is allowed to flow into the Agnekolor to a level high enough to wash the lip of the cover but not overflow the temperature-controlling well (no mean feat). After about 10 seconds of the wash period, the unit's light-tight cover is raised. The full length of the wash step is 2 minutes, but the

last 30 seconds are used as drain time. During the 1½ minutes in which fresh water is entering through the inlet hose, the Agnekolor's choke bar (the uppermost of the two plastic bars used to hold the sheet of paper in place) must be gently depressed and released several times to allow the wash water to remove any traces of blix from the bar. After doing this for a while, you then remove, reinstall (foam-side down), and alternately depress and release the choke bar several more times to cause the wash water to back up and flow over the back of the print in order to remove the blix from it. When no more blix can be seen on the print back, the choke bar is again removed, turned foam-side up, and reinstalled in its operating position. After all of this has been done, and the wash water has been completely drained, the pump's spigot is closed.

If, however, no running water or drain are available, the wash step is carried out as follows: with the cover in place, 11 ounces of wash water of the proper temperature are spilled from a pitcher over the area of the cover lip adjacent to the pump well, to wash all traces of blix from the lip. After 10 seconds, during which the unit's pump will circulate the 11 ounces of water and clean the underside of the cover's lip, the light-tight cover is raised (step 6) and the blix-contaminated wash water is drained from the pump spigot into a suitable container and then dumped from that container into a slop pail. Once the first 11 ounces of wash water is out of the machine, the spigot is reclosed and another 11 ounces of wash water are added to the pump well from the pitcher. This second wash-water charge is also allowed to circulate, with the cover in its raised position, for a 10 second period, during which the choke bar is alternately depressed and released to clean the blix from the bar. This water is drained and dumped, the pump's spigot closed, and another 11 ounce charge of fresh, clean temperature-controlled water is added to the pump well from the pitcher. During the 10 seconds this charge is allowed to circulate, before the pump's spigot is opened to drain it, the choke bar is flipped over, foam side down, and depressed and released to cause the wash water to back up and overflow the print to get the blix off its back. The wash is then drained through the pump's spigot, the spigot is closed, and the wash water is dumped. Now another 11 ounce charge of water is added to the pump well from the pitcher while the inverted choke bar is depressed and released

Step 1

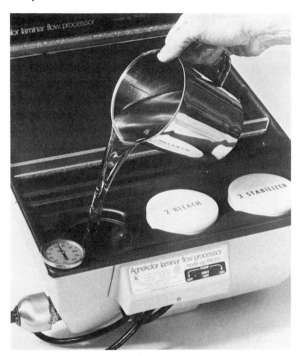

Step 2

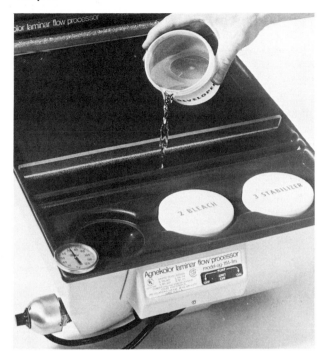

Step 3

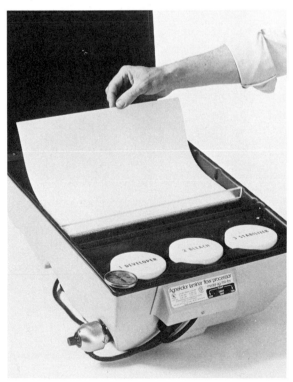

Step 4

Pour 46 ounces of water at the selected processing temperature into the temperature-controlling well (top left). Check the temperature of the developer. If it's what you've selected, pour all 11 ounces of it into the pump well (top right). Load the exposed paper into the machine, emulsion side down, in darkness or under a No. 10 or No. 13 safelight (bottom left). Drain the developer back into its container placed below the spigot (bottom right).

Step 5

Step 6

Step 7

Step 8

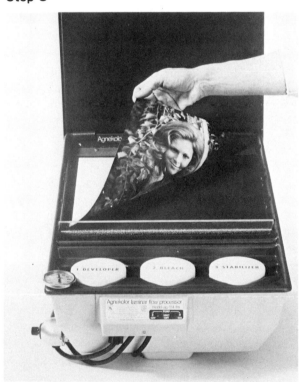

Replenish the developer container with fresh developer (top left). During the second washing procedure, raise the light-tight cover of the unit and drain the blix-contaminated wash water (top right). Remove the 11 ounce container of stabilizer from the tempering tub and spill it into the pump well (bottom left). Remove the print from the unit for drying (bottom right).

to further clean the print's back. After about 10 seconds of this, the choke bar is flipped back over and replaced and the wash water is drained from the pump's opened spigot. When all of the wash water has been drained, the spigot is closed and the machine is ready for the stabilizer cycle.

The 11 ounce container of stabilizer is removed from the tempering tub (step 7) and spilled into the pump well. The stabilizer is pumped under the print for the amount of time appropriate to the processing temperature being used. When your timer indicates that all of this period but 30 seconds has passed, the pump's drain spigot is opened and the stabilizer is allowed to drain back into its container (which you have placed beneath the spigot during the stabilizing cycle).

The print processing has now been completed and the print can be removed (step 8) from the Agnekolor, squeegeed, chamoised, and blown dry. However, several more steps are needed before the Agnekolor processor is ready to process the next print. First, the stabilizer container must be filled back up to the 11 ounce level and replaced in the tempering tub, then the machine must be cleaned.

Washing the Agnekolor with a source of running water is done by turning the water on, and, while the pump circulates it, pressing and releasing the choke bar to get all the stabilizer off; then turning the choke bar over so that its foam strip contacts the paper-supporting shelf when it is pressed. This dams up the flowing water to get traces of stabilizer off the support shelf and its sides. The flowing water must be directed to all portions of the machine that might possibly harbor a trace of stabilizer through any means which you can devise. After 1½ minutes of this, the water is turned off at the source, the pump is

turned off, and the machine is allowed to drain until dry through the open pump drain spigot. Finally, the spigot is closed.

When running water is not available, the washing procedure involves the use of four 11 ounce charges of fresh water to accomplish the stabilizer removal just described. Each 11 ounce charge of water is circulated with a closed spigot for 10 seconds, then drained for 30 seconds. After each drain, the contaminated wash water is dumped into a bucket. After the fourth wash step the pump motor is turned off, the pump well completely drained, and the spigot closed. Now the Agnekolor processor is ready to handle the next print.

This machine's initial cost is quite high, more than twice that of a 16″ × 20″ daylight drum and a motor base, and unlike that combination it can only handle a single 8″ × 10″ or 11″ × 14″ print at a time (a 16″ × 20″ drum will accommodate four 8″ × 10″ or two 11″ × 14″ prints). It must be used with chemical replenishment, and this is the least repeatable, least reliable, and least consistent of techniques for amateur or small-volume professional users who are not prepared to undertake periodic chemical analysis, to run control strips, and to keep the detailed records that are really required if replenishment is to be used with predictable results. The machine requires considerable manual manipulation during processing, sparing you nothing in that department. And, even if the extra-cost accessory heater is purchased for the Agnekolor, the unit's tempering well will only accommodate three chemical containers. This makes it necessary to use an auxiliary tempering device with the machine if a chemical process such as Kodak R-500, with its five (or six, if you count the potassium iodide rinse) solutions is used.

The Kodak Rapid Color Processor Model 11

The Model 11 consists of only a few major components. The heart of the machine is a large diameter stainless-steel drum with a diamond-pattern texture on its surface. The drum is driven, through a gear case, by a water-protected electric motor. The motor and gear case are mounted on one of the two vertical portions of the unit's stand. The drum, which can be

dismounted from the stand for ease of maintenance and cleaning, is supported and driven by the motor coupling at one end and is supported by a plastic cradle, in the other vertical portion of the stand, at its opposite end. The drum is rotated in a horizontal plane. Within the stand, between the two vertical supports, is a large tray that can be tilted. When the tray is in its normal

The Kodak Rapid Color Processor, Model 11.

horizontal position, it can hold several ounces of liquid. When the tray is tilted, the liquid is spilled out. The only other Model 11 components are a small glass rod-type thermometer, a plastic-tipped rubber hose with a faucet coupling at one end that is used to bring water from a temperature-controlled source to the hollow interior of the drum, and is also used for washing purposes, and an epoxy-coated nylon-mesh net, called a blanket, which is used to hold a print against the chemical on the surface of the rotating drum.

The complete machine is arranged so that there is a small space between the rotating drum and the tray below it. When a liquid chemical is spilled into the tray it fills this space and makes contact with the drum. The textured surface of the drum picks up the liquid chemical from the tray and an even coating of the chemical is distributed over the entire surface of the drum. When the drum is evenly coated with liquid, a piece of 8″ × 10″ or larger (up to 11″ × 14″) paper can be draped over its surface and held in place, hydroplaning on the film of liquid chemical on the drum, by the blanket. The blanket is, in turn, held in place by a metal bar, the ends of which, called lugs, hook into the frame of the machine. I realize that the machine I have just described (as best I could) sounds highly improbable, but there it is.

Before a new Model 11 can be used to process a print, several adjustments must be made to the machine and several operating requirements must be met. The machine, when operated in accordance with the maker's instructions, requires a source of running (½ gallon per minute *minimum* flow rate), temperature-controlled (100 ±½ F or 38 ±¼ C), water and a sink with a sewer-connected drain. A grounded 110 volt AC outlet is also required. If these requisites are met, the machine is set up in its operating location within the sink and the drum is leveled by means of a pair of leveling feet and a spirit level. This done, the tray height is then set by means of a pair of adjusting screws, then the unit is plugged into the wall outlet. The drum, the tray, and the blanket should now be thoroughly rinsed with warm running water. This is most easily done by connecting the rubber water tube to the outlet of the sink's thermostatically-controlled mixing valve, or to a faucet, and by using the long plastic tip of the hose to direct a stream of water over these portions of the machine (see photo). Once the entire apparatus has been thoroughly rinsed off, the plastic tip of the water tube is clipped into a bracket which directs the flow of water from the tube to the inside of the hollow stainless steel drum. Now the water supply is turned on and 100 F (38°C) water is allowed to flow into the drum. Once it is filled to its operating level, the temperature-controlling water will continuously spill from the open end of the drum. This overflow is measured with the thermometer, and when its temperature stabilizes within the specified range, the apparatus is ready to be used to process a print.

Tables 7–1 and 7–2 are from the instruction sheet supplied with this machine. They indicate the processing times and temperatures required to process 37 RC paper in Ektaprint 3 chemicals and Type 1993 paper in Ektaprint R-500 chemicals, respectively; but what they don't specify is the volume of these rather costly fluids required for *each* chemical step. The Model 11 requires 4 ounces each of the Ektaprint 3 chemicals and 7 ounces each of the chemical components of R-500. Since these chemicals are used once and then discarded, this is a very wasteful and expensive machine to process with.

A few more preprocessing steps are in order, however, before the Model 11 actually comes into use. Kodak advises pouring room temperature chemistry from its storage containers into smaller beakers, in the proper volumes for the process being used. It doesn't matter if the print being processed is an 8″ × 10″ or an 11″ × 14″, the volume of chemicals used will be the same. (Prints smaller than 8″ × 10″ should not be processed on a Model 11 because the friction between the blanket and drum will be excessive and cause the motor to overheat.) The beakers full of chemicals should be placed near the machine where they can be reached quickly. An 11″ × 14″ tray must also be placed close to the machine and filled with water at some temperature between 70 and 100 F (21 and 38 C). The blanket is placed in this water-filled presoak tray so that its lugs project over the sides of the tray and the green, epoxy-coated side of the blanket is facing up (see photo).

To wash the drum, tray, and blanket, connect the rubber water tube to the outlet of the sink's thermostatically controlled mixing valve, or to a faucet. Use the long plastic tip of the hose to direct a stream of water over these portions of the machine.

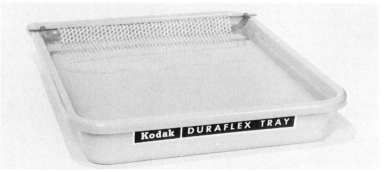

The blanket is placed in the pre-soak tray with the epoxy-coated side of the blanket facing up.

Table 7-1

PROCESSING SPECIFICATIONS
FOR KODAK EKTACOLOR 37 RC PAPER

PROCESSING STEPS	REMARKS	PROCESSING TIME* (MINUTES)	PROCESSING TEMPERATURE	
			C	F
1. Prewet	Agitate print in tray of water.†	½	21.1 to 38.9	70 to 102
2. Developer	Use Kodak Safelight Filter, No. 13 (amber) or No. 10 (dark amber) for first four steps.	2	37.8 ± 0.3	100 ± 0.5
3. First Water Wash	Running water.	½	37.8 ± 1.1	100 ± 2
4. Bleach-Fix	—	1	37.8 ± 1.1	100 ± 2
	The remaining steps of the process may be done in normal room light.			
5. Second Water Wash	Running water.	½	37.8 ± 1.1	100 ± 2
6. Stabilizer	No water wash or rinse after this step.	½	37.8 ± 1.1	100 ± 2
7. Dry	Air-dry the prints. Do Not Ferrotype.		Not over 107	Not over 225

*The time for each step, except the prewet, includes a 5-second drain time. The drain time after the prewet should be 10 seconds. In each case, start draining in time to end the processing step and start the next step on schedule.
†Agitate frequently during the prewet. Do not handle the dry print with wet fingers or the wet print with dry fingers. Plastic or rubber gloves are recommended. For prewetting the prints, always use fresh water; do not use the water that was previously used for cleaning the blanket and bar.

Caution: After completion of each processing run, thoroughly wash the blanket, bar, drum, and tray with water. Dump and rinse the prewet tray and fill the tray with fresh water.

Table 7-2

PROCESSING SPECIFICATIONS
FOR KODAK EKTACOLOR RC PAPER, TYPE 1993

PROCESSING STEPS	REMARKS	PROCESSING TIME* (MINUTES)	PROCESSING TEMPERATURE	
			C	F
1. Prewet	Total darkness. Agitate print in tray of water.†	1	21.1 to 38.9	70 to 102
2. First Developer	Total darkness.	1½	37.8 ± 0.3	100 ± 0.5
3. Stop Bath	Total darkness.	½	37.8 ± 0.6	100 ± 1
4. First Water Wash	Use Kodak Safelight Filter, No. 13 (amber), No. 10 (dark amber), or OA (greenish-yellow).	2	37.8 ± 1.1	100 ± 2
5. Color Developer		3	37.8 ± 0.6	100 ± 1
	The remaining steps of the process may be done in normal room light.			
6. Second Water Wash	—	½	37.8 ± 1.1	100 ± 2
7. Bleach-Fix	—	1½	37.8 ± 0.6	100 ± 1
8. Third Water Wash	—	1½	37.8 ± 1.1	100 ± 2
9. Stablizer	—	1	37.8 ± 0.6	100 ± 1
10. Rinse	—	¼	37.8 ± 1.1	100 ± 2
11. Dry	Air-dry the prints. Do Not Ferrotype.	—	49 to 66	120 to 150

*The time for each step, except the prewet, includes a 5-second drain time. The drain time after the prewet should be 10 seconds. In each case, start draining in time to end the processing step and start the next step on schedule.
†Agitate frequently during the prewet. Do not handle the dry print with wet fingers or the wet print with dry fingers. Plastic or rubber gloves are recommended. For prewetting the prints, always use fresh water; do not use the water that was previously used for cleaning the blanket and bar.

Caution: After completion of each processing run, thoroughly wash the blanket, bar, drum, and tray with water. Dump and rinse the prewet tray and fill the tray with fresh water.

Now the motor's switch is turned on and the drum begins to rotate. The first processing solution is poured into the center of the tray below the drum (see photo). (If the solution is poured into the tray while the drum is stationary, some of it will overflow and the tray and the remainder will be insufficient to evenly wet the entire drum.)

The room lights are turned off and safelights (No. 10 or No. 13) turned on, if 37 RC is to be processed. However, no safelights can be used to begin processing Type 1993 paper.

After the exposure has been made, the paper is placed in the presoak tray, along with the blanket, emulsion side down, and agitated for about half the presoak period called for in the tables. Then the piece of printing paper is turned over, emulsion side up, and lined up with the metal edge of the blanket. Ten seconds before the presoak period is up the paper and blanket are lifted from the tray, using both thumbs to hold the paper against the blanket's top bar. The pair are then held over the tray to allow the water to drip off them (see photo). The blanket's top bar is now rotated 180° and you must now, somehow, find your way with this dripping burden to the spinning drum. This is not excessively hard to do with a No. 13 safelight four feet overhead, but it may prove to be extremely difficult in total darkness. Let's assume you find your way—now you have to drape the combined blanket and print over the spinning, developer-covered drum (see photo) and manage to hook the blanket's lugs into a bracket in the machine so that the print will be held between the blanket on top and the spinning drum below it. Sometimes you can and sometimes you can't. The first few times you try this you will swear it can't be done. The next few times you will manage to get the print and blanket to stay on this weird apparatus, but part of the print will kind of slip out from under the blanket and manage to get unevenly processed or, worse yet, get thrown off the machine into the sink. After you have wasted a lot of time and paper you will, if you are a very well coordinated person, manage to get the print neatly and squarely sandwiched between the drum and the blanket. You will *probably* be able to repeat this thereafter, *if you use the machine reasonably often.* If, however, you are only an occasional processor, you will most likely have to go through the learning procedure time after time to rebuild the requisite manual dexterity needed to process prints on this incredible device.

Kodak recommends that the user start timing the development from the moment the emulsion side of the paper comes in contact with the chemical on the rotating drum. How the user is to do this they don't explain. Considering the difficulty sometimes encountered with getting the blanket lugs to stay put in the slots provided for them in the machine, to keep the print and blanket from being hurled off the drum and into the sink, you had better use a foot switch to start the timer, because your two hands will be rather busy at the moment the emulsion touches the chemical on the drum.

Once you have come this far, the rest will be relatively easy. I'll describe the sequence of events and procedures used for 37 RC and Ektaprint 3 below, but all of the chemical processing and wash steps used for any paper or any type of chemicals are identical to these; only the timing, type, and number of steps may be different.

Five seconds before the end of the developing step, the front of the tray is lifted to dump the developer from the tray, into the sink and down the sewer. The front of the tray is held raised during this 5 second period, and is then released and allowed to resume its normal, horizontal position.

As soon as the tray is released, 30 seconds is set on the timer (you supply it, you set it and you watch it) and the water tube is pulled from the plastic bracket, which holds it in a position to supply water to the inside of the drum, and directed at the print on top of the drum (see photo). The stream of water should be played over the back of the print and the entire surface of the drum for 25 seconds. During this time the rear edge of the tray must be occasionally raised, to dump the wash water that has collected in it. Perhaps a half-dozen dumps during this period will be sufficient. During the last 5 seconds of the wash period, the hose is reinstalled in its clip at the end of the drum opening and the tray's rear edge is lifted to drain the wash water from the machine. Might I remind you that the wash routine just described is carried out in the limited illumination provided by a safelight (and, in the case of reversal materials *in total darkness*—good luck!)

Now your timer is reset for 1 minute. Next you locate the beaker containing blix and pour it into the front of the tray with a sweeping motion,

The first processing solution is poured into the tray below the drum.

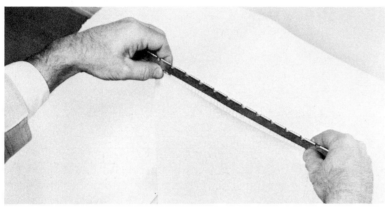

To remove the prewet print from its bath, lift the paper and the blanket from the tray, and hold the pair over the tray to allow the water to drip from them.

To put the print on Model II, drape the combined blanket and print over the spinning, developer-covered drum and hook the blanket's lugs into a bracket in the machine so that the print will be held between the blanket, on top, and the spinning drum below it.

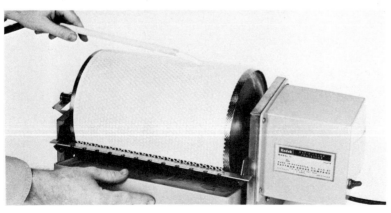

Direct the stream of wash water toward the back of the print during washing operations. Machine components must also be flushed with wash water.

from one side of the tray to the other, so that the chemical will be quickly and evenly distributed across the entire width of the drum and so that nothing overflows the tray before the drum can pick it up. After 55 seconds have elapsed you lift the rear of the tray and hold it elevated for 5 seconds. The preceding step, too, is performed under safelight illumination. But now the happy moment has arrived when you can turn the normal room lights back on. Now 30 seconds are set on the timer and another wash step is carried out as the first one was. Five seconds before the end of the wash step the hose is returned to the drum end and the rear of the tray is lifted and held (to dump the wash water) until the clock runs out.

Next, the timer is reset for 30 seconds and the beaker containing stabilizer is spilled into the tray with the same sweeping motion used for the blix. After the clock has run out, the switch is turned off and the drum stops rotating. The blanket is then removed from the drum and placed in the sink. The print is removed from the drum, squeegeed, chamoised, and blown dry. The tray of stabilizer is dumped. The hose is pulled from its clip and directed over the drum and tray to remove the stabilizer from them. Then the blanket, its support bar, and the presoak tray are all thoroughly washed. The machine is now ready to process another print.

While I am perfectly willing to admit to having loaded that description with a good deal of sarcasm and predjudice, I think that my reasons for doing so were legitimate and, hopefully, clear to the reader. This machine is very expensive and difficult to use. It requires constant attention and manipulation. It must be used in safelight illumination or total darkness during several complicated and difficult steps. And, while it does use the repeatable, predictable, and consistent one-shot chemical technique, each such shot will cost you dearly as the volumes of chemicals needed to make this machine work are grossly in excess of those needed for daylight drum operation. And finally, I do want to point out that this drum, more so than any other type of processor I am aware of, must be used in a very well-ventilated room as the drum acts as a very efficient evaporator and puts a maximum amount of chemical fumes into the darkroom air. As far as I am concerned, this machine has *no* redeeming features whatsoever.

Daylight Color Print Processing Drums

Enough has been said elsewhere in this book about the techniques and procedures involved with the use of daylight drum processors. Rather than go through yet another lengthy description of the simple, cheap, and efficient way that color prints are made in these inexpensive devices, I have instead illustrated the procedure called for in Chapter 4 for processing a print made on Unicolor's resin-base paper using that firm's R-2 chemicals. The hardware used in the accompanying illustrations consists of an 8″ × 10″ Unidrum daylight print-processing drum of the horizontal, ribbed type, a Uniroller motor base, a dial thermometer, a 1 gallon plastic pitcher, a 1 pint graduate, and four 4 ounce drinking glasses. I have also used two GraLab timers to illustrate the timing of each step. The motor base is plugged in to the timer on the left which is always set to establish the timing of the individual step illustrated. The timer on the right is provided for illustrative purposes only. It indicates the time remaining, at each step of the way, until the print has been completely pro-cessed. In actual practice, only the timer at the left would normally be used.

While the process illustrated and just outlined makes use of electrical energy to roll the processing drum about its long axis, the same agitating effect can be obtained through the use of human muscle. The drum, as explained in earlier chapters, can simply be rolled back and forth over any reasonably level surface that is covered with a towel or a sponge rubber pad to provide a bit of friction to insure that the drum rolls rather than slides. The procedures illustrated would be identical for this kind of manual operation except, of course, that the motor base would be replaced by a Turkish towel and your own two arms and ten fingers. The drum would stand on its own two legs, when it was to have a solution poured into it, and the timer would be started the moment the drum was rolled off its legs and manual agitation begun. To manually agitate the type of drum shown, it should be rolled as far as possible in one direction, until its legs touch the surface it is being rolled upon,

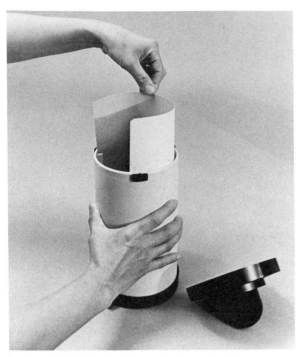

1. In safelight illumination or darkness, load the exposed sheet of paper into the clean, dry drum. Close the drum. Turn on the normal room lights.

2. Fill the one-gallon pitcher with water at 108F. Remove the thermometer and close the pitcher.

3. Fill each of the four-ounce glasses with two ounces of the chemical solution called for by its label.

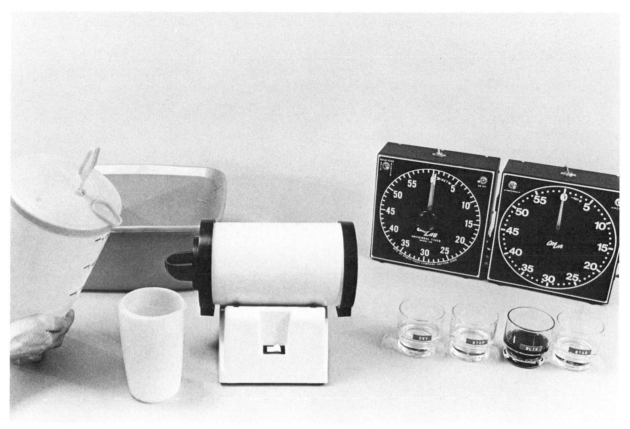

4. Pour one pint of water from the one-gallon pitcher into the one-pint graduate.

then it should be rolled back in the opposite direction until the other side of the legs touch the supporting surface.

There are several other types of manual agitation possible with some slightly different daylight drums. The Kodak London (not available in the United States) drum, which can be tightly capped at both ends, can be floated in a temperature-controlled water bath and spun in that bath to provide agitation. This same drum, and any of the vertical-type smooth-walled drums, can also be manually rolled on a dry surface.

One recent and interesting variation on these several methods is incorporated in Colourtronic's Turbo-Drive automatically driven daylight processor. These vertical smooth-walled drums are equipped with a band of impeller blades that fit over the center of the outside of the drum. The impeller-equipped drum is placed in a special tray that holds it in position to receive the output stream from a small electrically powered pump that busily recirculates a small

volume of temperature-controlling water within the tray. The stream of water from the pump hits the impeller blades and causes the drum to rotate within its supports in the tray and thereby agitates the contents of the drum.

All of these daylight drum alternatives have several definite features in common. Daylight drum processors are relatively cheap. They allow easy loading and print processing, if some electromechanical (or hydraulic) means of agitation is provided (though doing so does run the cost of the apparatus up to about half of that of the cheapest alternative). They use a minimum volume of processing chemicals, preferably in the one-shot manner, but they can also be used with a replenishment scheme (instead of dumping the used chemicals into a slop bucket, they can be dumped right back into their storage bottles) for those who (mistakenly) believe that economy can be obtained this way. Finally, they all keep the amount of processing chemical vapor in the darkroom air at a level of the barest minimum.

7-15

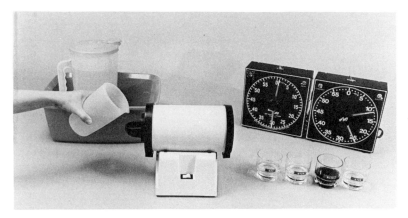

5. *Presoak.* Set the timer for 30 seconds. Pour the water from the one-pint graduate into the drum. Start the timer. (The motor base is plugged into the timer and will agitate the drum as long as the timer is running.)

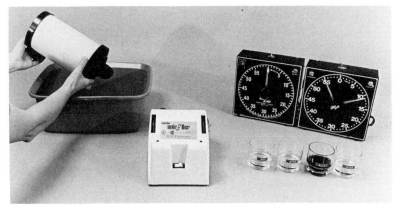

6. When the time set on the timer runs out, dump the water out of the drum into a slop bucket or down a sewer drain.

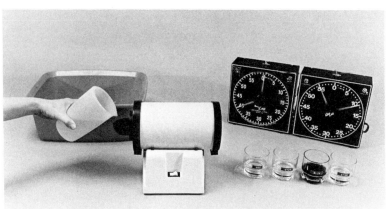

7. *Presoak.* Set the timer on 40 seconds. Measure another pint of water from the gallon pitcher into the one-pint graduate and pour the water into the drum. Start the timer.

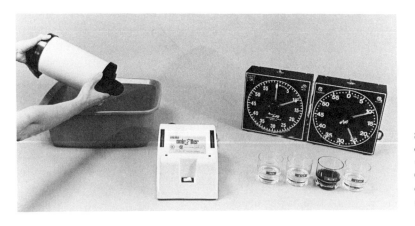

8. When the timer has 10 seconds to run, dump the water. Continue to drain the drum until the time set on the timer runs out. Gently shake the drum's spout during this drain period to get rid of as much water as possible.

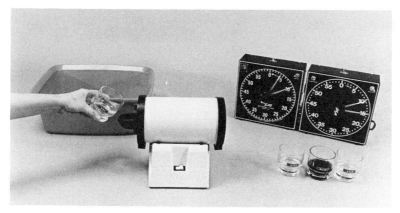

9. *Developer.* Set 4 minutes and 10 seconds on the timer. Pour two ounces of developer into the drum. Start the timer.

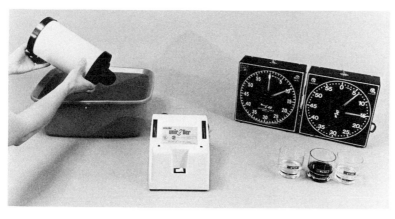

10. When 10 seconds remain on the timer, dump the used developer. Drain the drum, while gently shaking it until the time set on the timer runs out.

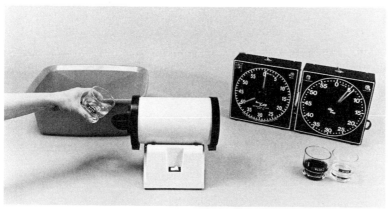

11. *Stop.* Set 40 seconds on the timer. Pour two ounces of stop bath into the drum. Start the timer.

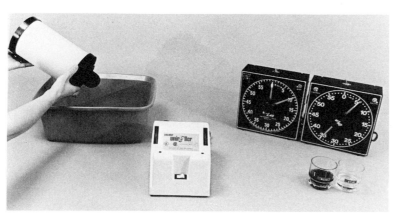

12. When 10 seconds remain on the timer, dump the stop bath. Drain the drum, while gently shaking it, until the time set on the timer runs out.

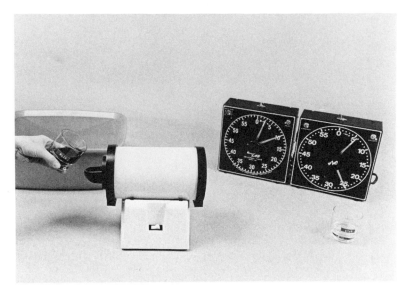

13.   *Blix.* Set 2 minutes and 10 seconds on the timer. Pour two ounces of blix into the drum. Start the timer.

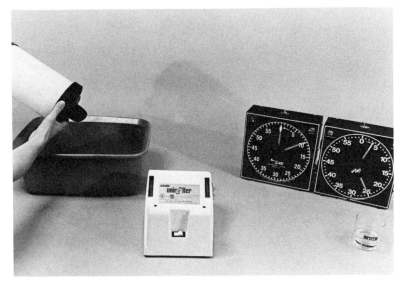

14.   When 10 seconds remain on the timer, dump the blix. Drain the drum, while gently shaking it, until the time set on the timer runs out.

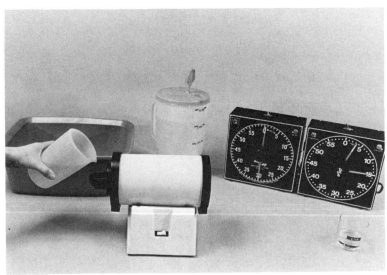

15.   *Wash.* Set 30 seconds on the timer. Measure eight ounces of the water remaining in the gallon pitcher into the one-pint graduate. Pour the water into the drum. Start the clock.

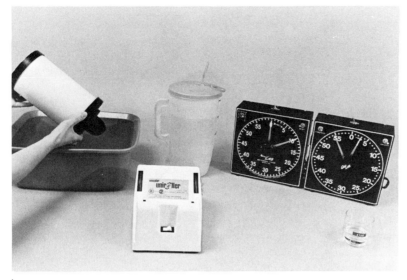

16. When 10 seconds remain on the clock, dump the water. Drain the drum, while gently shaking it, until the time set on the timer runs out. THREE ADDITIONAL WASH STEPS. Repeat the identical procedures illustrated and described in the wash procedure above, three more times.

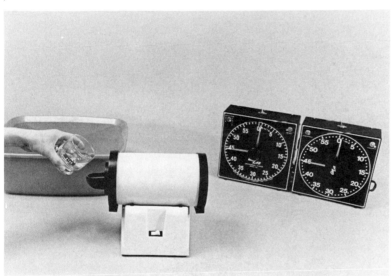

17. *Stabilizer.* Set the timer on 45 seconds. Pour two ounces of stabilizer into the drum. Start the timer. When 10 seconds remain on the timer, dump the stabilizer.

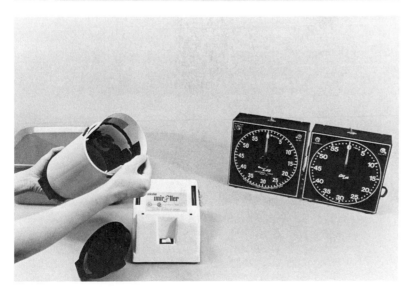

18. Open the drum. Remove the processed print. Dry the print. Wash the drum and its cap out thoroughly with warm water and dry them. The drum is now ready to process another print.

Temperature Control Techniques

The best temperature control is no temperature control. If you can work at room ambient temperature with speed sufficient to your needs (and temperament), then you will save yourself a great deal of trouble, money, and effort by ignoring temperature control completely. However, most of us are in too much of a hurry to put up with the long processing times required by low-temperature processing. And since most of us don't live in a tropical climate, we have little choice but to make use of one or more of the several alternative means of bringing our processing chemicals to an elevated temperature and maintaining them at that temperature during our print processing.

There is no one best way to achieve the degree of temperature control you need. The solution to your own particular problems will, in most cases, be found to be a function of the amount of money you feel you can afford to spend and the amount of ingenuity you can bring to bear on it. With a great deal of the latter, you will be able to keep the expense to a minimum.

Water Bath Temperature Controllers

The use of a water bath to control the temperature of processing chemicals or apparatus can involve a great deal of elaborate and expensive hardware—thermostatically controlled constant-temperature water-flow valves, water-pressure compensators, electronically controlled water-temperature regulating devices, pumps, hoses, remote-temperature sensors, etc.—or it can be done with nothing more than a large household dishpan, a pitcher, and a thermometer. The dishpan solution will, in most instances, be all that is really needed for most color printing requirements, although it may prove to be inadequate to film-processing needs.

To implement accurate temperature control with a dishpan, pitcher, and thermometer, first place the chemical containers, the film tank, the drum processor, or whatever piece of hard- or software you are trying to bring to some specific non-ambient temperature, into the dishpan. Then put your thermometer into the pitcher and run water into it from any convenient sink tap until the pitcher is filled with water at the desired processing temperature. Then spill the pitcher full of water into the dishpan. Continue to do this until you have as much water in the dishpan as you want, but not so much that half-filled chemical bottles tip over and begin to float in it. Now take the thermometer out of the pitcher and put it into the dishpan. You will note that the water temperature will begin to drop rapidly if the room's ambient temperature is well below the desired processing temperature. Correct this shift by scooping a pitcherful of water out of the dishpan and replacing it with more water, at, or a few degrees above, the desired processing temperature. It will take a considerable length of time to bring the apparatus you have placed in the dishpan to the desired temperature. You will have to keep an eye on the thermometer—a dial thermometer which is easy to read from a distance will help a great deal in this because it will allow you to go about your business, but still be able to tell at a glance how things are going in the dishpan—and continue to bring the tempering bath back up to the proper temperature for just as long as it takes. This monitoring and correcting process can be an ordeal, especially in an unheated basement darkroom during the winter months, when the room ambient temperature may be 55 F (12 C) and the desired processing temperature 100 F (38 C).

The next level of sophistication up from the dishpan-and-pitcher technique involves a greater expenditure of both dollars and energy. The dollars come out of your pocket and the energy will have to be provided by the consumption of one or another of the fossil fuels which seem to be in short supply.

If you can put your dishpan in a place where any overflow from it can drain into a sewer, you can leave your faucet set to allow water, at the desired processing temperature, to continuously run into the dishpan, overflow it, and run into the sewer drain. At this stage of elaborateness, the thermometer remains in the dishpan and you remain the controller of temperature changes (via the faucet's tap handles).

This standpipe is nothing more than a short length of pipe which fits snugly into the sink drain. The height of the pipe above the bottom of the sink determines the depth to which the water can rise in the sink before overflowing the top of the standpipe and running down the drain. Be sure to keep the top of a standpipe well below the level of the sides of any sink in which it is used or the water will overflow the sink instead of the top of the standpipe.

The next step toward a more sophisticated water-bath setup is to move the thermometer out of the bath and up to a well at the faucet outlet. This removes the temperature transfer, taking place in the bath itself, from your consideration and allows bringing fresh temperature-controlling water into the bath at precisely the right temperature, regardless of what the bath temperature may be at any given moment. At this level of sophistication you will have to spend a few more dollars for the needed thermometer well (for example: the Darkroom Plumber's Flo-Temp and the Leedal Econotemp).

If you find that a big dishpan is not large enough to accommodate everything you want to control the temperature of, you can easily use your entire sink to do the job. The only thing that will be required to convert any sink—processing, kitchen, laundry, etc.—to duty as a temperature-controlling bath, is a simple standpipe inserted into the drain. A standpipe is nothing more than a short length of pipe (of any material, but perhaps plastic is the simplest to work with), which fits snugly into the sink drain. The standpipe is cut to a length sufficient to give you the depth of water in the sink which you require for temperature-controlling purposes. When the standpipe is plugged into the drain, the water will fill the sink until it is deep enough to overflow the top of the standpipe and run down the drain.

The ultimate level of sophistication and

expense, in running water temperature-controlling systems is the replacement of a faucet (be it single lever or separate hot and cold taps) with a thermostatically controlled pressure-compensated water-mixing valve. Such devices take you out of the control loop all together. They do it all themselves. These expensive valves operate automatically to maintain a constant-temperature flow of water into your temperature-controlling bath, regardless of relatively wide variations of input water temperature and pressure. Any darkroom worker who has ever painstakingly set a pair of faucets to deliver exactly 68 F (20 C) water temperature, and then watched with horror as the temperature of the water flowing from the faucet shot up to 145 F (62 C) to cook his washing film because someone had the audacity to flush a nearby toilet and thereby drop the cold-water supply pressure to near zero, will know exactly how important it is to include pressure compensation in such a device. (The Meynell Photomix and ITT Lawler Series 9700 valves are typical of such units). These valves, however, must pass at least one-half gallon of water per minute to maintain their specified temperature-controlling accuracy, which is usually about $\pm\frac{1}{2}$ F ($\pm\frac{1}{4}$ C). Pouring one-half gallon of water, which has been heated from, let's say 65 F (19 C) to 100 F (38 C), down the drain every 30 seconds is a very expensive way of keeping your solutions at the proper processing temperature.

A cheaper and less energy-consuming method is to use an electrical device to maintain a fixed volume of water at the desired processing temperature. By working with a fixed, constantly recirculated volume of water, you are not simply throwing away heated water at the rate of one-half gallon per minute, but only supplying the temperature-controlling bath with whatever energy is needed to transfer heat to the materials within it and to make up for any energy losses to the surroundings. This method also has the added advantages of not requiring a sewer drain and of not wasting water. Here again, you can use any container from a dishpan up through a full-size processing sink. Perhaps the neatest, cheapest, most clever tempering-bath construction I have seen is the one recommended by the Photo-Therm Company in an application sheet.

PHOTO THERM MODEL 14: APPLICATIONS AND COMPONENTS

Typical of completely packaged integral, temperature-controlling tubs is this Photo-Therm Model 14 Constant-Temperature Bath. In one compact unit, at the side of the tub, are packaged the pump, heater, temperature sensor, and electronic control module.

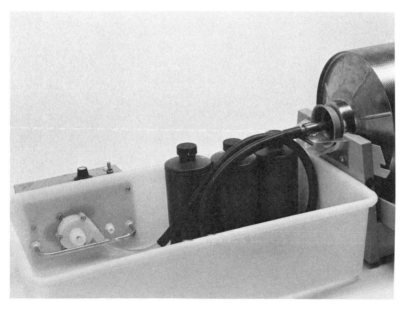

This is one way to get the maximum mileage out of an integral temperature-control bath. The Photo-Therm Model-14's pump is equipped with an outlet which can be easily coupled to a length of flexible tubing. As shown here, the flexible tube from the pump can then be coupled to the flexible tube leading to a Kodak Model 11 processor, to supply it with constant-temperature water. The water fills the Model 11's drum and runs back into the Photo-Therm Model-14's tub which has been strategically placed to catch it. The pump continually recirculates the water in this manner. The flowing water passes through a tiny pair of holes in the hollow fitting, just in front of the pump, where it flows over the temperature sensor. Note how the bar has been placed to prevent the chemical supply bottles, stored in the tempered water in the tub, from floating into a position where they could block the pump or the sensor inlets.

(They, of course, make all of the control components needed to implement such a system.) The company suggests cutting 1″ × 6″ boards to the dimensions of the temperature-controlling bath required, nailing the boards together, and then simply draping heavy gauge polyethylene sheeting over the board edges to form the sink. No bottom is needed as the supporting surface will act as the bottom of the container and hold up the plastic sheeting; nor do the joints, where the 1″ × 6″ boards meet, need waterproofing. The polyethylene sheet provides all the sealing necessary. (The sink, so formed, is sort of an open-topped water bed.)

Regardless of what kind of container you may choose to hold your temperature-controlled water bath, you will need several components to do the controlling. These are a pump, a heater,

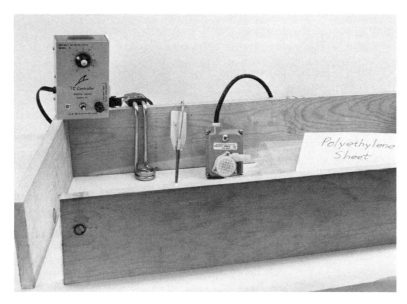

This is an illustration of Photo-Therm's design of an instant processing sink. The sink is nothing more than four 1″ × 6″ boards nailed together. A sheet of heavy plastic material is then simply draped over the edges of the board to contain the water. All of the necessary components are then arranged around the module and the heater, and everything is plugged in to create an instant sink.

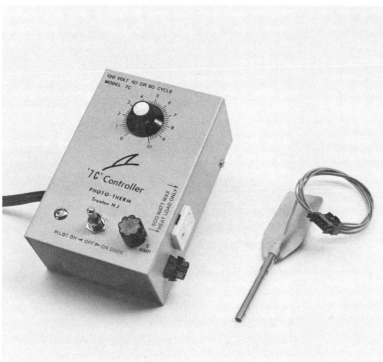

The heart of the instant sink, or any other electronically controlled–constant volume, re-circulated, constant-temperature bath is its temperature sensor water heater control module. This Photo-Therm "7C" unit accepts the sensor plug just below the standard, grounded, 110 volt outlet it provides for the heating coils.

and a control module. All of these components may be purchased: assembled and attached to a tub (the Photo-Therm Model 14 is a typical example); assembled and operated remote from the bath, via hoses (the Supertemp Model 150 fits this description), separately as individual modules that can be placed within the temperature-controlled bath itself (both Photo-Therm and Colourtronic market such modules).

Finally, it should be noted that with a bit of additional ingenuity, temperature-controlling baths, of either the recirculating or continuous flow type, can be made to perform as process-temperature controllers as well chemical-temperature regulators. Procedures for doing so can range from the simple use of a dishpan to hold not only chemical supply bottles, but also a capped drum processor (such as the Kodak London drum, which is not available in the U.S.), to a much more complicated arrangement of flexible hoses used to pipe water from the temperature controller's pump or valve outlet to the processor (typically a Kodak Model 11 or an Agnekolor); then used to return the water from the processor to the tub and from there back to the circulating pump or down the drain. While it may sound a bit complicated, in practice it just takes a bit of study to determine what will best suit your own individual needs and pocketbook.

While up until now I have only mentioned products specifically designed with photographic applications in mind, don't let that discourage any of you who may be handy but unable to afford these specialty components. You may also be able to lash up a perfectly workable recirculating temperature-controlling system making use of the cheaper components used to circulate and control the temperature of aquariums; though it will, most likely, take a bit of experimentation to be able to do so. If you do want to go this route, be sure to determine the capacities of each of the needed components, and their total cost, before purchasing anything. You may find that the difference in cost is not great enough to justify the bother and inconvenience of putting together a jury-rigged system.

Processing at Elevated Temperatures with Ambient Temperature Chemicals

While that subject heading may sound like it contains a contradiction in terms, it really doesn't. It is perfectly possible to process at "effective" temperatures well above the room ambient without ever bothering to regulate the temperatures of either the chemicals used or the environment in which the processing takes place. The Kodak Model 11 makes use of this technique. The operating instructions that accompany the machine specify that the chemicals used in it be loaded into the machine at room ambient temperature at the beginning of each processing step, regardless of what that ambient temperature may be. These same instructions provide time/temperature charts specifying processing times based on chemical temperatures of 100 F (38 C). This is possible because the big, hollow, stainless-steel drum of the Kodak machine is always half filled with water at the proper processing temperature. This temperature-controlled water heats the thin, highly heat-conductive shell of the drum and rapidly passes thermal energy from the water inside the drum to the room-temperature chemicals spread over the surface of the outside of the drum. Since there is a relatively small volume of processing chemicals to be heated, and a relatively large volume of temperature-controlled water to do the heating, the processing chemicals are quickly brought to, and then maintained at, the proper processing temperature.

It is also quite possible to do something very similar but even simpler with plastic daylight drum processors. Most daylight drum processors are made of plastic materials which have rather poor thermal conductivity. So, instead of trying to control the temperature of the processing chemistry poured into them by means of transferring heat from a water bath through the drum wall (such as is done in the case of the Kodak Model 11 and even recommended for the Kodak London daylight drum) the same effect can be achieved in just the opposite way. With a daylight drum, instead of bothering to maintain a constant source of temperature-controlled water, one small volume of water at some specific temperature can be used not only to heat the chemicals to the requisite temperature, but also to serve for all of the water washes needed during the entire processing procedure. Typically, about one gallon of water is needed to do both these jobs when processing an 8″ × 10″ sheet of printing paper in an 8″ × 10″ daylight drum.

The way this is accomplished is with a presoak bath. A presoak bath is a small volume of water, at a temperature somewhat higher than the processing temperature, which is poured into the paper-loaded processing drum and then agitated inside the drum for a relatively long period of time. This procedure permits heat to be transferred from the water to the drum walls and to the sheet of printing paper which is inside the drum. The presoak water is then poured out of the drum and a very small volume of the first room-temperature chemical is quickly poured into it. Thermal energy is retransferred from the printing paper itself, as well as from the walls of the drum, to the very small volume of chemistry which is being continually passed over the entire inside surface of the drum as the drum is rolled to provide agitation.

Even if the ambient temperature in the room in which the processing is taking place is quite low, this system will still remain a very effective means of allowing the processing to be carried out at an "effective" elevated temperature, as the heat loss from the drum walls to the air surrounding them is relatively low and the quantity of heat energy which can be stored in the relatively thick drum walls, and within the paper itself, is more than sufficient to both warm the chemicals inside the drum and to accommodate heat losses to the surroundings. You have undoubtedly noted that I have continually referred to processing at *"effectively"* elevated temperatures with this presoak technique. I have done so for a very definite reason, which I will illustrate with the example which follows. Let's assume that the processing temperature you wish to use is 100 F (38 C), the room ambient is 68 F (20 C), and you use a presoak water temperature of 125 F (52 C). It should be fairly obvious that after the presoak, when two ounces (60 ml) of the first room-temperature chemical is added to an 8″ × 10″ daylight drum, it will quickly be warmed to some temperature above the desired 100 F (38 C) processing temperature. Then it will gradually drop in temperature during the remainder of the processing step, as the drum walls slowly give up their heat to the surroundings, to some temperature which will, most likely, be below the desired processing temperature. The temperature

rise and subsequent fall will not take place at equal rates, so it is rather inappropriate to try to determine some time-based *average* temperature of the chemical within the drum. It is far more realistic to think in terms of the effective processing rate achieved with this procedure. If the processing carried out by a volume of room-ambient temperature chemical, added to a drum after an elevated temperature presoak, is the same as that which an equal volume of the same chemical at some specific, controlled and constant temperature will achieve, then the "effective" temperature of the room-ambient temperature chemical is that of the constant-temperature chemical.

Don't let anyone force you into believing that photographic chemical reactions are only properly carried out at a single, Kodak-given temperature. Kodak's photographic chemicals, like all others, will work properly over a temperature range, with the best results occurring at some target temperature. The speed at which these chemicals react is governed not by a corporate board, nor even a committee of chemical engineers, but only by the same physical laws which govern all chemical reactions.

Once the first chemical process in the drum has been completed, the remaining portion of the water that was used for the original presoak step is used for a rinse step. Since only one quart of the one-gallon quantity of presoak water was used, the remaining three quarts will have sufficient thermal inertia to remain quite close to the original presoak temperature during the brief period in which the first chemical process takes place. So there is no need to adjust its temperature prior to using it for the wash step. Now, if a sufficient volume of water is used for the wash it will not only serve to remove the previously employed chemical, but will also rewarm the walls of the drum and the sheet of printing paper inside to close to the original presoak temperature. When this wash water is poured off and the next room-temperature solution is poured into the drum, the same chemical heating takes place and the second chemical solution is brought up to the requisite "effective" processing temperature. Since each of the chemical steps involved with print processing can be followed by a water wash (in this process), each of the subsequent chemicals can be brought to an elevated "effective" temperature by the presoak water remaining. And since the temperature tolerance opens up considerably with each of the succeeding chemicals used in print processing, the slight cooling of the remaining volume of presoak water has no significant detrimental effect on this whole procedure.

Print Processing Nomographs

If I have been able to convince you that processing at "effective" elevated temperatures is both possible and practical, you are now worse off then you were before you read the preceding section, because now you know you can do it but you don't know how. It's all well and good for me to offer random examples of elevated presoak temperatures, but what you really need is a way to determine what temperature of presoak water is required to bring a small volume of the processing chemicals you prefer, at the temperature of your processing room, to the specific "effective" processing temperature recommended by the makers of the chemicals. And what would be even better would be some sort of device that would provide this information for not only one specific combination of these three temperatures, but for *any* combination within a reasonable range. Such a device exists; it is called a color print-processing nomograph.

Unfortunately, there is not one but several such devices, all easily available to the color printer and almost all of which disagree by a fair margin. The reasons for the disagreement among nomographs is that they were all developed empirically by the vendors of several different color printing products. It shouldn't be too hard to imagine that the thermal conductivity and mass of one maker's daylight drum is different from that of another's, or that one manufacturer's chemicals behave somewhat differently, under identical conditions, than another's. I think that to a very large extent, these are the basic reasons for the fairly wide disagreement among nomographs; however, I wouldn't be too surprised to find a bit of sloppiness and wishful thinking behind some of the disparity as well.

At any rate, before I continue on that tangent, let me hasten to explain just what a nomograph is, and how it is used. The device itself consists of nothing more than three parallel numerical scales: one for room (chemical) temperature, a second for processing temperature, and the third for presoak water temperature. These scales are usually arranged side by side on a single sheet of paper in such a way that all the user needs to have available is any two of the temperatures to be able to quickly obtain the third. For instance, it would be a dull printer indeed who didn't know the temperature of the room in which prints were to be processed. All that printer would have to do to get that temperature is to read a wall thermometer, or better yet, to stick a thermometer into one of the bottles of processing chemicals stored in the room. The processing temperature (or temperatures) specified by the maker of the chemicals being used is easily obtained by reading the label on the box the chemicals came in, or the data sheet packed inside. Now, armed with these two temperatures, all that the printer needs to do to obtain the third presoak water temperature is to put a straightedge down across the known value on the room-temperature scale and the known value on the processing-temperature scale, and simply note where the straightedge crosses the third presoak water-temperature scale. It is at that intersection point that the presoak water-temperature scale is read. And that is absolutely all there is to using a nomograph.

There is one rather handy variation on this theme. It is a device produced by the Paterson Company, for use with their processing drums, on which two of the scales are arranged on a single fixed surface of a sliderule device, and the third scale is printed on the center sliding member. This device is even simpler to use than the conventional nomograph because it eliminates the need for a straightedge. All you do to use the Paterson slide rule is line up the room

Note the discrepancy between the presoak water temperatures offered by this Beseler nomograph and this Paterson slide rule for the identical room and processing temperatures. Both devices are set for a room temperature of 75F (24C) and a processing temperature of 88F (37C). Beseler advises a presoak water temperature of 100F (38C), while Paterson recommends a 111F (42C) presoak. You can make either one work if you use it consistently.

ROOM TEMPERATURE (Chemical Temp.)	DESIRED PROCESSING TEMP.	WATER TEMP.
(F.)		• 138°
		• 136°
		• 134°
		• 132°
		• 130°
• 100°	• 110°	• 128°
	• 108°	• 126°
• 95°	• 106°	• 124°
	• 104°	• 122°
• 90°	• 102°	• 120°
	• 100°	• 118°
• 85°	• 98°	• 116°
	• 96°	• 114°
• 80°	• 94°	• 112°
		• 110°
• 75°	• 92°	• 108°
	• 90°	• 106°
• 70°	• 88°	• 104°
		• 102°
• 65°	• 86°	• 100°
	• 84°	• 98°
• 60°	• 82°	• 96°
	• 80°	• 94°
• 55°	• 78°	• 92°
	• 76°	• 90°
• 50°	• 74°	• 88°
	• 72°	• 86°
	• 70°	• 84°
	• 68°	• 82°
		• 80°
		• 78°
		• 76°
		• 74°
		• 72°
		• 70°

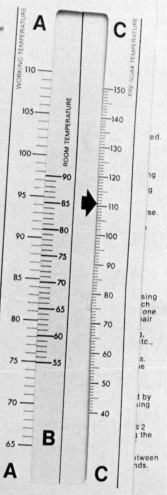

°F FAHRENHEIT SCALES

Scale A (working temperature) is the processing temperature recommended by the paper manufacturer. Scale B is your room temperature. Set this against scale A and read off the pre-soak temperature indicated on scale C.

PATERSON
Pre-soak Temperature Calculator

2 MINUTE COLOR PRINTS IN A DRUM

Load the exposed paper into a clean and dry processing drum and stand the drum on its feet on a level surface. Heat the chemistry to 125°F (STEP #1 and STEP #2). Pour STEP #1 into an ambient temperature drum and IMMEDIATELY begin continuous and vigorous agitation by rolling the drum from side to side at the rate of one complete left to right cycle per second during the first 20 seconds and then at the rate of 20 left to right cycles during the remaining 40 seconds of processing time.

Thoroughly drain the drum (shake it dry) and pour-in STEP #2. IMMEDIATELY begin continuous and vigorous agitation by rolling the drum from side to side at the rate of one complete left to right cycle per second during the first 20 seconds and then at the rate of 30 left to right cycles during the remaining 40 seconds of processing time. Pour-out STEP #2. You're all done processing. You've just made a 2 minute color print with just two chemical steps. With the exception of washing and drying your print, you're all done. It couldn't be easier (or faster)!

RE-USABLE CHEMISTRY (DRUM PROCESSING)

Another marvelous feature of the Beseler TWO-STEP Chemistry is that it is reusable up to four times within a period of a few hours. This re-usable feature dramatically lowers the cost of processing a color print in a drum.

For each re-use (8 x 10 print or equivalent), add ½ oz. of fresh STEP #1 to the used STEP #1 and ½ oz. of fresh STEP #2 to the used STEP #2 and increase processing times by 5% (STEP #1 and STEP #2). Discard the exhausted chemistry after it has been used four times. (For larger print sizes, add 1 oz. fresh chemistry per 11 x 14 print and add 2 oz. per 16 x 20 print. Always increase processing times 5% per re-use regardless of print size.)

8 x 10 PRINTS	STEP #1	STEP #2	PROCESS TIME Normal
#1	—	—	+ 5 %
#2	+ ½ oz	+ ½ oz	+ 5 %
#3	+ ½ oz	+ ½ oz	+ 5 %
#4	+ ½ oz	+ ½ oz	+ 5 %

TRAY PROCESSING AT AMBIENT TEMPERATURES

Only two trays are required. Pour one quart of ambient temperature STEP #1 into an 8 x 10 tray and one quart of ambient temperature STEP #2 into a second 8 x 10 tray. (Use ½ gallon for 11 x 14 trays and use one gallon for 16 x 20 trays.)

Consult the time/temperature chart for processing times in STEP #1 and STEP #2. Use plastic or stainless steel print tongs to totally immerse the exposed sheet of paper face down into tray #1 and agitate the print continuously for the recommended processing time.

3. Inconsistent agitation (STEP #2)
4. Insufficient drain (STEP #1): Drain thoroughly or add a cold water rinse after STEP #1.

Cyan Cast Over Entire Print (Cyan Borders):
1. Step #1 is contaminated: Wash all utensils in cold water and mix fresh STEP #1.
2. Print exposed to B & W safelight

3

temperature, on the central moving scale, with the processing temperature on the adjacent fixed scale. Then the presoak water temperature is read on the fixed scale adjacent to a large index arrow on the moving scale.

To the best of my knowledge, nomographs are now, or have previously been, supplied with the following products: Beseler chemicals and drums, Chromega chemicals, paper, and drums, and Paterson drums. There are significant divergences in the numerical results obtained with all of them. However, I have used all of them, with the products they were prepared for, and I have been able to achieve excellent results with all of them. I would suggest that you use the nomograph supplied with the drum or the chemicals you are using, or that you select one nomograph which seems to give you the best results, and stick to it regardless of what products you may use. Once again, I will repeat, *the most important quality a color printer can have is consistency.*

If you are going to process a print in Chromega chemistry in a Paterson drum and the two applicable nomographs disagree, toss a coin to determine the one you will use. Then use it consistently and everything will come out okay in the end.

Chapter 8

Electronic Color Analyzers

Principles of Operation

The accompanying figure represents a color analyzer reduced to the barest essentials and represented schematically. I won't be a bit surprised if your initial reaction to this sketch is "is that all there is?" But essentially, that *is* all there is: four filter windows in a rotating turret, a light-sensitive cell, four potentiometers (hereafter referred to as pots), a selector switch, a meter, and a battery.

The way this simple collection of hardware works is equally uncomplicated. The sketch shows the light-sensitive cell located under a solid portion of the filter turret, where it is shielded from the light falling on the turret from the enlarger lens. Now, if the turret is rotated clockwise, until the red-filter window is directly above the light-sensitive cell and directly below the enlarger lens, two things will happen: light from the enlarger will pass through the red filter and fall on the light-sensitive cell, and a mechanical linkage will turn the selector switch to its cyan position. The cell will respond to the red light falling on it by changing its resistance. Current from the battery will be able to pass through the light-sensitive cell in proportion to the intensity of light reaching it. From the cell, the current will flow to a bank of four parallel pots, then through a portion of the resistance element of the cyan pot, and through the pot's wiper to the wiper of the unit's selector switch set in its cyan position. From the switch the current flows to the galvanometer and causes the meter's needle to deflect in proportion to the amount of current passing through the galvanometer's coil.

When the filter turret is rotated to allow the enlarger's light to pass through the green-filtered window, the selector switch is automatically mechanically set to its magenta position and the meter deflection then noted is representative of the amount of green light hitting the light-sensitive cell. With the blue filter positioned over the cell and the selector switch automatically turned to its yellow position, the meter indicates the blue content of the light striking the light-sensitive cell. Finally, when the clear glass-filled window is rotated into position over the cell, the selector switch is automatically set to read white light and the meter indicates the amount of white light striking the cell.

All of that is well and good, but of no use whatever for color printing purposes unless we can devise some scheme to put the information obtained from the meter to some use. One way to do so is to use our simple machine to measure and record the properties of the light passing through a filter pack and a negative that we have previously used to make a perfect print. Then we can compare the properties of the light passing through another negative, which we have not as yet printed, to these recorded values, and if we find that they do not match the perfect print's data, we can adjust the printing filter pack and lens opening until they do.

This can be done as follows: Use the normal procedures, described in an earlier chapter, to make an *absolutely perfect* color print of your standard negative. When that's done, leave the enlarger set exactly as it was when the perfect exposure was made. Record the type of paper the perfect calibration print was made on, the paper's emulsion-batch number, the lens opening, the duration of the exposure, the type of chemistry used to process the print, the processor used, the processing variables (there may be a dozen or more of these, which I will return to later), the

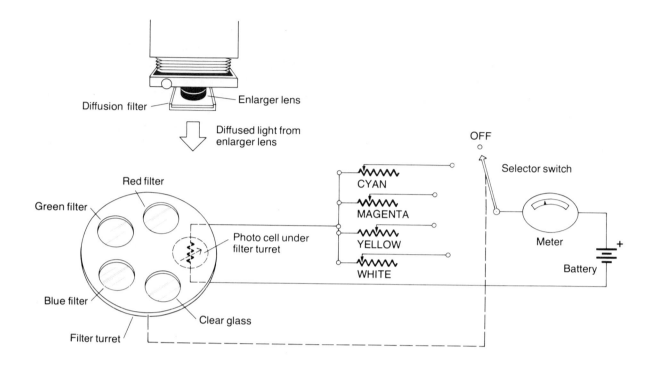

Diffusion filter — Enlarger lens

Diffused light from enlarger lens

Red filter

Green filter

OFF

CYAN

MAGENTA

Selector switch

Photo cell under filter turret

YELLOW

Meter

WHITE

Blue filter

Clear glass

Battery

Filter turret

age and condition of the chemistry, the type of film your standard negative was made on, and any other bit of data you think may be even remotely pertinent to the way you arrived at a producing the perfect print. Once all that has been done, the analyzer can be positioned on the enlarging easel in place of a sheet of printing paper. The standard negative is left in the carrier, all of the printing filters used remain in place, and the enlarger's head height and focus are set exactly as they were when the perfect exposure was made. The only difference between the enlarger setup used to make a perfect print and the one that will be used with the analyzer is that a diffusion filter is now placed in the enlarger's external filter holder and swung into position directly below the lens.

Now, the room lights and any safelights are turned off and the enlarger lamp is turned on. The light-sensitive cell is located on the easel so as to be directly below the center of the lens, and the analyzer's filter turret is rotated until the red filter is directly above the light-sensitive cell. The light from the enlarger lamp passes through the printing filter pack, the negative, and the lens, and is then integrated (thouroughly mixed) by the diffusion filter. This integration is required to

insure that light coming from different portions of the negative receives the photographic equivalent of homogenizing to average the color content of the focused image of the standard negative. This is done to prevent a situation in which, for example, a patch of cyan on the negative might be the only portion of the image focused directly on the entire area of the light-sensitive cell. This would cause the cell to see only light considerably more deficient in red than in blue and green content. The diffuser serves to scramble the entire image and to mix light reflecting all of the color content of both the standard negative and the printing filter pack to achieve an average, integrated distribution of them over the surface of the light-sensitive cell.

With the turret set to allow only the red component of the light leaving the diffusion filter to hit the light-sensitive cell, and the selector switch automatically positioned to cyan, the meter needle will be deflected by the current flowing in the circuit. Now, if the knob controlling the wiper (movable contact) of the cyan pot is adjusted so that the meter needle is positioned exactly in the center of the scale, the analyzer will be programmed for the red content of the scrambled light coming through your standard negative and through the printing filter pack you used to make a perfect print from it. This same programming procedure must also be carried out for each of the remaining three window positions on the filter turret. Each of the appropriate pot wipers must be adjusted until the analyzer is completely programmed so that its meter needle will deflect to the exact the center of its scale on each of its four channels: cyan (red filter), magenta (green filter), yellow (blue filter), and white (no filter).

Now, hopefully, we can put this combination of hardware and color procedure together and come up with something useful. Let's assume that you have another color negative on the same type of film, and you would like to know what filter pack to use to print it. From the preceding chapters you know that the most convenient, quick, and economical way to do this is by including the negative in a calibrated color contact sheet. But, for the sake of this example, let's go on and use this collection of electrical hardware to do the job instead. To do so, put the unknown negative in the carrier and put the same printing filter pack that you used to make your calibration print into the enlarger's filter drawer (or dial in the appropriate dichroic filters). Now, turn the enlarger lamp on; close your enlarger's lens down two stops from wide open; crank the enlarger's head up or down to get the magnification you want; compose and focus the image to be printed on the easel, then put the analyzer's filter turret on the easel; and swing the diffuser in under the lens. At this point, rotate the turret until the red filter window is directly under the lens and over the light-sensitive cell. Note the position of the meter needle. If it is not at the midpoint of the meter there is a difference between the amount of red light that is falling on the light-sensitive cell with the unknown negative in the carrier, and the amount that was measured as having passed through the standard negative. Cancel out this difference by opening or closing the enlarger lens' diaphragm until the meter needle settles at its midposition.

You go through a very similar procedure with the green and blue filter positions on the turret, but for these readings you don't center the needle by adjusting the lens opening. Instead, you add or subtract magenta filtration from the printing filter pack to center the needle when the

turret's green filter is in the light path, and you center the needle by changing the yellow filters in the printing filter pack when the blue filter is lined up with the light-sensitive cell. At this point you have used the analyzer to insure that the printing paper you expose will get the same proportions of red, green, and blue light that the calibration print of your standard negative did. All that now remains to be done is to adjust the exposure. To do this, rotate the filter turret until the window holding the piece of clear glass lines up directly under the lens, with the light-sensitive cell and, with the diffuser in place, note the position of the meter needle. If it is not at the center, bring it to that position by opening or closing the lens diaphragm.

In theory, you have just completely matched the color content and intensity of the light coming through the unknown negative to that which you found would, when it came through your standard negative, produce a perfect print. Since the unknown negative is on the same type of film (and, therefore, has the same type of built-in printing mask), and you have painstakingly matched the characteristics of the projected image to those of your standard negative, all you should have to do now is remove the analyzer from the easel, remove the diffuser from under the lens, put another sheet of the same kind of printing paper that you used to make your calibration print on the easel, expose the paper for the same length of time you used for the calibration print, remove the exposed sheet, process it exactly the way you did your calibration print and, at last, you *should* have a perfect print of your unknown negative. The odds are, though, that you won't. There are just too many things that can happen to foul up the simple analyzer and its comparative reading. Even if this device that I have used for illustrative purposes did manage to do its job faultlessly, any slight change in the myriad of printmaking variables would be enough to cause the print made on the basis of our instrument's readout to be considerably less than perfect.

Much of the remainder of this chapter is concerned with defining and describing the many problems inherent in the use of electronic color analyzers in color printing and examining some of the many refinements which have been incorporated in today's commercially available instruments to overcome these problems.

Analyzer Types

Perhaps the most obvious thing that may have occured to you as a definite limitation of my hypothetical analyzer is its need to operate with a diffuser in the light path. I've covered this limitation earlier in the text as it applied to the cheaper, simpler, and passive color printing calculators. My earlier reason, which is still valid, for disliking the use of a diffuser to scramble and integrate the color content of an "average" focused color image, was simply that there isn't any such thing as an average image.

The color analyzer I've illustrated and discussed so far has been based on the assumption that every color negative that you may ever want to analyze with it in the future will have the same *average* color content as your standard negative. This is a statistically valid, but often specifically incorrect assumption. A standard negative is always chosen for its *average* properties. It is shot with an eye toward a good, even distribution of color content. A negative containing an image of your uncle Irving seated in his fire-engine red Chevy is certainly not going to have the same sort of *average* color content. If you try to analyze this shot with the machine we've been using, you will run into a problem called subject failure, which is caused by a predominance of one color in the image.

There is an obvious way around this problem — that is, to develop a type of color analyzer other than the averaging (or "integrating") type we have been discussing until now. The quickest way to do this is to simply remove the diffusion filter from the schematic, as shown in the accompanying figure. Now the turret's filter windows will admit a small and specific portion of the focused image to the surface of the light-sensitive cell. Since the filter windows in the turret illustrated are fairly large, such a metering scheme would have to be referred to as a zone type, and such a machine would probably prove to have only very limited use. There are very few large areas, or zones, of a single uniform color in the vast majority of color negatives. But with the diffuser removed from the light path, it is just such uniform monochromatic areas of the negative that we will have to concern ourselves with when programming our newly modified, zone metering-type, electronic color analyzer.

Let's ignore that objection and see how a zone metering-type analyzer could be programmed to be more specifically useful than an averaging-type meter. Assume that you shoot a lot of landscape material and that you do much of your shooting during the summer when the landscape you shoot is of a fairly uniform color.

SIMPLE ANALYZER FOR ZONE READING

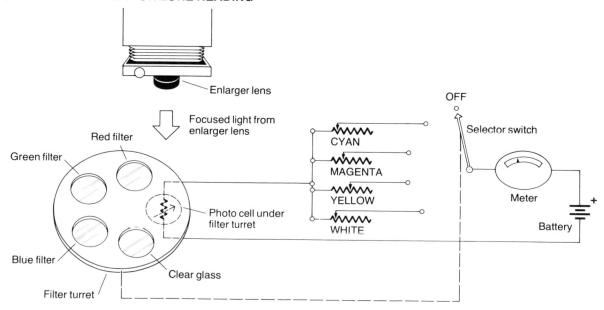

You can use a typical landscape negative as your programming standard. First, of course, you'll have to make a perfect print of the negative, using our tried-and-true methods from earlier chapters. Then, with the data used to make the perfect calibrated landscape print recorded, and the enlarger still set up with the landscape standard negative in the carrier with the same printing filter pack and mechanical settings that were used to make the calibration print, you can now position our zone metering-type analyzer's filter turret so that the area of the standard negative's focused image falling on the filter windows will be from an *average* portion of the green foliage of your landscape image. The entire programming procedure would then be run through as before, to put an *average* green foliage program into the machine. Then, any other shot, on the same negative material, containing a landscape with a lot of *average* green foliage can be set up in the enlarger so that the analyzer turret's filter windows look at the projected image of some of that *average* green foliage. The filter pack and the enlarger lens can then be adjusted so that the unknown negative's *average* foliage will be printed with light having the same color components and intensity as was used to make your perfect calibration print of the standard landscape negative.

Now, we all should know full well that there is no such thing as an *average* green foliage; but,

nevertheless, this sort of procedure is recommended for use with several zone metering-type electronic analyzers available today. If you are willing to accept the premise, you may well be willing to accept the machine.

The next level of refinement that we might wish to make to the basic analyzer, shown in the accompanying figure, is to simply close down the size of the windows in the filter turret to four very tiny holes. If we do this, then we won't have to look for a relatively large zone of a single, uniform, programmable color in the projected image. Instead, we can look for a much easier to find tiny spot of such color. This, then, is the basis of the spot-metering electronic analyzers. But it should also be immediately obvious that if you close down the filter windows, you will also limit the amount of light that can fall on the light-sensitive cell, regardless of the sensitive area of that cell. So one of the first problems we will have to overcome in the design of this new spot metering-type analyzer is that of the light sensitivity of the unit's sensor. For our purposes here, overcoming that problem is quite simple. We can just put an amplifier in the circuit to boost the output of the light-sensitive cell. In the real world of nuts and bolts and transisters, the solution may get to be a good deal more complicated, but we needn't worry too much about the real world here, except to mention that the more sensitive such real analyzer designs

SIMPLE ANALYZER FOR SPOT READING

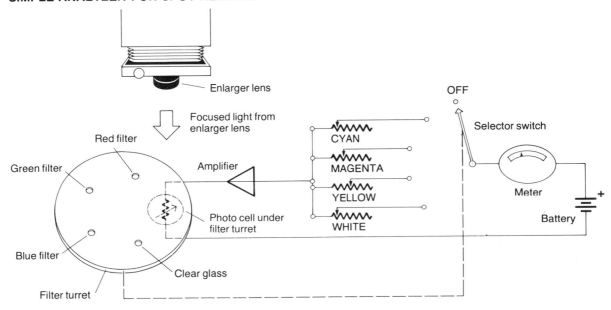

become, the less inherent circuit stability they tend to have.

Now that we have our analyzer boosted in power to the point where it can measure the intensity of the light passing through a tiny hole which is covered with a very dense additive primary filter, we can go about our programming and our unknown negative analysis a bit more selectively. For one thing, we can go back to using our normal standard negative to generate a perfect calibrated print, once again by the methods outlined earlier, and then use the standard negative, and the enlarger setup used to make it, to generate not one, but several programs. For example, we can place the analyzer's tiny light-measuring spot on an area of the focused image that contains only an evenly lit 18 percent gray card, and program the analyzer for 18 percent gray cards, which is always a very useful kind of program to have in any kind of machine, I might add. Or, we can place the sensitive spot so that it is directly under the projected image of a middle tone on a uniformly lit female Caucasian face, and put this program into our analyzer. Or, we can put the spot under the projected image of an area of the negative that contains any one of the color bars that are a good idea to include in any standard negative. Then we can program our spot-metering color analyzer, which will allow you to compare any such color bar in any future unprinted negative to the information stored in the analyzer's pots, and thereby set up your enlarger to produce a print that will have a perfectly rendered color bar. There is no limit to the number of programs you can set up with a spot-metering analyzer. Though I doubt the real, effective usefulness of all of them about as much as I do the simple averaging program we set up in the first example presented in this chapter, they will, at the very least, allow you to do a bit of cross-checking when analyzing any given negative.

There is a very large fly in this ointment. So far, I have only provided you with a hypothetical machine that can hold only a single fixed program. On the analyzer we have been using until now, you set the program into the machine by making four separate adjustments to four separate potentiometers. I haven't told you how you can use this machine with more than a single program at a time and how you would manage to set the pots. I'll do that right now.

While I have used at least one commercially available electronic color analyzer that required me to set its multiturn pots with a screw driver, most such machinery available today provides the person using it with a simple knob to turn to adjust each of the pots employed in the circuit. Most such units provide an index line on each knob and a scale surrounding each knob so that the pot settings can be noted and recorded on paper.

Now, I will similarly equip my hypothetical electronic color analyzer with the same knobs, index lines, and logging scales. With my machine so equipped, you might go through the 18 percent gray-card spot-programming procedure and find that the cyan pot-knob's index line pointed to 17 on its logging scale, the magenta pot-knob's index pointed to 1.5 on its scale, the yellow pot-knob's index was set at 44.3 on its scale and the white pot-knob's index pointed at 7 on its logging scale. If I carefully note each of these knob settings, I can then move the sensitive spot on the turret over a bit to look at, let's say, a middle tone in the female Caucasian-face portion of the image. Then I can program my machine for this without any concern for the fact that I am moving the pot's knobs off the settings I had so painstakingly established when programming the machine for 18 percent gray. I can twist the knobs with abandon because I have written each knob's index position in my lab record book and can quickly reestablish my 18 percent gray card program by simply looking up the recorded data and resetting the knob's index lines to the logging scale positions they had been at when I first programmed the machine.

I can do this with a degree of accuracy and repeatability which will be a function of the quality of the pots I use in my analyzer. If I use cheap pots with coarse windings, I will find it very difficult to get exactly the same program reestablished in the machine because the slightest movement of the knob will cause a large electrical difference to be introduced into the circuit. Obviously, then, since this is only a paper design which I don't have to sell at an attractive price, I will use only the very finest multiturn, zero-backlash (no mechanical error), gear-driven, digital-readout, knob-type pots in my analyzer. Unfortunately, few, if any, manufacturers of the real products can afford to use the finest parts available.

Analyzer Features

There are a large number of electronic color analyzers on the market at a wide variety of prices offering a number of different features which their several makers advise are of paramount importance to users. I'll do my best to explain some of them here, using my hypothetical electronic color analyzer whenever possible to simplify matters, but you should always be aware that the real product hardly resembles this crude little device. They are mechanically and electronically complex and are, in many cases, rather good examples of contemporary solid-state technology. I have included a number of schematics, circuit diagrams, and mechanical drawings of several of these products to illustrate this point. My continued reference here to my simple machine is aimed only at helping those readers who are not comfortable with the complexities of the actual devices.

Sensors

You have probably noticed that my analyzer has a sensor I have continually referred to as a "light-sensitive cell," without bothering to define it further. Real analyzer designers have to get a little more specific. They can incorporate light-sensitive cells of three different types: Cadmium sulfide (Cds) cells, photo diodes, and photo-multiplier tubes. I've listed the sensors in ascending order of their light sensitivity.

Cds cells are long familiar to users of 35mm SLR's with behind-the-lens meters. They are the same type of cells used in the metering systems of many of these cameras. Cds cells have the advantages of reasonably good sensitivity, high stability, and low cost, but they also suffer from being easy to "blind." The term "blind" refers to a phenomenon that causes a Cds cell to provide an incorrect response to light stimulation for a considerable period after the cell has been exposed to very bright light. Unfortunately, it is all too easy to blind the sensor of an electronic analyzer by inadvertently turning on the normal room lights in the darkroom while the analyzer is in use. To compensate for the relatively low sensitivity of Cds cells, the manufacturers of

BESELER PM2L COLOR ANALYZER BLOCK DIAGRAM

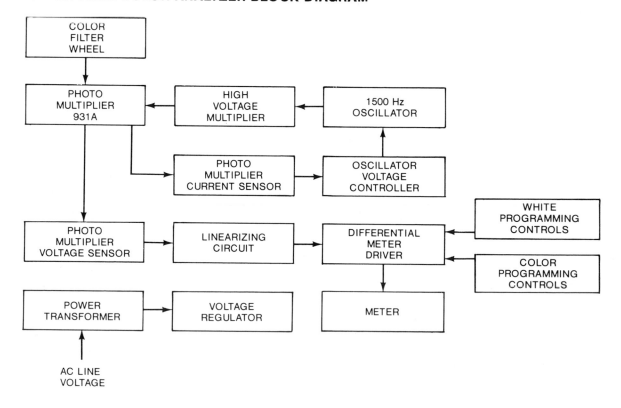

BESELER PM2 COLOR ANALYZER BLOCK DIAGRAM

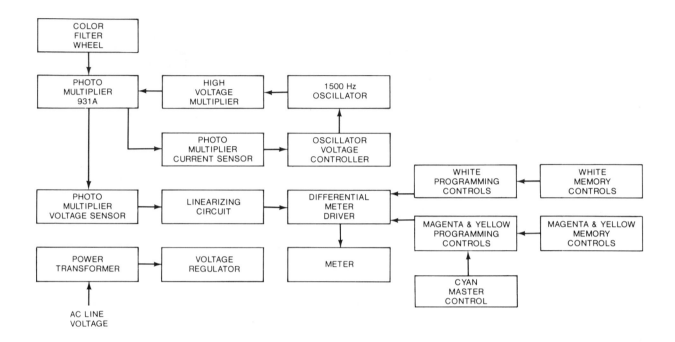

OPERATING CONTROLS OF THE SIMTRON II COLOR ANALYZER

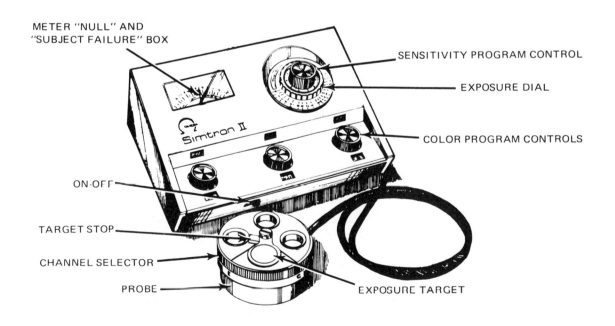

PARTS BREAKDOWN OF THE SIMTRON II COLOR ANALYZER

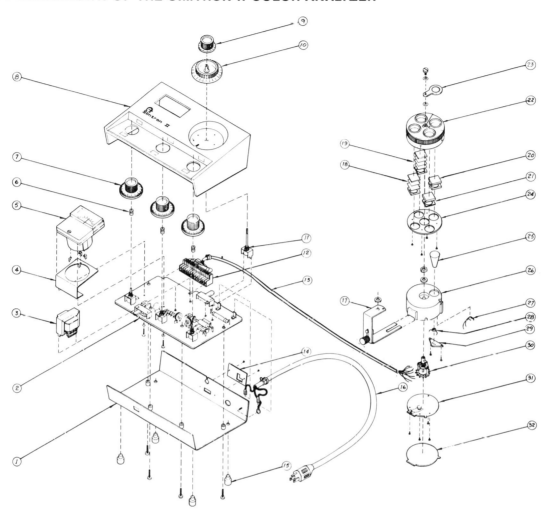

The parts breakdown of the Simtron II Color Analyzer includes: (1) a cover and spacer assembly; (2) a PC board assembly, which includes items 3, 4, 5, 11: (3) a transformer; (4) a meter mount; (5) a meter; (6) three shaft adapters; (7) three knob and skirt assemblies; (8) a housing and light pipe assembly; (9) a sensitivity and paper speed knob assembly; (10) an exposure dial assembly; (11) a potentiometer; (12) a right angle connector; (13) a cable; (14) a selector plate; (15) four bumpers; (16) a power cord; (17) a B22/Super C mounting bracket; (18) a magenta filter pack; (19) a cyan filter pack; (20) an exposure filter pack; (21) a yellow filter pack; (22) an upper housing; (23) a shutter assembly; (24) a retaining ring; (25) a light cone; (26) a lower housing; (27) a light bulb; (28) a photo cell; (29) a photo cell support; (30) a switch; (31) a bottom cover assembly; (32) and a pad.

several electronic color analyzers, which employ them, locate the cells directly under and adjacent to the enlarger lens in probes held in place by special brackets that attach directly to the enlarger or to the lens barrel itself. Cds cells are generally employed in integrated-light reading-type analyzers.

Photodiodes are the latest sensors to be used in electronic color analyzers and, like the Cds cells, are also familiar to users of 35mm behind-the-lens metering SLR's. Silicon photodiodes are now beginning to be used in the metering systems of these cameras on a widespread basis. The cells offer a virtual immunity to blinding and a considerably faster response time than Cds cells do. They can also provide much greater sensitivity than the Cds cells can; but to do so they require considerably more sophisticated circuitry, so they may be regarded as less stable than Cds cells. With enough clever high-quality

CHROMEGATRON PRO-LAB SCHEMATIC DIAGRAM

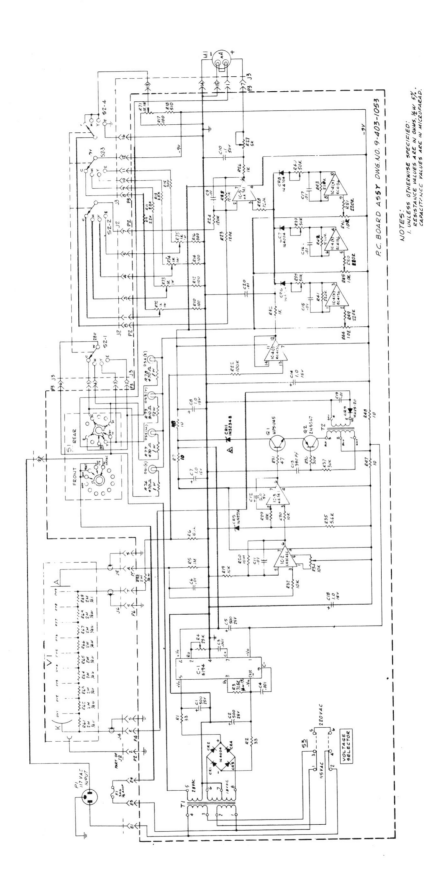

NOTES:
1. UNLESS OTHERWISE SPECIFIED:
   RESISTANCE VALUES ARE IN OHMS, 1/2W 5%.
   CAPACITANCE VALUES ARE IN MICROFARAD.

P.C. BOARD ASSY DWG.NO. 9-403-1053

8-10

THE SIMTRON II ELECTRICAL SCHEMATIC

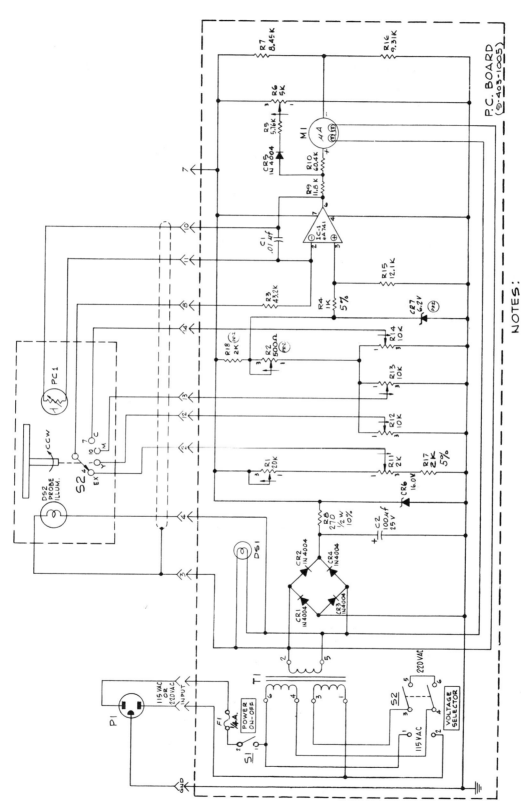

NOTES:
1. UNLESS OTHERWISE SPECIFIED:
   RESISTANCE VALUES ARE IN OHMS, ¼ WATT, 1%.
   CAPACITANCE VALUES ARE IN MICROFARADS.
2. DIRECTION OF ARROWS ON ALL VAR. RESISTORS
   INDICATES CLOCKWISE ROTATION.

P.C. BOARD
(9-405-1005)

CHROMEGATRON PRO-LAB SYSTEM BLOCK DIAGRAM

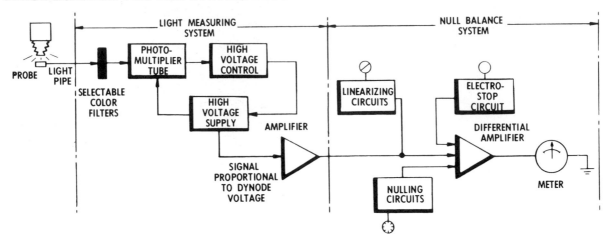

CHROMEGATRON PRO-LAB OPTICAL SCHEMATIC

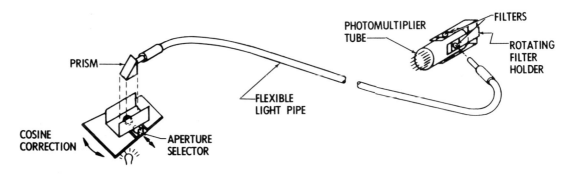

circuitry, however, this tendency can be completely overcome. The only commercially available electronic color analyzers I am presently aware of that employ these cells are the Minolta and the Cosar Mornick 328 Chroma Log. The Minolta analyzer is designed to operate only in conjunction with a special enlarger, also of Minolta's manufacture, which locates its light-sensitive silicon photodiodes within the bellows of the enlarger itself. I expect to see wider use made of photodiodes in other electronic analyzers in the not-too-distant future.

The most sensitive, but least inherently stable, of the several light-sensing devices used in electronic color analyzers is the photomultiplier tube. This vacuum tube sensor is useful down to incredibly low levels of illumination, but it is also very easy to overload ("blind") unless elaborate circuitry is employed to protect it. At the present state of color-analyzer technology, photomultiplier tubes are the units of choice for spot-metering-type color analyzers, primarily because of their extreme sensitivity. Like all vacuum tube devices, the photomultiplier tube is subject to damage from rough handling.

Probes

The filter turret of my hypothetical analyzer is its probe. In the real world probes are usually neatly packaged and a good deal more sophisticated than the unit I provided for my little illustrative machine. Probes fall into two broad categories: on-easel and off-easel. The type of probe that is placed on the enlarger's baseboard, or is mounted by a special bracket that holds it in a position immediately below and adjacent to the enlarger lens, is obviously in the off-easel category. The type of probe that sits directly on the easel is a member of the on-easel category.

Most probes are connected to the main cabinet of their associated electronic analyzer by an electrical cable of sufficient length to permit the user a bit of flexibility in the positioning of the cabinet. However, not all such connecting cables contain electrical wires. Some analyzers locate only their filter windows in their probes and then use a fiber-optic bundle to transmit photons (light), rather than electrons, back to the cabinet. There is an advantage in using such a light pipe with analyzers employing photomultiplier tubes in that the sensitive vacuum tube

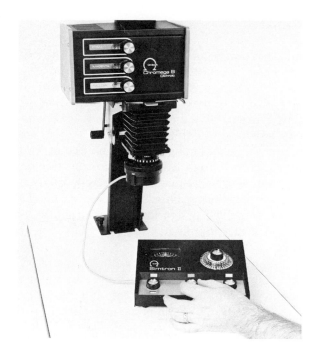

The Omega Simtron II's probe is rather unusual in that it is placed just *below* the lens for color programming and analysis.

Its probe is placed *on* the easel for exposure programming and analysis.

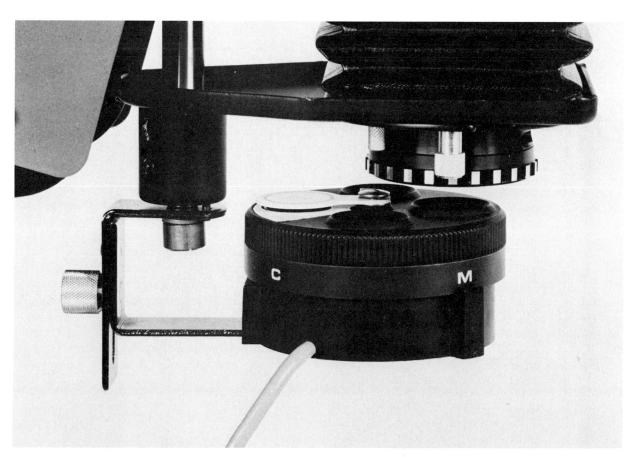

The turret-type probe of the Simtron II analyzer mounts on the red-safety-filter bracket of a Chromega B enlarger.

itself can be kept within the unit's cabinet and so be offered a high degree of mechanical protection. On the other hand, the difficulties and inconsistencies encountered with some fiber optic devices may well offset that advantage. I wouldn't care to try to judge the question.

It is very important that the user of any color analyzer be aware of how the probe for the particular unit in use is designed. The most common design calls for the probe to be placed flat down on the surface of the easel upon which the actual sheet of printing paper will later be placed. Other probes are designed to be placed on the surface of a piece of the same type of paper that will subsequently be exposed on the easel. Still other probes may be calibrated for placement on the enlarger's baseboard or for placement at some very specific distance from the front element of the enlarger lens. In general, you should be aware of exactly how your particular probe is intended to be used, as a deviation of only a few millimeters from this specific placement can influence the instrument's readings.

One probe feature allows for obtaining a partial reading correction when the probe must be placed well off the enlarger's optical axis in order locate it on some specific spot. To achieve this partial correction, often referred to as "cosine correction," the light-sensitive receptor can be tilted to receive light rays from the enlarger lens at an angle more nearly perpendicular to the surface of the receptor than if no tilting were possible. However, if this mechanical re-orienting of the probe is not accompanied by any electrical compensation to the circuit for the increased light-path length, only a partial cosine correction will be obtained.

Packaging and Components

All of the many components parts that are housed beneath the metal skin of an electronic analyzer's cabinet contribute directly to both the instrument's accuracy and its convenience of use.

You may have wondered, when I mentioned earlier that in order to program or to analyze with my device you would have to turn off all room lights and safelights, just how you were going to be able to see the meter needle in the dark to be able to carry out the necessary procedure. The answer is that you wouldn't be able to see the meter, unless, of course, I had put a little light bulb into the meter case itself to light up the dial whenever the filter turret, and, therefore, the selector switch, was turned to a reading position. Any color analyzer that employs a meter readout must provide for meter illumination. Your own eyes will have to determine if the units you are considering offer enough to suit your needs. And no matter how brightly it is lit, the meter face on any analyzer you are to use comfortably will have to be physically large enough so that you can read it with ease. The design limit here, of course, is that an overly illuminated meter could fog your paper.

Illumination of the machine's operating controls can also make the difference between a clumsy hard-to-use instrument and one that simplifies your darkroom procedure. Such things as probe-channel selectors, pot-knob scales, power switches, etc., can all be very difficult to deal with in the dark unless you are somehow able to first find them and then see enough of what you have to do with them to make the task possible.

Having just discussed meters, it is also important to note that even the largest of them, when viewed in brightroom light, can be very difficult to read accurately because of the parallax error which is introduced by viewing the thin meter needle from an angle rather than looking at it from a position directly in front of, and perpendicular to, the needle. A mirrored meter scale can help to overcome this problem, but a direct digital readout is even more foolproof. Some electronic analyzers use lights instead of meters as indicators. Obviously this type of readout is very easy to use in the dark, but the amount of information conveyed by such a system may be very limited.

You may have wondered, while I was describing the negative analyzing procedure used with my simple machine, what would happen if you ran out of lens openings when you were trying to bring the meter needle to its center position by adjusting the lens aperture. I simply failed to mention that it was a rather good possibility that you might often do just that, particularly with under- or over-exposed negatives. In the case of my machine, you would have to know enough to change the enlarger's head height and calculate the effect of the light-path change in *f*/stops. Fortunately, however, most contemporary electronic color analyzers don't require you to be smart, since they almost all provide some type of sensitivity-range extension, either through a mechanical change in the size of the aperture over the light-sensitive cell, or by means of electrical switching, or by indication on the meter scale. This sensitivity-range extension capability is often an important feature and one that should be looked for when selecting an instrument.

While discussing my simple analyzer, there was no need to consider the type of circuitry involved, as there was virtually no circuitry involved. But the cabinets of most of the electronic analyzers on the market are packed full of electronic components. Perhaps the best of these circuits are entirely solid-state (with the exception of the photomultiplier tube, where used, of course). In general, solid-state components can be expected to burn out quickly once the unit is turned on if they are defective, or last for a reasonably long time if they are satisfactory. This will usually tend to keep solid-state component failures well within the time limits of the unit's warranty. Most solid-state circuits also have the advantage of being available for operation soon after the power switch is thrown. Vacuum-tube units must be allowed to warm up and stabilize before they can be used.

While on the subject of stability, it should be mentioned that circuit stability is hardly only a matter of whether the components are solid-state or not, but more largely a matter of how well the components have been used in properly engineered circuits. The best of transistors and IC chips can be improperly applied in circuits which are inherently unstable. Any electronic analyzer that shows pronounced signs of meter-needle drift under steady-state conditions is one that will be all but unusable in the darkroom. Part of the way that circuit stability is achieved, in this era of electrical power brown-outs and over-loaded household circuits, is through the provision of voltage stabilization at the instrument's input. This is a very important feature that you should look for in any unit under consideration. A maximum of 1 percent output fluctuation for ± 10 percent line variation is a reasonable minimum level of voltage stabilization to look for. If more is provided, all the better. Unfortunately, however, unless your enlarger is also similarly provided with input voltage stabilization, your very stable analyzer is often going to give you

some very irrelevant readings. If you can afford to spend the amount of money required to buy a voltage-stabilized electronic analyzer, you would be well advised to also buy a constant-voltage transformer to power your enlarger.

In case this discussion of input voltage stabilization has confused you, you might look back to one of the drawings of my analyzer circuit. You will note that it is powered by a battery. It should be apparent that if that battery voltage drops, so will the meter reading. If the voltage can be stabilized, all other settings being equal, the meter reading will also remain constant. In the real world of most electronic color analyzers, the power source is not a battery but is the 110 volts of AC that comes out of your darkroom's wall outlet, and it, too, has its ups and downs, and needs to be stabilized.

If you will forgive me for repeating myself, I do want to mention once again that the accuracy and repeatability of programming with any instrument will depend, to a very large extent, on the quality of its programming pots and the accuracy and legibility of the faces of the pot-dial's indexes. You might want to try setting up a random program, then changing the pot settings, and then trying to reestablish the program a few times to note the ease, and particularly the accuracy, with which this can be done, when you are considering purchasing your own instrument.

One very useful feature in any analyzer is built-in electrical program storage. This feature which is a fairly inexpensive to build into a circuit, simply requires three or four additional pots and one additional position on a multiposition selector switch per program to be stored. As I will explain in a subsequent section of this chapter, creating and storing multiple programs is a virtual necessity for most electronic color-analyzer operators. There is nothing inherently wrong with storing programs in writing on a piece of paper, as we had to do with my machine, but it does always involve the inherent inaccuracies encountered when trying to reestablish programs on an instrument. Among units intended primarily for the amateur market, the Beseler PM2 is the only electronic color analyzer I am aware of that has a built-in capacity to store a total of three programs. The EPOI MM9 and the Cosar Mornick 328 Chroma Log analyzers, offer plug-in program storage modules.

Analyzer Benefits and Limitations

The primary benefit an electronic analyzer can bestow on a darkroom worker is speed. If you understand the instrument's limitations and can accommodate yourself to them, an electronic analyzer will save you a lot of time. However, it is very doubtful, when you compare the cost of an analyzer to the cost of paper and chemistry, that the use of an electronic analyzer will save you money over any reasonable span of time.

To understand why the benefits I've mentioned are so very limited, it will be necessary to take a detailed look at the machine's inherent limitations. To get any use out of an electronic color analyzer, you will have to be even more expert in all aspects of color printing than you would if you simply stuck to the various alternative approaches to color print analysis offered in the earlier chapters of this book, and never bothered to try to analyze your negative prior to making a print. This is so because when using an analyzer, you will not only have to understand all of the processes and procedures involved in color printmaking, but you will also have to understand all of the many things that can affect the operation of an analyzer.

Before you can so much as turn on the switch of any analyzer, you will have to be capable of producing an absolutely flawless color print of a standard negative, all by yourself, or perhaps with the rather limited aid available from a subtractive calculator. Once you have made your perfect print, you may program your analyzer with the data you painstakingly arrived at without its help. You must also be very careful to record everything pertinent to the many other variables involved in the exposure and processing of your calibration print, because *the program you load will be limited in its application to prints that are made with materials and processes identical to those used to make the calibration print.*

For example, if you make your calibration print on 37 RC paper in Beseler chemistry, the program so obtained won't be of any use whatever if you switch to Chromega paper or you decide to use Unicolor chemistry. As a matter of fact, the program won't be of any use even if you stick to the original materials but run out of paper and have to purchase a new supply from another emulsion batch.

Your program will also be limited to the use of the same enlarger and the same set (but not the same values) of filters. The program will apply only to the type of processor you used, and the particular way you used it (times, temperatures, agitation, procedures, etc.). It will only cover the enlarger lamp you used; if it burns out and needs replacement, the analyzer will have to be reprogrammed.

Perhaps most important of all, the program you load into your analyzer will apply only to the type of negative film your standard negative was made on. If your standard negative is on CPS and you want to analyze a Vericolor II negative, the CPS program won't work. (This is due to the rather gross differences in the printing masks—the orangy residual couplers which remain in the negative after processing—and the spectral absorption characteristics of the different dyes used in the several brands and types of color negative material which are offered by various manufacturers.

As if all this weren't enough, the analyzer's performance subsequent to being programmed is subject to all kind of vagaries. For example, your darkroom's temperature and its relative humidity may affect your analysis of a color negative; so may electrical power fluctuations, probe-cable configuration, ambient light in the darkroom (and, for all I know, evil spirits and sun spots—at least it has sometimes seemed that way to me).

Aside from all of the aforementioned problems, you also must consider the applicability of the program to the particular negative you want to analyze. You may recall the earlier mention of subject failure when using the integrated reading-type instrument as one case in point, but there are several others that can also haunt you when using a spot-reading type of instrument. For instance; let's assume you have loaded a middle-tone Caucasian-female skin-spot program and you have a negative of another Caucasian female to print. Even in the very unlikely circumstance that the model for your standard negative had a complexion remotely like that of the subject of the negative to be analyzed, it would be up to you to be smart enough to recognize an identical middle flesh-tone in the projection of the woman's image on the easel, and then to be able to position the probe in that exact spot. Even if you are that smart and able, it is doubtful if the projected image of the woman's head under consideration will be at exactly the same distance from the optical axis of the enlarger lens as the projected image of the model's head on your standard negative was. Since the distance at which a probe is placed from the optical axis will very definitely affect the readings obtained during negative analysis, you will either have to reposition the negative in the carrier or shift the lens board to bring the spot under analysis to the same position your programmed spot had, or be smart enough to guess the effect of the offset. (Don't bother calculating, your guess will probably be as accurate.)

Then too, there is always the problem of surface reflectance and texture to consider when doing a spot analysis. You may be clever and patient enough to load your analyzer with ten different programs for everything ranging from brick red to a distant mountain's purple majesty; but if the bricks or mountains shot in the negative under analysis had a different surface texture or reflectance or, heaven forbid, color, than your programmed brick or mountains had, you can forget the applicability of the program. It simply won't work properly. You have to be smart enough to realize all of this every time you turn on the analyzer or you might just as well not bother.

If you are that smart, and if you are willing to completely standardize all of your operations and materials, and to prepare separate programs to cover any and all changes in material, subject matter, ambient conditions (and evil spirits), then you will be able to do some very fast work indeed. Properly programmed and used, modern com-mercially available analyzers of good quality are easily capable of providing you with enough information to set your enlarger to make a commercially acceptable color print of a decently exposed negative in a matter of minutes. It is highly unlikely, though, that a really critical worker will settle for the print so obtained. At least I've not yet run across an analyzer that was able to put me right on the money. But with the analyzer operating to get you very close on your first print, it may be necessary to make only one or two more prints before a critically satisfactory image is obtained. All of which means that properly used, an analyzer may save you as much as a quarter of an hour and the cost of a sheet of paper and the chemicals to process it in *per print*. That is not an inconsiderable saving, but remember it is based on the *proper* use of the machine.

One final note on the limitations of color analyzers: To the best of my knowledge, you cannot use any of the machines presently on the market to perform color analysis of slides for use in reversal printing. You can, however, program and use any electronic color analyzer to determine the overall illumination (white light) level needed to obtain a perfect reversal print. Once you have made your calibration reversal print and programmed its illumination data into the analyzer, that determination is all that is really needed to produce prints from other slides *on the same kind of slide film*. This is subject, of course, to all of the same vagaries and limitations applicable to using such machines to analyze color negatives, as just described.

General Procedures for Use

Specific operating techniques differ for each manufacturer's electronic color analyzers, and even among models from the same manufacturer. In general, though, all of these machines are programmed in much the same way as my hypothetical little analyzer was in the section *"Principles of Operation."* There are, however, several general techniques of use that are applicable to any machine, regardless of manufacturer or design, and they are the ones I will concern myself with here.

Overall Gray Card Program

The most universally useful and applicable type of program I know of involves the use of an 18 percent gray card. It can be loaded into an integrated-reading or a spot-reading type of machine with equal facility and it is probably the most accurate and foolproof program available for use with analyzers. To develop such a program, it will be necessary to very carefully expose a frame of the type of film you most often shoot to render a frame-filling image of an evenly lit 18 percent gray card. Since most 35mm SLR's don't show you the entire frame you are shooting, be sure to get in close enough to more than fill the viewfinder window with the gray card's image even if doing so results in an out-of-focus image. Once the film is properly processed, a perfect print must be made by means explained elsewhere in this book. Be very careful to compare the prints you make to the card itself. Don't stop making prints until you get an excellent match with the actual gray card, making whatever allowances are necessary, of course, for differences in surface texture between the print and the card. This done, record all of the data pertinent to the way the calibration print was made and program your analyzer, be it integrated-reading or spot-reading, using the gray card negative and the procedure called for by the analyzer's operating manual. Now, in order to gain anything from the tedious work you have already put in, you will have to include the same 18 percent gray card in at least one frame of every roll which you shoot under controlled lighting, or in each frame that you shoot under variable lighting. If you follow this procedure you will always have a known standard to analyze. But I will admit that trying to get a gray card into every frame can be difficult, if not ridiculous.

Standardizing Procedures

It is essential to remember that the program you load for a calibration print made on paper from one emulsion batch, most often won't work for prints to be made on paper from another emulsion batch. If you intend to use an electronic color analyzer, it is a good idea to buy as much printing paper from a single emulsion batch as you can afford. Don't bother even considering the purchase of any quantity less than 100 sheets; buy several hundred if you can. Be sure to freeze the unopened boxes because, if you don't, the color qualities of the paper will change with time and you will be no better off than if each of your unopened and unrefriger-

ated boxes of paper had come from different emulsion batches. Once a box of paper has been opened, it is a good idea to put the sheets of paper in the box into a vapor-tight wrapper, if they are not already so packaged. When the remainder of the paper is to be stored between printing sessions, it is useful to expel as much air as possible from the inner wrapper and then refrigerate or refreeze the paper until you need it. Most paper manufacturers seem to recommend against this refreezing technique because of the damage that water vapor in the paper box can cause, but I have never found any problem with the procedure and I have found that paper so stored seems to undergo color shifting at a considerably slower rate than unfrozen paper. If you haven't any freezing facilities, refrigeration will help. Follow the warm-up directions of the manufacturer before using the paper.

It is probably helpful to burn in a new enlarger lamp for about half an hour before making any calibration prints for programming purposes. This is more necessary for ordinary incandescent enlarging lamps than it is for the tungsten-halogen-type bulbs now used in many color enlargers, but even with these the burn-in period will probably be useful. This burn-in is needed because the color temperature of incandescent lamps drops as the lamps age. The most pronounced change takes place when the bulb is brand new. Once the burn-in is over, the bulb's aging rate decreases continually until the filament finally fails. It is also useful to make new calibration prints, from time to time, as a precaution against the bulb's color shifting and also as a precaution against acetate-filter fading (if you use CP filters).

Special Analyzer Techniques

It is possible to use an electronic color analyzer for a large number of special applications. Some are capable of determining the contrast-grade of paper a black-and-white negative should be printed on, checking the color balance of studio lighting, or suggesting which PC filter to use with polycontrast black-and-white paper.

It is not practical to try to suggest the exact procedure that should be used with specific analyzers to fulfill any of these tasks; there would simply be too many to cover. But several manufacturers do offer such data in their instru-

ment's operating manuals, or upon request. If you do have an application that you feel your analyzer can fill, it might be useful to correspond with the instrument's manufacturer for their suggestions on how to proceed. Or, you can simply think of the device you own as a sensitive light meter that is able to see light through three selectable, additive-primary filters and one selectable, unfiltered aperture. It probably won't take too long to work out a scheme to use your analyzer for anything from a reflection densitometer to the front end of a color-code-operated, electric-garage-door opener.

Chapter 9

Manufacturer's Product Data

One of the hardest things about color printing is simply keeping abreast of the latest useful and worthwhile hardware and software that is available. Those of you who have only started color printing rather recently may not be able to appreciate just how important keeping up with new products really is. But those of us who go back a little way know that it has only been within the very recent past that simple, easily controllable, reasonably priced amateur color printing software has become readily available. In the days before plastic-coated printing papers, two-step processing, and good, workable direct-reversal products—in other words, as recently as the early 1970s—color printing was significantly more difficult to practice in an amateur darkroom. Far fewer amateur printers chose to try it, and fewer still were very successful. It is the revolutionary new materials that contemporary technology has provided that have made color printing as simple as it presently is, and have swelled the ranks of color printers enormously.

So, while this chapter is little more, in places, than a sort of catalog, and in others simply a collection of manufacturers' data, its importance shouldn't be underestimated.

Since this listing should be as up-to-date as possible, I fully expect some significant portion of each supplement to this book to cover new items being made available to color printers.

Enlargers

This is one area where contemporary hardware has made an enormous difference to color printing and to color printers. Contemporary enlargers designed primarily to print color material, and only secondarily to do black-and-white printing, can influence not only the ease with which color prints may be made, but also the quality the prints will exhibit. Modern color enlargers provide dichroic filters which their makers state do not fade and change their printing characteristics with time. They use quartz-halogen bulbs, which provide a somewhat higher and much more constant color temperature, and diffused illumination rather than the sharply focused illumination found in condenser enlargers; thereby decreasing the need for drastic color spotting. (If you've ever done much color spotting you know just how important that is.) These new enlargers also offer operational conveniences unthought of only a few years ago. With a modern color enlarger you simply twist a few knobs to add or subtract filtration from the printing filter pack. With condenser-type enlargers that have color drawers built into their heads, CP acetate filters must be physically added to or subtracted from a pile of such filters in a drawer or on a shelf in the enlarger head to affect changes to the printing filter pack. While this is not such a hardship, the process is time consuming and does require that you have a fairly large number of CP filters on hand. Keep in mind that acetate CP printing filters tend to fade and change their printing characteristics with time.

Condenser enlargers are desirable for black-and-white printing, particularly for small-format work, and diffusion enlargers with dichroic filtration are a boon to color printing; but, unfortunately, many of us are unable to keep one of each type in our darkrooms. Both the cost and space requirements of maintaining two separate enlargers can be prohibitive. Fortunately, there are a number of enlargers available which feature simple, quick convertibility from one type to the other. Some enlarger manufacturers make their own conversion kits while others make only basic condenser machines, and a color head manufactured by another firm must be purchased to affect the change. Some of these machines are quite simple to convert back and forth between black-and-white and color, while others require considerably more effort.

The material that follows is an alphabetical listing of what I believe is a representative sample of the enlargers, widely available in the U.S., which fit the several categories just described and are primarily intended for amateur or low-volume professional color printing work, or can easily be adapted to it.

My omission here of the many fine but unconvertible condenser enlargers with filter drawers above their negative stages is not intended as a slight to these machines. I haven't included them here simply because I never intended to catalog all the world's enlargers. I had to draw an arbitrary line somewhere and this is where I chose to draw it. If you own such a piece of equipment, you needn't be concerned that it isn't a functional piece of color printing hardware. It most certainly is. On the other hand, if you do not already own an enlarger, and you do intend to use the machine you purchase primarily for color printing work, or at least you want to keep that option open to yourself, perhaps the types of enlargers listed here may offer you some added benefits.

In addition to all of the information on enlargers I have omitted, there is a truly staggering amount of data concerning the many optional accessories available for many of the enlargers listed, which I have simply had to omit for lack of space and energy. However, I believe I have managed to provide sufficient information to be of assistance to you in comparing the various machines. I have also provided data on each enlarger's marketer so that you can contact each directly for full specifications and any other data you may feel is pertinent.

Another type of information I have not even attempted to provide here is price. The rate at which prices are continually changing would make any entry obsolete by the time it reaches you. I suggest that you contact your local dealer for pricing data.

Convertible Enlargers

Convertible enlargers can be user-converted from condenser illumination to diffusion illumination, with dichroic filtration, and subsequently reconverted at will. Descriptions of convertible enlargers follow.

Beseler 23C/Beseler 23CD
Converter—Beseler 23dga Colorhead

Type:	Convertible
Distributor:	Beseler Photo Marketing Co., Inc.
Formats:	8 mm–2¼″ × 3¼″
Illumination:	23C—double condenser with variable positioning
	23CD—diffusion
Lamp Type:	23C—type 111, 110 volt incandescent, 75 watt bulb
	23CD—type EJL, 24 volt quartz-halogen, 200 watt bulb
Cooling:	23C—conduction/convection
	23CD—fan
Filtration:	23C—drawer in head for CP acetates; drawer between negative stage and lens for CC gelatins
	23CD—dichroic, dialable, M+Y+C, 0–160; white-light lever provided
Carriers:	22 models for all formats within range, in both glass and glassless types; special mechanical transport models in 35mm and 120/220
Projection:	Vertical and horizontal
Max. Mag. w/50mm:	14×
Other Data/ Optional Equip.:	Lensboard tilts, 11 lensboards, 4 extension cones, column extension, voltage-stabilized power-transformer option 35mm intensifier for 23 dga, others
Remarks:	This is a very quick and simple enlarger to convert back and forth between color and black-and-white operation.

The Beseler 23C Enlarger

The Beseler Dichro 23dga Colorhead

The Beseler 23CD Enlarger

Beseler 45M/45MXD
Converter—Dichro dg Colorhead

Type: Convertible
Distributor: Beseler Photo Marketing Co., Inc.
Formats: 8mm–4″ × 5″
Illumination: 45M—double condenser with variable positioning

45MXD—diffusion via two interchangeable mixing chambers; one for formats to 35mm, one for larger formats

Lamp Type: 45M—type 212, 110 volt incandescent, 150 watt bulb.

45MXD—two type EJL, 200 watt, 24 volt quartz-halogen bulbs

Cooling: 45M—conduction/convection

45MXD—fan with flexible exhaust hose

Filtration: 45M—drawer in head for CP acetates; drawer between negative stage and lens for CC gelatins

45MXD—dichroic, dialable, M+Y+C, 0–130; white-light lever provided

Carriers: 30 models for all formats within range, in both glass and glassless types; special mechanical transport models in 35mm and 120/220

Projection: Horizontal and vertical
Other Data/
Optional Equip.: Lensboard tilts, electrically powered head-height adjustment, 11 lensboards, rheostat and voltmeter, 400 watt CVT, point source, 35mm mixing chamber, others

The Beseler 45M Enlarger

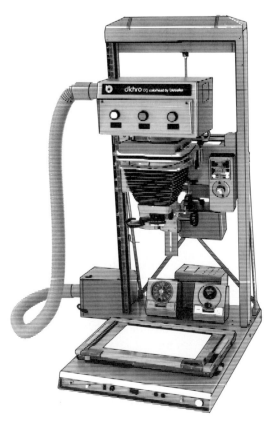

The Beseler 45MXD Enlarger with Dichro dg Colorhead

Bogen 22A Special/22A Dichro Special
Converter — Bogen Dichro

Type:	Convertible
Distributor:	Bogen Photo Corp.
Formats:	8mm–2¼″ × 2¼″
Illumination:	22A — 2-element fixed condensers
	22A dichro — diffusion
Lamp Type:	22A — type 211, 75 watt, 110 volt incandescent bulb
	22A dichro — 75 watt, 12 volt, quartz-halogen bulb
Cooling:	22A and 22A dichro — conduction/convection
Filtration:	22A — drawer in head for CP acetates
	22A dichro — dichroic, dialable, M+Y+C, 0–150
Carriers:	7 glassless types covering the available formats
Projection:	Vertical and horizontal
Max. Mag. w/50mm:	11.8×
Other Data/ Optional Equip.:	Interchangeable lenses, board has Leica thread

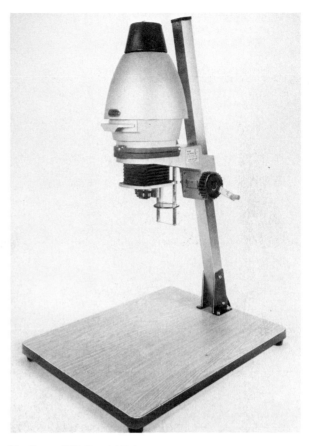

The Bogen 22A Special Enlarger

Bogen 67 Special/67 Dichro Special
Converter—Bogen Dichro

Type: Convertible
Distributor: Bogen Photo Corp.
Formats: 35mm–2¼" × 2¾"
Illumination: 67 Special—2-element fixed
  condensor plus one
  supplementary condenser
  for lenses of 50mm or
  shorter focal length
  67 Dichro Special—diffusion
Lamp Type: 67 Special—type 211, 75 watt,
  110 volt incandescent bulb
  67 Dichro Special—75 watt,
  12 volt, quartz-halogen
  bulb
Cooling: 67 Special—conduction/
  convection
  67 Dichro Special—
  conduction/convection
Filtration: 67 Special—drawer in head
  for CP acetates
  67 Dichro Special—dichroic,
  dialable, M+Y+C, 0–150
Carriers: 5 glassless types covering the
  available formats
Projection: Vertical and horizontal
Max. Mag.
 w/50mm: 12.5×
Other Data/
Optional Equip.: Interchangeable lenses, board
  has Leica thread

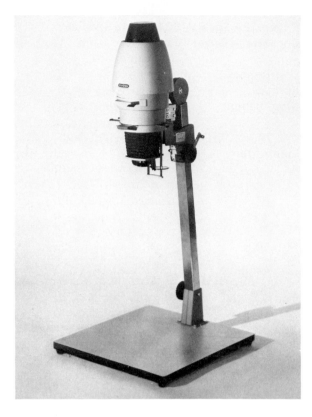

The Bogen 67 Special Enlarger

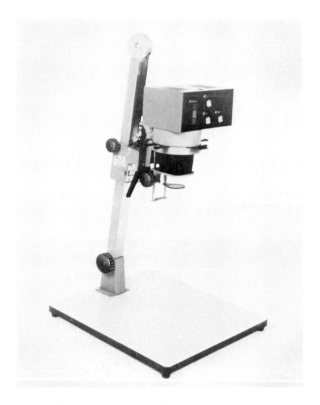

The Bogen 67 Dichro Special Enlarger

**Durst M-301/M-301 Color
Converter—CLS 35 Colorhead**

Type: Convertible
Distributor: Durst (USA) Inc.
Formats: 8mm–35mm
Illumination: M-301—2-element fixed
                     condenser, reflex system
                     (with mirror) with movable
                     lamp
                     M-301 Color—diffusion
Lamp Type: M-301—type 211, 75 watt,
                     110 volt incandescent bulb
                     M-301 Color—type ELB, 80
                     watt quartz-halogen, 30 volt
                     bulb
Cooling: M-301 and M-301 Color—
                     conduction/convection
Filtration: M-301—drawer in head for
                     CP acetates
                     M-301 Color—dichroic,
                     dialable, M+Y+C, 0–100 as
                     well as drawer in head for
                     added CP acetates (see
                     remarks)
Carriers: 6 glassless types covering
                     several formats
Projection: Vertical and horizontal
Max. Mag.
  w/50mm: 11.5×
Other Data/
Optional Equip.:   3 lensboards with Leica
                     thread, Schneider adapter,
                     extension column for 17×
                     on baseboard, filter sets,
                     copying equipment, others
Remarks: This is a fairly simple enlarger
                     to convert back and forth
                     between black-and-white
                     and color operation; but the
                     filtration range of the color
                     head may, at times, be too
                     limited for new emulsions
                     without additional CP
                     acetates being used in
                     conjunction with the
                     dichroic filters. The lamp's
                     30 volt power supply has
                     built-in voltage
                     stabilization. The dichroic
                     filters' dial calibrations do
                     not coincide with standard
                     values used in the U.S.

The Durst M-301 Color Enlarger

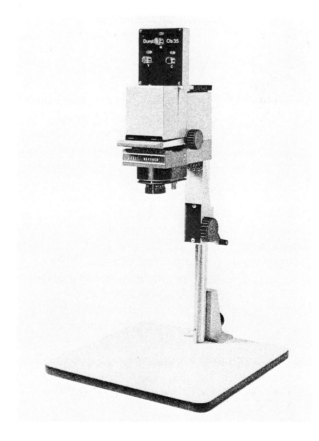

The Durst M-301 Color Enlarger with CLS 35 Colorhead

Durst M-601/M-601 Color Converter—CLS 66 Colorhead

Type:	Convertible
Distributor:	Durst (USA) Inc.
Formats:	8mm–2¼″ × 2¼″
Illumination:	M-601 — 2 element, 3-component, interchangeable reflex (with mirror), condenser system with movable lamp M-601 Color — diffusion via two interchangeable mixing chambers; one for 35mm (optional) one for 2¼″ × 2¼″ standard
Lamp:	M-601 — types 211 (75 watt) or 212 (150 watt) 110 volt incandescent bulbs M-601 Color — type ELB, 80 watt, 30 volt, quartz-halogen bulb
Cooling:	M-601 and M-601 Color — conduction/convection
Filtration:	M-601 — drawer in head for CP acetates M-601 Color — dichroic, dialable, M+Y+C, 0–100 as well as drawer in head for added CP acetates (see Remarks)
Carriers:	Standard carrier is glass with 4 independent masking bands; 18 others available in glassless type; anti-Newton glass available for standard carrier
Projection:	Vertical and horizontal
Max. Mag w/50mm:	15.5×
Other Data/ Optional Equip.:	Lensboard tilts and shifts, 6 lensboards with threads for Leica, Schneider, or Wollensak converter; filter sets, copying equipment, others
Remarks:	This is a fairly simple enlarger to convert back and forth between black-and-white and color operation; but the filtration range of the color head may, at times, be too limited for new emulsions without additional CP acetates being used in conjunction with the dichroic filters. The lamp's 30 volt power supply incorporates built-in voltage stabilization. The dichroic filters' dial calibrations do not coincide with standard values used in the U.S.

The Durst M-601 Enlarger

The Durst CLS 66 Colorhead

The Durst M-601 Color Enlarger with CLS 66 Colorhead

**Durst M-800/M-800 Color
Converter—CLS 80 Colorhead**

Type:	Convertible
Distributor:	Durst (USA) Inc.
Formats:	8mm–2½″ × 3½″
Illumination:	M-800—2-element, 6-component, interchangeable (in pairs), reflex (with mirror) condenser system with movable lamp
	M-800 Color—diffusion via 3 interchangeable mixing boxes.
Lamp Type:	M-800—type 211 (75 watt) or 212 (150 watt), 110 volt incandescent bulbs
	M-800 Color—type ELC, 250 watt, 24 volt, quartz-halogen bulb
Cooling:	M-800—conduction/convection
	M-800 Color—fan
Filtration:	M-800—drawer in head for CP acetates
	M-800 Color—dichroic, dialable, M+Y+C, 0–100 as well as drawer in head for added CP acetates
Carriers:	Standard carrier is glass type with four independent masking bands; 9 others available in glassless type; anti-Newton glass available for standard carrier
Projection:	Vertical and horizontal
Max. Mag. w/50mm:	18×
Other Data/ Optional Equip.:	Lensboard shifts and tilts, 7 lensboards, tubes adapters, etc. filter sets, cold light head, condenser sets, copying equipment; 35mm mixing box and 6cm × 9cm mixing box optional; 6cm × 6cm mixing box standard

Remarks: This is a fairly simple enlarger to convert back and forth between black-and-white and color operation; but the filtration range of the color head may, at times, be too limited for new emulsions without additional CP acetates being used in conjunction with the dichroic filters. The lamp's 24 volt power supply has built-in voltage stabilization. The dichroic filters' dial calibrations do not coincide with standard values used in the U.S.

The Durst M-800 Enlarger

Omega B 600/Chromega B 600
Converter—Chromega B Dichroic Lamphouse

Type: Convertible

Distributor: Berkey Marketing Companies, Inc.

Formats: 35mm–2¼″ × 2¼″

Illumination: B 600—2-element fixed condenser with supplementary condenser for lenses of 50mm or shorter focal length

Chromega B 600—diffusion

Lamp Type: B 600—type ph 140 (GE), 75 watt, 110 volt incandescent bulb

Chromega B 600—75 watt, 27 volt, quartz-halogen, type ELB

Cooling: Omega B 600 and Chromega B 600—conduction/convection

Filtration: B 600—drawer in head for CP acetates

Chromega B 600—dichroic, dialable, M+Y+C, 0–170

Carriers: 6 glassless carriers in full range of formats; one 2¼″ × 2¼″ glass carrier

Projection: Vertical

Max. Mag. w/50mm: 11×

Other Data/ Optional Equip.: Fixed, Leica-threaded lensboard, supplementary condenser, voltage stabilizer (Chromega B 600)

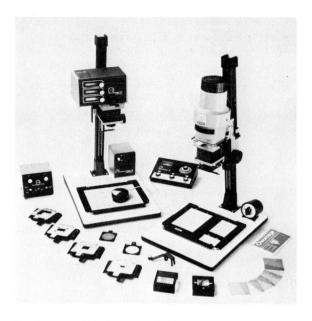

The Omega B 600/Chromega B 600 Enlarger with Chromega B Dichroic Lamphouse

Omega B22/Chromega B
Converter—Chromega B Dichroic Lamphouse

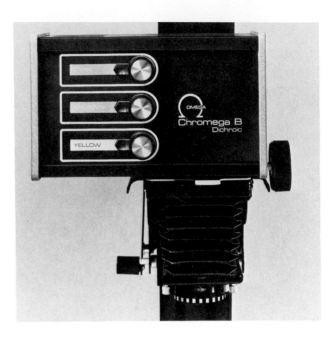

The Omega B Dichroic Lamphouse

Type:	Convertible
Distributor:	Berkey Marketing Companies, Inc.
Formats:	8mm–2¼″ × 2¼″
Illumination:	B22—2-element fixed condenser system with supplementary condenser for lenses 50mm and shorter focal length
	Chromega B—diffusion
Lamp Type:	B22—type 111A, 75 watt, 110 volt incandescent bulb
	Chromega B—75 watt, 27 volt, quartz-halogen, ELB bulb
Cooling:	B22 and Chromega B—conduction/convection
Filtration:	B22—drawer in head for CP acetates
	Chromega B—dichroic, dialable, M+Y+C, 0–170
Carriers:	5 glassless carriers available to cover the applicable formats
Projection:	Vertical
Max. Mag. w/50mm:	11.8×
Other Data/ Optional Equip.:	6 lensboards to mount various lens thread sizes, diffusion glasses (B22), voltage stabilizer (Chromega B), long column, others
Remarks:	This enlarger is no longer manufactured, but there are still many available. It is not an easy machine to convert back and forth between black-and-white and color operation, but it can be done.

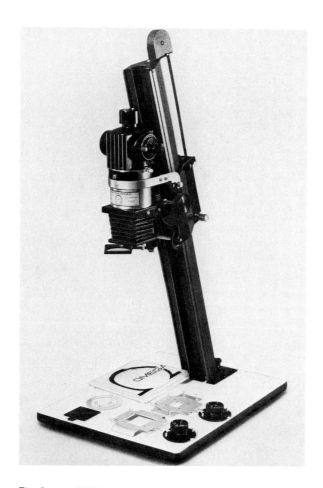

The Omega B22 Enlarger

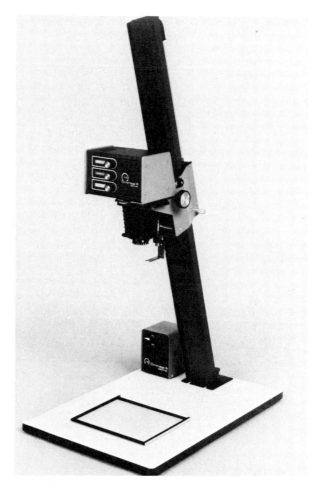

The Chromega B Enlarger

Omega Pro-Lab B-66/Chromega B Converter—Chromega B Dichroic Lamphouse

Type:	Convertible
Distributor:	Berkey Marketing Companies, Inc.
Formats:	8mm–2¼″ × 2¼″
Illumination:	B-66—2-element condenser system with supplementary condenser for lenses of 50mm and shorter focal length Chromega B—diffusion
Lamp Type:	B-66—type ph 140 (GE), 75 watt, 110 volt incandescent bulb Chromega B—75 watt, 27 volt, quartz-halogen, ELB bulb
Cooling:	B-66 and Chromega B—conduction/convection
Filtration:	B-66—drawer in head for CP acetates Chromega B—dichroic, dialable, M+Y+C, 0–170
Carriers:	5 glassless carriers available to cover the applicable formats
Projection:	Vertical
Max. Mag. w/50mm:	12.5×
Other Data/ Optional Equip.:	6 lensboards to mount various thread sizes and focal lengths, voltage stabilizer (Chromega B), long column, others

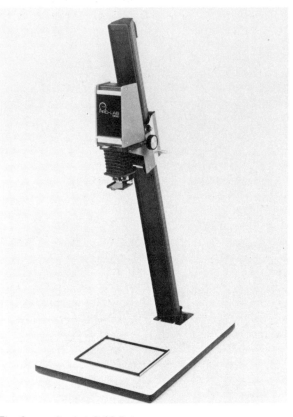

The Omega Pro-Lab B-66 Enlarger

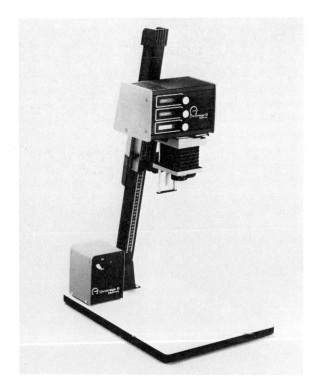

The Chromega B Enlarger

Omega D Series/Super Chromega D Series Converter—Chromega D Dichroic Lamphouse and mounting kit

Type: Convertible
(There are several models among the Omegas, including the D5-V and D5-VXL. All of these models can be converted to the Super Chromega D Dichroic II.)

Distributor: Berkey Marketing Companies, Inc.

Formats: 8mm–4″ × 5″

Illumination: Omega D's—2 fixed-condenser elements and 1 variable-condenser element
Chromega Ds—diffusion via two interchangeable mixing chambers; one for negatives to 4″ × 5″, the other to 2¼″ × 2¾″, white-light lever

Lamp Type: Omega Ds—type 211 (75 watts) or type 212 (150 watts) 110 volt incandescent bulbs
Chromega Ds—type ELC, 250 watt, 22.5 volt quartz-halogen bulb

Cooling: Omega Ds—conduction/convection
Chromega Ds—fan

Filtration: Omega Ds—drawer in head for CP acetates
Chromega Ds—dichroic, dialable, M+Y+C, 0–170

Carriers: 29 glassless types, 7 glass types, 2 special purpose types, 1 mechanical transport type for formats to 70mm, 1 two-pin registration type for 4″ × 5″ separations

Projection: Vertical (forward or reversed) or horizontal with optional projection attachment

Max. Mag. w/50mm: 17.7×

Other Data/
Optional Equip.: There are a staggering number of lens-mounting provisions possible for the D series machines. There is also a wide range of other accessories including a wall-mounting kit, voltage stabilizers, negative masking devices, diffusion glasses, lens turret, micrometer focusing, point-source head, pulsed xenon head, floor stand, and others.

Remarks: These machines are not converted easily back and forth between black-and-white and color configurations, though it can be done.

The Omega Super Chromega D Dichroic II Lamphouse

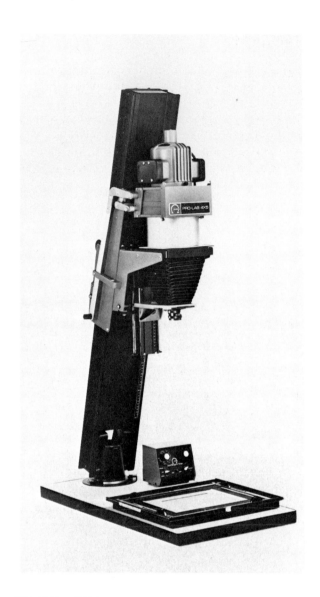

The Omega D Enlarger

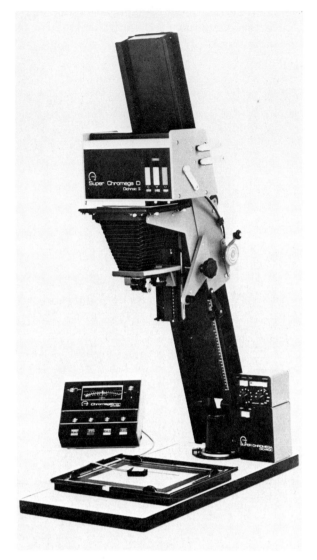

The Super Chromega D Enlarger with Chromega D Dichroic
Lamphouse

Diffusion-Only Enlargers

The several machines in this category were designed specifically to print color first and foremost and to print black-and-white material only secondarily. None of these enlargers can be equipped with the condenser illumination system *I feel* is necessary to small-format black-and-white work, but they will all print black-and-white material reasonably well. In general, their greatest black-and-white printing drawback is a lack of contrast. This can be overcome, to a degree, by using harder contrast-grade black-and-white printing materials. If your primary printing requirements are for color work, then any of these machines might be very attractive to you.

Super Chromega-C

Type:	Diffusion only
Distributor:	Berkey Marketing Companies, Inc.
Formats:	8mm–2¼″ × 2¾″
Illumination:	Diffusion via two interchangeable mixing chambers; one for negative formats up to 35mm, the other for larger formats, white-light lever
Lamp Type:	150 watt, 21 volt quartz-halogen bulb
Cooling:	Fan
Filtration:	Dichroic, dialable, M+Y+C, 0–170
Carriers:	8 glassless, to cover the range of formats, 1 glass type
Projection:	Vertical
Max. Mag. w/50mm:	15.5×
Other Data/ Optional Equip.:	5 lensboards for various focal lengths and thread sizes, wall mount, 35mm mixing chamber, others
Remarks:	No condensers are available for this machine. The lamp's 21 volt power supply has built-in voltage stabilization.

The Super Chromega C Enlarger

Cosar Mornick 371 Enlarger

Type:	Diffusion only
Distributor:	Cosar Corp., Mornick Div.
Formats:	8mm–2¼″ × 2¾″
Illumination:	Diffusion
Lamp Type:	Type ELB, 80 watt, 30 volt quartz-halogen bulb
Cooling:	Conduction/convection
Filtration:	Dichroic, dialable, M+Y+C, magenta and cyan range 0–170; yellow range 0–200
Carriers:	6 glassless types available to cover range of formats
Projection:	Vertical
Max. Mag. w/50mm:	14×
Other Data/ Optional Equip.:	Choice of voltage-regulated or unregulated power supply; lensboards (blank, pilot hole, or clearance for 39mm Leica thread) attach magnetically and/or mechanically
Remarks:	No condensers are available for this machine. A portable, tent-type, darkroom accessory is available for this enlarger. It enables the machine to be used in full room light.

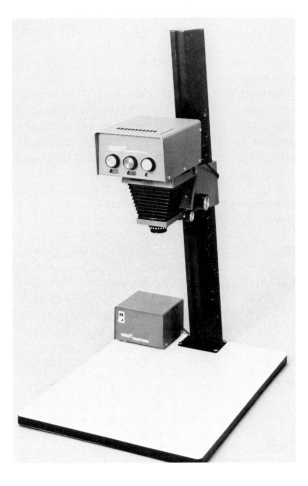

The Cosar Mornick 371 Enlarger

Minolta Color Enlarger Mod I and Mod III

Type: Diffusion only

Distributor: Minolta Corp.

Formats: 110–2¼″ × 2¾″

Illumination: Mod I and Mod III — diffusion via two interchangeable mixing chambers; one for negative formats to 35mm, the other for larger formats

Lamp Type: Mod I and Mod III — EKG type, 80 watt, 19 volt quartz-halogen bulb

Cooling: Mod I and Mod III — conduction/convection

Filtration: Mod I — drawer between lamp module and mixing box for CP acetate filters

Mod III — dichroic, dialable, M+Y+C, 0–150; fits between lamp and mixing-box modules

Carriers: 4 glassless carriers in the several formats covered, one 35mm glass-type carrier

Projection: Vertical

Max. Mag. w/50mm: 15×

Other Data/ Optional Equip.: One Leica-threaded lensboard (flat); optional (35mm or 2¼″ × 2¾″ mixing chambers; accepts special integral color analyzer

Remarks: No condensers are available for this machine. The lamp's 19 volt power supply features built-in voltage stabilization.

The Minolta Color Enlarger Mod I Diffuser

The Minolta Color Enlarger Mod I Diffuser with Lamphouse and 24 × 36 mm Mixing Chamber

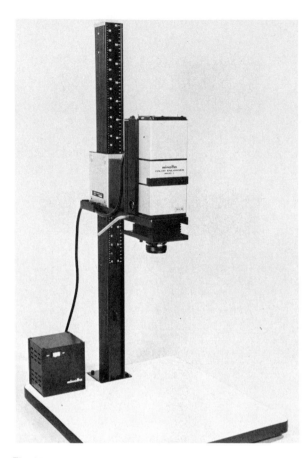

The Minolta Color Enlarger Mod I

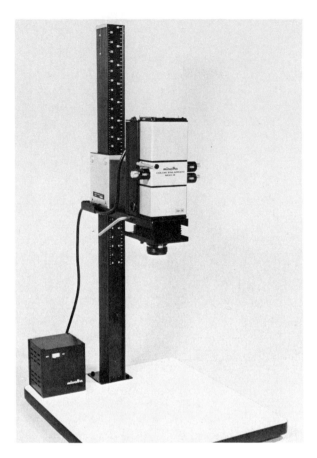

The Minolta Color Enlarger Mod III

The Minolta Color Enlarger Mod III Dichroic Filtration Section

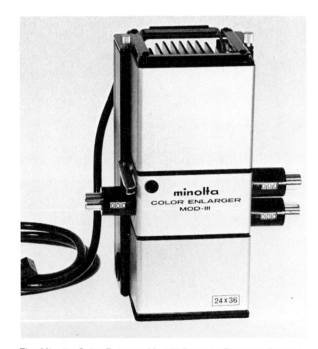

The Minolta Color Enlarger Mod III Dichroic Filtration Section with Lamphouse and 24 × 36 mm Mixing Chamber

Color Printing Filters

The hardware described here falls into two categories: dichroic-filtration conversion kits and CP acetate and CC gelatin filters. The dichroic conversion units are not suitable for use with all enlargers. If no mention is made here of a machine you may wish to convert, I suggest that you contact the marketer of the conversion kit directly for further data.

CP acetate filters are often sold in kits containing a wide assortment of density grades in two or three of the subtractive primary colors and also often include an ultraviolet cutoff filter. Such kits are often offered by the marketers of specific enlargers, already cut to the proper size to fit their machine's drawer. Purchasing filters in such sets may or may not be a money-saving step. It is a good idea to check several prices before deciding

on the filters you purchase. Filter quality should also be kept very much in mind when making your selection, as should the availability of special filters that are particularly suited to certain manufacturer's printing materials. Typical examples would be the applicability of Kodak's CP Cyan-2 filters to printing that firm's negative-to-positive materials, while their CP Cyan filters are better suited to printing Kodak's reversal materials. Kodak is the only manufacturer of sensitized materials that makes sensitometric data on their filters and on the filter requirements of their sensitized material widely available to darkroom workers. For further, and very detailed data on filters and filtration, I recommend Kodak's Publication B-3, *Kodak Filters for Scientific and Technical Uses*.

Independently Manufactured Dichroic-Filtration Conversion Heads

These units are intended to do one or both of the following: provide dialable dichroic filtration to an enlarger which was originally designed to use acetate CP filters in a drawer in its head; and/or provide diffusion illumination to an

enlarger that was designed to use condenser illumination. To my way of thinking, it hardly pays to provide only the former capability when the latter is also available. Descriptions of conversion heads follow.

Mornick 360 Diffusion Dichroic Color Head

Type:	Dichroic (diffusion) conversion head
Distributor:	Cosar Corp., Mornick Div.
Illumination:	Diffusion
Lamp Type:	Type ELB, 80 watt, 30 volt quartz-halogen bulb.
Cooling:	Conduction/convection
Filtration:	Dichroic, dialable over the following ranges: cyan and magenta, 0–170; yellow, 0–200
Other Data:	Choice of stabilized (at extra cost) or unstabilized power supplies. Illuminated color-dial faces.

Enlargers that can be converted with this device: Beseler 23C, 67, 69, 22A, T35; Meopta Ophemus and Axomat; Omega B22 and B66; Vivitar E33 and E36

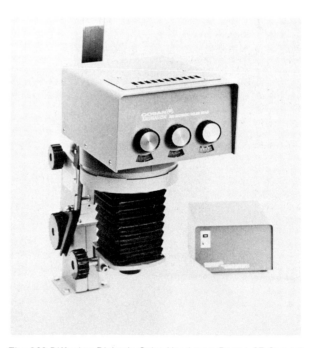

The 360 Diffusion Dichroic Color Head on a Bogen 67 Special Enlarger

Cosar Mornick 340 Condenser Dichroic Color Head

Type: Dichroic (condenser) conversion head

Distributor: Cosar Corp., Mornick Div.

Illumination: The conversion head utilizes the converted enlarger's existing condenser system. A light-mixing chamber is employed to integrate the light prior to its reaching the condensers.

Lamp Type: Type ELH, 300 watt, 120 volt quartz-halogen bulb

Cooling: Separate exhaust fan, connected by hose to the head

Filtration: Dichroic, yellow and magenta filtration can be dial selected over the following ranges: yellow, 0–200; magenta, 0–150; cyan filtration is only available in two rather indefinite values of approximately 30 and 60; these values are selected by moving a lever

Other Data: The unit can be powered directly from household current or by an optional 300 watt CVT. Enlargers that can be converted with this device: Beseler 23C and 45; Bogen 67, 69, 22A, and Super Pro; Omega B22, B7, and D Series: Leitz Focomat IC, IIC and Valoy; Meopta Ophemus and Axomat; Vivitar E74

Remarks: The limited availability and indefinite values of cyan filtration may be a difficult situation to overcome with some enlargers that can't take additional CP acetates in a filter drawer when this unit is attached to the enlarger. The condenser illumination system is not the most desirable one for color printing because of its tendency to sharply focus minute dirt particles or blemishes on negatives or transparencies.

The Cosar Mornick 340 Condenser Dichroic Color Head

Color Filters

If you already have a perfectly good condenser-illuminated enlarger with a drawer somewhere in its lamphouse that will accept CP acetate filters, or even with a below-the-lens filter holder that can be used to carry CC gelatins and you don't want to spend any more than is absolutely necessary for equipment needed to make color prints, the products listed here will interest you.

In addition to the various CP and CC filters and the IR and UV absorbing filters described in the following material, you may also want to consider experimenting with simply removing your enlarger's condensers altogether and replacing them with a diffusion glass. Many enlarger manufacturers offer such glasses for their machines. Doing so will decrease your enlarger's printing speed, but it will also help to reduce the need for spotting your color prints. Not all condenser-illuminated enlargers can be satisfactorily modified in this way. Some of them will not provide even illumination without their condensers. Descriptions of color filters follow.

Beseler Color Printing Filter Sets

Distributor:	Beseler Photo Marketing Co., Inc.
Type:	One set of 22 filters, and one set of 7 filters, all CP acetates
Sizes:	3″ × 3″, 5½″ × 5½″, and 6″ × 6″
Colors:	One set contains yellow, magenta, and cyan, plus an ultraviolet filter; a second set contains only red filters
Density Dist.:	In the subtractive-primary set there is one filter in each subtractive primary color in each of the following densities: 02.5, 05, 10, 20, 30, 40, and 50. The red filters in the red filter set are in the following densities: 02.5, 05, 10, 20, 30, 40, and 50.
Other Data:	The filter sets are packaged in cartons containing individual tab-indexed locations for each filter. Beseler also markets heat-absorbing glasses in the sizes just mentioned.
Remarks:	The 5½″ × 5½″ filters fit the Beseler 23C with no need for trimming. The red filters are useful for printing Kodak's new negative emulsions on condenser-type enlargers with minimum exposure time requirements.

The Color by Beseler Color Printing Filter Set

Premier Color Printing Filter Set

Distributor:	Photo Materials Co.
Type:	Set contains 15 CP acetate filters
Sizes:	3″ × 3″ and 6″ × 6″
Colors:	Yellow and magenta; a UV absorbing filter is also included
Density Dist.:	Filters in both colors are supplied in the same densities, namely: 02.5, 05, 10, 20, 30, 40, and 50
Other Data:	None
Remarks:	This filter set will have to be supplemented with cyan and/or cyan-2 filters to perform many necessary color printing tasks.

Unicolor Color Printing Filter Set

Distributor:	Unicolor Div., Photo Systems Inc.
Type:	The set contains 22 CP acetate filters
Sizes:	3″ × 3″ and 6″ × 6″
Colors:	Yellow, magenta, cyan, and red; a UV absorbing filter is also included in the set
Density Dist.:	Magenta and yellow: one each in 02.5, 20, 40, and 50; three each in 05; cyan: one each in 02.5, 05, 10, 20, and 40; red: two each in 50
Other Data:	The 3″ × 3″ set is packaged in a steel file box with individual tab-indexed dividers for each filter.

Chromega Color Printing Filter Set and Tri-Color Filter Kit

Distributor:	Berkey Marketing Co., Inc.
Type:	The set contains 22 CP acetate filters
Sizes:	3″ × 3″
Colors:	Yellow, magenta, and cyan; an ultraviolet absorber is also included in the set
Density Dist.:	There is one filter in each of the subtractive primary colors in each of the following densities: 02.5, 05, 10, 20, 30, 40, and 50.
Other Data:	A Chromega Tri-Color Filter Kit is also available. It contains a bracket by which the device may be clamped directly to the barrel of many enlarger lenses, a sliding bar with red, green, and blue filter windows, a swing-away diffuser, and a tri-color printing calculator. Chromega also markets heat-absorbing glasses in several sizes and shapes.
Remarks:	If you really insist on color printing with the tri-color system with its long serial-exposure requirements, the Chromega tri-color kit provides all of the filtration you will need and offers a printing calculator to get you started.

The Unicolor Subtractive Color Printing Filter Set

Kodak Color Printing Filters; Wratten Filters; Kodak Color Compensating Filters; Kodak Infrared Cutoff Filters

Distributor:	Eastman Kodak Co.
Type:	CP acetates, CC gelatins, UV absorbers in acetate and gelatin; IR reflectors are dichroic on glass substrate
Sizes:	CP acetates: 5″ × 5″, 6″ × 6″, 8″ × 8″, 12″ × 12″, and 8″ × 10″ CC gelatins: 2″ × 2″, 3″ × 3″, 4″ × 4″, 5″ × 5″, 6″ × 6″ 2E gelatin: 5″ × 5″ 301A dichroic: 2″ × 2″, 3″ × 3″, and 4½″ × 4½″
Colors:	CP acetates: yellow, magenta, cyan, cyan-2, and red CC gelatins: yellow, magenta, cyan, cyan-2, red, green, and blue
Density Dist.:	CP acetates: 02.5, 05, 10, 20, and 40; no 02.5 density available in red and cyan; an 80 density available in yellow CC gelatins: 05, 10, 20, 30, 40, and 50
Other Data:	No complete sets are available; 2B and 2E can be had in either acetate or gelatin
Remarks:	Kodak offers complete sensitometric data for all of its filters.

Colourtronic Color Printing Filter Sets

Distributor:	Colourtronic
Type:	The set contains 14 CP acetate filters.
Sizes:	3″ × 3″, 4″ × 4″, 6″ × 6″, and 70mm × 70mm
Colors:	Yellow, magenta, and cyan (only one cyan filter is provided); a UV filter is also included in the set
Density Dist:	Yellow: 02.5, 05, 10, 20, 40, 45, and 80; magenta: 02.5, 05, 10, 20, and 40; cyan: 40
Other Data:	None
Remarks:	Additional cyan or cyan-2 filters will have to be purchased from another source to perform many necessary color printing tasks.

Durst Color Printing Filter Set

Distributor:	Durst (USA) Inc.
Type:	The set contains 10 CP acetate filters.
Sizes:	7cm × 7cm, 3″ × 3″, and 4¾″ × 4¾″
Colors:	Yellow, magenta, and red; a UV absorbing filter is also provided
Density Dist.:	Yellow and magenta: 05, 10, 20, and 40; Red: 40
Other Data:	None
Remarks:	This filter set will have to be supplemented with cyan and/or cyan-2 filters to perform many necessary color printing tasks.

Chapter 7 was devoted, in large part, to the two presently available color print-processing machines that do not incorporate daylight drums: the Agnekolor Laminar Flow Processor and the Kodak Rapid Color Processor, Model 11. Nothing would be gained by offering further outline data on either of these machines, as they are dealt with in some detail in that chapter. Chapters 3 and 6 offer data on several general categories of daylight drum processors, so such redundant information will be kept to a minimum here. Since there are a large number of such drums commercially available, I will, however, offer outline data on the many choices to facilitate comparison of them.

Daylight processing drums are little more than light-tight hollow tubes. The print to be processed is curled up, emulsion side facing the center of the drum, and placed inside of the drum. Then one or both of the drum's light-baffled liquid-pouring end caps is placed on the drum and all subsequent processing operations are carried out in normal room light. All of the drums now commercially available are made of plastic materials that have low thermal conductivity. There are two general categories of drums: vertical and horizontal. Horizontal drums have a pair of legs, one leg at each end. The drums are placed on these legs, in a horizontal position, and the chemicals are added through a snout-like protuberance on one end cap. The solutions flow, by this means, through the cap's light baffle and into a trough of some sort inside the drum. Properly used, none of the chemicals added to a horizontal drum will contact the print inside it until the drum is deliberately rolled off its legs.

Vertical drums have no legs, nor do they have any snouts. They are stood up vertically, on end, to add chemicals. One end of a vertical drum looks like the wide-mouthed portion of a funnel, while the other end often looks like the narrow end of a funnel (in the center of the drum in a recess in the end cap). Vertical drums are designed so that as soon as they are stood up vertically, whatever chemical is in them spills out the bottom cap. While this is occurring, the next chemical can be added to the opposite end of the drum. This is possible because there is a reservoir under the cap's light baffle that catches the solution being poured in and keeps it from the surface of the contained print until the drum is drained and deliberately placed in a horizontal position. This arrangement is most often quite satisfactory for the small volumes of chemical to be added to a daylight drum, but it can be awkward and hard to deal with when larger volumes of presoak or wash water have to be added to or removed from such a drum.

Another significant factor in daylight drum design is whether their inside walls are completely smooth, or if they have raised "ribs" running the length of the drum. Completely smooth-walled drums are not well suited to the wash step that always follows bleaching and fixing (blixing). Because of this, smooth-walled drums are generally unloaded after the bleach-fix step and washes and stabilization are carried out in trays external to the drum. This allows large quantities of smelly, eye and lung-irritating stabilizer vapor to get into the darkroom air—a fate worse than death as far as I am concerned. On the positive side, though, smooth-walled drums are, theoretically, capable of being used with somewhat smaller volumes of chemicals. Another negative aspect of smooth-walled drums is that they are not suitable for processing multiple prints, in my experience. This is because these drums have nothing to mechanically restrain the prints that may shift during processing and partially cover one another. This results in improper processing of the covered prints.

Most drums have end caps, which are simply pressed on and remain in place through friction. While I say they are *simply* pressed on, I should go on to explain that many such caps must be properly oriented (often aligned with a pin) before they can be properly installed. This can be a difficult thing for some people to do in the dark. Only two commercially available drums differ in this respect: the Paterson with a screw-threaded closure, and the Unidrum with an excellent bayonet closure system.

That, in a rather large nutshell, covers most of the major factors concerning daylight drum design, and should provide enough information to help in interpreting the necessarily brief descriptions of the several products that follow. If further clarification is needed, reference to the chapters mentioned or contacting the distributor of the product in question should help.

Daylight Print Processing Drums

Descriptions of the available hardware follow.

Beseler Print-Processing Drums

Distributor: Beseler Photo Marketing Co., Inc.

Type: Horizontal, semi-smooth walls (only 3 ribs — two fixed paper guides and one removable one), separators, both end caps removable, elevated chemical trough

Sizes: 8″ × 10″, 11″ × 14″, 16″ × 20″, and 20″ × 24″

Paper sizes: 8″ × 10″—one 8″ × 10″, two 5″ × 7″, four 4″ × 5″
11″ × 14″—one 11″ × 14″, two 8″ × 10″, four 5″ × 7″, eight 4″ × 5″

Other data: The maker states that 1½ fluid ounces of chemicals are all that is required when processing with the 8″ × 10″ drum. The pouring spout is double baffled for quick, accurate emptying.

Remarks: This drum is too short to fit on Chromega motor bases and only marginally operable on the Uniroller motor base.

The Beseler Print-Processing Drums

Chromega Daylight Color Processors

Distributor:	Berkey Marketing Co., Inc.
Type:	Horizontal, ribbed walls, variable paper guides, one friction-fitted end cap, separators, cam-shaped end caps for transverse agitation
Sizes:	8″ × 10″, 11″ × 14″, and 16″ × 20″
Paper sizes:	8″ × 10″ — one 8″ × 10″, two 5″ × 7″, and four 4″ × 5″ 11″ × 14″ — one 11″ × 14″, two 8″ × 10″, four 5″ × 7″, six 4″ × 5″ 16″ × 20″ — one 16″ × 20″, one 11″ × 14″, four 8″ × 10″, eight 5″ × 7″, and eight 4″ × 5″ Extra tracks are provided for the variable paper guides to accommodate metric-size paper as well as sizes listed
Other data:	This is the only drum design which, when rolled on a level surface, will provide both radial and transverse agitation to the chemicals inside. The friction-fitted end cap is pin located.
Remarks:	These drums are manufactured for Omega, by Simmard, in Canada where they are sold as Simmard drums.

Cibachrome Color Processing Drum

Distributor:	Ilford Inc.
Type:	Vertical, smooth-walled, two friction-fitted end caps.
Sizes:	8″ × 10″, and 11″ × 14″
Paper sizes:	8″ × 10″ — one 8″ × 10″ 11″ × 14″ — one 11″ × 14″
Other data:	Only a new center tube is needed to convert the 8″ × 10″ model to an 11″ × 14″ model as the tube diameters are identical and both end caps are removable.
Remarks:	This drum tends to air lock if placed in a puddle in a sink during the drain period.

FR One-Shot Drum Processor

Distributor:	FR Chemical/Div., Cinemagnetics
Type:	Vertical, smooth-walled, only one end cap removable, O-ring closure
Sizes:	8″ × 10″
Paper sizes:	8″ × 10″ — one 8″ × 10″
Other data:	Very nicely finished overall.
Remarks:	The pour-out end of this drum is castellated to prevent air locking.

Kodak (London, England) Printank

Distributor:	Eastman Kodak Co.
Type:	Vertical, smooth-walled, only one end cap removable, but both ends seal to make this tank airtight and allow it to be floated in a water bath
Sizes:	8″ × 10″
Paper sizes:	8″ × 10″ — one 8″ × 10″
Other data:	Plastic caps are provided to close the tank's end caps to make the drum airtight. This allows the drum to be floated in a constant-temperature bath. It can be used the same way other drums are used. Construction is very heavy.
Remarks:	Air locking is no problem with this vertical drum. The Kodak Printank is not sold in the U.S. but can be mail ordered from English photo-supply dealers.

Colourtronic Daylight Processors

Distributor: Colourtronic

Type: Vertical, with longitudinal flutes and dividing ribs, both end caps, removable and friction-fitted.

Sizes: 8″ × 10″, 11″ × 14″, 16″ × 20″, 20″ × 24″, 30″ × 20″, and 30″ × 40″

Paper sizes: 8″ × 10″—one 8″ × 10″
11″ × 14″—one 11″ × 14″, two 8″ × 10″
16″ × 20″—one 16″ × 20″, four 8″ × 10″
36″ × 24″—one 20″ × 24″
36″ × 20″—one print to a maximum of 20″ × 36″, two 16″ × 20″
30″ × 40″—one 30″ × 40″

Other data: Only a new center tube is needed to convert an 8″ × 10″ drum to an 11″ × 14″ drum as the tube diameters are identical and both end caps are removable.

Remarks: Older models of these drums were smooth walled. These drums tend to air lock if placed in a puddle in a sink during draining.

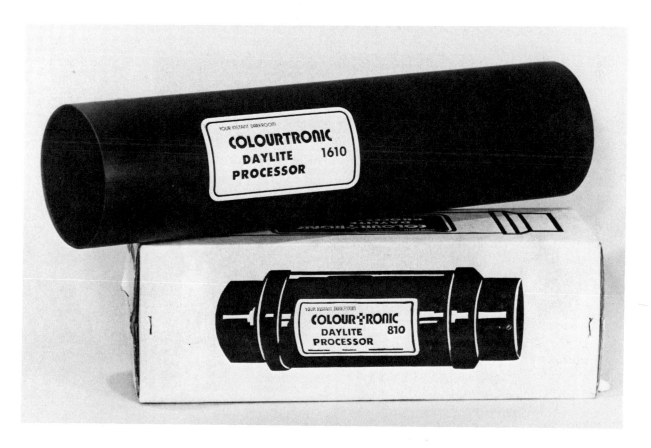

The Colourtronic Daylight Processors

Paterson Color Print Processors

Distributor: Braun North America

Type: Vertical, smooth-walled, only one end cap removable, screw-threaded cap with crushable gasket. Tank and special cradle are integral. Cradle permits tank to be agitated by a built-in crank and causes transverse chemical agitation of chemicals in drum during normal, cranked, rotary agitation.

Sizes: 8″ × 10″ and 11″ × 14″

Paper sizes: 8″ × 10″—one 8″ × 10″
11″ × 14″—one 11″ × 14″

Other data: This is the only tank available that permits the user to disassemble the light-trapped pour-in reservoir for thorough cleaning.

Remarks: The spiral groove cut into the end of this tank, which engages a pin in its cradle to enable transverse agitation to be achieved, is of very light construction, as are several other components, and may be damaged through rough handling.

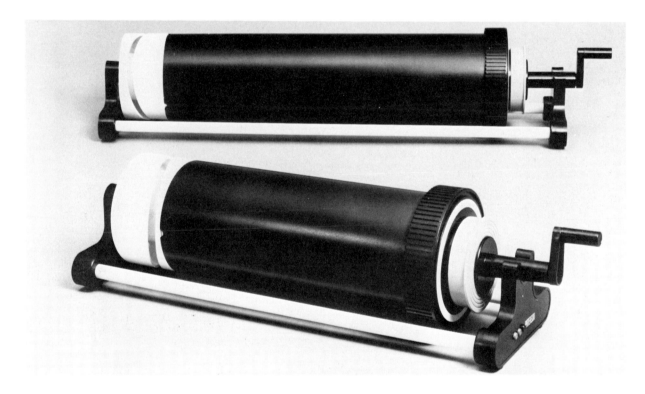

The Paterson Color Print Processors

Unidrum II Daylight Color Print Processors

Distributor: Unicolor Div., Photo Systems Inc.

Type: Horizontal, longitudinal ribs and multiple, fixed paper-locating flanges. Only one end cap removable. Cap closure system incorporates a bayonet, twist-lock construction.

Sizes: 8″ × 10″, 11″ × 14″, and 16″ × 20″

Paper sizes: 8″ × 10″—one 8″ × 10″, two 5″ × 7″, four 4″ × 5″
11″ × 14″—one 11″ × 14″, two 8″ × 10″
16″ × 20″—one 16″ × 20″, two 11″ × 14″, four 8″ × 10″, two 8″ × 10″ plus one 11″ × 14″

Other data: While flanges are supplied to hold prints against rotary motion, no separators are provided to keep multiple prints apart.

Remarks: From a practical standpoint I have found the lack of separators to be of no importance in these drums when making multiple prints.

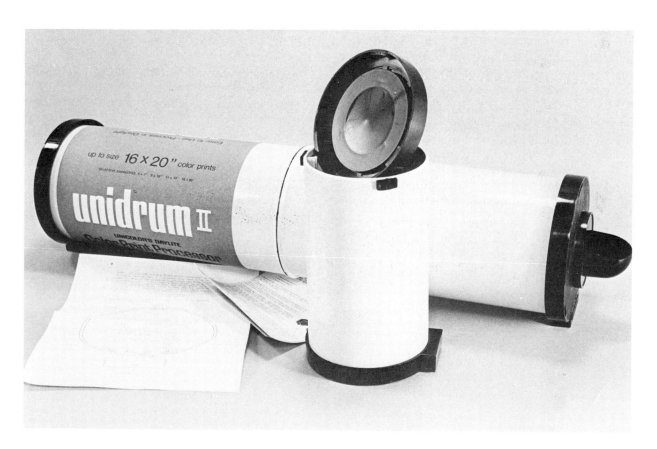

The Unidrum II Daylight Color Print Processors

Print-Processing Drum Agitators

Daylight print-processing drums must be rotated to keep the tiny chemical puddle inside in continual motion over the surface of the print. Without agitation only the area under the stationary puddle within the drum will be processed, and that area typically represents less than five percent of the image. Even with agitation, the quality of a print processed in a daylight drum will depend, to a considerable extent, on the type of agitation it receives while in the drum. A print that has been drum processed with irregular, or inadequate, or too much agitation will be improperly processed. Duplicate prints made in drums which have been manually agitated are seldom exactly alike because manual agitation is extremely difficult to do with perfect uniformity.

It is no fun to roll a drum from side to side for 10 or 12 minutes. It is tiring, boring, and generally unpleasant. The best of color printers may manage to agitate a drum through one or two complete processing cycles with good uniformity, but beyond that number of prints there are few people indeed who can fight off the boredom and ignore the charley-horsed muscles and fatigue well enough to obtain good uniformity for the third or fourth print and beyond.

Even printers who choose the Paterson drum system, which includes a cradle and a crank with which the drum may be rotated within the stationary cradle, will soon find themselves with cramped fingers and will be very bored by the repetitive motion required to keep the drum turning and the chemical puddle moving.

The only way out of this agitation problem involves a significant cash outlay. You have to purchase some sort of mechanical device to do your agitating for you. The majority of these devices are called motor bases. They are little more than a set of motor-driven, rubber-rimmed wheels mounted in a base and aligned, across a V-shaped notch in that base, with a set of idler wheels so that the drum to be turned can be placed between the driver wheels and the idlers. The motor then takes over the dull chore of rotating the drum about its longitudinal axis.

There is, at present, one variation on this simple theme. It is a device that consists of a trough, a pump, and an impeller collar. The collar fits over a daylight drum, the drum and impeller sit in the trough, and the pump continually recirculates water inside the trough by pumping a stream of it against the impeller blades attached to the tank. The stream of water impinging on the impeller blades causes the drum, which is partially afloat in the trough, to rotate, and thereby agitate the chemical inside. Descriptions of the available hardware follow.

Colourtronic Turbo-Drive Processors, Models TD 800 and TD 1410

Distributor: Colourtronic

Type: Hydraulic, consists of a trough, and impeller band for the drum to be agitated, a pump (and, optionally, a heater and a temperature sensor/regulator). A stream of water, recirculated in the trough by the pump, drives the impeller blades attached to the drum (which is afloat in the trough), causing the drum to rotate and thereby agitating the chemical inside the drum.

Drive motion: Rotary motion is unidirectional.

Drive speed: The manufacturer specifies it as being variable, depending on the depth of water within the trough; however, neither normal speed nor speed limits are provided in the unit's specification sheet.

Drum sizes: The TD 800 will accommodate a single 8″ × 10″ Colourtronic drum. The TD 1410 agitates a single Colourtronic 11″ × 14″ drum. Other manufacturers' drums or other sizes of Colourtronic drums cannot be handled. Models TD 810 and TD 1410A include appropriately sized drums along with the components already mentioned.

Other data: The trough may also be used to temper the processing chemicals. The maker claims a 40 percent time reduction for processing is possible with these units, but does not explain how this is obtained.

Remarks: It is difficult to understand how the rotational rate can be varied by varying the trough's water level. It is harder still to see how the use of this device could reduce processing time by 40 percent unless by means of temperature control. Of course, that option is open to any agitating device through presoaking.

The Colourtronic Turbo-Drive Processor, Model TD 800

Beseler Motor-Base Agitator

Distributor: Beseler Photo Marketing Co., Inc.

Type: Motor-driven rubber-rimmed drive wheels opposite rubber idler wheels on either side of a V-slot.

Drive motion: Rotary motion is unidirectional

Drive speed: Approximately 4.1 inches per second (rotary)

Drum sizes: Any

Other data: Unidirectional, high-speed rotation causes drums to walk off the base. This necessitates adding a pair of thick rubber bands (supplied with the motor base) to the drum to be agitated to keep it from being thrown off the base.

A screw-type leveling foot and a cord-storage slot are provided. The unit is Underwriters' Laboratories Inc. (U.L.) listed and approved.

Remarks: This is the narrowest motor base I know of. Its dimensions were tailored to the Beseler 8″ × 10″ drum which is the shortest drum I know of. The Beseler motor base is the only motor base narrow enough to rotate the Beseler 8″ × 10″ drum without occasional interference problems. This unit affords only rotational agitation. No provisions for transverse agitation are offered.

The Beseler Motor Base Agitator

Chromega Dual-Action Agitator

Distributor: Berkey Marketing Co., Inc.

Type: Motor-driven rubber-rimmed drive wheels opposite rubber idler wheels on either side of a V-slot.

Drive motion: Rotary motion is unidirectional. Eccentrically mounted drive wheels also provide an end-to-end rocking motion.

Drive speed: Approximately 3.8 inches per second (rotary)

Drum sizes: Any size but Beseler 8″ × 10″. However, all drums need special stabilizing bands which are only available for Chromega drums (see the following).

Other data: Unidirectional, high-speed rotation and constant drum rocking, due to the eccentrically mounted drive wheels, provide forces which quickly walk drums off this motor base unless they are equipped with the special molded-plastic stabilizing bands, which are only available in sizes to fit Chromega drums. This base is, then, effectively limited to use with Chromega drums. The unit is U.L. listed and approved.

Remarks: This is the only motor base I am aware of that provides both rotary and transverse agitation.

The Chromega Dual-Action Agitator

Uniroller

Distributor:	Unicolor Div., Photo Systems Inc.
Type:	Motor-driven rubber-rimmed drive wheels opposite rubber idler wheels on either side of a V-slot.
Drive motion:	Rotary motion is bidirectional. Motion is reversed every 3.5 seconds.
Drive speed:	Approximately 1.7 inches per second (rotary)
Drum sizes:	Any conventional diameter; however, the Beseler 8″ × 10″ drum is a very tight fit so far as length is concerned.
Other data:	This unit is the only available motor base that can accommodate any drum without any concern over whether the drum will walk off the base. The constantly reversed, low-speed motion does not cause any detectable drum shifting on the rollers. The unit is U.L. listed and approved.
Remarks:	While this unit has a relatively low rotational speed, the constant reversal of motion seems to provide any additional agitation that the low speed requires. The unit functions extremely well.

The Unicolor Uniroller

I'd gladly trade all the 747s in the world for just one rigid airship like the Shenendoah, but, alas, I seem to be almost alone in my preference. This Goodyear blimp, the Mayflower, and a few more like her will just have to do until the real thing comes along. The shot was made on Kodachrome II and printed on Ektachrome Type 1993 paper.

NEGATIVE-TO-POSITIVE RING-AROUND

+40 RED

+2 STOPS

+40 YELLOW

+20 RED

+1 STOP

+20 YELLOW

+10 RED

+½ STOP

+10 YELLOW

+40 GREEN

+20 GREEN

+10 GREEN

PERFECT

+10 MAGENTA

+20 MAGENTA

+40 MAGENTA

+10 BLUE

-½ STOP

+10 CYAN

+20 BLUE

-1 STOP

+20 CYAN

+40 BLUE

-2 STOPS

+40 CYAN

C4-2

POSITIVE-TO-POSITIVE RING-AROUND

+40 YELLOW

+40 MAGENTA

+40 CYAN

+20 YELLOW

+20 MAGENTA

+20 CYAN

+10 YELLOW

+10 MAGENTA

+10 CYAN

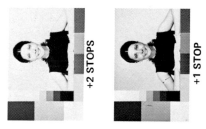

+2 STOPS   +1 STOP   +½ STOP   PERFECT   -½ STOP   -1 STOP   -2 STOPS

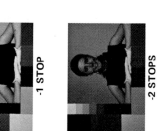

+10 RED

+10 GREEN

+10 BLUE

+20 RED

+20 GREEN

+20 BLUE

+40 RED

+40 GREEN

+40 BLUE

PRINTS MADE WITH VARIOUS COLOR-PRINTING TECHNIQUES

▲ With a sunset like this one, over Canada's Northumberland Strait, it would be hard to miss making an interesting image. This shot was recorded on Kodachrome II and later printed on Ektachrome Type 1993 paper.

▼ Sometimes bad lenses accidentally make interesting images. This shot, of a gull following a Lake Constance steamer, was made with a fast 50mm lens that produced a lot of flare on Agfa CT 18. The deep saturation possible with Cibachrome printing material provides an attractive graphic image, but much of the subtlety of the original gets lost in the translation.

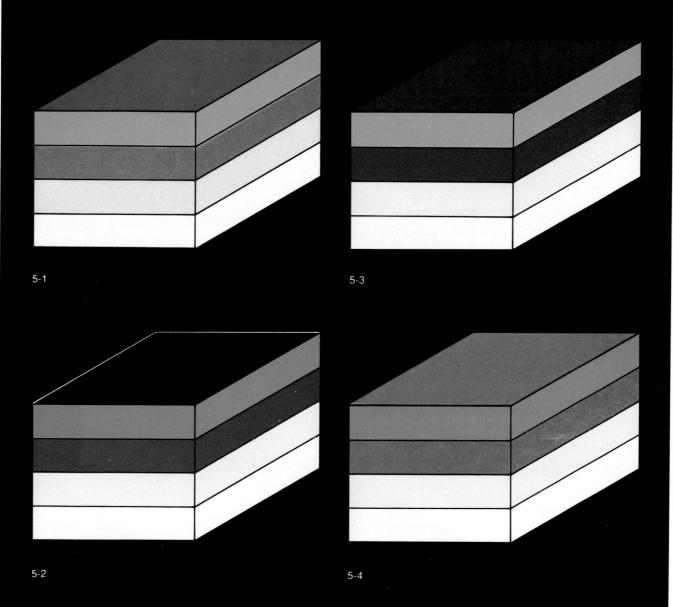

5-1

5-3

5-2

5-4

Fig. 5-1—Three layers of partially saturated dye yield neutral density. The low-density cyan layer absorbs some red. The low-density magenta layer absorbs some green. The low-density yellow layer absorbs some blue. The remainder of the light reflected from the white paper base is seen as gray at the surface.

Fig. 5-2—When the three dye layers are saturated, they absorb all white light before it can leave the print. Therefore, your eyes perceive black, the absence of light.

Fig. 5-3—Here, the yellow magenta layers are well saturated, but the cyan layer is weak. As less red light is absorbed than blue and green light, the eye perceives the surface of this print to be reddish-gray.

Fig. 5-4—Strong cyan and yellow dye layers, plus a weak magenta dye layer, make the surface of this print look greenish-gray.

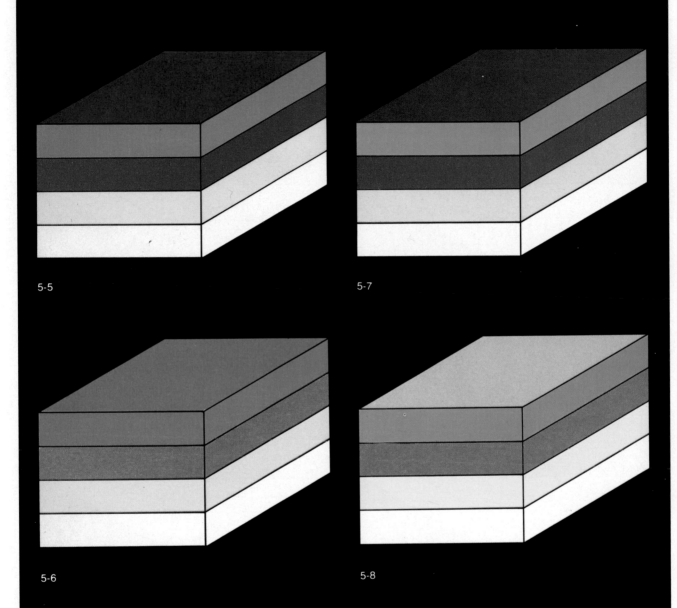

5-5

5-7

5-6

5-8

Fig. 5-5—Weak yellow and strong cyan and magenta dye layers cause the surface of this print to appear to be bluish-gray.

Fig. 5-6—This print has one strong dye layer, cyan, and two weak ones, magenta and yellow. Since less green and blue than red light is absorbed, the surface appears cyanish-gray. (Cyan is blue plus green.)

Fig. 5-7—This is another case of two weak dye layers and one strong one. Here, cyan and yellow have a low density. The magenta layer has a high one. This print will look magentaish-gray. (Magenta is a combination of red plus blue.)

Fig. 5-8—Here the cyan and magenta dye layers are weak and the yellow layer is strong. The surface appearance of this print will be yellowish-gray. (Yellow is red plus green.)

VIEWING FILTERS FOR COLOR PRINTING

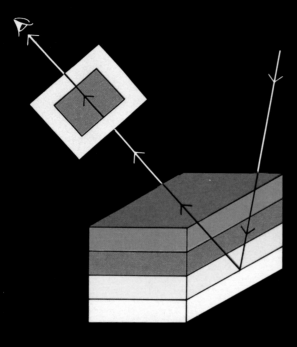

Fig. 5-9—For you to properly see a color print, it must be illuminated from above. A light ray enters the print from above, passes through all three dye layers, is reflected back from the brilliant white, optically-brightened paper base and then makes a second pass through the dye layers before it leaves the surface of the print on its way to your eye. The dyes in a color print need only be half as dense as those in a color transparency, which is for direct viewing by transillumination. (The light source is placed behind a transparency so that light rays get only one chance to pass through its three dye layers.) The viewing filter, shown here, is placed so that the light ray makes only one pass through it. If the viewing filter is, for example, a CC 10M, and it corrects the greenish-gray problem, for a negative-to-positive printing process you only subtract an 5 magenta filter from the printing filter pack because, by doing so, you will increase the density of the print's magenta layer by 5. Since light rays pass through this 5 density twice, the effect of this change will be (theoretically) identical to that brought about by viewing the print through a 10M viewing filter positioned so that the light rays from the print surface pass through the viewing filter only once.

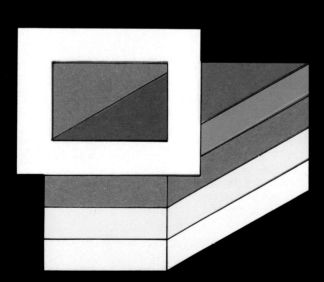

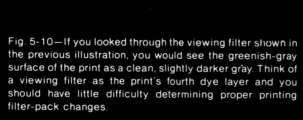

Fig. 5-10—If you looked through the viewing filter shown in the previous illustration, you would see the greenish-gray surface of the print as a clean, slightly darker gray. Think of a viewing filter as the print's fourth dye layer and you should have little difficulty determining proper printing filter-pack changes.

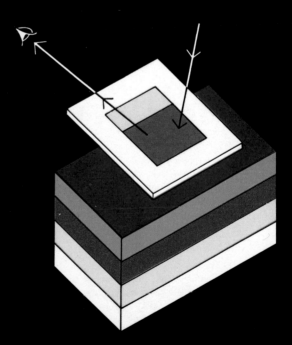

Fig. 5-11—When you must place a viewing filter on top of a print to correct a problem, as shown here where a yellow filter clears up the bluish-gray color cast of the print, be aware that white light is passing through the viewing filter twice; once on the way into the print surface, and once on its way out of the print surface to your eye.

VIEWING FILTERS FOR COLOR PRINTING

Fig. 5-12

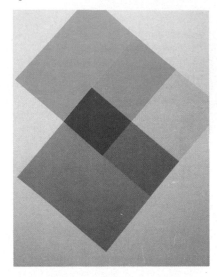

Fig. 5-13

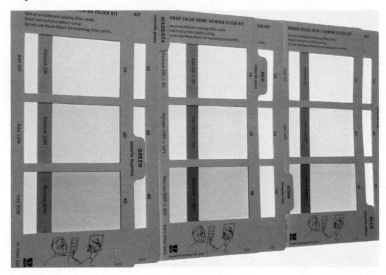

Fig. 5-12—By overlapping cyan, magenta, and yellow subtractive primary color filters, you create neutral density. Where only two of these subtractive primaries overlap, an additive primary is formed. You can use this technique to form additive primary viewing filters. (Yellow plus magenta makes red, yellow plus cyan makes green, and cyan plus magenta makes blue.)

Fig. 5-13—This Kodak viewing filter set is laid out in pairs of complements. Note that where cyan and red, magenta and green, yellow and blue filters overlap, the result is neutral density (gray).

MAKING A CALIBRATION PRINT OF A STANDARD NEGATIVE

Fig. 5-14—Unicolor sent me their new resin-coated type-A paper and their new R-2 chemistry to play with. I had no idea of how it would print so I started to calibrate the paper with a Vericolor II "Shirley," by using a 40M+60Y filter pack, and an exposure time of 10 seconds at f/5.6 for a 5× enlargement. This overexposed dark color print was the result.

Fig. 5-15—When you are more than one half-stop over or underexposed there is little point in trying to make any color correction. Reprint to get the density right, then worry about the color as I did with this print. I used the same pack and exposure time, but closed down my enlarging lens to f/8. This print is close enough to being properly exposed so that viewing filters can be used to determine the problem-color cast. I had to lay a 20C filter flat down on the print to get one of the density wedges to look almost neutral gray, rather than the reddish-gray that appears here.

Fig. 5-16—This print resulted from the pack change called for by the viewing filter used on the previous illustration. The pack used was 65M+85Y. I held the f/8 lens opening,

but cut the printing exposure to 7½ seconds to see what a bit less density would look like. It's close but not perfect. The viewing filters again told me what the problem was. I had over-corrected and driven poor Shirley to cyan. This time a 20R filter, held so the light from the print made only one pass through the viewing filter, made the density look "right." But poor Shirley looks pale at 7½ seconds, so I decided to increase my exposure slightly to pep her up—see the next print.

Fig. 5-17—Here's our girl printed through a 55M+75Y pack and an f/8 lens opening for 10 seconds. The color balance is good but a 9 second printing time would have been a trifle better, and probably would have cleared the slightly red tinge out of the second wedge. All of this goes to prove that viewing filters are an effective tool, and that Unicolor has come up with a winning pair of materials. Their new resin-coated paper (actually Mitsubishi makes it for them) is a bit contrastier than Kodak 37 RC and, considering the inherent low contrast of Vericolor II and Kodacolor II, the extra contrast of Unicolor is much appreciated by this printer.

MAKING A CALIBRATION PRINT OF A STANDARD NEGATIVE

Fig. 5-14

Fig. 5-15

Fig. 5-16

Fig. 5-17

A CALIBRATED COLOR CONTACT SHEET

Fig. 5-18—This is a typical calibrated color contact sheet. Note that the author mistakenly put his standard negative into his contact frame emulsion side down, so that it has printed here as a mirror image of the way it should have appeared; but I believe you will get the idea of what the whole procedure is about in spite of this error. Shirley, nevertheless, has been reproduced with the proper density and color balance to assure that the exposure and processing used for this sheet were perfect. The other images, shot at dusk, can all be quite easily judged against the standard negative's image, and printing judgements on their density, color balance, aesthetic appeal, etc., can be readily made. An acceptable print of any frame can be made, on the first try, with the aid of the Color Printing Computer and a set of viewing filters. Note that a file number is included on the face of the sheet, for ease in filing and retrieval.

This example of a successful print of two images sandwiched together suggests the devastation of a forest fire. There is certainly nothing to recommend either of its component images, but it should be evident that sandwiching can sometimes serve to put dull and otherwise uninteresting slides to some constructive use. The printing exposure required for this sandwich was quite long. The print, made on Ektachrome Type 1993 paper and processed in R-500 chemicals, needed a four-minute exposure. The central portion of the "flame" was dodged for the last one and one-half minutes of exposure time. The enlarger data was: $6\times$ magnification; $f/2.8$ lens opening; 2E, 301A, and 10Y + 30M filters.

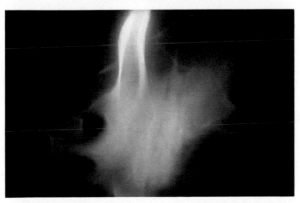

(Above) This basically unmoving image of a beautiful Nova Scotia sunset offered the perfect opportunity for trying out some print-manipulation techniques. I decided to add a boat, using multiple-printing, to make a more interesting composite image.

(Below) This cull from the same Nova Scotia series seemed to offer a likely-looking boat to add to the sunset image. The challenge was to figure out a way to add the image of the boat to the precise spot on the sunset print where it would look best.

I photographed a very beautiful sunset over the Bay of Fundy, but the image returned from the lab was so unmoving that I laid it aside. When next I looked at the photo, it occurred to me that adding a boat might help, so I decided to use multiple printing to make a composite image. I started by printing the 35mm slide of the sunset on Ektachrome Type 1993. I used a two-minute exposure at 6× magnification, through an f/2.8 lens opening. I dodged the lower-right corner of the image for about 50 seconds to darken this area still further (leaving the emulsion essentially unexposed and available for the image of a boat). Once the print was made, I removed the sheet of printing paper from the easel and cut off one of its corners so that I could reorient it properly on the easel again. Then I stored it in a black plastic bag. I next placed a focusing sheet on the easel and, while projecting the sunset onto it, I used a pencil to circle the area of the sunset image in which I wanted to put the boat. I then found a likely-looking boat on another cull from the same Nova Scotia series, removed the sunset slide, and put the second 35mm slide into the enlarger's carrier. I projected the image of the boat onto the focusing sheet, moving the easel until the boat fell inside

the pencil-circled area. I found that the boat fitted the area quite well at the same 6× magnification I had used for the first print, so the enlarger head height remained unchanged. I cut a small hole in a piece of black paper to provide a burning tool, focused the image sharply, removed the focusing sheet, turned off the enlarger lamp, and got the original sheet of paper from its light-tight bag. I felt the sheet to find the cutoff corner and placed that corner in the easel's paper grips. Then, using the black paper-burning tool, I projected only the image of the boat into the lower-right corner of the sheet, through the same lens opening, for 45 seconds. The printing filter pack used for both exposures was identical: a 301A, a 2E, and 10Y + 30M. The processed composite print showed a fairly large area of light blue water all around the boat. I eliminated most of that with the dry-dye technique, using Kodak's Flexichrome dyes; however, I left some of this area undarkened to provide a slightly mysterious setting for the boat. All in all, it was a lot of work for a middling image, but it did provide me with a good illustration of several manipulative techniques that could be used to produce an overall improved composite image.

C6-3

Occasionally the Sabattier Effect will turn a dull image into an arresting one; so when I found the straight print that I made of the George Washington Bridge to be insipid, I tried reversing the colors. Unfortunately, even inside out, this image is nothing to write home about. Its technical details are, perhaps, of more interest than its aesthetics. The shot was made on Eastman Type 5247 color negative film. The straight print called for a 22.5M pack and a 15 second exposure at 7× magnification through an f/4 opening in a 50mm lens. The reversal was made with the identical exposure; but after four-fifths of the development was completed I opened the drum, removed the print, and reexposed it to the light of a 15 watt frosted bulb for one second. Then I put the print back in the drum and completed the development and the rest of the processing steps as I normally do. The printing materials used were Unicolor R-2 chemicals and their Resin-Base paper.

ENHANCEMENT AND MANIPULATION OF COLOR PRINTS

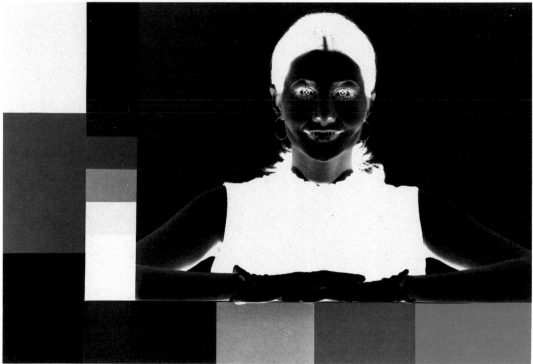

It is easy to reverse the colors of an image on transparency film. To do so, you simply print the slide directly on the type of paper you normally use to make prints from color negatives. This unreversed image was made from a Kodak Standard (Ektachrome-X) Transparency, printed on Ektachrome Type 1993 paper and processed in Ektaprint R-500 chemicals. The reversed print was made with the same slide in the negative carrier, but it was exposed on Unicolor's Resin-Base paper and processed in that firm's R-2 chemistry. The printing filter pack used to make the reversed print was 90Y. Note that good color reversals were obtained from the red, cyan, and yellow color bars, but the green used in the Ektachrome-X transparency seems to be a poor match for the Unicolor materials as the green color bar left only a weak reversed (magenta) image. Note also the extreme contrast of the reversed image, which it typical of prints made with this reversal technique.

This rather dull and dreary image is a reject from a series I shot of this peculiar storybook building and garden, on the island of Minou, in the Boden-see. I dislike this particular frame intensely, but being a frugal person by nature, I try to conduct my photographic affairs so that absolutely nothing goes to waste. In order to improve this cull, shot on Kodachrome II, I decided to see if it might not look considerably more interesting as an abstract image.

I suspected that a simple color reversal and a lot of contrast would help. To find out if I was right, I put the slide into my enlarger's negative carrier, set the machine's yellow filtration dial to 90, and made a 30 second exposure on Unicolor Resin Base paper (which is normally used for making prints from color negatives) at a 6× magnification, through an f/4 opening in a 50mm lens. Nothing went to waste—I was pleased enough with the result to show it here.

Printing Calculators

Printing calculators are, for the most part, little more than collections of many tiny pieces of color printing filters, all put together in a logical pattern. There is an additional section included on most calculators that is, in effect, an extinction scale in either red or neutral density.

All color printing calculators are based on the often invalid assumption that any subject you may photograph will fall within a well proven statistical norm and reflect an average distribution of light of the colors of the three additive primaries, red, green, and blue into your camera's lens. The calculators also assume that you will be smart enough to follow the directions packed with them; that you will use them in conjunction with an enlarger with a 75 watt lamp of reasonable color temperature (about 3000 K); that you will print with CP acetate filters; and that you will put a diffusion screen (supplied with the calculator) under the lens while you make a contact print of all of the tiny little filter segments on the calculator. The contact print is made with light coming from your enlarger lamp, passing through an IR, a UV, and whatever other filters the instructions call for, and then through your color negative or slide, your lens, and finally, through the diffuser and then the calculator itself.

When you process and dry a contact print of a calculator, you should, if you have followed the manufacturer's instructions, see a printed matrix of little colored areas corresponding to the filter sections on the calculator. Among those areas, if you get lucky, will be one or more which appear to be gray. You visually confirm the grayness of the areas with a comparator, also always supplied with the unit, and then go through a decoding procedure to determine what the particular position in which you have located the gray area means in relation to the filters that are going to be needed in your enlarger's printing filter pack to make a print of the negative or slide in the carrier that will be properly (statistically) balanced.

Sometimes learning to use a calculator is considerably harder than reading the pertinent portions of this book and learning to print; other times learning to use a calculator is quite simple. It's really very much a function of how well the calculator has been designed for ease of use, and how well the instructions that go along with the device have been written.

Once you have determined the proper filter pack to use, you refer to the portion of the contact print that contains the image of the extinction scale to determine the last numeral on that scale you can read. With that information, you once again go through a decoding procedure which may be painfully simple or grossly complicated, again, depending on how well the unit you are using has been set up for ease of operation and how well its instructions have been written.

Once you have obtained all of the data the instrument can provide, you will know what filter pack, lens opening, and printing exposure time to use to make a print of the unknown negative or slide in the enlarger's negative carrier, for the particular set of printing variables at hand (paper, magnification, processor, and processing, etc.). Using this data you will most often obtain a commercially acceptable print. If you are particular, it will probably take you about two or three more tries using the methods explained earlier, to get exactly the right filter pack and exposure, based on results obtained with the calculator's best efforts.

A reasonably experienced color printer is able to do as well or better using viewing filters to check a calibrated contact sheet, as he or she can do with a calculator. And relying on the contact sheet will save you the time and expense of having to make a contact print of the calculator. Color printing calculators are really little more than crutches for people without the confidence to trust their own judgment, or who haven't the experience to have developed any judgment. The danger in using them is that you may find that you like using this kind of a crutch, and if you continue to do so you may never develop the judgment that will enable you to throw it away. A description of several such devices follows.

Color by Beseler Subtractive Calculator

Distributor: Beseler Photo Marketing Co., Inc.

Type: For negative-to-positive printing only, integrated reading

Filter matrix: 130 section matrix in two subtractive colors: yellow and magenta. Values of yellow from zero to 120 in steps of ten are available; values of magenta from zero to 90, in steps of ten, are available.

Extinct. scale: Neutral-density type with a four-stop range.

To interpret: Simple. Direct reading of contact print for filtration requirements. One simple calculation for exposure. Color check of zero/zero matrix box and simple table reference when no gray section is printed.

Other data: Continuous-tone gray comparator. Clear, easy to use, well written instructions.

Remarks: This is the simplest calculator to use of those I have had the opportunity to try. Results seem to be equal to those obtainable with more complicated units. The lack of cyan filtration information may, in some few instances, prevent this device from providing essential data; however, with the newer emulsions these occasions should be rare.

The Color by Beseler Subtractive Calculator

Colourtronic Color Balancer Numbers 1, 3 and 4

Distributor: Colourtronic

Type: For negative-to-positive printing only, integrated reading.

Filter matrix: No. 1 — 308 section matrix in two subtractive primary colors, yellow and magenta; values of yellow to 105 and of magenta to 65, both in steps of 05 density, are available

No. 3 — 96 section matrix in two subtractive primary colors, yellow and magenta; values of yellow to 55 and of magenta to 35, both in steps of 05 density, are available

No. 4 — 96 section matrix in two subtractive primary colors, yellow and magenta; values of yellow to 110 and of magenta to 70, both in steps of 10 density, are available.

Extinct. scale: None

To interpret: Simple, and the same for all three units. Direct reading of contact print for filtration requirements. If no gray matrix section is evident, cyan must be added to the starting pack. No exposure determination provisions are offered.

Other data: Positive-determination gray comparator insures that proper gray section has been located on the contact print.

Remarks: All of the three different models offered are designed to provide only filtration data, and only data involving yellow and magenta filters. The lack of cyan filtration information may, in some instances, prevent these devices from providing essential data; however, with the newer emulsions these occasions should be rare. Lack of an extinction scale requires that the printer make test strips after first having made a contact print of the calculator. This is a very time-consuming and expensive procedure. The instructions for the use of these units are clearly written and easy to follow.

Chromega Subtractive Color Calculator Kit

Distributor: Berkey Marketing Co., Inc.

Type: For negative-to-positive printing only, integrated reading

Filter matrix: 88 section matrix in all three subtractive colors. Values of yellow and magenta of 0, 05, 10, 20, 30, 40, and 50; values of cyan of 0, 05, 10, and 20.

Extinct. scale: Neutral-density type with two-stop range

To interpret: Simple, numbered matrix sections are easy to locate on the contact print. Checking a single table is required for filtration data and to provide a multiplier used in a simple calculation to determine exposure requirements. Color check of zero/zero matrix box and reference to a simple table when no gray section is printed.

Other data: 8 section gray comparator. Clear, easy to use, well written instructions.

Remarks: This is a simple, effective calculator to use.

The D.P.C. Calculator

Distributor:	The Camera Barn
Type:	For positive-to-positive printing only; direct reading
Filter matrix:	120 section matrix in all three subtractive primary colors. Repeated combinations of density values of 10, 20, and 40 in all three subtractive primary colors, as well as several unfiltered sections.
Extinct. scale:	None
To interpret:	The D.P.C Calculator is placed on top of the slide to be printed, in the enlarger's negative carrier. The enlarger is focused on the calculator's image. A reversal print is made. The printed image of the calculator is compared to the calculator image itself to determine the best color match among the 120 sections of the matrix.
Other data:	Clear and easily followed instructions.
Remarks:	No real provisions for exposure determination are offered by this device.

Unicolor Mitchell Duocube

Distributor:	Unicolor Div., Photo Systems Inc.
Type:	For both negative-to-positive and positive-to-positive printing; integrated reading.
Filter matrix:	There are two filter matrixes; a 5-step array and a 20-step array. The 5-step is used exclusively for negative-to-positive printing. It contains 61 sections in all three of the subtractive primary colors. Yellow, magenta, and cyan values from zero to 20 in steps of 05 density, are available. The 20-step array is used for both negative-to-positive and for positive-to-positive printing. It too contains 61 sections in all three of the subtractive primaries. This array provides yellow, magenta and cyan values from zero to 80 in steps of 20 density.
Extinct. scale:	Negative-to-positive—neutral density type with a four-stop range. Positive-to-positive—red filter type with three-stop range
To interpret:	Somewhat complicated and confusing. Checking a table is required to determine filtration requirements, but the matrix sections are not identified on the contact print. A second table check and a simple calculation are required to determine exposure requirements.
Other data:	6 segment gray comparator; complicated, oddly organized instructions.
Remarks:	This is not a difficult device to use, and it does work satisfactorily when compared with others which are available; but it is a bit overwhelming until you get used to the procedure required for its use and interpretation. A similar device, applicable to negative-to-positive printing only, called the Unicolor Mitchell Unicube preceded the present Duocube model on the market. The Unicube had a larger (91 section) matrix in all three subtractive primaries, in 05-density steps from zero to 40 values of filtration. It also had a red filter, 2⅓ stop range, extinction scale for exposure determination. It too was a rather overwhelming and complicated device to get used to.

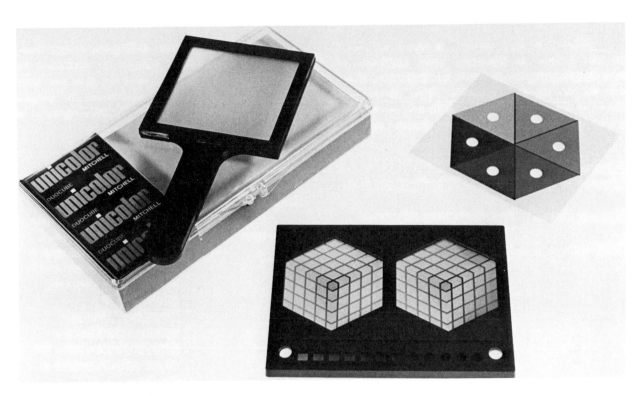

The Unicolor Mitchell Duocube

Electronic Color Analyzers

Chapter 8 was entirely devoted to covering the subject of electronic color analyzers in very broad and general terms, so, hopefully, there will be no need to redefine these devices in detail. If you do have some difficulty in making sense of the necessarily brief outline description of the specific items of hardware listed here, the preceding chapter should be reviewed for clarification. If you can't find the data you need there, contact the unit's distributor to request more complete specifications. Descriptions of representative hardware items follow.

Beseler PM Color Analyzer

Distributor:	Beseler Photo Marketing Co., Inc.
Reading modes:	Spot (3.2mm) or integrated (with diffuser under lens)
Probe type:	Relatively large on-easel probe (2⁹⁄₁₆″ H × 7″ L × 1⅜″ D) with photomultiplier tube within probe housing. Channel-selector switch is mounted in the probe housing. An electrical cable connects the probe to the chassis.
Sensitivity:	0.00002 footcandles
Circuit:	All solid state (except photomultiplier tube), needs no warm-up, internally voltage-stabilized, consumes 10 watts
Meter size:	3¼ inches
Illuminated components:	Meter face
No. programs:	One
Other data:	Grounded metal case; electronic protection of photomultiplier tube against blinding.
Remarks:	Manufacture of this model has been discontinued.

Beseler PM1 Color Analyzer

Distributor:	Beseler Photo Marketing Co.
Reading modes:	Spot (3.2mm) or integrated (with diffuser under lens)
Probe type:	This unit has no separate probe. The reading spot is in the upper portion of the instrument's relatively small (6¾″ W × 7″ L × 3″ H) cabinet. The light-sensitive element is a photomultiplier tube. The entire cabinet is used on the easel.
Sensitivity:	0.0001 footcandles.
Circuit:	All solid state (except photomultiplier tube), needs no warm-up, internally voltage-stabilized, consumes 10 watts
Meter size:	Small (not specified)
Illuminated components:	Meter face
No. programs:	One
Other data:	Grounded metal case; electronic protection of photomultiplier tube against blinding.

The Beseler PM Color Analyzer

The Beseler PM1 Color Analyzer

Beseler PM2 Color Analyzer

Distributor:	Beseler Photo Marketing Co., Inc.
Reading modes:	Spot (3.2mm) or integrated (with diffuser under lens)
Probe type:	Relatively large, on-easel probe (2⁹⁄₁₆″ H × 7″ L × 1³⁄₈″ D) with photomultiplier tube within the probe housing. The channel selector switch is mounted in the probe housing. The electrical cable connects the probe to the chassis.
Sensitivity:	0.00002 footcandles
Circuit:	All solid state (except photomultiplier tube), needs no warm-up, internally voltage-stabilized, consumes 10 watts
Meter size:	4½ inches
Illuminated components:	Meter face and color-channel indicators.
No. programs:	Three
Other data:	Range-expansion provisions built in to circuit and readout on meter face; grounded metal case; electronic protection of photomultiplier tube against blinding.

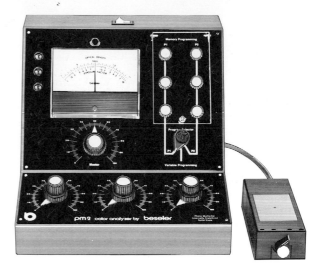

The Beseler PM2 Color Analyzer

Beseler PM2L Color Analyzer

Distributor:	Beseler Photo Marketing Co.
Reading modes:	Spot (3.2mm) or integrated (with diffuser under lens)
Probe type:	Relatively large, on-easel probe (2⁹⁄₁₆″ H × 7″ L × 1⅜″ D) with photomultiplier tube within probe housing. The channel selector switch is mounted in the probe housing. The electrical cable connects the probe to the chassis
Sensitivity:	0.00002 footcandles
Circuit:	All solid state (except photomultiplier tube), needs no warm-up, internally voltage-stabilized, consumes 10 watts
Meter size:	4⅛″
Illuminated components:	Meter face
No. programs:	One
Other data:	Meter has mirrored band for parallax error prevention; range expansion provisions built in to circuit and readout on meter face; grounded metal case; electronic protection of photomultiplier tube against blinding.

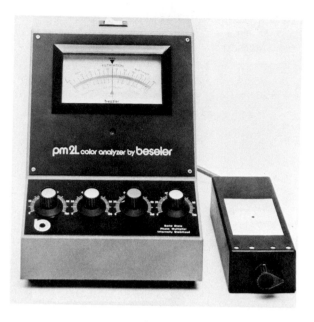

The Beseler PM2L Color Analyzer

Simtron II Color Analyzer

Distributor:	Berkey Marketing Co., Inc.
Reading modes:	Integrated (with diffuser on probe, immediately above the light-sensitive cell) for color channels, zone for exposure
Probe type:	Turret-type probe which mounts directly under the lens for integrated color-channel programming and analysis, and is used on the easel, with the diffuser swung away, for exposure-programming and analysis; Cds cell in probe; electrical cable to the chassis
Sensitivity:	Not specified
Circuit:	All solid state, needs no warm-up, internally voltage-stabilized, fused, consumes 8 watts.
Meter size:	2½ inches
Illuminated components:	Probe's channel selector, meter face, exposure-dial index
No. programs:	One
Other data:	Electronic range correction, subject failure-correction provisions, operates on 120/220 volts.

The Simtron II Color Analyzer

**Chromegatron Pro-Lab Professional
Color Analyzer and Exposure Meter**

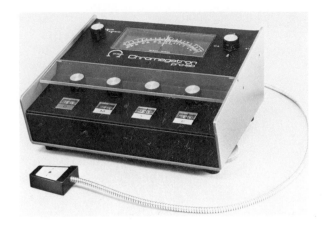

Distributor:	Berkey Marketing Co., Inc.
Reading modes:	Selectable, spot (3mm), zone (5mm), or integrated (diffuser under lens)
Probe type:	Small on-easel probe containing a prism, two selectable apertures and a cosine-correction (partial) tilting plate, connected by fiber-optic armored cable to photomultiplier tube in the instrument's cabinet.
Sensitivity:	0.000001 footcandles
Circuit:	All solid state (except photomultiplier tube), requires no warm-up, internally voltage-stabilized, fused, consumes 10 watts
Meter size:	5½ inches
Illuminated components:	Color-channel selector switch, color and exposure selector dials, meter face
No. programs:	One
Other data:	Continuously variable electronic-range adjustment; cosine correction (partial) for off-optical axis readings; mechanical protection for program knob settings; operates on 120/220 volts; electronic protection against photomultiplier tube blinding.

The Chromegatron Pro-Lab Professional Color Analyzer and Exposure Meter

Cosar Mornick 321 Color Analyzer

Distributor: Cosar Corp., Mornick Div.

Reading modes: Spot (³⁄₁₆″), zone (⁷⁄₁₆″), integrated (diffuser under lens)

Probe type: Relatively large on-easel probe with photomultiplier tube within probe housing; aperture is selected by reversing probe's top panel; channel selector is mounted on probe housing

Sensitivity: Not specified

Circuit: Solid state (except for photomultiplier tube), however 15 minute warm-up is called for; internal voltage stabilization is provided.

Meter size: 3½ inches

Illuminated components: Meter face, channel-selected indicator

No. programs: One

Other data: Optional fiber-optic probe for reading close to the paper plane. Optional reflection probe to convert the instrument to a reflection densitometer. Diffusion filter and a standard negative and transparency are included with the instrument. Coarse and fine settings.

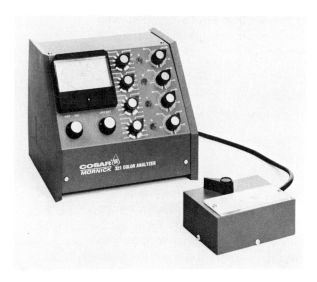

The Cosar Mornick 321 Color Analyzer

Cosar Mornick 322 Color Analyzer

The Cosar Mornick 322 Color Analyzer

Distributor:	Cosar Corp., Mornick Div.
Reading modes:	Spot (⅛″), zone (¼″), or integrated (½″) with diffuser under lens
Probe type:	Relatively large, on-easel probe with photomultiplier tube within probe housing; channel selector mounted on probe housing; aperture is selected by reversing or removing the probe's top panel (fastened with two screws)
Sensitivity:	Not specified
Circuit:	All solid state (except for photomultiplier tube), no warmup required, internally voltage stabilized
Meter size:	5 inches
Illuminated components:	Meter face
No. programs:	One
Other data:	Optional fiber-optic probe for reading close to the paper plane; optional reflection probe to convert the instrument to a reflection densitometer; diffusion filter and standard negative and transparency are included with instrument.

Cosar Mornick 328 Chroma-Log Color Analyzer

Distributor:	Cosar Corp., Mornick Div.
Reading modes:	Spot (3mm), zone (5mm), integrated (with diffuser below lens)
Probe types:	Medium size (2″ × 3″ × 1″), on-easel probe with planar silicon photodiode sensor on tilting plate within probe housing; two selectable apertures available; probe connected by electrical cable to chassis
Sensitivity:	Not specified
Circuit:	All solid state with internal voltage stabilization
Meter size:	8 inches
Illuminated components:	Meter face (electro-luminescent), channel-selected indicator, plug-in-memory-in-use indicator
No. programs:	Unlimited, with optional plug-in memory modules
Other data:	4-stop electronic range adjustment; cosine correction (partial) for off-optical-axis probe placement; both coarse and fine program control for all channels.
Remarks:	This is an excellent design from the standpoint of mechanical program reinsertion, as both coarse and vernier pots are provided for initial program and for reprogramming. Twenty-turn pots are also used in the optional plug-in memory modules. Optional probe converts instrument for use as reflection densitometer.

The Cosar Mornick 328 Chroma-Log Color Analyzer

EPOI MM-7 Color Analyzer

Distributor:	EPOI Inc.
Reading modes:	Spot (3mm) and zone (8mm); zone readings for color balance; spot readings for exposure.
Probe type:	Relatively large, on-easel probe with a photomultiplier tube within the probe housing. The channel and aperture selector is mounted on the probe housing. An electrical cable connects the probe to the chassis.
Sensitivity:	0.005 footcandles for full meter deflection on the zone exposure channel.
Circuit:	All solid state except for the photomultiplier tube. However, the manufacturer's instructions call for continuous operation in order to achieve stability. Internal voltage stabilization is provided for ±10 percent input voltage fluctuation. Power consumption is 17.25 watts. The circuit is fused.
Meter size:	4½ inches
Illuminated components:	Meter face
No. programs:	One
Other data:	Electronic range control (4 to 5 stops); provisions for both mechanical and electrical meter zeroing; an aperture cover plate is provided, and must be manually opened to allow light to reach the photomultiplier tube, and shut to prevent blinding the tube when room lights are turned on.

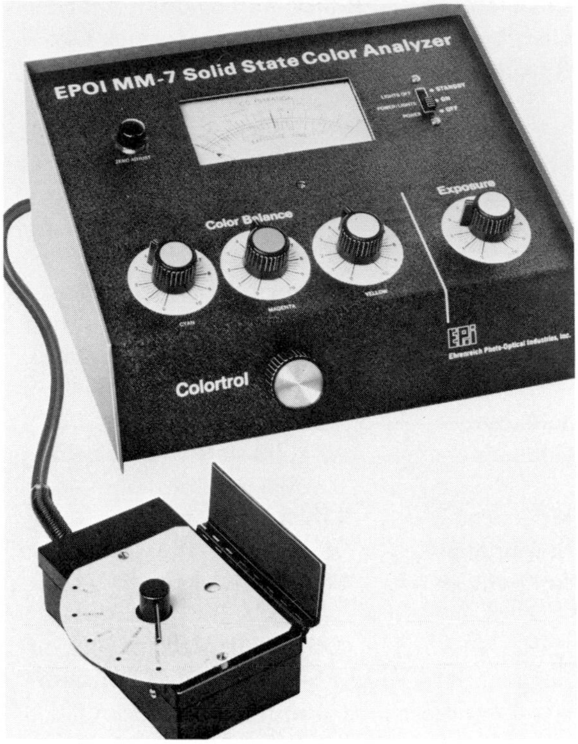

The EPOI MM-7 Color Analyzer

EPOI MM-9 Color Printing Analyzer

Distributor: EPOI Inc.

Reading modes: Spot (2.4mm) and zone (11.1mm), both apertures are below an integrating diffusion disk mounted on the probe

Probe type: Relatively large, on-easel probe with a photomultiplier tube within the probe housing; the channel and aperture selector is mounted on the probe housing; an electrical cable connects the probe to the chassis

Sensitivity: 0.0005 footcandles

Circuit: All solid state (except for photomultiplier tube), however 30 minute warm-up is called for; internal voltage stabilization is provided; power consumption is 17 watts; fused

Meter size: 6 inches

Illuminated components: Meter face, channel-selected indicator

No. programs: Unlimited, with optional plug-in program modules; two with single module supplied

Other data: Both coarse and fine programming controls for all color channels and for both separate sets of exposure controls (spot and zone); electronic range control (high and low); provisions for both mechanical and electrical meter zeroing; manual shutter built-in to probe housing to protect photomultiplier tube from blinding; an aperture cover plate is also provided.

Remarks: This is an excellent design from the standpoint of mechanical program reinsertion as both coarse and vernier pots are provided for initial programming. Multi-turn pots are also used on the plug-in modules.

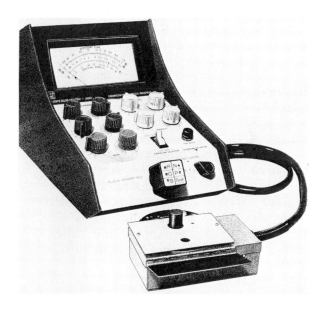

The EPOI MM-9 Color Printing Analyzer

Minolta Color Analyzer

Distributor: Minolta Corp.

Reading modes: Integrated (within the Minolta enlarger's bellows) on all color channels; spot (4mm) exposure channel readings

Probe: Silicon photodiode sensing elements for color channels contained on special lensboard which retrofits the Minolta enlarger; exposure reading probe is of medium size (1.1″ × 2.1″ × 4.4″), is used on-easel and contains a silicon photodiode within the probe housing; the probe is connected to the chassis via an electrical cable

Sensitivity: 0.186 foot candles

Circuit: All solid state; fused; power consumption is 2.5 watts

Meter size: Not specified

Illuminated components: Meter face, channel-selected indicator

No. programs: One

Other data: Analyzer mounts directly on Minolta enlarger carriage; probe hangs from analyzer; this packaging frees the normally crowded area around the baseboard of unnecessary clutter.

The Minolta Color Analyzer

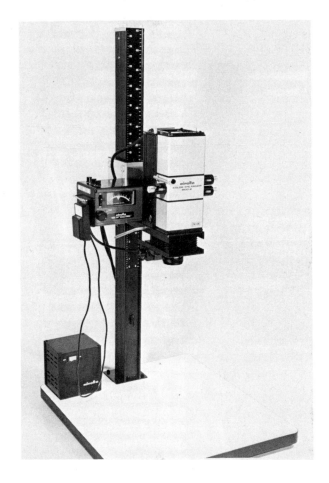

The Minolta Color Enlarger Mod III with Minolta Color Analyzer

Software

Software is the single term I've used throughout this book to refer to all of the products involved with the color darkroom which are normally consumed in processing. The two most important software items a color printer must consider are printing papers (or plastics, in the case of Cibachrome) and the various chemicals used to process them. There is no shortage of variety of either commodity as is evidenced in the list of products that follow.

Color Printing Papers

The materials color prints are made on fall into several major catagories. First and foremost, of course, is whether the paper is intended for the production of prints from color negatives, or if it is to be used to make prints directly from slides. Beyond this basic distinction there are several other important color printing-material variables to consider; prime among them is the matter of the paper's quality, dependability, and consistency from emulsion batch to emulsion batch, from box to box, and from year to year.

Another less important color printing-material property is the type and number of surface finishes available for any given material. Frankly, so far as I am concerned, anything other than glossy is, at the present state of the art of plastic-coated color paper making, a complete waste of time—yet many workers prefer a non-glossy surface. Glossy paper permits better resolution and color saturation to be obtained in a print than any of the textured, semi-matte, or matte surfaces do. If you are the type of photographer who is chronically out of focus when shooting, perhaps a textured surface will provide you with a bit of diffusion to help hide your mistakes. There are, I'm told, lots of printers who think "silk" surfaces to be attractive. To each his own.

As discussed in Chapter 2, color printing materials are provided in two basic types; A and B. The differences between the types have to do with the way the color couplers are incorporated in the paper's emulsion layers. The mechanically retained couplers in type-B paper allow it to be reasonably well evaluated for both density and color while it is still wet (though unless it is absolutely necessary to do so, better results will be obtained if type-B paper is dried before image evaluation is undertaken). The oil encapsulated couplers in type-A paper prevent any color or density evaluation of the paper from being made while the paper is wet (unless it is chemically treated). With baryta-base papers this is still an important factor to consider; however, with the new plastic-coated materials, which can be dried in a minute or two, it has become much less of a consideration.

Unfortunately, no one has yet figured out a way to make a plastic-coated paper that will produce a surface finish, when dry, as beautiful as that which can be obtained with a glossy paper-based print which has been air dried rather than ferrotyped; but, perhaps in the not-too-distant future, this too shall come.

Other considerations, including available sizes, chemical requirements for processing, and dry-mountability, are noted in the following.

Negative-to-Positive Papers

Colourtronic Paper — Resin-Coated

Distributor:	Colourtronic
Type:	A
Base:	Resin-coated paper
Safelight:	No. 10 or No. 13 with a 15 watt bulb at least four feet away
Surfaces:	Glossy; dries glossy with heat, semi-glossy when air dried
Sizes/Pkg.:	8″ × 10″ in 10 and 25 sheet packages
	11″ × 14″ in 10 sheet packages
	16″ × 20″ in 10 sheet packages
	20″ × 24″ in 10 sheet packages
Other data:	Colourtronic Universal Chemistry is available for processing this material. Mounting may be difficult.

Unicolor B Color Print Paper

Distributor:	Unicolor Div., Photo Systems Inc.
Type:	B
Base:	Baryta-base paper
Safelight:	No. 10 or No. 13 with a 15 watt bulb, at least four feet away
Surfaces:	Semi-glossy, fine grain, and silk
Sizes/Pkg.:	5″ × 7″ in 25 sheet packages
	8″ × 10″ in 25 and 100 sheet packages
	11″ × 14″ in 10 sheet packages
	16″ × 20″ in 10 sheet packages
Other data:	Unicolor offers two sets of chemicals to process this material; either Unicolor B, or Unicolor Pro B, Prints From Negatives Chemistry. The paper is manufactured by Mitsubishi in Japan.

Chromega Resin-Coated Paper

Distributor: Berkey Marketing Co., Inc.
Type: A
Base: Resin-coated paper
Safelight: No. 10 or 13 with a 15 watt bulb, at least four feet away
Surfaces: Glossy, silk, matte, and brilliant
Sizes/Pkg. 5" × 7" in 25 sheet packages
8" × 10" in 25 and 100 sheet packages
11" × 14" in 10 sheet packages
16" × 20" in 10 sheet packages
Other data: Dries relatively quickly and remains relatively flat after drying.
Remarks: The paper is manufactured by GAF as are the recommended Chromega Color Print-Processing Chemicals. This material presents some mounting difficulties, but can be satisfactorily drymounted.

Kodak Ektacolor 37 RC Paper

Distributor: Eastman Kodak Co.
Type: A
Base: Resin-coated paper
Safelight: No. 10 with a 7½ watt bulb, or No. 13 with a 15 watt bulb, at least four feet away
Surfaces: Smooth glossy (F), smooth lustre (N), silk lustre (Y)
Sizes/Pkg.: 8" × 10" in 25 (in F&N) and 100 (in F, N & Y) sheet packages
8½" × 11" in 50 (in F&N) sheet packages
11" × 14" in 10 (F&N) and 50 (F, N & Y) sheet packages
14" × 17" in 50 (N) sheet packages
16" × 20" in 10 (F&N) and 50 (F, N & Y) sheet packages
20" × 24" in 10 and 50 (F&N) sheet packages
30" × 40" in 10 and 50 (F&N) sheet packages
Other data: Kodak calls for processing this material in Ektaprint 3 or 300 chemicals (Ektaprint 300 is recommended for drum processing).
Remarks: Dries relatively quickly and remains fairly flat. This paper presents some mounting difficulties, but it can be successfully drymounted.

Kodak Ektacolor 74 RC Paper

Distributor: Eastman Kodak Co.
Type: A
Base: Resin-coated paper
Safelight: No. 13 with a 7½ watt bulb at least 4½ feet away
Surfaces: Fine-grained lustre (E), smooth glossy (F), smooth lustre (N), silk lustre (Y)
Sizes/Pkg: 8" × 10" in 10, 25, and 100 sheet packages
8½" × 11" in 50 sheet packages
10" × 10" in 50 sheet packages
11" × 14" in 10 and 50 sheet packages
14" × 17" in 50 sheet packages
16" × 20" in 10 and 50 sheet packages
20" × 24" in 10 and 50 sheet packages
30" × 40" in 10 and 50 sheet packages
Other data: Kodak calls for processing this material in Ektaprint 2 or Ektaprint 3 chemicals (Ektaprint 2 is recommended for drum processing).
Remarks: This paper is stated by Kodak to be 50 percent faster than 37 RC. My own observations have been that a two-stop (70 percent) speed increase over 37 RC is more typical for this material. The paper is somewhat brighter than 37 RC. It dries quickly and remains fairly flat. Like all plastic-coated papers it presents some dry-mounting difficulties, but it can be properly drymounted. with a minimum of care.

Unicolor Resin-Base Color Print Paper

Distributor: Unicolor Div., Photo Systems
Type: A
Base: Resin-coated paper
Safelight: No. 10 or No. 13 with a 15 watt bulb, at least four feet away

Surfaces: Glossy, matte, and silk
Sizes/Pkg.:   5″ × 7″ in 25 sheet packages
                8″ × 10″ in 25 and 100 sheet
                  packages
                11″ × 14″ in 10 sheet
                  packages
                16″ × 20″ in 10 sheet
                  packages
Other data: Unicolor specifies their R-2
                chemicals as being the only

ones appropriate for processing this paper. The paper is manufactured by Mitsubishi in Japan.

Remarks: Dries relatively quickly and remains fairly flat. The paper presents some mounting difficulties, but it can be successfully drymounted.

Positive-to-Positive Color Printing Papers

Descriptions of several available brands of positive-to-positive color printing paper follow.

Cibachrome Color Print Material—Type A

Distributor: Ilford, Inc.
Type: Dye bleach
Base: Cellulose triacetate (plastic)
Safelight: None, handling should be
               done in total darkness
Surfaces: Glossy
Sizes/Pkg.:   8″ × 10″ in 20 sheet packages
               11″ × 14″ in 10 sheet
               packages
Other data: At present this material can only be processed in Cibachrome Chemistry Kit Process P-12 materials. The material is manufactured by Ciba-Geigy in Switzerland.
Remarks: Dries about half as fast as most resin-coated papers. Dries fairly flat. This material is extremely difficult to successfully drymount with a conventional press, and can be drymounted only with considerable care and expertise on a hard-bed press.

Kodak Ektachrome RC Paper, Type 1993

Distributor: Eastman Kodak Co.
Type: A
Base: Resin-coated paper
Safelight: None, handling should be
               done in total darkness
Surfaces: Smooth glossy (F) and silk
               high-lustre (Y) in rolls only.
Sizes/Pkg.:   8″ × 10″ in 25 and 100 (F)
               sheet packages
               11″ × 14″ in 50 (F) sheet
               packages
               16″ × 20″ in 50 (F) sheet
               packages
               20″ × 24″ in 50 (F) sheet
               packages
               30″ × 40″ in 50 (F) sheet
               packages
Other data: Kodak calls for processing this material in Ektaprint R-5 or R-500 chemicals. Ektaprint R-500 is recommended for drum processing.
Remarks: Dries fairly quickly and remains relatively flat. This paper presents some mounting difficulties, but it can be drymounted successfully.

Color Printing Chemicals

Perhaps in no other area of color printing is there as much confusion and so many strange claims as in the marketing of chemicals to process color printing materials. Color printing chemicals seem to me to often be sold the way that razor blades or automobiles are: on the basis of a lot of wishful thinking neatly packaged to make the customer believe he or she is not only going to get something for nothing if a particular brand of chemicals is purchased, but that the prints processed in these miracle brews will be "better," "faster," "easier," "sexier," or whatever. To the best of my knowledge, there are no miraculous color print-processing chemicals. There are some kits of chemicals which have fewer ingredients than others. Some processing chemicals call for fewer steps than others. Some processes are quicker than others. But for each one of these advantages several drawbacks may also be encountered. Kodak has eliminated the stabilizer from its Ektaprint 2 chemicals for basket processing. Beseler has, for some time, marketed Tetenal chemicals which do not include a stabilizer. Other manufacturers, however, continue to offer not only a stabilizer but a stop bath as a part of their negative-to-positive print-processing soups. It is up to the poor, hapless consumer to decide whether skipping a few steps is necessary. Good luck in making your choice.

In order to help, though, I do want to suggest a few general considerations. My first bit of advice is to avoid very rapid, very high-temperature processing. It is the type of processing that is least well suited to amateur and low-volume professional use because it is the least controllable and most inconsistent type. If you must produce a fair volume of prints in a short period of time, it is far better to do multiple print processing in a large daylight print-processing drum than it is to try to grind out individual prints quickly at elevated temperatures.

In my own experience, I've never found a negative-to-positive color print-processing sequence that couldn't be improved from the standpoint of consistency and performance through the use of a suitable stop bath after the developer.

I feel that the possible benefits to be obtained through the use of a stabilizer, to prolong the life of a color print, make it worth putting up with the foul-smelling, eye and throat-irritating stuff. Color prints have only a limited time to live after you have completed your processing, drying, mounting, and framing. They carry the seeds of their own destruction with them in the form of very unstable dyes. Color prints begin to deteriorate from the moment you complete them. Exposure to light—particularly the ultraviolet component of sunlight or flourescent light, and air—especially that which is full of pollutants and humidity, all work to bleach your prints into nonexistence. There is very little you can do about this sad state of affairs but to place your prints in a vapor-tight container and store them in a dark freezer. Since this is not what color print making is about, I strongly suggest that you take the meager alternative that is available to you and stabilize your prints, for whatever small amount of good it may do.

Another matter worthy of your attention is convenience packaging and price. Just as it has in the food industry, convenience packaging has arrived in the color darkroom; and just as with the price of convenience-packaged food, the price of convenience-packaged color printing chemicals may be almost double the cost of buying the individual chemical components in larger quantities.

There are, at present, three manufacturers of chemicals to process Kodak's Ektachrome RC, Type 1993 paper. Kodak and Unicolor offer chemicals which do not require reexposure of the partially processed print to white light during processing.

In the description of the several available print-processing chemicals offered in the following section, I have presented data on the products which I have abstracted from each manufacturer's instruction sheet. Since data of this nature often changes fairly rapidly (such changes will be reflected in future supplements whenever possible), it is suggested that the reader not rely solely on this data, but check it against the material that is provided with the chemicals when they are purchased. If in doubt, the manufacturer's data, packaged with the materials you have on hand, should always take precedence over the information offered here.

Negative-to-Positive Processing Chemicals

Descriptions of several available brands of negative-to-positive color print-processing chemicals, as well as one type (Unicolor Total Color) that can be used to first process color negative film, and then reused to process negative-to-positive color printing paper, follow.

Color By Beseler 2-Step Color Print Chemistry

Distributor:	Beseler Photo Marketing Co., Inc.
Materials:	The manufacturer states: "... Kodak Ektachrome RC and similar type-A color papers of other manufacturers."
Components:	Sold in kits containing all necessary chemical components. All components are mixed with tap water to produce working-strength chemical solutions. Step No. 1 (color developer) is packaged as one liquid and three solid (powder) components. Step No. 2 (bleach-fix) is packaged as two solid (powder) components.
Packaging:	Three different kits of all components, to make one quart, one gallon, or three and one-half gallons, are available
Shelf life:	Unopened packages of component chemicals are guaranteed to remain fresh for one year from the date of purchase. Working-strength chemical solutions have an 8 to 10 week shelf life when stored in tightly capped, filled, brown glass bottles; no data offered for partially filled storage containers.
Process data:	Instructions packaged with the chemicals cover both one-shot and replenishment processing in daylight drums at ambient or elevated temperatures or with an elevated temperature presoak. Data on processing in trays and on the Kodak Model 11 processor are also provided. No minimum volume of chemicals required for one-shot processing is offered. Representative one-shot drum-processing data from the manufacturer's instructions follow.
Remarks:	These chemicals are manufactured by Tetenal of West Germany. The manufacturer states that prints processed in these chemicals and washed according to directions have "excellent fade resistance properties."

Table 9-1 TIME/TEMPERATURE CHART

ROOM TEMP. °F.	ROOM TEMP. °C	PROCESSING TIME (MINUTES)	
		STEP 1	STEP 2
107	42	1	1
101	38	1½	1
96	36	2	1
92	33	2½	1
89	32	3	1½
86	30	3½	1½
83	28	4	1½
81	27	4½	2
79	26	5	2
77	25	5½	2
75	24	6	2½
72	22	7	2½
70	21	8	2½
68	20	9	3
66	19	10	3

Wash each print individually immediately after processing. Wash for 2½ minutes at approximately 85F (30C) or 5 minutes at 75F (24C) in a tray of rapidly changing water. These times should not substantially be exceeded. Batch washing or keeping prints in holding trays should be avoided.

TROUBLE SHOOTING

Uneven Development:
1. Not enough solution (STEP 1.)
2. Rolling (agitation) surface not level.
3. Waited too long before beginning agitation (STEP 1.)
4. Agitation rate too slow during first 20 seconds (STEP 1.)
5. Inconsistent agitation (STEP 1.)

Localized Blue Streaks or Stains:
1. Waited too long before beginning agitation (STEP 2.)
2. Agitation rate too slow during first 20 seconds (STEP 2.)
3. Inconsistent agitation (STEP 2.)
4. Insufficient drain (STEP 1): Drain thoroughly or add a cold water rinse after STEP 1.

Cyan or Green Cast Over Entire Print (Cyan or Green Borders):
1. Step 1 is contaminated. Wash all utensils in cold water and mix fresh STEP 1.
2. Print exposed to black and white safelight.
3. If STEP 1 is greatly contaminated you may see a reddish-purple cast over the print and in the borders.

Pinkish Cast Over Entire Print (Pink Borders):
1. Forgot to drain out STEP 1. Repeat exposure and use a fresh 3 oz. of STEP 1 and STEP 2 to process.
2. Step 2 is contaminated. Wash all utensils in cold water and mix fresh STEP 2.

Yellow or Reddish Areas:
1. Paper is light-fogged.

Blue Splotches on Face of Print:
1. Trace quantities of STEP 1 trapped between drum walls and back of paper: (1) Use a water pre-soak before STEP 1. (2) Use a cold water rinse after STEP 1.

Color Shift When Re-Using Chemistry:
1. Forgot to add ½ oz. (15cc) fresh STEP 1 and ½ oz. (15cc) fresh STEP 2 for each re-use in a drum (8 × 10 prints.)
2. Forgot to add 1 oz. (30cc) fresh STEP 1 and 1 oz. (30cc) fresh STEP 2 for each re-use in a tray (8 × 10 prints.)

Density Shift (Lighter) When Re-using Chemistry:
1. Forgot to increase processing time 10% for each re-use in a drum.
2. Forgot to increase processing time 10% for each five prints processed in a tray.

Wide Tolerance

All processing times quoted represent actual processing times with continuous agitation at the recommended rate. To these actual processing times you must add the "drain and fill" times in drum processing and the "drain" time in tray processing. (About 5–20 seconds with either method.)

Shorter processing times are not recommended but longer times (up to 25% longer in STEP 1 and up to 100% longer in STEP 2) will have virtually no adverse effect.

PRESOAK CHART

Room (chemical) temperature (F)	Processing temperature (F)	Water temperature (F)

Follow this example: If the room temperature is 70F and the desired processing temperature is 101F, then the correct temperature for the presoak water is about 117F. (Dotted line is example only. Make your own line for other temperature conditions.)

Color by Beseler 2-Step, 2-Minute
Color Print Chemistry

Distributor: Beseler Photo Marketing Co., Inc.

Materials: The manufacturer advises that these chemicals process Agfa and other type-B papers.

Components: Sold in kits containing all necessary chemical components. All components are mixed with water to produce working-strength chemical solutions: Step No. 1 (color developer)— packaged as three solid (powder) components. Step No. 2 (bleach-fix)— packaged as two solid (powder) components.

Packaging: Three different kits are available to make one quart, to make four one-quart quantities, and to make a one-gallon quantity.

Shelf life: Unopened packages of component chemicals are guaranteed to remain fresh for one year from the date of purchase. Working-strength chemical solutions have an 8 to 10 week shelf life when stored in tightly capped, filled, brown glass bottles; no data offered for partially filled containers of working-strength solutions.

Process data: Instructions packaged with the chemicals cover both one-shot and replenishment processing in daylight drums at ambient and elevated temperatures or with an elevated temperature presoak. Data on processing in trays and on the Kodak Model 11 processor are also provided. No minimum volume of chemicals required for one-shot processing is offered. Representative drum-processing data from the manufacturer's instructions follow.

Remarks: These chemicals are manufactured by Tetenal of West Germany.

Table 9-2
OPTIONAL HEAT SOAK CHART

Room (chemical) temperature (F)	Desired processing temperature (F)	Water temperature (F)
		138
		136
		134
		132
		130
		128
	110	126
100	108	124
	106	122
95	104	120
90	102	118
	100	116
85	98	114
	96	112
80	94	110
	92	108
75	90	106
	88	104
70	86	102
	84	100
65	82	98
	80	96
60	78	94
	76	92
55	74	90
	72	88
50	70	86
	68	84
		82
		80
		78
		76
		74
		72
		70

AMBIENT TEMPERATURE PROCESSING

Ambient (room) temperature processing is the simplest and most repeatable method of processing a color print. Since both the chemistry and the processing instrument (drum or tray) are used at existing room temperature, absolutely no temperature control of any kind is required.

Simply find the processing times on the time/temperature chart and process for the indicated times in STEP 1 and STEP 2.

AMBIENT TEMPERATURE DRUM PROCESSING

Load the exposed paper into a clean Color by Beseler or other brand of processing drum and stand the drum on its feet on any reasonably level surface. Consult the TIME/TEMPERATURE chart and pour in the required amount of STEP 1 chemistry at ambient temperature. *Immediately* begin continuous and vigorous agitation by rolling the drum from side to side at the rate of one complete left to right cycle per second for the first 20 seconds and thereafter at the rate of 30 cycles per minute for the remainder of the processing time.

At the end of the recommended processing time, thoroughly drain the drum (shake it dry) and pour-in STEP 2. *Immediately* begin continuous and vigorous agitation by rolling the drum from side to side at the rate of one complete left to right cycle per second for the first 20 seconds and thereafter at the rate of 30 cycles per minute for the remainder of the processing time.

At the end of the recommended processing time, drain out STEP 2. Processing is now complete. The print may be individually washed and dried at this time, or it may be placed in a holding tray, filled with ambient temperature water, to which may be added up to nine additional prints for subsequent "batch" washing and drying.

OPTIONAL PRE-SOAK
(for ambient temperature drum processing)

If you wish to pre-soak (and pre-condition) the paper and then to process at ambient temperature, simply stand the drum on its feet and fill it with 16 ounces of ambient temperature water (32 ounces to 11 × 14 and 16 × 20 driving). Rotate the drum for one minute and then drain-out ALL of the pre-soak water so as not to dilute the STEP 1 chemistry. (Shake the drum absolutely dry).

Stand the drum on its feet and pour-in the required quantity of ambient temperature STEP 1 chemistry. Process according to instructions.

OPTIONAL HEAT-SOAK
(for high-temperature drum processing)

If you wish to pre-soak the paper and to pre-heat the drum, just lay a straightedge from the ROOM TEMPERATURE column to the DESIRED PROCESSING TEMPERATURE. The point of intersection of the WATER TEMPERATURE column indicates the correct temperature of the pre-soak water.

Stand the processing drum on its feet and fill it with 16 ounces of pre-soak water of the required temperature (32 ounces for 11 × 14 and 16 × 20 drums). Rotate the drum for one full minute and then drain out *all* of the pre-soak water. (Shake the drum absolutely dry, so as not to dilute STEP 1 chemistry.)

Stand the drum on its feet and pour in the required quantity of ambient temperature STEP 1 chemistry. Process according to instructions.

TROUBLE SHOOTING
Uneven Development:
1. Not enough solution (STEP 1).
2. Rolling (agitation) surface not level.
3. Waited too long before beginning agitation (STEP 1).
4. Agitation rate too slow during first 20 seconds (STEP 1).
5. Inconsistent agitation (STEP 1).

Localized Blue Streaks or Stains:
1. Waited too long before beginning agitation (STEP 2).
2. Agitation rate too slow during first 20 seconds (STEP 2).
3. Inconsistent agitation (STEP 2).
4. Insufficient drain (STEP 1): Drain thoroughly or add a cold water rinse after STEP 1.

Cyan Cast Over Entire Print (Cyan Borders):
1. Step 1 is contaminated: Wash all utensils in cold water and mix fresh STEP 1.
2. Print exposed to black and white safelight.

Pinkish Cast Over Entire Print (Pink Borders):
1. Step 2 is contaminated: Wash all utensils in cold water and mix fresh STEP 2.

Yellow or Reddish Areas:
1. Paper is light-fogged.

Blue Splotches on Face of Print:
1. Trace quantities of STEP 1 trapped between drum walls and back of paper: 1) Buy a Color by Beseler processing drum. 2) Use a cold water rinse after STEP 1.

TIME/TEMPERATURE CHART
Table 9-3

ROOM TEMP.	PROCESSING TIME (MINUTES)	
	STEP 1	STEP 2
108 F	1 minute	1 minute
100 F	1½ minutes	1 minute
95 F	2 minutes	1 minute
91 F	2½ minutes	1½ minutes
87 F	3 minutes	1½ minutes
84 F	3½ minutes	1½ minutes
82 F	4 minutes	1½ minutes
79 F	5 minutes	2 minutes
77 F	6 minutes	2 minutes
74 F	7 minutes	2 minutes
72 F	8 minutes	2½ minutes
70 F	9 minutes	2½ minutes
68 F	10 minutes	2½ minutes

Chromega Color Print Chemistry

Distributor: Berkey Marketing Co., Inc.

Materials: The instructions state: "For Chromega and other type-A Resin-Coated Color Papers."

Components: Sold in kits containing all necessary chemical components. All components are mixed with tap water to produce working-strength solutions: developer—packaged as two liquid components; bleach-fix—packaged as two liquid components; stabilizer—packaged as a single liquid component; and a one-ounce and a six-ounce graduate are included in each kit.

Packaging: A one-gallon (of working-strength solutions) kit of all necessary components is available.

Shelf life: Unopened bottles of concentrated component solutions are stated to have a shelf life of one year, but kits are not dated to indicate when they were manufactured. Opened and partially filled bottles of concentrated component solutions have shelf lives stated as follows: developer—3 months; bleach-fix—3–4 months; stabilizer—3–4 months. Working-strength solutions in partially filled, tightly stoppered bottles have shelf lives stated as follows: developer—2–4 weeks; bleach-fix—8–10 weeks; stabilizer—8–10 weeks.

Process data: Instructions packaged with the chemicals cover tray processing at several temperatures and one-shot processing on the Kodak Model 11 (or 16K) Processor and in drums. A minimum of 3 fluid ounces of developer and bleach-fix and 2 fluid ounces of stabilizer, per print, are called for when processing in an 8" × 10" drum. Representative processing data from the manufacturer's instructions follow.

Remarks: These chemicals are produced by GAF.

PRESOAK TEMPERATURE NOMOGRAPH

To use this chart: (Step 1) Determine the temperature of the chemistry. (Step 2) Align the straightedge from the Chemical Temperature column to the Specified Temperature column. (Step 3) Bring the presoak water to the temperature indicated where the line intersects. The broken line on the nomograph, for example, indicates that chemicals at 75F require 125F presoak temperature water.

Table 9-4 KODAK MODEL 11 OR 16K PROCESSORS

Follow the loading and handling procedures recommended. All processing times include a 5-second draining time.

PROCESSING	TIME (IN MINUTES) (88°F)	TIME (IN MINUTES) (100°F)	REMARKS
Pre-Wet	1	½	In a tray of water
Developer	3½	1¾	
Stabilizer	1	½	
Wash	1	½	
Bleach-Fix	2½	1	
Wash	3	2	Use running water
Stablizer	1	½	
Dry			

Table 9-5   PROCESSING INSTRUCTIONS

For Chromega Color Print Processor or similar type drums (at 100° temperatures)

STEP	SOLUTION	TEMPERATURE	TIME	REMARKS (FOR 8 × 10 DRUMS)
1	Presoak water	From nomograph	1 minute	In darkness, load exposed paper into dry, clean processor. Replace cap on drum. Turn on lights. Stand drum on end and fill completely with heated water (as specified on nomogram). Let stand for 1 minute, then drain into a clean graduate for reuse in subsequent wash steps.
2	Developer	Room temperature	3 minutes	Place drum in horizontal position or on agitator and pour the developer into the spout. Use a minimum of 3 oz. of solution. Roll (agitate) as prescribed in your drum instructions. Drain through pouring spout at end of step.
3	Stabilizer	Room temperature	½ minute	Pour 3 oz. of stabilizer in and agitate. At the end of step, drain.
4	Wash	Use pre-soak water	½ minute	Pour 8 oz. of water recovered from step 1 and agitate drum for 15 seconds. **Dump.** Repeat again. Drain completely.
5	Bleach-Fix	Room temperature	2 minutes	Pour 3 oz. of Bleach-Fix in and agitate. Drain at end of step.
6	Wash	Use pre-soak water	2 minutes	Pour 8 oz. of water recovered from step 1 and agitate for 20 seconds. **Dump.** Repeat four more times using 8 oz. of water each time. **Drain.** Open drum and remove print.
7	Stabilizer	Room temperature	½-1 minute	Use 8 × 10 print tray and fill with 12 oz. of fresh, unused stabilizer*. Place print in tray and agitate for 1 minute. Remove and drain print. Sponge print and dry. Processing is completed. **Note:** A bluish cast on a wet print is normal. Dry print fully to judge the color. (See drying instructions below.)

(*Enough for six prints)

Drying: Chromega and other Type-A Resin-Coated Color Papers can be air-dried, or dried with an ordinary hair blower. To speed drying time, sponge prints first.

Table 9-6   TROUBLESHOOTING

PROBLEM	POSSIBLE CAUSE	SOLUTION
Magenta mottle and stained	Developer contaminated with Bleach-Fix	Mix fresh developer. Cover developer bottles whenever working with Bleach-Fix.
Yellow stain	Stabilizer contaminated with Bleach-Fix	Check your wash after Bleach-Fix.
	Old or improperly stored paper	Color print paper should be stored at 50F or lower.
Reddish or pink stain	Oxidized Developer	Developer should be stored in an air-tight bottle. Mix fresh developer.
Bluish patches or blotches	Printing while paper is still cold from storage	Allow printing paper to warm to room temperature before use.
Red spots, irregular in size and shape	Emulsion surface touched before processing	Do not touch emulsion surface while wet or damp. Handle by the edges.
Stains on edge of print	Contamination caused by chemicals left in drum from previous development	Chromega Processors have removable holders to make cleaning easy.
White spots	Water droplets on emulsion surface before development	Use care in handling paper and solution to prevent spattering.

PROBLEM	POSSIBLE CAUSE	SOLUTION
Muddy or grayish yellow patches	Insufficient treatment in Bleach-Fix	Check your time and temperature for Bleach Fix.
Yellow or yellow-brown streaks	White light fog	Check darkroom for leaks. Check closures on paper containers.
Blue or bluish-magenta streaks, stains, etc.	Safelight fog	Do not use OA or OC safelight. Use Wratten No. 10 or No. 13 filtered safelights with not more than a 15 watt bulb.
Uneven stains on print and borders	Paper not thoroughly presoaked	Follow processing instructions.
	Too little chemistry used or rolling surface not level	Use twice as much chemistry.
Small prints with portions not fully developed	No separators used to keep small prints from overlapping during development	Chromega Color print processors have multi-size paper holders and separators to hold prints in place.
Spots — reddish or pink	Bleach-Fix spattered on paper surface near end of process	Use care when processing to prevent splashing of any solution.
	Permanent type paper holders may be hard to clean	

Colourtronic Universal Chemistry

Distributor: Colourtronic

Materials: The instructions packaged with this product state: "This chemistry will yield excellent results with all type-B and Resin-Coated color printing papers." (This does not include reversal papers such as Ektachrome RC, Type 1993.)

Components: Sold in kits containing all necessary chemical components. All components are mixed with tap water to produce working-strength chemical solutions: developer — packaged as one solid (powder) component and one liquid component. Only the solid component is used for type-B papers. Both components are used for type-A resin-coated papers; stop bath — packaged as a single liquid component; bleach-fix — packaged as a single solid (powder) component; stabilizer — packaged as one solid (powder) and one liquid component.

Packaging: Two different kits are available: a two-quart and a one-gallon size. Components are packaged to be mixed in one-quart batches.

Shelf Life: No shelf life is specified for unopened packages of component chemicals. Working-strength developer, stored at temperatures below 75 F. (24C), in amber, tightly capped, filled bottles is stated to have a shelf life of 3 to 4 weeks. No data provided for working-strength stop bath. Working-strength bleach-fix is said to require no special storage conditions and to have a useful life of over 3 months under normal room-temperature conditions. Stabilizer in working-strength dilution is said to be quite stable and to provide a useful life of approximately one year when stored under normal room-temperature conditions.

Process data: The processing data provided in the instructions packaged with these chemicals follow.

Table 9-7 RAPID PROCESSING AT VARIOUS TEMPERATURES

All processing steps should be done at the same temperature

STEP	TIME INCLUDING 10 SECOND DRAIN TIME	*QUANTITY FOR C810 PROCESSOR
1. Pre-wet	30 sec.	4 oz.
2. Developer	See Fig. A	2 oz.
3. Stop bath rinse	30 sec.	2 oz.
4. Water rinse	30 sec.	4 oz.
5. Bleach Fix	2 min. or Fig. B	2 oz.
6. Water rinse	30 sec.	4 oz.
If working with a test print dry and evaluate.		
For a color print with maximum durability:		
7. Water wash	1 min. 30 sec.	Running water
8. Stabilizer	2 min.	Tray
9. Dry print		

Note: If the above processing is conducted in either trays or a canoe, the lights may be turned on at the completion of step 5 (Bleach Fix). For drum processing the print may be removed from the drum or left in the drum for subsequent steps.

For other processors follow manufacturer's recommendations.

Figure A

DEVELOPER (D-8)
TIME/TEMPERATURE CURVE

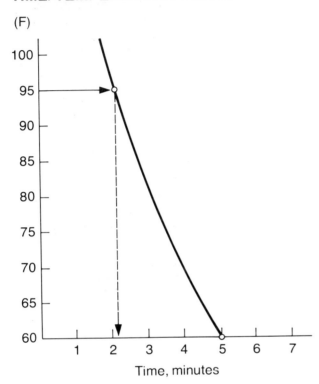

(F)

Time, minutes

Example: At 95F, the Development time is 2 minutes 15 seconds.

Figure B

BLEACH-FIX (B-8)
TIME/TEMPERATURE CURVE

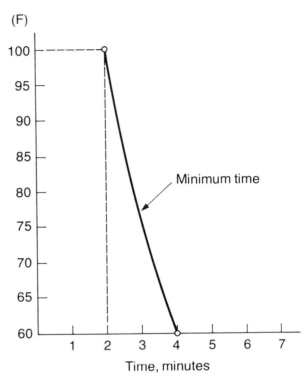

(F)

Minimum time

Time, minutes

Example: At 100F, the Bleach-Fix time is 2 minutes (minimum).

RECOMMENDED 100 F PROCESSING CYCLE

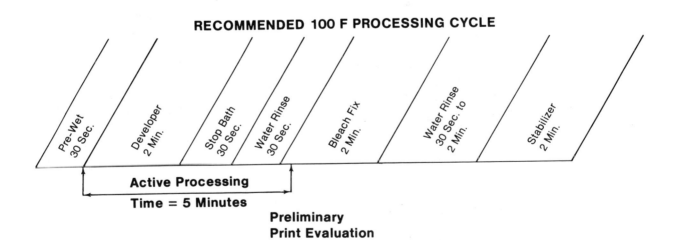

Pre-Wet 30 Sec.

Developer 2 Min.

Stop Bath 30 Sec.

Water Rinse 30 Sec.

Bleach Fix 2 Min.

Water Rinse 30 Sec. to 2 Min.

Stabilizer 2 Min.

Active Processing
Time = 5 Minutes

Preliminary
Print Evaluation

9-64

**Kodak Ektaprint 3 Chemicals
(Ektaprint 300 Developer)**

Distributor:	Eastman Kodak Co.
Materials:	Kodak Ektacolor 37 RC Paper
Components:	Sold as individual component chemicals and also as kits of all necessary chemical components. All concentrated liquid components are mixed with tap water to produce working-strength chemical solutions: developer—packaged as three liquid components; bleach-fix—packaged as two liquid components; and stabilizer—packaged as one liquid component.
Packaging:	Three different kits are available: a one-quart, a one-gallon, and a three and one-half-gallon size. All of these kits contain Ektaprint 3 developer which must be mixed to produce 20 percent less than the volumes just stated if used to process prints either on Kodak's Model 11 Processor or in daylight drums. (The one-quart kit's developer would yield 25.5 fl. oz.; the one-gallon kit's developer would yield 102.5 fl. oz.; and the three and one-half-gallon kit's developer would yield 358.5 fl. oz.) Separate component chemicals are also available to make one-quart, one-gallon and three and one-half-gallon quantities. A separate Ektaprint 300 developer is also available. It is designed for use with the Model 11 and drum processors. No special mixing is required. It is packaged in one-gallon and three and one-half-gallon sizes. The one-gallon size is designed to be mixed in two half-gallon lots. Special replenishers are also packaged for each of these chemicals. Replenishers are packaged in rather large quantities (25 gallons is typical) and are not practical for amateur or low-volume professional use.
Shelf life:	Kodak provides no data on the shelf life of unopened bottles of concentrated component solutions; however, the boxes the components are packaged in are coded to indicate the date of manufacture. No data is provided for partially filled bottles of concentrated solutions; however, Kodak's mixing directions call for mixing the full amount of their liquid concentrates rather than making smaller batches. Working-strength solutions in filled, tightly capped glass bottles have the following stated shelf lives: developer—6 weeks; bleach-fix—8 weeks; and stabilizer—indefinite. Working-strength solutions in partially filled, tightly capped, glass bottles have the following stated shelf lives: developer—3 weeks; bleach-fix—6 weeks; and stabilizer—8 weeks.
Process data:	Numerous Kodak publications offer processing instructions for these chemicals. See Chapter 7 for processing instructions for the Model 11 Processor. Representative daylight-drum processing data from Kodak's Publication Z-204 follow.

Table 9-8   GENERAL PROCESSING SPECIFICATIONS

Nominal solution temperature of 88F (31C)

PROCESSING STEP		*TIME IN MINUTES	ACCUMULATED TIME IN MINUTES	AMOUNT OF SOLUTION
I. Prewet		½	½	†500 ml. of water
2. Developer		3½	4	70 ml. developer
3. Stop Bath (use stabilizer)		½	4½	40 ml. stabilizer
4. Wash		½	5	†500 ml. water
5. Bleach-Fix		1½	6½	40 ml. bleach-fix
‡After the bleach-fix step, carefully remove the print from the tube and continue the wash and stabilizer steps in an 8″ × 10″ tray.				
6. Wash	Pour into	½	7	500 ml. water
7. Wash	tray,	½	7½	500 ml. water
8. Wash	agitate,	½	8	500 ml. water
9. Wash	and dump,	½	8½	500 ml. water
10. Stabilizer	4 times.	1	9½	●500 ml. stabilizer

Important: Always clean and dry the processing tube thoroughly after each process to help prevent contamination.

Dry—Prints can be dried at room temperature, on racks, or in air-impingment dryers. A simple hair dryer or other type forced circulation of air up to 200 F (93 C) may be used for faster drying. Use of a squeegee may also be beneficial. **Never ferrotype RC paper prints.**

500 ml = approximately 17 fluidounces
70 ml = approximately 2.4 fluidounces
40 ml = approximately 1.4 fluidounces

All times include a 10 second drain time (to avoid excess solution carryover). Some processing tubes may require a slightly longer drain time. Be sure to allow enough time to make certain the tube is drained and to add the next solution on time for the next step. The next step begins when the solution contacts the paper.

†*Some processing tubes will not hold 500 ml. Fill with as much water as possible in these two steps.*

‡*The wash and stabilizer steps can be completed in the processing tube; however, without adequate wash in steps 6, 7, 8, and 9, brown bleach-fix stain may result. If the bleach-fix is transferred to the emulsion, it can adversely affect image stability.*

●*This 500 ml of stabilizer may be reused, but should be discarded after processing twenty 8″ × 10″ prints. Do not save or reuse the stabilizer used in the Stop Bath step.*

Table 9-9   PROCESSING PROBLEMS

TROUBLE	POSSIBLE CAUSE
1. High contrast, cyan stain and/or high cyan contrast (pink highlights and cyan shadows).	1. Contamination—bleach-fix in developer or in prewet. 2. Developer temperature too high.
2. Magenta-blue streaks.	1. Insufficient stopping action (stop is bad or no stop was used).
3. Light and dark streaks (uneven development).	1. Prewet not used. 2. Insufficient developer agitation. 3. Processor tube not level.
4. Blue-blacks.	1. Diluted developer (mix concentration). 2. Insufficient developer time. 3. Insufficient drain time after prewet.
5. Low contrast (especially magenta-pink highlights and green shadows).	1. Diluted developer. 2. Insufficient volume of developer. 3. Not enough agitation. 4. Developer temperature too low.

Kodak Ektaprint 2 Chemicals

Distributor: Eastman Kodak Co.

Materials: Kodak Ektacolor 74 RC Paper

Components: Sold as individual component chemicals and also as kits of all necessary chemical components. All concentrated liquid components are mixed with tap water to produce working-strength chemical solutions: developer—packaged as four liquid components and bleach-fix—packaged as two liquid components.

Packaging: Two different kit and component-quantity packages are available: a one-gallon and a three and one-half-gallon size. Replenishment chemicals are also available in 5, 25, 75, and 150-gallon sizes.

Shelf life: Kodak provides no data on the shelf life of unopened bottles of concentrated component solutions; however, the boxes the components are packaged in are coded to indicate the date of manufacture. No data are provided for partially filled bottles of concentrated solutions; however, Kodak's mixing directions call for mixing the full amount of their liquid concentrates rather than making smaller batches. Working-strength solutions, in filled, tightly capped glass bottles have the following stated shelf lives: developer—6 weeks and bleach-fix—8 weeks. No data are provided for working-strength solutions in partially filled, tightly capped, glass bottles, though partially used, unreplenished working-strength chemicals in tanks with floating covers are specified as having the following shelf lives: developer—one week and bleach-fix—6 weeks.

Process data: These materials are intended for use in trays, baskets, continuous processing machines, and drums. Kodak does not recommend their use with Kodak Model 11 Processors. The maker also advises that a stop bath (Kodak Stop Bath SB-1, composed of 48 ml of 28 percent acetic acid in one liter of water) may be required to prevent streaking, and that Ektaprint 3 Stabilizer may be used with Ektaprint 2 chemicals, if desired. The drum processing data offered here is based on Kodak's publication Z-207. When used for drum processing, Ektaprint 2 developer is to be mixed to 20 percent greater concentration (to 3 liters of working-strength solution, rather than to one gallon).

Table 9-10
GENERAL PROCESSING SPECIFICATIONS—ALL SOLUTIONS AT 91.5 ± ½F (33 0.3 C)

PROCESSING STEP	PROCESSING TIME IN MINUTES	AMOUNT OF SOLUTION (ml)
1. Prewet	½	500
2. Developer*	3½	70
3. Stop Bath	½	70
4. Wash	½	500
5. Bleach-Fix	1	70
6. Wash	½	500
7. Wash	½	500
8. Wash	½	500
9. Wash	½	500

*Developer is to be mixed to 20 percent greater than normal concentration (use concentrates which normally are diluted to make one gallon of working strength solution to make only three liters or 102 fluid ounces).

Table 9-10A
PROCESSING PROBLEMS

PROBLEM	POSSIBLE CAUSE
Cyan stains and/or high cyan contrast (pink highlights and cyan shadows)	Bleach-fix contamination of developer or prewet. Developer temperature too high.
Magenta-blue streaks	Insufficient stop-bath action (exhausted stop bath or non-use of stop-bath step).
Light and dark streaks (uneven development)	Prewet not used. Too little developer agitation. Unlevel drum.
Bluish cast to blacks	Diluted developer (failure to drain prewet water completely, also see note on Table 9-10). Too little development time. Developer temperature low.
Low contrast (magenta-pink highlights and green shadows)	Diluted developer (failure to drain prewet water, also see note on Table 9-10). Too little developer agitation.

Unicolor Aᵣ Chemistry

Distributor: Unicolor Div., Photo Systems Inc.

Materials: The instructions state that these chemicals will process Kodak 37 RC paper.

Components: Sold in kits containing all necessary chemical components. All liquid concentrated components are mixed with tap water to produce working-strength solutions: developer—packaged as two liquid components; stop bath—packaged as a single liquid component; blix (bleach-fix)—packaged as two liquid components; and stabilizer—packaged as a single liquid component.

Packaging: Three different kits are available: a one-quart, a one-gallon, and a four-gallon size.

Shelf life: Unopened bottles of concentrated component solutions are stated to have a shelf life of up to two years, but kits are not dated to indicate when they were manufactured. Opened and partially filled bottles of concentrated component solutions have shelf lives stated as follows: developer activator—3 to 4 months; all other components—4 to 6 months. Working-strength solutions in tightly capped, filled containers have the following stated shelf lives: color developer—1 week; all other components—8 weeks. Working-strength solutions in partially filled, tightly capped containers have the following stated shelf lives: color developer—up to 1 week; all other component solutions—up to four weeks. All shelf-life data listed is based on storage temperatures between 60 and 80 F (16–27C).

Process data: Instructions packaged with the chemicals cover tray processing at several temperatures and one-shot processing in drums. A minimum of two fluid ounces of each of the chemicals is called for when processing in an 8″ × 10″ drum. Processing data follow.

Table 9-11 — PROCESSING INSTRUCTIONS UNICOLOR Aʳ CHEMISTRY IN UNIDRUM™

Processing may be done completely in daylight after paper is properly loaded in Unidrum™. See note below for processing with Kodak Model 11 or 16 Processors.

STEP	USE THIS SOLUTION OR PROCEDURE	AT THIS TEMP.	TIME	AT THIS TEMP.	TIME	WITH THIS TECHNIQUE
		NORMAL PROCESS		RAPID PROCESS		Note: The chemistry working solution quantities in this column are for the 8 × 10 **UNIDRUM™** only. If you are using an 11 × 14 or 16 × 20 **UNIDRUM™** or another drum-type processor, see the quantity requirements in instructions for **UNIDRUM™** or other processor.
1.	Water	105-110F (40-43C)	1 min.	105-110F (40-43C)	1 min.	Load exposed paper into clean dry **UNIDRUM™ with lights off.** Replace top (cap) on drum. **Lights on.** Fill **UNIDRUM™** through pouring spout, with water. Set drum vertically on end and allow to stand 1 full minute. Drain completely through pouring spout. Place drum on legs (horizontally) in processing area.
2.	Developer	75-80F (24-27C)	3½ min.	105-110F (40-43C)	2 min.	If **UNIDRUM™** working (rolling) surface is level use 2 oz. of chemistry in this and all following steps except washes; if surface is not absolutely level use 4 oz. of all chemicals and **reuse once.** Add developer through pouring spout, roll (agitate) as prescribed in **UNIDRUM™** (other processor) instructions. Drain through pouring spout at end of step.
3.	Stop Bath	70-90F (21-32C)	½ min.	90-110F (32-43C)	½ min.	Add chemistry through pouring spout and roll **UNIDRUM™** per Step 2. Drain Stop Bath through pouring spout at end of step.
4.	Blix	70-90F (21-32C)	2 min.	90-110F (32-43C)	1½ min.	Add chemistry through pouring spout and roll **UNIDRUM™** per Step 2. Drain Blix through pouring spout at the end of step.
5.	Water	70-90F (21-32C)	2 min.	90-110F (32-43C)	1 to 2 min.	Add 8 oz. water and roll (agitate) **UNIDRUM™** for 15-20 seconds. Dump. **Repeat four (4) more times** using 8 oz. of water and rolling **UNIDRUM™** approximately 15-25 seconds each time. Dump water from final wash. Open **UNIDRUM™** and remove print.
6.	Stabilizer	70-90F (21-32C)	1½ to 1 min	70-90F (21-32C)	½ to 1 min.	Place print in Stablizer Tray . . . agitate 30 seconds to 1 minute and remove print. Wipe off print and dry . . . there is **no additional washing** . . . processing is completed. Note: bluish cast of wet prints is normal for RC papers. All prints must be dry to judge the final color. See drying details above.

Table 9-12 — PROCESSING PROBLEMS

PROBLEM	PROBABLE CAUSE(S)	REMEDY
Fingerprints or smudges, generally reddish in color.	Emulsion surface touched before processing. Water or chemistry on fingers.	Handle RC paper only by edges and/or back with clean hands . . . or wear dry rubber or plastic gloves.
Stained prints borders . . . may extend into body of print, generally bluish-magenta in color.	Paper not presoaked in UNIDRUM® Insufficient rinse and/or stop between developer and Blix. Too little chemistry used or rolling surface not level.	Read and follow instructions per Table 9-11. Use twice as much chemistry and reuse once. Use more water and/or Stop Bath volume or time.
Cyan-Blue cast over entire print.	Paper exposed to black and white safelight.	Use only Wratten No. 10 or No. 13 Safelight with not more than 15 watt bulb . . . or no safelight.
Magenta or Cyan Blue cast over entire print.	Developer contaminated with Blix.	Mix new developer.
Yellowish-brown case . . . generally localized and darker towards an edge.	Stray light reflected off nearby object during exposure (such as enlarger post) Light leak in paper box (or bag).	Eliminate reflections. Secure closure on paper container when not in use.
On dry print . . . magenta-blue "opalescence" not correctable by filtration.	Underdevelopment or developer weak or old.	Follow prescribed techniques of time, temperature, etc. Mix chemistry per instructions and do not overextend capacity of shelf-life.
"Muddiness," generally grayish-purple, over entire print.	Insufficient Blixing.	Same as above.

Unicolor Universal A' Chemistry

Distributor: Unicolor Div., Photo Systems Inc.

Materials: The instructions state that these chemicals will process Kodak Ektacolor 37 RC Color Print Paper and may also be used for Unicolor B (not RB) and Agfacolor (B) type papers.

Components: Sold in kits containing all necessary chemical components. All liquid concentrated components are mixed with tap water to produce working-strength solutions: developer—packaged as two liquid components; stop bath—packaged as a single liquid component; blix (bleach-fix)—packaged as two liquid components; and stabilizer—packaged as a single liquid component.

Packaging: A one-quart kit is available.

Shelf life: Unopened bottles of concentrated component solutions are stated to have a shelf life of up to two years, but kits are not dated (in user-readable terms) to indicate when they were manufactured. Opened and partially filled bottles of concentrated component solutions have shelf lives stated as follows: developer activator—3 to 4 months; all other components — 4 to 6 months. Working-strength solutions in tightly stoppered, filled containers have the following stated shelf lives: color developer—1 week; all other components up to 12 weeks. No data are provided for working-strength solutions stored in partially filled containers. All shelf-life data provided is based on storage temperatures of between 60 and 80F (16–27C).

Process data: Instructions packaged with the chemicals cover tray processing at several temperatures and one-shot processing in drums and on the Kodak Models 11 and 16K Processors; replenishment data also provided. A minimum of two fluid ounces of each of the processing chemicals is called for when using an 8″ × 10″ drum. Representative processing data from the manufacturer's instructions follow.

Table 9-13 PROCESSING PROBLEMS

PROBLEM	PROBABLE CAUSE(S)	REMEDY
Fingerprints or smudges, generally reddish in color.	Emulsion surface touched before processing. Water or chemistry on fingers.	Handle RC paper only by edges and/or back with clean hands . . . or wear dry rubber or plastic gloves.
Stained prints borders . . . may extend into body of print, generally bluish-magneta in color.	Paper not presoaked in UNIDRUM® Insufficient stop between developer and Blix Too little chemistry used or rolling surface not level.	Read and Follow instructions per Table 9-13. Use twice as much chemistry and resue once. Use more water and/or Stop Bath volume or time.
Cyan-Blue cast over entire print.	Paper exposed to black and white safelight.	Use only Wratten No. 10 or No. 13 safelight with not more than 15 watt bulb . . . or no safelight.
Magenta or Cyan blue cast over entire print.	Developer contaminated with Blix.	Mix new developer.
Yellowish-brown cast . . . generally localized and darker towards an edge.	Stray light reflected off nearby object during exposure (such as enlarger post); Light leak in paper box (or bag).	Eliminate reflections. Secure closure on paper container when not in use.
On dry print . . . magenta-blue "opalescence" not correctable by filtration.	Underdevelopment or developer weak or old.	Follow prescribed techniques of time, temperature, etc. Mix chemistry per instructions and do not overextend capacity of shelf life.
"Muddiness," generally grayish-purple, over entire print.	Insufficient Blixing.	Same as above.

Table 9-14

PROCESSING INSTRUCTIONS ... UNICOLOR UNIVERSAL A^r CHEMISTRY ... IN UNIDRUM®

Processing may be done completely in daylight after paper is properly loaded in Unidrum®. See note below for processing with Kodak Model 11 or 16 Processors.

STEP	USE THIS SOLUTION OR PROCEDURE	AT THIS TEMP.	TIME	AT THIS TEMP.	TIME	WITH THIS TECHNIQUE
		NORMAL PROCESS		RAPID PROCESS*		Note: The chemistry working solution quantities in the column are for the 8 × 10 **UNIDRUM**® only. If you are using an 11 × 14 or 16 × 20 **UNIDRUM**® or another drum-type processor, see the quantity requirements in instructions for **UNIDRUM**® or other processor.
1.	Water (Presoak)	105-110F (40-43C)	1 min.	105-110F (40-43C)	1 min.	Load exposed paper into clean dry **UNIDRUM**® **with lights off.** Replace top (cap) on drum. **Lights on. Fill UNIDRUM**® through pouring spout, with water. Set drum vertically on end and allow to stand 1 full minute. Drain completely through pouring spout. Place drum on legs (horizontally) in processing area.
2.	Developer	75-80F (24-27C)	3½ min.	105-110F (40-43C)	2 min.	If **UNIDRUM**® working (rolling) surface is level use 2 oz. of chemistry in this and all following steps except washes; if surface is not absolutely level use 4 oz. of all chemicals and **reuse once.** Add developer through pouring spout, roll (agitate) as prescribed in **UNIDRUM**® (other processor) instructions. Drain through pouring spout at end of step.
3.	Stop Bath	70-90F (21-32C)	½ min.	90-110F (32-43C)	1½ min.	Add chemistry through pouring spout and roll **UNIDRUM**® per Step 2. Drain Stop Bath through pouring spout at end of step.
4.	Blix	70-90F (21-32C)	2 min.	90-110F (32-43C)	½ min.	Add chemistry through pouring spout and roll **UNIDRUM**® per Step 2. Drain Blix through pouring spout at the end of step.
5.	Water (Rinse)	70-90F (21-32C)	2 min.	90-110F (32-43C)	1 to 2 min.	Add 8 oz. water and roll (agitate) **UNIDRUM**® for 15-20 seconds. Dump. **Repeat four (4) more times** using 8 oz. of water and rolling **UNIDRUM**® approximately 15-25 seconds each time. Dump water from final wash. Open **UNIDRUM**® and remove print.
6.	Stabilizer	70-90F (21-32C)	½ to 1 in.	70-90F (21-32C)	½ to 1 min.	Place print in Stabilizer Tray ... agitate 30 seconds to 1 minute and remove print. Wipe off print and dry ... there is **no additional washing** ... processing is completed. Note: bluish cast of wet prints is normal for RC papers. All prints must be dry to judge the final color. See drying details above.

Universal A^r Chemistry on Kodak Model 11 and 16K Processors ... The user must have running water at 100F (38C) for rinsing and to temper the processor. **The drum temperature is 100F (38C)** for all steps. Use the **Rapid Process Times** in the above table. Prewet the print in a tray of water between 75-100F (24-38C) for 1 minute before putting on apron.

*Do not use Rapid Process for Agfacolor Paper

Unicolor B Chemistry

Distributor: Unicolor Div., Photo Systems Inc.

Materials: The instructions state that these chemicals will process Unicolor, Mitsubishi and Agfacolor print papers (type B).

Components: Sold in kits containing all necessary chemical components. All components mix with tap water to produce working-strength solutions: developer—packaged as two liquid components; blix (bleach-fix)—packaged as two liquid components; and stabilizer—packaged as a single liquid component.

Packaging: A one-gallon (of working-strength solutions) kit of all necessary components is available.

Shelf life: Unopened bottles of concentrated component solutions are stated to have a shelf life of up to 18 months, but kits are not dated to indicate when they were manufactured. Opened and partially filled bottles of concentrated component solutions have shelf lives stated as follows (at storage temperatures between 60 and 80 F 16–27C): developer activator (in dark glass)—3 to 4 months; all other components (in high-density plastic)—4 to 6 months. Working-strength solutions in filled, tightly capped containers have the following stated shelf lives: color developer—1 week; all other components—8 weeks. Working-strength solutions in partially filled, tightly capped containers have the following stated shelf life: color developer—up to 1 week; all other component solutions—up to 4 weeks.

Process data: Instructions packaged with the chemicals cover tray processing at several temperatures and one-shot processing in drums. A minimum of two fluid ounces of each of the processing chemicals is called for when working in an 8″ 4 10″ drum. Representative processing data from manufacturer's instructions follow.

Table 9-15 PROCESSING INSTRUCTIONS ... UNICOLOR B CHEMISTRY WITH 8 × 10 UNIDRUM™

May be done completely in daylight after paper is properly loaded in capped UNIDRUM™

STEP	USE THIS SOLUTION	AT THIS TEMPERATURE	TIME	WITH THIS TECHNIQUE
				NOTE: The chemistry working solution quantities in this column are for the 8 × 10 UNIDRUM™ only. If you are using an 11 × 14 or 16 × 20 UNIDRUM™ or another drum-type processor, see the quantity requirements packed with the UNIDRUM™ or other processor.
1.	Water	92 ± 2F	1 minute	Load exposed paper into a clean, dry UNIDRUM™ **with lights off.** Replace top (cap) on drum. **Lights on.** Fill UNIDRUM™ through pouring spout, with water 92 ± 2F. Set drum vertically on end and allow to stand 1 full minute. Drain completely through pouring spout retaining water for subsequent wash steps. Place drum on legs (horizontally) in processing area.
2.	Developer	70 ± 4F	2 minutes	If UNIDRUM™ working (rolling) surface is absolutely level use 2 oz. of all chemicals in this and all following steps except washes: if surface is not absolutely level use 4 oz. of all chemicals and **reuse once.** Add chemistry through pouring spout. Smartly knock drum off legs and roll (agitate) vigorously back-and-forth ... see UNIDRUM™ instructions for rolling technique detail. Drain developer through pouring spout at end of step.
3.	Water	Saved from Step 1	1 minute	Add 8 oz. of water saved from Step 1 and roll (agitate) UNIDRUM™ vigorously for 15-20 seconds. Dump. **Repeat two (2) more times** using 8 oz. of water and rolling UNIDRUM™ 15-20 seconds each time. After third wash place drained UNIDRUM™ back on its legs in processing area. **This wash step is very important toward assuring there will be no stains on print or in borders.**
4.	Blix™	70 ± 4F	2 minutes	Add chemistry through pouring spout and roll UNIDRUM™ per Step 2. It is important the full ... 2 minutes ... time interval be observed for Step 4 ... going beyond the 2 minutes will have no adverse effect; however, care should be exercised not to process for less than 2 minutes. Drain Blix™ through pouring spout at the end of step.
5.	Water	Saved from Step 1	2 minutes	Add 8 oz. of water saved from Step 1 and roll (agitate) UNIDRUM™ vigorously for 15-20 seconds. Dump. **Repeat four (4) more times** using 8 oz. of water and rolling UNIDRUM™ approximately 25 seconds each time. Dump water from final wash. Open UNIDRUM™ and remove print.
6.	Stabilizer (in tray)	Room Temperature (70-80F)	1 minute	It is permissible to stabilize print in UNIDRUM™, however, if the print is removed at the conclusion of Step 5, and if the UNIDRUM™ is clean and need only be dried to proceed to next print. If print is stabilized in UNIDRUM™ then drum must be thoroughly washed and dried before proceeding to next print. After print has been placed in Stabilizer Tray ... agitate for 30 seconds to 1 minute and remove print. Squeegee print and dry ... there is **no additional washing** ... processing is completed. Air-dried prints assume a semi-glossy finish ... ferrotyped prints assume a glossy finish. It using heat for drying keep below 200F. Color prints may be dry mounted in the conventional manner ... keep heat low.

Table 9-16   PROCESSING PROBLEMS

PROBLEM	PROBABLE CAUSE(S)	REMEDY
Stained print borders or Uneven stains or mottling on print	Paper not presoaked in UNIDRUM™ before development Too little chemistry used or UNIDRUM™ rolling surface not level Too little or inconsistent agitation Insufficient rinsing between developer and Blix™	Load paper in UNIDRUM™ before heat soaking. See Table 9-15 . . . Step 1. Use twice as much chemistry and reuse once. (4 oz. in 8 × 10 UNIDRUM™). Agitate vigorously and consistently in all steps. Use more water and vigorous agitation with UNIDRUM™; use running water if tray processing. Read washing techniques in processing instructions Table 9-15.
Cyan cast over entire print	Paper exposed to black-and-white safelight	Use only Wratten No. 10 safelight with not more than 15w bulb . . . or no safelight.
Yellowish cast over entire print	Stray light reflected off enlarger post or walls	Eliminate stray light.
Grayish cast over entire print	Insufficient Blix™ time; Blix™ too weak or exhausted	Blix per time in instructions; mix per instructions; do not use beyond capacity.
Magenta-blue "opalescent" cast to print colors not correctable by filter pack or R, G, B exposure changes	Underdevelopment or Developer weak or old	Follow correct techniques, times, and temperatures per processing instructions. Mix developer per instructions and do not use beyond capacity or life.
Same as above but cast includes borders	Developer contaminated by Blix™	Mix new developer.
Blue "measle-like" dots on print	Print processed in drum with smooth inside wall (no ribs). Chemistry sometimes traps between back of paper and drum wall . . . does not get properly washed.	Buy a UNIDRUM™
Red "measle-like" dots on print	Print dried on pitted ferrotype plate	Replace ferrotype plate

Unicolor Pro-B Chemistry (cf1,10,12

Distributor: Unicolor Div., Photo Systems Inc.

Materials: The instructions state that these chemicals will process Unicolor, Mitsubishi and Agfacolor print papers (all type B).

Components: Sold in kits containing all necessary chemical components. All components are mixed with tap water to produce working-strength solutions: developer — packaged as two liquid components; stop bath — packaged as a single liquid component; blix (bleach-fix) — packaged as a single liquid component; and stabilizer — packaged as a single liquid component.

Packaging: Two different kits are available: a one-gallon size and a four-gallon size.

Shelf life: Unopened bottles of concentrated component solutions are stated to have a shelf life of up to 18 months, but kits are not dated to indicate when they were manufactured. Opened and partially filled bottles of concentrated component solutions have shelf lives stated as follows: developer activator (in dark glass) — 3 to 4 months; all other components (in high-density plastic) — 4 to 6 months. Working-strength solutions in tightly capped, filled containers have the following stated shelf lives: color developer — 1 week; all other components — 8 weeks. Working-strength solutions in partially filled, tightly capped containers have the following stated shelf lives: color developer — up to 1 week; all other component solutions — up to 4 weeks. All shelf life data listed is based on storage temperatures between 60 and 80 F (16-27C).

Process data: Instructions packaged with the chemicals cover tray processing at several temperatures and one-shot processing in drums. A minimum of two fluid ounces of each of the processing chemicals is called for when working in an 8″ × 10″ drum. Representative processing data from the manufacturer's instructions follow.

Table 9-17   PROCESSING INSTRUCTIONS . . . UNICOLOR PRO-B CHEMISTRY WITH 8 × 10 UNIDRUM™

May be done completely in daylight after paper is properly loaded in capped UNIDRUM™

STEP	USE THIS SOLUTION	AT THIS TEMPERATURE	TIME	WITH THIS TECHNIQUE
				NOTE: The chemistry working solution quantities in this column are for the 8 × 10 UNIDRUM™ only. If you are using an 11 × 14 or 16 × 20 UNIDRUM™ or another drum-type processor, see the quantity requirements packed with the UNIDRUM™ or other processor.
1.	Water	92 ± 2F	1 minute	Load exposed paper into a clean, dry UNIDRUM™ with lights off. Replace top (cap) on drum. **Lights on.** Fill UNIDRUM™ through pouring spout, with water at 92 ± 2F. Set drum vertically on end and allow to stand 1 full minute. Drain completely through pouring spout retaining water for subsequent wash steps. Place drum on legs (horizontally) in processing area.
2.	Developer	70 ± 4F	2 minutes	If UNIDRUM™ working (rolling) surface is absolutely level use 2 oz. of all chemicals in this and all following steps except washes; if surface is not absolutely level use 4 oz. of all chemicals and **reuse once.** Add chemistry through pouring spout. Smartly knock drum off legs and roll (agitate) vigorously back-and-forth . . . see UNIDRUM™ instructions for rolling technique detail. Drain developer through pouring spout at end of step.
3.	Stop Bath	70 ± 4F	1 minute	Add chemistry through pouring spout and roll UNIDRUM™ per Step 2. It is important the full . . . 1 minute . . . time interval be observed for Step 3 . . . going beyond 1 minute will have no adverse effect; however, care should be exercised not to process for less than one minute. Drain stop bath through pouring spot at the end of step.
4.	Blix™	70 ± 4F	2 minutes	Add chemistry through pouring spout and roll UNIDRUM™ per Step 2. It is important the full . . . 2 minutes . . . time interval be observed for Step 4 . . . going beyond the two minutes will have no adverse effect; however, care should be exercised not to process for less than two minutes. Drain Blix™ through pouring spout at the end of step.
5.	Water	Saved from Step 1	2 minutes	Add 8 oz. of water saved from Step 1 and roll (agitate) UNIDRUM™ vigorously for 15-20 seconds. Dump. **Repeat four (4) more times** using 8 oz. of water and rolling UNIDRUM™ approximately 25 seconds each time. Dump water from final wash. Open UNIDRUM™ and remove print.
6.	Stabilizer (in tray)	Room Temperature (70-80F)	1 minute	It is permissible to stabilize print in UNIDRUM™, however, if the print is removed at the conclusion of Step 5, the UNIDRUM™ is clean and need only be dried to proceed to next print. If print is stabilized in UNIDRUM™ then drum must be thoroughly washed and dried before proceeding to next print. After print has been placed in Stabilizer Tray . . . agitate for 30 seconds to 1 minute and remove print. Squeegee print and dry . . . there is no additional washing . . . processing is completed. Air dried prints assume a semi-glossy finish . . . ferrotyped prints assume a glossy finish. If using heat for drying keep below 200F. Color prints may be dry mounted in the conventional manner . . . keep heat low.

Table 9-18   PROCESSING PROBLEMS

PROBLEM	PROBABLE CAUSES(S)	REMEDY
Stained print borders or Uneven stains or motting on print	Paper not presoaked in UNIDRUM before development Too little chemistry used or UNIDRUM™ rolling surface not level Too little or inconsistent agitation Insufficient Stop Bath between developer and Blix™	Load paper in UNIDRUM™ before heat soaking. See Table 9-17 . . . Step 1. Use twice as much chemistry and reuse once. (4 oz. in 8 × 10 UNIDRUM™). Agitate vigorously and conssitently in all steps.
Cyan cast over entire print	Paper exposed to black-and-white safelight	Use only Wratten No. 10 Safelight with not more than 15w bulb . . . or no safelight.
Yellowish cast over entire print	Stray light reflected off enlarger post or walls	Eliminate stray light.
Grayish cast over entire print	Insufficient Blix™ time; Blix™ too weak or exhausted	Blix per time in instructions; mix per instructions; do not use beyond capacity.
Magenta-blue "opalescent" cast to print colors not correctable by filter pack or R, G, B exposure changes	Underdevelopment or developer weak or old	Follow correct techniques, times, and temperatures per processing instructions. Mix developer per instructions and do not use beyond capacity or life.
Same as above but cast includes borders	Developer contaminated by Blix™	Mix new developer.
Blue "measle-like" dots on print	Print processed in drum with smooth inside wall (no ribs). Chemistry sometimes traps between back of paper and drum wall . . . does not get properly washed.	Buy a UNIDRUM™
Red "measle-like" dots on print	Print dried on pitted ferrotype plate	Replace ferrotype plate

Unicolor Total Color

Distributor: Unicolor Div., Photo Systems Inc.

Materials: Color Negative Films—Kodacolor II, Vericolor II, Sakuracolor II, Fuji F-II, Eastman type 5247
Color Print Papers—Unicolor RB, Kodak 37 RC, Agfa RC

Components: Sold as separate chemical components. All liquid concentrated components are mixed with tap water to produce working-strength solutions: developer—packaged as four liquid components; optional stop bath—packaged as a single liquid component included in the blix components; blix—packaged as four (including the stop bath and stabilizer components) liquid components; and optional stabilizer—packaged as a single liquid component included among the blix components.

Packaging: Developer components are packaged to produce 24 fluid ounces of film-processing, working-strength solution and/or 48 fluid ounces of print-processing, working-strength solution. Blix components are packaged to produce 24 ounces of working-strength film-processing blix solution and/or 48 ounces of working-strength print-processing solution. Additional components carried in the blix packaging produce 24 ounces of working-strength film-processing stabilizer and 48 ounces of working-strength print-processing stabilizer solution, as well as 48 ounces of working-strength print-processing stop bath solution.

Shelf life: Unopened bottles of concentrated component solutions are stated to have a shelf life of up to two years, but kits are not dated (in user-readable code) to indicate when they were manufactured. Working-strength solutions of all components have a one-week shelf life.

Process data: Instructions packaged with the chemicals cover film processing in conventional film tanks as well as in the Unicolor Film Drum. Paper processing in trays and in daylight drums is also covered. Representative processing data from the manufacturer's instructions follow.

Remarks: These chemicals are specifically designed to *first* be used for processing film, *then* to be replenished and slightly modified for reuse in processing paper. When so used, they offer good economy and good processing results. However, when used for paper processing alone, these chemicals may prove to be more expensive to use than the other single-purpose materials listed in this section.

Table 9-19 TOTAL COLOR FILM PROCESSING TIMES

For: Kodacolor II, Vericolor II and Sakuracolor II. See below for Fujicolor F-II and Eastman Type 5247. Processing Times in Fresh Chemistry . . . See General Instructions on Reuse of Chemistry.

STEP	SOLUTION	TIME	TEMPERATURE
1.	Water preheat (Unicolor Film Drum only)	1 minute	*100°F (38°C)
2.	Developer (time & temperature in this step are critical)	3¼ minutes	100°F (30°C)
3.	Blix	6 minutes	95-105°F (35-41°C)
4.	Running Water Rinse (lights on OK)	3 minutes	95-105°F (35-41°C)
5.	Stabilizer (optional) (lights on OK)	30 seconds	Room Temp. to 105°F (41°C)

*Processing Fujicolor F-II: Same as above but development time (fresh chemistry)=3 minutes.
Processing Eastman Type 5247:
Water preheat and developer temperature = 104F (40C)
Development time (fresh chemistry)=3¼ minutes.
Times & temperatures for remainder of process are identical to those above.

Note on water rinse: Type 5247 film has a carbon rem-jet backing on the base side which must be removed during rinse step. Remove film from reel and thoroughly rub off backing with fingers or sponge.

Table 9-20 TOTAL COLOR PRINT PROCESSING TIMES IN UNIDRUMS

(See Other Side for Tray Processing)
Development time: Consult nomograph.
Glix and Water Rinse Times: Use times belor if solutions are between 70-100°F (21-38°C).
Above 100°F (38°C) . . . you can use 1 minute each for Blix and water rinse.

STEP	SOLUTION	TIME
1.	Water Presoak	1 minute
2.	Developer	See nomograph
3.	Stop Bath (or water rinse)	15-30 seconds
4.	Blix	2 minutes
5.	Water rinse	2 minutes
6.	Stablizer (optional)	½-1 minute

If stablizer is omitted . . . double rinse time above (Step 5). Stabilize in tray only.

TOTAL COLOR PRINT PROCESSING TIME/TEMPERATURE NOMOGRAPH

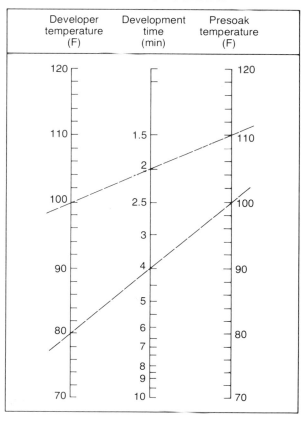

Unicolor R-2 Chemistry

Distributor:	Unicolor Div., Photo Systems Inc.
Materials:	Unicolor Resin-Base Color Print Paper
Components:	Sold in kits containing all necessary chemical components. All liquid concentrated components are mixed with tap water to produce working-strength solutions: developer— packaged as three liquid components; stop bath— packaged as a single liquid component; blix (bleach-fix)—packaged as a single liquid component; and stabilizer—packaged as a single liquid component.
Packaging:	Two different kits are available; a one-quart and a one-gallon size.
Shelf life:	Unopened bottles of concentrated component solutions are stated to have a shelf life of up to two years, but kits are not dated to indicate when they were manufactured. Opened and partially filled bottles of concentrated component solutions have shelf lives stated as follows: color developer part A—3 to 4 months; all other components—4 to 6 months. Working-strength solutions in filled, tightly capped containers have the following stated shelf lives: color developer—1 week; all other components—up to 12 weeks. No data is provided for working-strength solutions in partially filled containers.
Process data:	Instructions packaged with the chemicals cover tray and deep-tank processing (with and without replenishment) at several temperatures; one-shot

processing on Kodak Model 11 and 16 Processors; and one-shot processing in drums at several temperatures. A minimum of two fluid ounces of each of the processing chemicals is called for when processing in an 8″ × 10″ drum. Representative processing data from the manufacturer's instructions follow.

Table 9-21   PROCESSING PROBLEMS

PROBLEM	PROBABLE CAUSE(S)	REMEDY
Fingerprints or smudges, generally reddish in color.	Emulsion surface touched before processing. Water or chemistry on fingers.	Handle RC paper only by edges and/ or back with clean hands . . . or wear dry rubber or plastic gloves.
Stained prints borders . . . may extend into body of print, generally bluish-magenta in color.	Paper not presoaked in UNIDRUM®	Read and Follow instructions per Table 9-21.
	Insufficient stop between developer and Blix	Use twice as much chemistry and resue once.
	Too little chemistry used or rolling surface not level.	Use more water and/or Stop Bath volume or time.
Cyan-Blue cast over entire print.	Paper exposed to black-and-white safelight.	Use only Wratten No. 10 or No. 13 safelight with not more than 15 watt bulb . . . or no safelight.
Magenta or Cyan-Blue cast over entire print.	Developer contaminated with Blix.	Mix new developer.
Yellowish-brown cast . . . generally localized and darker towards an edge.	Stray light reflected off nearby object during exposure (such as enlarger post)	Eliminate reflections.
	Light leak in paper box (or bag).	Secure closure on paper container when not in use.
On dry print . . . magenta-blue "opalescence" not correctable by filtration.	Underdevelopment or developer weak or old.	Follow prescribed techniques of time, temperature, etc. Mix chemistry per instructions and do not overextend capacity of shelflife.
"Muddiness," generally grayish-purple, over entire print.	Insufficient Blixing.	Same as above.

Table 9-22 PROCESSING INSTRUCTIONS...UNICOLOR R2 CHEMISTRY...IN UNIDRUM®

Processing may be done completely in daylight after paper is properly loaded in Unidrum®. See note below for processing with Kodak Model 11 or 16 Processors.*

STEP	USE THIS SOLUTION PROCEDURE	AT THIS TEMP.	TIME	AT THIS TEMP.	TIME	WITH THIS TECHNIQUE
		NORMAL PROCESS		RAPID PROCESS		Note: The chemistry working solution quantities in this column are for the 8 × 10 UNIDRUM® only. If you are using an 11 × 14 or 16 × 20 UNIDRUM® or another drum-type processor, see the quantity requirements in instructions for UNIDRUM® or other processor.
1.	Water (Presoak)	105-110F (40-43C)	1 min.	105-110F (40-43C)	1 min.	Load exposed paper into clean dry UNIDRUM® with lights off. Replace top (cap) on drum. Lights on. Fill UNIDRUM® through pouring spout, with water. Set drum vertically on end and allow to stand 1 full minute. Drain completely through pouring spout. Place drum on legs (horizontally) in processing area.
2.	Developer	75-80F (24-27C)	4 min.	105-110F (40-43C)	2½ min.	If UNIDRUM® working (rolling) surface is level use 2 oz. of chemistry in this and all following steps except washes; if surface is not absolutely level use 4 oz. of all chemicals and reuse once. Add developer through pouring spout, roll (agitate) as prescribed in UNIDRUM® (other processor) instructions. Drain through pouring spout at end of step.
3.	Stop Bath	70-90F (21-32C)	½ min.	90-110F (32-43C)	½ min.	Add chemistry through pouring spout and roll UNIDRUM® per Step 2. Drain Stop Bath through pouring spout at end of step.
4.	Blix	70-90F (21-32C)	2 min.	90-110F (32-43C)	1½ min.	Add chemistry through pouring spout and roll UNIDRUM® per Step 2. Drain Blix through pouring spout at the end of step.
5.	Water (Rinse)	70-90F (21-32C)	2 min.	90-110F (32-43C)	1 to 2 min.	Add 8 oz. water and roll (agitate) UNIDRUM® for 15-20 seconds. Dump. Repeat four (4) more times using 8 oz. of water and rolling UNIDRUM® approximately 15-25 seconds each time. Dump water from final wash. Open UNIDRUM® and remove print.
6.	Stabilizer	70-90F (21-32C)	½ to 1 min.	70-90F (21-32C)	½ to 1 min.	Place print in Stabilizer Tray ... agitate 30 seconds to 1 minute and remove print. Wipe off print and dry ... there is no additional washing ... processing is completed. Note: bluish cast of wet prints is normal for RC papers. All prints must be dry to judge the final color. See drying details above.

Note: R2 Chemistry on Kodak Model 11 and 16K Processors ... The user must have running water at 100F (38C) for rinsing and to temper the processor. The drum temperature is 100F (38C) for all steps. Use the Rapid Process Times in table 9-21. Prewet the print in a tray of water between 75-100F (24-38C) for 1 minute before putting on apron.

Table 9-23 TIME AND TEMPERATURE PROCESSING IN THE UNIDRUM

For processing in the Unidrum at temperatures other than those given in Table 9-20, use the times listed below:

USE THIS SOLUTION (In order of use)	AT THIS TIME AND TEMPERATURE								
	70-75F	75-80F	80-85F	85-90F	90-95F	95-100F	100-105F	105-110F	110-115F
1. Water (Presoak)	At same temperature as developer 1 minute								
2. Developer	13 min.	10 min.	8 min.	6½ min.	5 min.	4 min.	3¼ min.	2½ min.	2 min.
3. Stop Bath	½ minute								
4. Blix	2 minutes					1½ minutes			
5. Water (Rinse)	2 minutes					1 to 2 minutes			
6. Stabilizer	½ to 1 minute								

A note of caution ... When processing by the Time & Temperature method with any color chemistry it is normal to find a slightly different color balance (requiring a different printing filter pack) at 75F, for example, as opposed to 100F and so on. Thus we restate our cardinal rule of CONSISTENCY! Pick a processing mode (time & temperature) and stay with it. This will eliminate color shifts and save time and materials.

Positive-to-Positive Processing Chemicals

A number of brands of positive-to-positive color printing-processing chemicals are available on the market. Descriptions of several of those brands follow.

Color by Beseler RP5 Reversal Print Chemistry

Distributor: Beseler Photo Marketing Co., Inc.

Materials: Kodak Ektachrome RC Type 1993 Color Paper

Components: Sold in kits containing all necessary chemical components. All concentrated liquid components are mixed with tap water to produce working-strength solutions: first developer—packaged as a single liquid component; first stop bath—packaged as a single liquid component; color developer—packaged as three liquid components; second stop bath—packaged as a single liquid component; bleach-fix—packaged as three liquid components; and stabilizer—packaged as a single liquid component.

Packaging: A one-quart size kit is available.

Shelf life: No data is provided on: the shelf life of the unopened concentrated solutions; the shelf life of partially filled bottles of concentrated solutions, though the user is advised to mix all of concentrates at one time; or for partially filled containers of working-strength chemicals. Working-strength chemicals, in filled, tightly capped, brown glass bottles have stated shelf lives as follows: first developer—about 4 weeks; first stop bath—about 2 months; color developer—about 4 weeks; second stop bath—about 2 months; bleach-fix—about 2 months; No data is provided for the stabilizer solution.

Process data: Instructions packaged with the chemicals cover drum processing at ambient and elevated temperatures in some detail. The summary data, presented next, does not include drain times, which must be added to each step, or data on the required reexposure of the print to white light during the first wash step. The reexposure is done with the print in the wash tray. Both sides of the print must be exposed to a 100 watt bulb at a distance of 18 to 24 inches, for not less than 15 seconds per side. Ambient temperature processing requires a minimum of 1½ ounces of processing chemicals. Elevated temperature processing calls for a minimum of 2½ fluid ounces of the processing chemicals. Representative processing data from the manufacturer's instructions follow.

Table 9-24

COLOR BY BESELER RP5
TIME/TEMPERATURE CHART

ROOM TEMP.		FIRST DEVELOPER	FIRST STOP BATH	FIRST WASH*		COLOR DEVELOPER	SECOND STOP BATH	BLEACH FIX	FINAL WASH*
C°	F°								
37.5	100	1	½	2		2	½	2	2
35.6	96	1½	½	2		2¼	½	2	2
33	92	2	1	2	*Re-expose*	2½	1	2	2
30	86	3	1	2		3	1	3	2
28	82	3½	1	2		3½	1	3	2
26	79	4	1	2		4	1	3	2
24.5	76	4½	1	4		4½	1	3	4
23	73	5	1	4		5	1	3	4
21	70	5½	1	4		5½	1	3	4
20	68	6	1	4		6	1	3	4

*Wash time: 2 minutes between 82–100F, and 4 minutes at a temperature lower than 82F.

Note: After all processing steps are completed, place the print in a tray of stabilizer solution and agitate for one minute.

Table 9-25

COLOR BY BESELER RP5
CHEMISTRY PRE-HEAT CHART

PRE-HEAT DEVELOPER TEMPERATURE		FIRST DEVELOPER	FIRST STOP BATH	FIRST† WASH		COLOR DEVELOPER*	SECOND STOP BATH	BLEACH FIX	FINAL WASH†
43C	110F	1	½	2	*Re-expose*	2	½	2	2

*Pre-heat to 110F (43C) before using.
†Wash time: 2 minutes between 82–100F, and 4 minutes at a temperature lower than 82F.

Note. After all processing steps are completed, place the print in a tray of stabilizer solution and agitate for one minute.

PROBLEM	CAUSE	SOLUTION
UNEVEN DEVELOPMENT (areas of greater or lesser density than the rest of the print):	1) Not enough solution.	Follow your drum manufacturer's recommendations. Measure volumes carefully.
	2) Agitation rate too slow during first 20 seconds	Follow agitation recommendations in this instruction sheet.
	3) Inconsistent agitation.	Follow agitation recommendations in this instruction sheet.
	4) Rolling surface not level.	Check it and correct.
FINGERPRINTS OR SMUDGES	1) Print emulsion touched before processing. Water or chemistry on fingers.	Handle paper by edges only. Wash and dry hands. Wear cotton or plastic gloves.
MAGENTA (PINKISH) CAST OVER ENTIRE PRINT, LOW CONTRAST	1) Insufficient time in first developer.	Check instructions for proper time/ temperature. Check thermometer.
	2) Oxidized, exhausted, contaminated first developer.	Do not attempt to reuse this chemistry. Store in full stoppered brown glass bottles.
RED/PURPLE SHADOWS AND BORDERS, WEAK COLORS	1) Insufficient time in color developer.	Check instructions for proper time/ temperature. Check thermometer.
	2) Oxidized, exhausted, contaminated color developer	Do not attempt to reuse this chemistry. Store in full, stoppered brown glass bottles.
BROWN METALLIC OR MAGENTA CAST OVER ENTIRE PRINT	1) Insufficient time in Bleach Fix.	Follow processing instructions
	2) Bleach Fix contaminated or exhausted.	Do not attempt to reuse this chemistry.
BLACK SPOTS OR MARKS ON PRINT	1) Dust or scratches on color slide.	Clean slide before printing.
YELLOW OR BLUISH AREAS (Partial or complete print)	1) Paper is light fogged.	Do not use a safelight when exposing or loading the print in the drum. Check your darkroom for light leaks.
	2) Yellow fog — insufficient time in second stop bath.	Follow processing instructions.
	3) Cyan fog — color developer temperature too high.	Follow processing instructions.
WHITES NOT WHITE	1) Insufficient time in first developer 2) First developer oxidized or exhausted. 3) Print was underexposed.	Follow processing instructions. Store in full, stoppered brown glass bottles. Increase print exposure.
WHITE PRINT, ALMOST NO IMAGE	1) First stop bath and second stop bath reversed	Check order of chemicals and labeling of bottles.

PROBLEM	CAUSE	SOLUTION
BLACKS NOT BLACK	1) Insufficient time in color developer.	Follow processing instructions.
	2) Insufficient time in first stop bath.	Follow processing instructions.
	3) Inadequate re-exposure.	With 100W bulb 18'' to 24'' above tray, expose print for at least 15 seconds front and back.
	4) Print was overexposed.	Decrease print exposure.
	5) Contaminated color developer	Clean drum, graduates, etc. Process a second print. If problem persists, mix fresh color developer.
LOW PRINT CONTRAST	1) Insufficient time in first or color developer.	Check processing temperature. Follow processing instructions.
	2) Contaminated first or color developer.	Clean drum graduates, etc. Process a second print. If problem persists, mix fresh chemistry.
DENSITY OR COLOR SHIFT FROM ONE PRINT TO NEXT	1) Process times not maintained the same for each print.	Follow the instructions carefully for processing times in first developer and color developer.
	2) Processing temperatures not maintained the same for each print.	Check to see if temperature has changed. Check thermometer. Follow the instructions for a specific time/ temperature. Try to always process at approximately the same time/ temperature for all prints.
	3) Agitation different from print to print.	Try to agitate per instructions the same way each time. Consider purchasing No. 8921 Motor Base Drum Agitator.
	4) Variations in voltage to enlarger lamp.	Make prints from 10 a.m. to 4 p.m. or after 7 p.m. when others are less likely to turn on appliances. Purchase a voltage stabilizer.
	5) Different volumes of chemistry used for each print.	Use the amount of chemistry required by the drum maker. Measure volumes carefully. Use the same amount of chemistry each time.

Cibachrome Chemistry Kit Process P-12

Distributor: Ilford Inc.

Materials: Cibachrome Color Print Material-Type A

Components: Sold in kits containing all necessary chemical components. All concentrated components are mixed with tap water to produce working-strength solutions: developer—packaged as two liquid components; bleach—packaged as one solid (powder) and one liquid component; and fixer—packaged as one liquid component (in two containers of equal volume). Bleach Neutralizer powder is also provided with the kit. It takes no part in the processing reactions, but is made available to reduce the acidity of the bleach before it is discarded to prevent serious corrosion problems in the darkroom's sewer drain lines.

Packaging: A half-gallon size kit is A half-gallon-size kit is components are packaged to conveniently be diluted in two one-quart batches.

Shelf life: The shelf-life information offered in the data that accompanies the kit of chemicals is sufficiently vague to warrant my quoting it here: "All Cibachrome chemicals should be stored at room temperature in well-sealed glass or polyethylene bottles. The concentrated stock solutions will keep for several months in tightly sealed bottles. Part 1B of the developer may turn yellowish on extended storage, but this will not affect its strength nor cause staining of prints. Storage life of the working solutions at room temperature and in well-sealed bottles is as follows: developer—up to 3 weeks; bleach—up to 5 weeks; fixer—up to one year."

Process data: Instructions that accompany the kit of chemicals cover processing in both drums and trays. While the procedures for each type of processing differ somewhat, they are both, in general, extremely simple. The time and temperature data that follow is identical for both drum and tray processing. It and the table of exposure and processing faults that follow are from Ilford's *Cibachrome Color Print Manual.*

Table 9-27   PROCESSING DATA

It is important that in any given processing run the temperature of all solutions and of the wash water be kept within 3° of each other.

	60F ± 3F (20C ± 1½C)	75F ± 3F (24C ± 1½C)	82F ± 3F (28C ± 1½C)
Developer	2½ min.*	2 min.*	1½ min.*
Bleach	4½ min.*	4 min.*	3½ min.*
Fix	3½ min.	3 min.	2½ min.
Wash	3½ min.	3 min.	2½ min.
Total time:	14 min.	12 min.	10 min.

*Includes 15 second drain and rinse.

Note: An increase or decrease in image contrast equal to about one grade of paper can be achieved through variations in developing time up to ± ½ minute. Shorter times will yield lower contrast at some sacrifice in speed, and vice versa.

Table 9-28   EXPOSURE AND PROCESSING PROBLEMS

PROBLEM	CAUSE	REMEDY
Picture dark reddish in tone and image reversed	Partial or complete exposure through the back of the print material.	Reprint the picture. Be careful to have emulsion side up. Use a black printing support (enlarging easel).
Blue spots	Due to static, mainly in dry atmosphere.	Handle print material carefully when removing from the envelope.
Black picture, or no picture	No exposure, or ommission of Part A or B in either developer, or bleach, or omission of developing step, or omission of bleaching step.	Reprint under correct conditions. Follow directions closely.
Fogged and dull print	Probably due to incorrectly mixed bleach solution (too diluted), or insufficient bleaching due to low temperature or insufficient bleaching time, or	Check if bleaching conditions were correct and mixing instructions carefully followed.
	developer not drained before bleach was added, or	Reprint and follow correct processing procedures.
	traces of fixer in the developer (for example, drum not sufficiently rinsed before reuse), or	Reprint and follow correct processing procedures.
	reversal of fixer and bleach steps.	Reprint and follow correct processing procedures.
Formation of yellow stain after relatively short time	Insufficient final wash.	Wash print to stop further degradation.
Dark and flat print	Developing time too short.	Reprint and follow correct processing procedures.
Yellowish appearance of the print	Bleach not drained before fixer was added, or	Reprint and follow correct processing procedures.
	fixing omitted or fixing time too short.	Repeat fixing step and final wash.
Light print with loss of maximum density	Developing time too long.	Reprint and follow correct processing procedures.
Streaky and irregular appearance of the print	Insufficient agitation during processing, or insufficient volume of solutions.	Reprint and follow correct processing procedures.

Kodak Ektaprint R-500 Chemicals

Distributor: Eastman Kodak Co.

Materials: Kodak Ektachrome RC Paper, Type 1993

Components: Sold as individual component chemicals and also as kits of all necessary chemical components. All concentrated liquid components are mixed with tap water to produce working-strength chemical solutions: first developer—packaged as one liquid component; stop bath—packaged as one liquid component; color developer—packaged as three liquid components; bleach fix—packaged as two liquid components; and rinse (potassium iodide)—packaged as one liquid component in some kits and as a solid (crystals) in other kits, and when purchased as an individual component; stabilizer—packaged as a single liquid component.

Packaging: Two different kits are available; a one-quart and a one-gallon size. Separate component chemicals are also available to make one-gallon quantities. Potassium iodide crystals are packaged in 25 gram containers. This quantity yields three quarts of stock solution or about seven and one-half-gallons of working-strength rinse.

Shelf life: Kodak provides no data on the shelf life of unopened bottles of concentrated component solutions; however, the boxes the components are packaged in are coded to indicate the date of manufacture. No data are provided for partially filled bottles of concentrated solutions; however, Kodak's mixing directions call for mixing the full amount of their liquid concentrates rather than making small batches of working-strength chemicals. Working-strength solutions in full, tightly capped, glass bottles are stated to have the following shelf lives: first developer—4 weeks; stop bath—8 weeks; color developer—4 weeks; bleach fix—8 weeks; stabilizer—8 weeks; and rinse—6 months. Working-strength solutions in partially full, tightly capped bottles are stated as having the following shelf lives: first developer—2 weeks; stop bath—8 weeks; color developer—2 weeks; bleach-fix—8 weeks; stabilizer—8 weeks; and rinse—6 months.

Process data: Numerous Kodak publications offer processing instructions for these chemicals in Kodak Model 11 and 16K Processors, Kodak Model 30A automatic tube processors and drum processors. Another type of chemistry, Kodak's Ektaprint R-5 Chemicals, are used for basket, tank, and tray processing. (Model 11 processing instructions will be found in chapter 7). Representative daylight drum processing instructions from Kodak's publication KP 69283 6-75 follow.

Table 9-29 GENERAL PROCESSING SPECIFICATIONS

Nominal solution temperature of 100F (38C)

PROCESSING STEP	*TIME IN MINUTES	ACCUMU-LATED TIME	SOLUTION IN MILLILITERS
1. Prewet (water)	½	½	150
2. First Developer	1½	2	70
3. Stop Bath	½	2½	70
4. Wash	½	3	150
5. Wash	½	3½	150
6. Color Developer	2	5½	70
7. Wash	½	6	150
8. Bleach-Fix	1½	7½	70
9. Wash	½	8	150
10. Wash†	½	8½	150
11. Stabilizer	½	9	70
12. Rinse	¼	9¼	150

*All times include a 10-second drain time (to avoid excess solution carryover). Some processing tubes may require a slightly longer drain time. Be sure to allow enough time to make certain the tube is drained and to add the next solution on time for the next step. The next step begins when the solution contacts the paper.

†An additional wash step (new step 11) may be required, depending on the processing tube you are using. To determine, see preliminary processing steps.

Table 9-30 TROUBLESHOOTING

PROBLEM	CAUSE	SOLUTION
Black spots or specks	Dust	Clean the transparency to remove all dust.
Streaks or nonuniformity	Improper agitation	Follow tube manufacturer's recommendations.
	Tube not level	Check to see that the tube is level during process.
	Solution poured into tube incorrectly	Follow tube manufacturer's recommendations.
	Insufficient solution volume	Use more of each solution.
Stain (overall or partial)	Contamination	Use each container for one solution only; wash thermometer between solutions.
	Potassium iodide wash not used after color developer	Follow the directions.
Washed-out color, not caused by exposure problem	Insufficient drain time	Be sure to drain the tube completely between steps.

Unicolor PFS (Prints From Slides) Chemistry

Distributor: Unicolor Div., Photo Systems Inc.

Materials: Kodak Ektachrome RC Paper, Type 1993

Components: Sold in kits containing all necessary chemical components. All components are mixed with tap water to produce working-strength solutions: first developer — packaged as one solid (powder) and one liquid component; stop bath — packaged as a single liquid component; color developer — packaged as two liquid components; PFS Rinse — packaged as a single solid (powder) component; blix (bleach-fix) — packaged as a single liquid component; and stabilizer — packaged as a single liquid component.

Packaging: Two different kits are available: a one-quart and a one-gallon size.

Shelf life: Unopened bottles of concentrated component solutions are stated to have a shelf life of up to one year. Unopened packets of solid components are stated to have a shelf life exceeding five years. However, the kits are not dated to indicate when they were manufactured. Opened and partially filled bottles of concentrated component solutions have shelf lives stated as follows: color developer, part B — 3 to 4 months; all other solutions — 4 to 6 months. Working-strength solutions in filled, tightly capped, brown glass bottles are stated to have the following shelf lives: first and color developers — 1 week; all other solutions — up to 12 weeks. No data are provided for working-strength solutions in partially filled containers.

Process data: Instructions provided with the chemicals cover drum processing techniques. Representative data from the manufacturer's instructions follow.

Table 9-31 PROCESSING INSTRUCTIONS . . . UNICOLOR PFS CHEMISTRY . . . IN UNIDRUM

Processing may be done completely in daylight after paper is properly loaded in Unidrum. We do not recommend trays for this process. See note below processing with Kodak Model 11 or 16 Processors.

STEP	USE THIS SOLUTION OR PROCEDURE	AT THIS TEMP.	TIME	WITH THIS TECHNIQUE
				Note: The chemistry working solution quantities in this column are for the 8 × 10 **UNIDRUM** only. If you are using an 11 × 14 or 16 × 20 **UNIDRUM** or another drum-type processor, see the quantity requirements in instructions for **UNIDRUM** or other processor.
1.	Water	105-110F (40-43C)	1 min.	Load exposed print (emulsion side in) into a clean dry **UNIDRUM with lights off.** Replace top (cap) on drum. **Lights on.** Fill **UNIDRUM** through pouring spout with water at 105-110F (40-43C). Set drum vertically on end and allow to stand 1 full minute. Drain completely through pouring spout. Place drum on legs (horizontally) in processing area. See note below.
2.	First Developer	75-80F (24-27C)	2 min.	**UNIDRUM** working (rolling) surface must be level. Use 2 ounces of chemistry in this and all following steps except washes. Add developer through pouring spout, roll (agitate) as prescribed in **UNIDRUM** (other processor) instructions. Drain through pouring spout at end of step.
3.	Stop Bath	70-80F (21-27C)	½ min.	Add chemistry through pouring spout and roll **UNIDRUM** per step 2. Drain Stop Bath through pouring spout at end of step. **Print is no longer sensitive to room light. UNIDRUM cap may be removed for step 4 or any succeeding steps.**
4.	Water	70-110F (21-43C)	2 min.	There are several ways to wash print: The easiest is to stand the **UNIDRUM** on end with lid off and run water into it with a hose or tap leaving print in place. You can also use fill and dump method: Add 8 oz. of water and roll (agitate) **UNIDRUM** for 15-20 seconds. Dump. Repeat until 2 minutes time cycle is completed (4-6 changes of water). **Note:** At end of rinse, leave drum filled with 105-110 water to preheat drum for color development (step 7).
5.	Reexposure	—	15 sec. per side	Remove print from **UNIDRUM** and expose to No. 2 photoflood (500 watt) for 15 seconds on each side with paper 18-24 inches from lamp. **Do not splatter water drops on lamp during re-exposure** . . . lamp could explode. Replace print in **UNIDRUM.**
6.	Water (Preheat No. 2)	105-110F (40-43C)	1 min.	**Note:** This is not really a separate operation (you started it at the end of step 4). We are just reminding you that the drum should be preheating at this stage. Replace cap and drain **UNIDRUM** at end of step.
7.	Color Developer	70-80F (21-27C)	3 min.	Add chemistry through pouring spout and roll **UNIDRUM** per step 2. Drain Color Developer through pouring spout at end of step.
8.	PFS Rinse	70-110F (21-43C)	1 min.	Add 8 oz. PFS rinse, agitate 30 seconds and dump. **Repeat one time. (Use working solution only . . . not stock solution).**
9.	Blix	70-80F (21-27C)	2 min.	Add chemistry through pouring spout and roll **UNIDRUM** per step 2. Drain Blix through pouring spout at end of step.
10.	Water	70-110F (21-43C)	1½ min.	Follow rinse techniques in step 4. If using the fill and dump method use at least three (3) changes of water. At end of step remove print from **UNIDRUM.**
11.	Stabilizer	70-80F (21-27C)	1 min.	Place print in Stabilizer Tray . . . agitate 30 seconds to 1 minute and remove print. Wipe print with soft paper towel and dry . . . there is **no additional washing** . . . Processing is completed. **Note:** Bluish cast of wet prints is normal for RC papers . . . prints must be dry to judge the final color. See drying details on **page 2.**

Note: Refer to Kodak Publication E-96 for more complete printing and processing procedures and sample prints showing processing defects.

Table 9-32 RAPID PROCESSING PFS CHEMISTRY IN UNIDRUM

Prewet and rinse water should be 105-110F; 1st developer should be 75-80F; and all other chemicals (including PFS rinse) should be 105-110F.

STEP	USE THIS SOLUTION	FOR THIS TIME	WITH THIS TECHNIQUE
1.	Water	—	Fill Unidrum with water at 105-110F before exposing print. Then expose print and load in Unidrum. Replace cap and drain water. This step pre-wets paper and warms Unidrum to operating temperature.
2.	1st Developer	2 minutes	Standard technique per Step 2 of PFS Instructions—Table 9-31.
3.	Stop Bath	½ minute	Standard technique per Step 3 of PFS Instructions—Table 9-31.
4.	Water	1 minute	Add 8 oz. water, roll (agitate) Unidrum two revolutions on Uniroller and dump. Repeat three times. Leave Unidrum filled with 105-110F water in preparation for Step 6 (color developer).
5.	Reexposure	15 seconds per side	Standard technique per Step 5 of PFS Instructions—Table 9-31.
6.	Color Developer	2 minutes	Dump water remaining in Unidrum from Step 4; then use standard color developer technique per Step 7 of PFS Instructions Table 9-31.
7.	PFS Rinse	½ minute	Add 8 oz. PFS rinse (working solution), roll (agitate) Unidrum two revolutions on Uniroller and dump. Repeat one time.
8.	Blix	1½ minutes	Standard technique per Step 9 of PFS Instructions—Table 9-31.
9.	Water	¾ minute	Add 8 oz. water, roll (agitate) Unidrum two revolutions on Uniroller and dump. Repeat two more times.
10.	Stabilizer	½ minute	Standard technique per Step 11 of PFS Instructions—Table 9-31.

Note: PFS Chemistry on Kodak Model 11 and 16K Processors ... The user must have running water at 100F (38C) for rinsing and to temper the processor. The drum temperature is 100F (38C) for all steps. The times remain the same as in the above table. Prewet the print in a tray of water between 75–100F for 1 minute before putting on apron.

A word of warning ... No safelight should be used with Kodak Type 1993 paper.

Table 9-33 PROCESSING PROBLEMS

PROBLEM	PROBABLE CAUSE(S)	REMEDY
Fingerprints or smudges	Emulsion surface touched before processing water or chemistry on fingers	Handle RC paper only by edges and/or back with clean hands ... or wear dry rubber or plastic gloves.
Color balance OK, but print has "dirty" yellowish blotches or yellowish overcast	Underexposure, too little first development, or first developer weak or old.	Increase exposure. Follow times, and temperature per table 9-31.
Color balance OK, but print colors seem flat, blacks are weak and bluish	Insufficient or no re-exposure Insufficient color development or color developer weak or old	Follow all techniques as prescribed in table 9-31.
Magenta overcast or stain ... usually associated with greenish-black borders	Excess chlorine in water used for processing	Consult local water-softening dealer about removal techniques.

Notes: 1. For 11 × 14 Unidrum ... use 16 oz. water in Steps 4 and 9; also use 16 oz. PFS Rinse in Step 7.
2. For 16 × 20 Unidrum ... use 32 oz. water in Steps 4 and 9; also use 32 oz. PFS Rinse in Step 7.

Index

Index-4